THE PERFECT BOOK TO HAVE BEFORE THE WEDDING— ESSENTIAL READING AFTER IT

THE FIRST YEAR OF Marriage

"This intelligent, clearly written, down-to-earth book describes both the superficial and deep sources of difficulty in early marriage and provides a variety of possible solutions. The authors manage to combine an excellent basic course in human relations with a trouble shooting and repair manual for the newly wedded. This book will be helpful not only to those in their first year of marriage, but to those hesitantly considering that step and many who have gotten well beyond that year."

—**Arnold M. Cooper, M.D.**
Past President of the
American Psychoanalytic Association

"This lively and well written book is filled with useful and practical advice that makes it a must read for newlyweds and those considering the joys and perils of marriage."

—**Allen Frances, M.D.**
Professor of Psychiatry and Director of the Outpatient
Department at Payne Whitney Clinic, New York Hospital

"This book is an invaluable guide through either the first year or later in one's lifetime commitment to the most intimate of partnerships."

—**Rave Reviews**

"Excellent work . . . a vast number of topics are included: the marriage mystique, conflicts, power struggles, money, families, communication, sex, intimacy—in fact, just about every issue that comes into play in marriage. . . . It also manages to be a 'good read'—no mean feat!"

—**Beverly Lowy,** *On the Issues* **magazine**

"Offers psychological insights in its anecdotal case notes, plus questionnaires, work-sheets, and checklists to help in identifying problems and solving them."

—*Washington Jewish Week*

*Featured in *Bride's* magazine and *New Woman* magazine, and on the Mutual Radio Network and the CBS Morning Program, as well as on many other radio and television programs across the country.

ABOUT THE AUTHORS

MIRIAM AROND was formerly a feature writer at the *New York Daily News* and on the editorial staff at *Bride's* magazine. She has published articles in magazines and newspapers nationwide, often focusing on psychological and family issues. She holds a B.A. degree in English literature from the University of Pennsylvania, where she was graduated Magna Cum Laude and elected to Phi Beta Kappa. She obtained her master's degree in journalism from New York University, where she was a two-time winner of the Sigma Delta Chi Deadline Club Award.

SAMUEL L. PAUKER, M.D., is a psychiatrist in private practice in Manhattan, a Clinical Instructor of Psychiatry at Cornell University Medical College, and a Clinical Affiliate at New York Hospital/Payne Whitney Clinic. He is also affiliated with the Columbia University Center for Psychoanalytic Training and Research, a member of the American Psychiatric Association, and an affiliated member of the American Psychoanalytic Association. He has published and lectured nationally on a broad range of psychiatric topics.

Married to each other, the co-authors base their literary and marital partnership in New York City.

THE FIRST YEAR OF
Marriage

WHAT TO EXPECT, WHAT TO ACCEPT, AND WHAT YOU CAN CHANGE

VITAL & REASSURING ANSWERS TO THE QUESTIONS YOU'RE AFRAID TO ASK BY

MIRIAM AROND AND
SAMUEL L. PAUKER, M.D.

WARNER BOOKS

A Time Warner Company

A word about our usage of *they* and *their* throughout this book. We've employed these pronouns at times in order to avoid endlessly repeating "he or she" and "his or her." Theodore M. Bernstein has noted in his *Dos, Don'ts and Maybes of English Usage* that "pronouns . . . tend to change over the centuries so perhaps the word *they* someday will become a legitimate singular. The pronoun *you* originally was only a plural word, the objective form of *ye*, which was exclusively plural. Maybe that word will eventually become a 'precedent.'" In the meantime, he suggests, "everyone should write whatever she thinks is best." Although our solution is not ideal, our intention has been to avoid using the sexist language we've all inherited.

The people in this book who shared their thoughts and experiences about their marriages are real, but their names and identities have been changed for the purpose of confidentiality. Any similarities between the pseudonyms used here and present-day persons and marriages are purely coincidental.

Grateful acknowledgment is made to the following for permission to reprint published material: Anniversary Waltz by Al Dubin and Dave Franklin. Copyright © 1941 by Mayfair Music Corp. & Chappell & Co., Inc. Copyright renewed and assigned to Chappell & Co., Inc. International Copyright secured. ALL RIGHTS RESERVED. Used by permission.

Warner Books, Inc., 666 Fifth Avenue, New York, NY 10103

 A Time Warner Company

Library of Congress Cataloging-in-Publication Data

Arond, Miriam.
  The first year of marriage.

  Bibliography: p.
  1. Marriage.   2. Interpersonal relations.
I. Pauker, Samuel L.   II. Title.
HQ734.A685   1987   646.7'8   86-4014
ISBN 0-446-38722-3 (U.S.A.) (pbk.)

Printed in the United States of America

First Trade Paperback Printing: June 1988

10 9 8 7 6 5 4 3

Cover design by Suzanne Noli
Book design by Nick Mazzella

*For Sarah Frances and
Elizabeth Paulette*

CONTENTS

ACKNOWLEDGMENTS

It was Barbara Tober, editor-in-chief of *Bride's* magazine, who introduced us to the person whose enthusiasm for this project got it off the ground, Larry Kirshbaum, president of Warner Books. To both, our deep gratitude for their interest in and support of this book.

We are indebted to the hundreds of people nationwide who filled out our questionnaires and who met with us to share their feelings about and experiences in their first year of marriage. We are especially grateful to those men and women who agreed to be interviewed repeatedly throughout their newlywed year, often rearranging work schedules and skipping lunch breaks to do so. While their names have been fictionalized, these people—with their candor and thoughtfulness—are the ones who made this book possible. Our thanks cannot be overstated.

Many people helped us obtain names of newlyweds to contact. We'd like to thank the Reverend Marion J. Hammond, Rabbi Barry Dov Schwartz, Helen Latner, Belle Steinberg, Kathy Mullin, Anne O'Malley, Marie Barry, Cotton Timberlake, Mark Levenstein, Allison Leopold, Margaret Farley, Dinah Prince, Betsey McGee, Deborah Purcell, Vivian Goldman, Gail Birnbaum, Robin Reif, Ken Ruge and Madeline Rogers.

Marc Glassman, Ph.D., was invaluable in helping us devise our statistical questionnaire and interpret our findings, as was Dawn Siegel, who was in charge of organizing the mailing and coding of our surveys. Sheryl Feldinger and Gretchen Haas, Ph.D., were also influential in the design of our survey. Candice Shicona assisted us by providing hours of library research.

When working on a project over a long period of time, it is difficult to keep a perspective and remain objective. We want to thank those people who read drafts of chapters and whose comments, questions, and suggestions helped us clarify and improve the manuscript: Clifford J. Sager, M.D., Ronald Blank, M.D., Sally Severino, M.D., Sandy Rosen, Lisa Steinberg, Raina Grossman, Neil Baim, Phyllis Krulik, Judah Deutsch, and Carol and Harold Finkel. Others who listened generously to our thoughts and observations about our research were Lee Wexler, Susan Sturm, Jane Starr, and Linda and Gary Jacobs.

Advice from our editor, Claire Zion, was always thoughtful, insightful, and most important, offered with a gentle and respectful manner that we much appreciated. Also our thanks to her assistant, Beth Lieberman, our copyeditor Julie Garriott, and the other people at Warner Books who helped make this book a reality. Charlotte Sheedy, our literary agent, and Vicky Bijour, her assistant, continually made themselves available throughout the book process.

We've each been fortunate to have a mentor whose encouragement has had a profound and guiding influence on our lives. These people are Nora Magid and Leonard Diamond, M.D. Our thanks also to colleagues, teachers, and friends at Columbia University Center for Psychoanalytic Training and Research and Cornell Medical College/Payne Whitney Clinic for hours of thoughtful discussion that contributed directly and indirectly to the ideas developed in this book.

To our families it is difficult to adequately express our appreciation. Lionel and Irma Arond's encouragement of their daughter's writing long precedes this book and has continued to be a sustaining force. Much of this book was written in Lionel Arond's office. It was wonderful to be greeted by a warm, welcoming face each day. Elsa and Irving Pauker's loving support was, as ever, shown in a multitude of ways.

Sarah and Elizabeth, our daughters, are truly the sunshine of our lives and make us forever grateful that we survived and have thrived beyond the first year of marriage.

One last mention: This book has special meaning for us because we did it together. As husband and wife, we found it a rich and rewarding experience to have shared in each other's area of expertise. Our thanks and love to each other.

THE FIRST YEAR OF
Marriage

INTRODUCTION

If you're about to be married or were recently wed, you may have realized by now that although your friends and relatives are excited about your decision, they haven't told you much about what to expect. Sure, you may have been warned that "the first year is the hardest" or advised that "marriage takes work." But old adages and trite generalities aren't a lot of help when you're trying to anticipate what your newlywed year will be like, or when you're embroiled in your first—or your hundredth—marital argument.

Of course, you simply may have assumed that marriage wouldn't be all that different from the relationship you've already been enjoying with your mate—especially if you've dated or lived together for years.

But like many of the men and women we interviewed about their first year of marriage, you may discover that, although you are eager and ready to accept the new roles and responsibilities of marriage, you are not immune from the changes that marriage brings. Suddenly, you may find yourself wondering:

- Is my mate *really* the right match for me?
- What do my doubts about my mate mean for our marriage?
- Why have family tensions escalated around the wedding?
- How can I avoid repeating the mistakes I've seen others make in their marriages?

In researching this book, we contacted hundreds of men and women who shared with us their experiences of adjusting to marriage. We spoke with newlyweds in their teens, newlyweds who are almost senior citizens, newlyweds who married interracially and interreligiously, newlyweds who married people much younger and much older than themselves, newlyweds who have children from a previous marriage, and newlyweds gaining stepchildren.

We found that regardless of age, reason for marrying, cultural and family background, or previous marital history, there *are* issues that newlyweds universally face. Inherent in the intimacy of marriage are practical, everyday questions of handling money and dividing household chores, as well as such complex emotional matters as trying to balance the need for closeness with the desire to maintain one's individuality. It is, in fact, in addressing and resolving these and other issues that you establish and solidify your identity as a married couple.

We wrote this book to explore the common issues that contemporary newlyweds confront. By presenting a wide spectrum of newlywed experiences and by drawing on psychological theory to explain the underlying reasons for many of the emotionally charged conflicts that arise in the first year of marriage, we hope to help readers prepare for and evaluate their own marital situations.

The seeds of this book were planted several years ago when we observed a similar pattern among many people we knew who had recently married. With one of us a psychiatrist and the other, at the time, on the editorial staff of a bridal magazine, we heard many stories of the joys and travails of adjusting to marriage. Despite the differences in age and background of newlyweds, many shared the same concerns: a recognition that marriage had changed things; doubt about whether their marital experience—or specifically, their marital conflict—was normal; and a sense of isolation, due to the fear that by sharing their worries they would be disloyal to their mates and be admitting that they weren't as blissful as newlyweds are supposed to be.

The fact is, it can be difficult to judge what's "normal" in marriage, because most people don't talk about what is *really* going on inside their marriages. Sure, married friends may gripe to you about a spouse's sloppiness or reveal the details of a big blowup at home. But people rarely divulge their innermost fears—the ones that strike the most sensitive chords—like "Did I marry the right person?" or "Why do I feel different toward my mate than I did before we got married?"

Once you've made a marriage commitment, you yourself may have begun feeling less comfortable about confiding details of your personal life to friends. In fact, more than one-third of the newlyweds we surveyed stated that they *did not confide to anyone* about their marital doubts and arguments. And many of the newlyweds we interviewed, feeling too disloyal, embarrassed, or fearful to admit to friends their marital doubts and confusion, told us it was a relief to be able to speak freely with us in a relatively anonymous situation.

While most people spend a considerable amount of time preparing to buy a house, car, or computer, many devote astonishingly little time in anticipating the realities of such a serious undertaking as marriage. It is important to know what to expect, to understand how and why marriage can change a relationship, and to be prepared for the challenges of marriage as well as the rewards.

In our study we found that people who enter marriage unprepared for any problems, disappointments, or adjustments sometimes panic that their marriage is not as it should be, that perhaps they aren't "made for each other," that maybe they made a big mistake. In fact, the difference between those couples who split up early in marriage and those who stay together is often their *attitude* toward their problems. Those who separated had found themselves shocked and horrified by the conflicts that arose, and fled, thinking this was *not* the way marriage was supposed to be. The newlyweds who stayed together were less thrown by their frustrations and arguments, or more determined to work things out.

Because the styles of marriage today are so varied, the challenge for newlyweds may be greater than before. There are no universal rules to follow, and so you may find that you have no role models upon which to pattern the type of marriage you'd like to create. And the increased prevalence of divorce may lead you to feel particularly threatened by whatever problems arise in your new marriage. With the option of "getting out" easily available, it's not just a matter of choosing whom to marry; it becomes obligatory to *reaffirm,* to yourself and to each other, your choice to stay together day after day.

Much of what we say in this book is practical advice for recognizing and handling problematic situations as they arise in your marriage. *Setting positive patterns early on is important.* How you and your spouse act and react toward each other as newlyweds will set a tone, possibly for years to come. Many people believe that, given time, problems smooth themselves out; but problems *don't* just disappear. With time attitudes harden, and spouses become accustomed to ways of behaving that make it more and more difficult for them to be flexible and compromise. That's not to say that negative patterns can't be changed, or that a contented newlywed year guarantees a lifetime of marital bliss. But if you establish a mode of relating and behaving that enables you to meet the needs of both parties in your partnership, you'll be setting a strong foundation that can only benefit you in the future.

Because we value the "first-blush" experience *and* the long-term perspective, we sought in our research not only the thoughts of newlyweds, but also the recollections of people who could look back over a long span of time. When listening to people reminisce, we were struck by how vividly many recalled their newlywed experience. Some people talked about it with sarcasm, some with hope, some with disappointment, and some with fondness. But for everyone it seemed to have an emotional weight and significance.

Even if you've dated your spouse for years, lived with your mate before your wedding, or are marrying for the second time, the first year of marriage is a fresh start—filled with hope and expectation. For most brides and grooms there is a tremendous burst of excitement and energy in committing themselves to marriage. The key to making the most of the newlywed year is to use that energy productively—to create a home life in which disagreements can be aired and resolved, and to cultivate a relationship that encourages the expression and fulfillment of your need to love and be loved.

Making the transition into marriage isn't always easy, but the problems, even crises, that commonly arise during the first year of marriage are a normal part of the painful process of growth. The task of the first year is to meet each challenge with the strength and understanding and maturity that enable growth—both as individuals and as a couple.

We don't pretend that every newlywed's experience is like every other's, or that anyone getting married can know exactly what lies ahead. As the philosopher Martin Buber wrote: "All journeys have secret destinations of which the traveler is unaware." Nevertheless, by probing the feelings, decisions, and dilemmas that often confront newlyweds, and by offering guidelines for coping with issues that might be expected to arise in your first year of marriage, we hope to illuminate the path that lies ahead after you say "I do."

PART 1

THE MARRIAGE MYSTIQUE

What greater thing is there for two human souls than to feel that they are joined for life. . . .

George Eliot
George Eliot Letters

CROSSING THE THRESHOLD

Making the Transition from Being Single to Being Married

WHAT IS ALL THE FUSS ABOUT?

No matter what kind of wedding you decide to have—large or small, traditional or nontraditional—you're probably aware that it represents a major rite of passage, if not in your own view, then at least in the eyes of your family, the community, society. But *what,* you may ask, is the big deal about the first year of marriage—especially if the two of you have been living together or dating "forever."

Well, no matter what you may think, being married is different from dating or living together. All our research confirms that marriage is a developmental process—which involves change, adjustment, growth. The following are just a few of our findings among the newlyweds we surveyed—half of whom had lived together prior to their wedding:

- 51 percent* of newlyweds reported that the number of arguments they had with their mate changed after their wedding.
- 52 percent of newlyweds reported that their tendency to be critical of their mate changed.
- 54 percent of newlyweds said that their feelings of self-confidence changed.
- 47 percent of newlyweds reported that their relationship with their own family changed.
- 58 percent of newlyweds reported that their attitude about their work changed.
- 54 percent of newlyweds said that their interest in having an attractive home changed.

*Percentages noted in all chapters of this book have been rounded to the nearest whole percent.

- 59 percent of newlyweds said that their relationship with their spouse's family changed.

In other words, newlyweds, who on average had been married six months when surveyed, and who for the most part had known each other quite well before marriage, discovered that saying "I do" had altered their lives and relationships.

Years ago, when marriages were arranged by the parents of young men and women, it was assumed that the first year would bring adjustments. In biblical times the special status of "bride and groom" lasted a full year. "When a man takes a new wife, he shall be deferred from military duty, he shall not be charged with any business. He shall be free for his house one year. . . ." (Deuteronomy 24:5) It was recognized that the first year would be one of learning, sharing, and adapting.

And even in twentieth-century America—until the late 1960s—couples who married were generally young and inexperienced, and expected that marriage would change their lifestyle. For those men and women, marriage was their first opportunity to live on their own, set up house, manage finances, develop a sexual relationship. As one woman, married in 1962, told us, "Part of what made me so excited about getting married was buying my own pots and pans and dishes. It was a thrill to get to play house for real!"

But if you are marrying today, chances are that you are marrying at a later age[1] and that you are more experienced and more established than was the typical newlywed of previous decades. Our sample of newlyweds represents this phenomenon.

Of the newlyweds we surveyed:

- 85 percent made love together before marrying.
- 63 percent vacationed together before marrying.
- 48 percent shared household expenses before marrying.
- 22 percent bought a house or car together before marrying.[2]

It's easy to understand why, if you've shared such a history together, you don't expect the "simple fact" of marriage to significantly alter the nature of your relationship, or the course of your life in general.

But familiarity before marriage seems to have little to do with how easily a couple adapts to marriage. In our survey, we found almost no relation* between whether or not spouses vacationed together,[3] bought a house or car together,[4] or how long they knew each other before their wedding,[5] and whether or not their adjustment to marriage had been easy or difficult.

Even living together probably isn't as much preparation for marriage as you might think. Our findings show no relationship between whether or not a couple lived together and how easily they adjust to marriage,[6] how happy they are in marriage,[7] how satisfied they are with their sex life in marriage.[8] In fact, a study undertaken by others found that couples who lived together before marriage had significantly *lower* marital satisfaction than those who did not cohabit before the wedding.[9]

Reverting to our own survey, it's also worth noting that neither living together[10] nor knowing each other a long time[11] before marriage affords any guarantee against having doubts in the weeks before the wedding as to whether you are marrying the right person.[12] Although the average newlywed in our survey was 27 years old (and so, presumably, old enough to know their own mind) and knew their spouse between two and four years before marrying, *41 percent* reported having doubts before their wedding about whether they were marrying the right person. It's also apparent that the reason somebody marries has almost no impact on whether or not they suffer premarital doubts.[13] Just the very fact that so many people put off marrying illustrates that there is a psychological and symbolic significance to marriage that sets it apart from "steady" dating or even living together.

JUST HOW IS BEING MARRIED SO DIFFERENT FROM DATING OR LIVING TOGETHER?

In his book, *The Family in Cross-Cultural Perspective,*[14] William Stephens defines marriage as "a socially legitimate sexual union, begun with a public announcement and undertaken with some idea of permanence; it is assumed with a more or less

---

*Unless otherwise stated, all relations noted are based on correlations drawn from our statistical survey, details of which are included in the Notes provided at the end of this book.

explicit marriage contract, which spells out the reciprocal rights and obligations between spouses, and between the spouses and their future children."

Stephens makes marriage sound serious—and it is. No matter how well an unmarried couple know each other, they have made no *public* commitment, no *pledge* for the future, no *official* pronouncement of love and responsibility. Theirs is essentially a private arrangement based on an emotional bond. Marriage, on the other hand, is much more than a love partnership. It is a public event that involves legal and societal responsibilities. It brings together not just two people, but also two families and two communities. It is not just for the here and now; it is, most newlyweds hope, "till death do us part." Getting married changes what you expect from your mate and yourself, the way you relate to your friends and family, and the way your friends, relatives, and work colleagues treat you.

One man we interviewed, who lived with his wife for seven years before they married, had not anticipated that marriage would change their relationship. But six months into marriage, the 32-year-old groom told us he felt different.

> I feel like my wife and I are even closer than before. We're much more accepted by each other's families. We're on better behavior—we're not fighting as much. My parents never fought, and I guess I think if you're married you should try to have a calm, stable relationship. We're also planning to buy a house—something we never even talked about before. To me, being married means being rooted in a community. I suppose you could say that getting married has made us a lot more settled and future-directed.

Marriage changes a relationship because it brings along with it a host of conscious—and unconscious—expectations. It triggers underlying fears and hopes and needs and desires that often have lain dormant for many years.

The experience of Jack and Michelle Grant, a couple in their thirties and married seven years when we spoke with them, clearly exemplifies this phenomenon. Said Michelle:

> For us, living together for two years before marrying was counterproductive. When I got married, my ex-

pectations of Jack totally changed, but I didn't realize it for quite some time. Before we were married I didn't care that Jack had dropped out of law school and was hanging out at the beach all day while I was going to business school. But when we got married, I started to resent it. I started thinking, What will my life be like years from now? It also started to bother me when Jack announced that he was taking off on his motorcycle for a two-week trip. Before we got married I never allowed myself to think I had a right to get angry about such things. But as a wife I feel *entitled* to a more predictable and stable life.

Jack Grant, now a lawyer, told us that marriage also affected his attitude toward Michelle.

When we lived together, I never minded when Michelle went out at night with her girlfriends. But after our wedding I felt that if she went out socially I should go with her. I became more demanding. And even though I still desired my freedom to take off when I wanted, I became more possessive of her time.

Months had passed before the Grants realized that marriage had changed what they wanted from their relationship.

Psychologist Mary Ainsworth[15] points out that marriage brings together the three major attachments of adult life: a sexual pairing; the major intimate love relationship of adult life; and a caretaking bond—which, historically, has been a stepping-stone to parenting.[16] It is inevitable that people have significant emotions associated with all three of these components of marriage—emotions connected with what they observed in their parents' relationship and how they felt about it, and what their own hopes are for themselves.

Your living together with your lover may be a rebellion against your parents, but in marrying, you and your mate step into the shoes of your parents—the first husband-and-wife team you ever had a chance to observe. As a newlywed you may suddenly find yourself repeating patterns, or thinking you *should* emulate your parents' relationship. On the other hand, you may feel uncomfortable assuming the adult roles you associate with your parents. If their relationship is not one you admire or deem successful, then you may feel at a loss for a positive model for marriage.

Because of the close, familial quality of marriage, getting married may revive many of the emotions you haven't felt since childhood—feelings of deprivation, of neediness, of dependency.[17] Marriage not only stirs up the problems and conflicts experienced in childhood, but often also becomes a force for working them out.

The expectations that you bring to marriage stem not only from your family experience, but also from childhood fantasies and dreams. Many newlywed women reported to us that intertwined with their idea of marriage is the image of the knight in shining armor carrying them off to live "happily ever after." Dr. Clifford Sager,[18] a noted marital therapist, has observed that some men and women marry with the expectation that marriage will rejuvenate a long-term relationship that has faded in intensity during the years that they were dating or living together. Almost always, they are disappointed. While marriage may draw you closer as a couple and bring much joy, it does not magically solve problems or recapture lost romance. Because people tend to expect of marriage a degree of perfection that often they do not expect to achieve in a living-together arrangement, they may feel devastated when their marriage does not fulfill that expectation.

The security of the marriage certificate sometimes has the effect of freeing newlyweds, enabling them to let down their guard, express their need to be loved and their desire to love. One woman married a month exclaimed to us:

> Nobody told me how wonderful marriage was going to be! I was terrified of getting married. But now I feel so filled with love. I guess I couldn't know how great it would be until I took the leap.

For this woman, being married felt safe and reassuring. Convinced of her mate's love and commitment, she was able to be more giving, to make herself more vulnerable.

But the notion that "marriage is forever" looms heavy over newlyweds who feel stifled, choked, threatened by the permanence and intimacy of marriage. Frightened that there is no longer an escape hatch—that it's no longer so easy to "get out"— they may be forced to confront qualities in themselves and each other that they had previously managed to deny. In choosing to marry, you inevitably go through a mourning process—for you are giving up your former life, giving up your childhood, giving up all the other people "out there" whom you might marry instead. Because by marrying you are ruling out other possible lifestyles, taking that step forces you to come to terms with the limitations you place on yourself in choosing to wed.

It is for all these reasons that the initial phase of marriage is so emotionally charged—and that some people who live together for years break up soon after getting married. Saying "I do" does do *something!* Just as adolescence is a developmental phase that forces certain issues to the fore, so too is the beginning of marriage a developmental stimulus. It catapults a person, often rapidly and abruptly, into a position of having to face issues connected with separation from family, problems of intimacy, the handling of aggression, the need to be loved, the desire for and hesitancies about having a sexual relationship.

It is only in relation to others that we define ourselves.[19] Because marriage is such a close relationship, it will inevitably prompt you to discover things about yourself that you may or may not be ready to see. You can't know if you're a cooperative person unless you have someone to cooperate with, and you can't know if you're a sharing person unless you have someone to share with. How giving, how understanding, how communicative, how loving you are are all hypothetical until you actually have a partner with whom to interact. Marriage challenges you to be the best person you can be, a challenge that may be exciting and frightening at the same time.[20]

ADAPTATION TO MARRIAGE: FIVE NEWLYWED SILHOUETTES

As we've noted, many people don't anticipate that marriage will be different from dating or living together. In fact, some men and women don't want to recognize even after the wedding that changes occur.

Your attitude toward the adjustments you experience following your wedding will have a lot to do with the expectations you bring to marriage. In our interviewing, we began to notice that newlyweds typically adapt to marriage in one of five ways.

The category a newlywed "falls into" depends primarily on the hopes and assumptions they have. The silhouettes are these:

The Inseparable Sweethearts

The sweethearts are honeymooners who have long anticipated falling in love and getting married. Swept up in the excitement of their dream-come-true, they leap at the chance to change their lives in whatever ways they think marriage *should* change things. They neglect friends in favor of togetherness and enmesh themselves in each other and each other's lives. There is a womblike quality to their relationship; and whatever conflict they may feel inside or between themselves gets projected onto relatives, friends, the outside world—who become "the bad guys." During the honeymoon it's typical for newlyweds in general to act the "incurable romantics." But although togetherness is often viewed as the marital ideal, the danger in carrying this twosome attitude too far—the hazard in being so eager to change your life for your marriage—is that you lose sight of who you are and what you are giving up by immersing yourselves utterly in a shared identity.

The Disappointed Dreamers

Dreamers have tremendous expectations of their new union. Because they idealize their mate as well as the institution of marriage, often they run into marriage without knowing their mate very well, and assume it will all work out. For them the realization that their mate is a three-dimensional human being with foibles as well as strengths is a rude awakening. Those who marry more for money or "power" than for love may be disappointed once they discover that their spouse's financial status or prestige is not enough to satisfy their longings for emotional fulfillment. Also numbered among the Dreamers are those who hope that marriage will perk up a dying romance or remedy a problematic relationship. That marriage is not a panacea for all ills comes as a terrible letdown.

The Fearful Fleers

Some newlyweds run out on marriage—either literally or emotionally, via alcohol or drug abuse—because the intensity and intimacy of married life frighten and bewilder them. These are people who've often kept their distance in previous relationships or have been hurt in the past. They don't know how to handle their feelings of aggression and anger. For them it is easier to escape marriage than to confront their mates or themselves with their furious, terrifying, and confusing feelings.

The Ho-Hum Honeymooners

Newlyweds who have lived together or dated for many years before marrying sometimes don't want to acknowledge that marriage has changed anything. They usually don't make too big a deal out of their wedding, don't plan to take a honeymoon, and try not to change any of their premarriage routines regarding how often they see friends, how much time they spend alone, etc. It's not that they're not happy to be married— most often, they are! But they liked their relationship the way it was before marriage and don't see any reason for things to change. Some may figure that since *this* is how they've been relating to each other until now, it would be phony to change their behavior because they're married. Others, feeling it might be better to do things differently, nonetheless decide not to rock the boat because their relationship up to now has worked, to a degree. These newlyweds' avoidance of doing anything too typically "married" may also stem from their rejection of their parents' or society's notion of what marriage is. There's nothing wrong with not making a fuss about being married, but there *are* hazards in denying that marriage has altered their expectations and needs. Acting as if you're not married when you are can lead to an avoidance of crucial issues. We found, however, that by the end of their newlywed year, most "ho-hummers" admit to themselves that marriage has shifted things. Once they feel assured that they can maintain one's individuality and autonomy in marriage, they can acknowledge that in marriage they share a closeness deeper and more complex than any they knew in their previous relationship with each other.

The Realistic Romantics

Realistic romantics go into marriage loving not only deeply but also practically. They accept that marriage demands adjustment, take responsibility for trying to understand and cope with marital problems that arise, and go along with, rather than bemoan, the inevitable ebb and flow, highs and lows, of marriage. Sometimes these are newlyweds who've shared a stormy relationship before getting married. Because they've already weathered and resolved problems as a couple, their relationship lacks the innocence of a new infatuation but has a strength and solidness instead. The attitude of such couples is ideal because it truly prepares the partners for the realities of marriage. Such newlyweds recognize that marriage is not the cure-all for all life's woes but will be what they make of it. They can appreciate the positives in their relationship, but at the same time acknowledge and deal with the anger and conflict.

We found that during their first year of marriage, couples often shift attitudes, fitting into one silhouette and then another. During their early months a couple may be "Inseparable Sweethearts," then feel like "Disappointed Dreamers," consider becoming "Fearful Fleers," and end up as "Realistic Romantics." Of course, two spouses may not adapt to marriage in the same way. A "Realistic Romantic" may make a mistake and marry a "Fearful Fleer," not realizing their mate is both more anxious and less mature than they are.

While it is natural to go through different stages of development, people who get stuck in any one of them—with the exception of the "Realistic Romantic" stage—may have difficulty. Essentially, the more realistically romantic you are, the better able you will be to set a foundation for the rest of your marriage. In fact, the process of growth that ideally you will go through is one of *becoming* "realistically romantic"—of aligning your marital expectations with reality. As many couples approach the end of their newlywed year (see chapter 13), they experience a sense of enrichment and contentment because they feel a more realistic appreciation of their mate and have found mutual goals to work toward. In the following chapters, as we explore the adjustments that marriage entails, we will see how very much adaptation to marriage has to do with matching one's expectations to reality.

ABOUT OUR NEWLYWED
SURVEY

We based our research on a nationwide study of 455 new-lyweds and 75 longer-married people looking back on their first year of marriage. Of this sample, we conducted in-depth interviews with over 50 first-time newlyweds and over 35 newlywed "veterans." We interviewed seventeen of the newlyweds (including seven couples) repeatedly, from the point of either just before or right after their wedding to the occasion of their first anniversary. The purpose of conducting longitudinal interviews was to chart how issues developed during marriages. We were interested in finding out how couples resolved issues over time, why problems escalated for certain couples, how couples dealt with the fears, doubts, and conflicts in their marriages. Generally we interviewed spouses separately, since people seemed to feel freer to speak about what was on their minds without their mate listening in on their thoughts.

In selecting whom to interview, we sought out newlyweds of various ages, occupations, backgrounds, and circumstances. They were either referred to us by word of mouth from clergy, friends, or coprofessionals, or were contacted in a follow-up to questionnaires they had filled out for us. None of the newlyweds we mention in this book represent therapy cases from clinical practice, although wisdom gained from patients who have related their life experiences in clinical treatment has obviously enriched the authors' understanding of the trials, tribulations, and triumphs of adult marital bonds.

Generally we spoke with our interviewees in their offices or their homes, sometimes by phone. When quoting those we interviewed or those who answered our questionnaire, we use fictitious names to protect the privacy of the men and women who so generously shared their experiences with us. In many instances we also change the occupation and hometown of our interviewees to further protect their privacy.

In addition to conducting interviews, we devised two questionnaires for newlyweds, as well as a questionnaire for people looking back on their first year of marriage. (The latter was sent to a "convenience sample"—meaning, people whom we reached conveniently, through friends, colleagues, and notices in local newspapers.)

Our initial newlywed questionnaire was designed for short-essay responses and sent to newlyweds who answered notices we placed in national and regional publications.[21] The 56 newlyweds who responded to that survey helped set the stage for our study by expressing their thoughts, fears, and problems regarding their adjustment to marriage.

We mailed a second survey, from which we generated statistical results, to a list of two thousand newlyweds nationwide whose names we procured from a mailing list–broker, who compiles the names of recently married people from wedding announcements and marriage records. It was from this survey—based on the responses of 346 newlyweds—that we drew percentage findings and correlations, which we refer to throughout this book.[22] This questionnaire, upon which our findings were based, is in Appendix B.

In Appendix A to this book we give a full breakdown of our sample, but here is some basic information about our newlywed respondents:

- 41 percent were male.
- 59 percent were female.
- The ages of our newlywed respondents ranged from 17 to 64.
- 54 percent lived with their mate before marriage.
- 23 percent were married before.
- 14 percent have children from a prior marriage.
- Newlywed respondents had been married anywhere from one month to 18 months (with the average being six months) at the time they filled out our survey.

Overall, the newlyweds we surveyed were a satisfied group:

- 35 percent said they could not be happier about their marriage.
- 45 percent said they were very happy.
- 11 percent said they were pretty happily married.
- Only 5 percent rated their feelings about their marriage as fair.
- Only 3 percent described themselves as being very unhappy in their marriage.

Nevertheless, despite their overall satisfaction, of the newlyweds we surveyed:

- 49 percent reported having significant marital problems.

- 42 percent said that marriage was harder than they had expected.

That marital happiness can coexist with marital difficulties shows that even as marriage brings joy, it also can trigger many internal and external struggles. Following in the next chapters is an exploration of the problems and challenges faced by newlyweds. As you'll notice, four larger sections follow this one. The first three—"Family," "Conflict," and "Intimacy"—focus on the central areas in which newlywed issues arise. The final section, "Reflections," provides a look back at the newlywed year from several perspectives.

We deal with each marital issue—such as sex, money, housework, friendships—in a separate chapter, because there are indeed specific problems that newlyweds confront routinely, and for different couples a different issue emerges as "the big one." In almost every marriage, though, at least one area is highly emotionally charged, rife with tension for both spouses.[23] For some, family issues might painfully touch upon the deepest needs and conflicts; for another couple, the focus of concern might become job-related matters. No matter what the big issue, it usually functions as a metaphor for a couple's evolving relationship—indicating their deep-seated conflicts, their mode of negotiation, their capability for tolerance and acceptance.

As we explore the most common newlywed issues chapter by chapter, we examine the underlying reasons for the conflicts that men and women confront early in marriage, and present guidelines for coping with them. Throughout the book we've included checklists and exercises that we hope will serve as a launching point for contemplation and discussion in, or prior to, your own marriage. Finally, we include, in their own words, stories of many of the newlyweds we spoke with across the country.

We hope that all readers find themselves within the pages that follow.

PART 2

FAMILY

Therefore shall a man leave his father and his mother, and shall cleave unto his wife: and they shall be one flesh.

Genesis 2:24

SEPARATION FROM FAMILY

Finding the Right Distance

Many men and women are surprised, even shocked, by the
emotions that overcome them when they decide to get married,
plan their wedding, and actually marry. They've anticipated
that the wedding period will be filled with joy shared between
themselves and celebrated with others. But they're frequently
astounded and become quite anxious when bittersweet feelings
enter the picture. Often, much of that bittersweet quality has
to do with family.

> As soon as we announced that we were getting married
> I became like a little girl. That night I cried on my
> father's shoulder and had this terribly sad feeling that
> I was leaving my family forever. I looked at David, my
> fiancé, and thought, Who is this man who is taking me
> away?
>
> —a 28-year-old social worker

> One of the most emotional moments of my wedding
> day was during the drive I took with my father to the
> church to get married. I became very nostalgic. I started
> telling my father how much I loved him and that I
> hoped he would be around to see my children grow
> up. We were both very teary. I think I was just over-
> come by the fact that he was getting older and I was
> getting older. I wanted to let him know how thankful
> I was for everything he had done for me.
>
> —a 32-year-old male lawyer, married
> several months

> My mother was totally frenetic and nervous the week
> before my wedding and was really getting on my nerves.
> All I could think about was how happy I was to be
> getting away from her.
>
> —a 24-year-old female painter

MAKING THE BREAK

It's really not surprising that feelings fly high around wedding time. Sure, finalizing details about floral centerpieces, making certain the tuxedos are rented, and arranging for out-of-town guests are part of the emotional frenzy. But underneath all that are a lot of feelings having to do with leaving one's family. After all, marriage is not just the beginning of a new family, but also the ending of an old one. Forty-seven percent of the newlyweds we surveyed reported that their relationship with their families changed since the wedding. No matter how many years earlier you may have left home physically, to attend college, perhaps, or to live on your own, getting married signifies an emotional leavetaking—an end to the tight family unit of one's childhood.[1]

The sadness experienced by many brides and grooms is a kind of mourning. In fact, quite a few people reported to us that in the weeks before their wedding they dreamt or harbored thoughts about their parents dying. Unconsciously, newlyweds may feel guilty about "abandoning" their parents—shifting their allegiance to their marriage partner. Or they may feel ambivalent about moving on, leaving the family nest, assuming the adult roles of husband and wife. As one 30-year-old, recently engaged woman told us:

> I waited two years for Les to propose to me, but when we finally became engaged one of the first things that hit me was that I felt old. I had spent my whole life wondering in the back of my mind who I was going to marry. Now that I know, it seems like there is something more finite about my life. I don't feel like such a kid anymore.

Even a man who had raised three children and was remarrying at the age of 46 acknowledged to us that marrying again—after leading a freewheeling life as a divorcé for ten years—signified to him an act of maturity, a "growing up."

> I started thinking about marrying again when I was stuck in bed for a week with a bout of the flu. The enforced hours of thinking made me aware that I was no spring chicken anymore. It really made me think of my mortality.

No matter how eager you are to marry, it's natural to feel a little afraid of making the change, or a little wistful about relinquishing the role of the cared-for "child" or the carefree adult. Ambivalence characterizes any transitional stage. A child beginning to walk is eager to try out his new skill but, at the same time, fearful of his independence. Frightened of the distance his new mobility creates between him and Mommy, he goes back to her for frequent assurance and comforting. An adolescent, on the verge of adulthood, is similarly both excited and hesitant about the meaning and responsibilities encompassed in growing up.

One bride told us that the only time she felt any mixed emotions during her wedding was right at the end, when the limousine was waiting outside for her and her groom. She wouldn't leave the reception hall until her father, who was busy paying the caterer, came out and kissed her goodbye. "I hugged him and cried, and I felt like both of us were saying goodbye to his little girl," she remembered.

Most of us aren't conscious of the passing of time except when major milestones occur—births, deaths, graduations, marriages. A wedding is a reminder that life continues, that things never stay the same. Newlyweds whose parents or grandparents died before the wedding told us of their sadness in not having those loved ones present at such a special time. In fact, researchers have noted the phenomenon of people meeting their spouse or deciding to marry within six months of a major change in their family of origin.[2] Upheaval in one's family apparently leads to the desire to replace or re-create the relationship that was lost or diminished.

Of course, not everyone experiences bittersweet feelings upon marrying. Many brides and grooms report feeling purely exuberant at their weddings. They are thrilled and relieved to have found a life partner to love and be loved by, someone with whom they can share the joys and the burdens of life. Some people who marry may be more conscious of bringing their spouse *into* their family, rather than of leaving their family. Others may rejoice that they have found a mate who provides the love, nurturance, or other desirable quality missing in their relationships with their own family.[3]

There are those who don't walk, but—at least emotionally—fly down the wedding aisle, thrilled to be escaping from their families. One woman told us that rather than make her nostalgic for her old family life, getting married rekindled her old anger.

> My parents are very controlling people and I was always very threatened by them. I felt they would swallow me up. I've always seen guys as a way to buffer me from them. On my wedding day I was in my glory. It felt like I was telling my parents, "I'm not yours anymore." My husband is so supportive and loving that marrying him emphasized to me everything my parents are not. But it's a little sad that on the happiest day of my life I was filled with so much anger toward them.

Whatever feelings you have regarding your family when you marry—no matter how mixed your emotions might be—it's quite normal for deep and intense emotions to be stirred. Getting married symbolizes a breaking away. And it's a change that affects not just you but your entire family. Just as you may feel different toward them, they may also be sensitive to the shifting family dynamics. As happy as they may be that you are marrying, they may also be sad about "losing" their child. Sure, they waited years to see you marry, but when that moment arrives, it sets off a whole series of questions and personal crises in them. They are reminded that they themselves are aging, and caused to wonder what direction their lives will take now that parenting is not their central concern.

One groom told us how disappointed he was by his mother's reaction when he told her he was engaged. He had been certain that she would be elated at the news. But instead of the hugging and kissing he expected, his mother just stayed in her seat and said, "Congratulations." He eventually realized that his mother, whose husband had died two years before, was experiencing his marriage as her loss. Without the support of her husband, his mother found it difficult to give up her only son to another woman.

Another groom admitted that his mother would have viewed as a threat to their relationship anyone whom he, the oldest child, might have married.

> My mother's very jealous. I chose a wife who is very different from the members of my family—she's more

reserved, much calmer, not as openly emotional. My mother sees her as distant. She feels I've made a choice to side with my wife and I'm leaving her out in the cold. I want to be a loving son and I want my parents to love my wife. But they've made it so difficult for us to plan our wedding that I've just ended up resenting them.

WHOSE WEDDING IS THIS, ANYWAY?

Much of the push-and-pull that parents and child feel between wanting to let go and *not* wanting to let go gets played out in a tug-of-war around the wedding. It's interesting and ironic that, while marriage involves a separation between parent and child, the planning of the wedding often brings the two generations into more intimate proximity with one another than they've experienced in years. The wedding is usually a family event and, especially if you are planning the wedding along with your parents, there are endless decisions that need to be negotiated—from how large a wedding to have and who is to be invited, to which invitations to select and what type of music to play. It's not unusual for all of the ambivalence and internal conflict felt by family members to come pouring out around the decisions that need to be made. Although you are taking a major step toward independence by marrying, if your parents are controlling the purse strings for the wedding, you may be thrust back into a dependent role. Even if you and your mate are planning and paying for the wedding yourselves, your parents may feel they have a right to voice their opinions and exercise their "rights."

It's important to look at the feelings and problems that arise during the wedding period, because frequently they crystalize family dynamics that have held sway for years and foreshadow conflicts that may crop up in years to come. Because weddings involve so much money, so much emotion, so much planning, it makes usually subtle family tendencies much more obvious. As one woman said, "The whole process of getting married brought out all the old family patterns I had long tried to deny—the ambivalence of my mother, the jealousy of my stepsisters, the absence of my father."

Wedding struggles don't just reflect on the past—they also hint at the future. Any competitiveness, intrusiveness, or hostility that family members demonstrate during the planning months before the wedding inevitably offer a clue to what will follow after you say "I do." If you're marrying someone who has children or if you have children from a previous marriage, the attitudes that the children adopt toward your wedding will reflect the feelings they harbor about your new marriage. So the more you understand about the family dynamics that emerge during the prewedding period, the better able you'll be to prepare and exercise ways to cope with relatives during your first year of marriage.

Here are three stories of people we interviewed whose conflicts with relatives during the wedding planning period highlighted important forces at work in family relations.

Roberta and Andrew

When Roberta and Andrew Parker married four years ago Roberta was 24 years old and her parents had been separated for six years. Her father had left her mother for another woman. Her mother, still angry and bitter about being deserted, announced immediately upon Roberta's engagement that neither Roberta's father nor Roberta's father's mother or brother could attend the wedding.

Roberta felt devastated. She couldn't imagine getting married without her father in attendance. Andrew, Roberta's fiancé, also did not want those close relatives to be slighted. Both tried to convince Roberta's mother that she was wrong, and even had the family rabbi talk to her in an attempt to change her mind. But Roberta's mother remained steadfast, saying she would not come to the wedding if Roberta's father was there.

Not knowing what to do, Roberta and Andrew finally resolved to get married twice. First they married in the rabbi's study, with Roberta's father, grandmother, and uncle there. Then they married again, in a large temple, with 130 guests taking part. Roberta satisfied her mother, and to a degree herself, in meeting her own need to have her father see her married. But four years later both she and Andrew still feel a certain bitterness on thinking back to their wedding. Said Andrew:

The wedding was beautiful, but I will always remember that there were people hurt in a very tangible way. It was a preposterous arrangement, and the way Roberta's mother acted was indicative of the long-standing problems we've had with her since. She did not want to let go of her favored child and she still doesn't. I feel that Roberta's mother has extensive influence over Roberta. She was outrageously demanding then and she still is.

If we look at what went on around the time of the wedding, certain things emerge clearly. Roberta's mother demonstrated then that she felt free to impose her own feelings on her daughter and son-in-law and knew how to manipulate her daughter in order to achieve her own ends. Roberta felt caught between her love for her two parents, yet cleverly managed to maintain her attachment to both, although at some risk of making herself unhappy. Finally, Andrew wanted to please his wife and therefore supported her in the way she decided to handle her estranged parents. On the other hand, he found Roberta's mother annoying, demanding, and intrusive.

According to the couple, all of the family dynamics operating at the time of the wedding are still very much apparent four years later. Roberta's mother is still very demanding, sometimes calling up Roberta and Andrew in the middle of the night to discuss some minor detail of concern to her. Roberta still resents her mother's wishes—and is still giving in to them. Andrew continues to accept Roberta's attachment to her mother but feels it's a definite problem in their marriage. Roberta and Andrew see Roberta's mother as a source of disruption in their marriage, but they continue to accept the situation as best they can, trying not to let her ruin their relationship.

Natalie and Vincent

By the time we met Natalie and Vincent Rizzo, shortly before their first anniversary, they seemed to have overcome the family tensions sparked by their wedding. But nothing had yet dimmed the memory of what Natalie described as her "wedding disaster."

Quite simply, I had a very different wedding in my mind than the one envisioned by my husband and his parents—and I guess *my* parents, too. I wanted a simple brunch, and they wanted a circus for two hundred and fifty of our "nearest and dearest," which is what we eventually had.

My in-laws are struggling immigrants, and I married their only child. They said they lived to see the day their son married. It was very hard for me to stand up to them. Even my parents thought I should give in and have a big, traditional wedding. I've always been a "good girl." I always had good grades, nice friends, was a good athlete. I'm also an only child, and I've never disappointed my parents. Probably because I know how invested my parents are in me, I understood how invested my husband's parents are in him. But to this day I get furious when I think about my wedding. I should have backed out from the big ceremony and done something simple. I was uncomfortable with the ostentation, uncertain about the tradition, and constantly bothered about bridesmaids' dresses and flowers—none of which I wanted. I got hysterical, crying halfway through my wedding because I felt like it *wasn't my wedding*. I felt like a fake. Getting drunk helped tremendously.

Although Natalie followed her in-laws' wishes in having the kind of wedding they wanted, she asserted herself to them once she got married.

When we first got married, they ignored me and tormented my husband about me. They didn't like me. We finally stormed out of their house one weekend when we were visiting, and simply said that we'd stop visiting or calling. They changed quickly.

The question of who was in control of Natalie's wedding really brought to the fore the issue of her desire always to please people. But in making everybody else happy about her wedding, Natalie couldn't help but realize that she had made herself miserable. The experience emphasized to her that if she was to be happy in marriage, she needed to assert herself more strongly. And, as she said to us, "Something very valuable came out of the whole mess. My husband realized that *if I'm miserable, he's miserable*—even if he gets what he wants. That's not the worst lesson to take through your marriage!"

Jacki and Earl

Jacki Robbins, a pretty, 24-year-old black woman who works as a secretary in Chicago, thought her whole wedding was planned—that is, until, two months before the wedding, when her future mother-in-law arrived from her native Trinidad and moved in with her and Earl, Jacki's fiancé. Since Earl, a restaurant chef, often worked late, Jacki found herself spending evenings listening to Earl's mother voice her opinions about their wedding. We first spoke to Jacki several days before her wedding. She reported to us with amazement:

> I had already decided how many people I was going to have in my wedding party, then *she* decided she wanted to throw all her granddaughters in the wedding party and just went out and bought them dresses. I asked her, "What are you doing?" Then, she wanted to have Earl's brother give me away at the wedding because my father died when I was young. And I said, "Well, we can't do this either because I have brothers and uncles who would also like to give me away."

Jacki told us she tried to elicit support from Earl in the month before their wedding but he just responded with "Well, tell her off."

"But I couldn't," said Jacki to us. "I told her nicely, 'I appreciate your thoughts, but we feel that we've already set it up.' "

Although Earl's mother didn't end up having her way about a lot of wedding decisions, according to Jacki, she did play the role of "queen bee" at the wedding by holding up the ceremony a half hour because she insisted on getting dressed in the bridal room. Interestingly, Jacki said that on the day of the wedding, Earl fought with *her* mother, accusing her of butting in by asking the band to play disco music. He also charged Jacki's maid of honor with being too bossy with Jacki. Although the wedding went off well and Jacki felt that the guests had a great time, she told us she felt sick about all the spats that took place. "I was spending the whole time trying to be a peacemaker."

According to Jacki, after Earl's mother returned to Trinidad, Earl did explain to Jacki that it had been difficult for him to deal with a lot of the relatives and friends who visited for the wedding—people he hadn't seen since his youth. "Now I understand him a lot better, especially things about his childhood," she commented to us, and then added with a laugh, "And now I know why he wanted to get married very quietly without saying anything to anybody."

Although Earl eventually apologized to her mother, Jacki remarked to us that even months later her mom still hadn't forgotten that Earl yelled at her at the wedding. What Jacki's mother didn't realize, of course, was that Earl had really displaced onto her and Jacki's maid of honor his anger at his own mother, to whom he was afraid to speak up. With his mother and other relatives vying for control of the wedding, he had felt out of control and lashed out in anger.

TIPS FOR WRESTLING WITH WEDDING POWER STRUGGLES

It's not always possible to avoid conflicts during the wedding planning period, but power struggles between family members can be minimized by being alert to your and your mate's feelings as well as to the concerns of your relatives. It's worth taking the trouble to prevent bad feelings from arising in connection with the wedding, because any resentments stirred then are likely to be remembered for years to come. Keep in mind that the wedding is important not just to you and your mate; it is a major event in the lives of both families.

Here are some guidelines aimed at keeping wedding planning peaceful and at setting positive precedents for dealing with relatives after you marry:

1. Think ahead. Imagine how family members will react, and plan accordingly.

Martin and Deborah, both 31, knew that Deborah's mother would take over the planning of their wedding if given any say in the matter. By keeping their engagement a secret for two months, they had time to decide what type of wedding they wanted, who'd be invited, and where the wedding would be held. When they eventually announced their engagement and presented their wedding plans, Deborah's parents realized that the couple knew their own minds, and went along with their wishes. It was a matter of not only getting the kind of wedding they wanted but also, even more important, showing both sets of parents that they, Martin and Deborah, were adults and wanted to be respected as such. By thinking things through beforehand, they avoided a power struggle.

2. *Take other people's feelings into consideration.* Try to understand and empathize with other family members—your parents, siblings, in-laws, children, stepchildren, and future spouse. Think about what it is they are reacting to: Is it jealousy toward a new sister-in-law or brother-in-law? sadness about losing a child? fears about gaining a new stepparent? One woman we spoke with was extremely bitter that her husband's parents— who were quite wealthy—did not offer to share in paying for the wedding, leaving her parents, who were less affluent, with the entire tab. Although she was unaware of it, a key factor in her anger was that she had no idea why her in-laws had not made an offer. Was it just cheapness on their part? Did they have old-fashioned notions about the bride's family paying for the wedding? Did they not realize what a financial burden the wedding was going to be for her parents? Or was there yet some other reason? Rather than just remain silently angry at her husband's family, she might have tried to find out the reason for their behavior.

3. *Include family members in your plans.* If you see that relatives are eager to take part in your wedding planning, share your ideas with them so that they feel included. But if they try to influence you with their opinions, state that you and your mate are planning to make all final decisions. You might also make relatives feel involved by assigning them tasks that can ease your mind—such as finding hotel rooms for out-of-town guests and picking up guests at the airport.

4. *Decide what is important to you and what isn't.* A certain amount of compromise may be necessary, especially if parents are paying for the wedding.

Mary, a 29-year-old film editor, discovered that her mother's notion of a wedding was totally unlike what she wanted. Her mother wanted to invite everyone from her parish, and all of her father's business associates. Mary decided to go along with her mother's wishes. "I really didn't particularly like my wedding, but it didn't bother me. My attitude was that *the wedding is for my parents, my marriage is for me.*" While that attitude is certainly not for everybody, it suited Mary and her husband.

5. *Assert yourself in a tactful manner.* Sharing your feelings with your own and your mate's relatives can be a healthy start to an open relationship, but be careful how you express yourself. An insult from a blood relative may well be quickly forgotten, but the same from an in-law will rarely be forgiven. One groom got along famously with his future mother-in-law until right before the wedding, when he boldly told her that she was becoming too interfering in his, and her daughter's, wedding plans. For at least eight months into the marriage, that couple has rarely seen the wife's mother, although they live quite near each other. When last we checked in with these newlyweds, the husband was embarrassed that he blew his cool, the mother-in-law was ashamed that she became so demanding about the wedding—but neither felt comfortable about making amends. Expressing yourself firmly but politely is crucial.

6. *Discourage rivalry between parents-in-law.* Some parents feel very competitive toward their child's "new" parents and try to vie for the couple's favor. One bride commented that right after her parents gave her and her husband a piano as a wedding gift, her husband's parents offered the couple a car. She knew that her in-laws were not nearly as well off as her own parents, and felt terrible that they were attempting to compete.

Rather than letting each set of parents feel that they should match the other's behavior, show that you appreciate their differences and accept them for who they are. Of course, it may be impossible to quell the jealousy and resentment that one or both sets of parents have for the other. Some parents can just never find a good word to say about their child's in-laws. If this is your situation, then try to stay uninvolved by offering both sets of parents little opportunity to draw you into the conflict.

7. *Make your loyalty to your mate clear to your family.* Some anxious relatives may try to test your love for them against your love for your new spouse by posing their demands against those of your spouse's. Don't let them! Show them that you still love them very much, but also make it obvious that your mate is your highest consideration. Cut them short if they begin to bad-mouth your spouse—or they will play on any of your uncertainties at a time when you're trying to establish a stable and permanent relationship.

8. Talk to your mate. It's important for you to impart to one another your feelings about your own family and your spouse's. In the case of Jacki and Earl, whom we introduced earlier, a lot of the bad feelings that emerged from the planning of their wedding might have been avoided if they had communicated more openly. If Earl had told Jacki before the wedding that he didn't feel comfortable confronting his mother, she probably would have been more understanding of his behavior before and during the celebration. Or she might even have convinced him beforehand to discuss his feelings with his mother in a calm way, and he then might not have felt a need to project his anger upon others.

9. Remember that your marriage is your highest priority. It's nice to take everyone else's feelings into consideration, but the most important aspect of the wedding ceremony is that it is the start of your marriage together. Under circumstances when it's impossible to please everybody, make sure that you at least please yourselves.

One couple we know simply eloped when they realized that the groom's parents were terribly opposed to his marrying and would poison the spirit of any wedding the young couple planned. They decided it was not worth taking the chance of having his parents ruin their wedding day.

CHECKUP:
MARRIAGE AND FAMILY

Your wedding is, of course, just the beginning. Whether or not your family was involved in planning it, whether or not family tensions mounted in the months preceding your wedding ceremony, you'll probably find that your families will play an important role in your marriage. By marrying, you and your spouse are entering new families and altering your own family structure. Even if you live miles away from your relatives, those changes are bound to set off all kinds of feelings and reactions in you.

The following is a list of statements commonly made by newlyweds about their own and their spouse's families. Place a check next to *each and every statement* that applies to you. Please note that this is *not* a multiple choice quiz. Check all the statements that apply to you—or none at all, if none apply. For some readers the "family" mentioned in these statements will refer to parents or in-laws. For others it will apply more to children or stepchildren. As you go through the checklist, just keep in mind which family members apply in your own situation.

I feel that my spouse is:
- [ ] too close with their family
- [ ] not close enough with their family

My spouse feels that I am:
- [ ] too close with my family
- [ ] not close enough with my family

I wish:
- [ ] I felt more comfortable with my spouse's family
- [ ] my spouse felt more comfortable with my family

My spouse and I disagree over:
- [ ] how much time to spend with family
- [ ] whose family to visit for the holidays

I sometimes feel pulled between:
- [ ] what my family wants from me and what my spouse wants from me
- [ ] my loyalty to my own family and my loyalty to my spouse's family

Since our wedding, my relationship with my own family:
- [ ] has changed for the better
- [ ] has changed for the worse

Since our wedding, my relationship with my spouse's family:
- [ ] has changed for the better
- [ ] has changed for the worse

Now look at the statements beside which you placed check marks. Don't be concerned if you checked quite a few. This Checkup is not a pass-or-fail test, and it's not a competition in which one spouse "wins" over the other. You both, however, *should* win *with* it. It is an invitation to greater self-knowledge, and a deeper understanding of one another. *Often we don't know what our feelings are until we try to articulate them,* until we discuss feelings and ideas with others. This Checkup (along with other devices in the book) is a springboard for airing (and ultimately resolving) those feelings and ideas.

Keep in mind that it is natural to have a lot of feelings stirred up about family—especially early in marriage, when you're trying to sort out what kind of relationships you want to have with your own family and your spouse's family. In fact, family is (after money) the second major cause of arguments among newlyweds,[4] probably because so many feelings about family are triggered during the marriage process.

It is vital to be aware of your feelings about family—especially at the start of marriage. The relationships you establish with family members, as a couple and as individual human beings, are ones that will continue for many years. Understanding the emotions you experience and focusing on what role you want relatives to play in your marriage are important goals to keep in mind.

In the following sections we look into many of the issues suggested by the statements in the Checkup above. You'll find it easier to implement changes when you recognize the reasons for your internal and marital conflicts having to do with family. At the end of this chapter we offer guidelines to help you integrate family relationships into your marriage in a way that suits your needs.

FAMILY TIES

The task of the first year of marriage is to establish yourselves as a married couple—to become comfortable with your identity as a married pair and to adapt to dealing with others as married partners. That challenge is often complicated, however, by relatives who, well meaning though they may be, want to make certain that they still play a central role in your lives.

Presenting a united front as husband and wife to relatives who can be intrusive is crucial, though difficult. Here are some of the problems—some dealt with successfully, some not so successfully—that newlyweds we interviewed faced from intervening family members.

The Parent Pull

If your parents or your spouse's parents have always been the type to intervene in your lives, consider it unlikely that they will suddenly stop when you get married. And even if they aren't the kind to butt in, seeing their child marry may prompt fears that they are losing their parental hold and spark them to intercede in ways that you may feel threaten your marital relationship.

In many instances, it will be your job to remind your parents that you need to be respected as a couple.

Francesca, a 24-year-old newlywed, told us of the time her mother visited her at home when Francesca was sick and her husband was off at work. While she lay in bed, her mother went into the living room and rearranged all the furniture. When Francesca ventured out of her bedroom later in the day, she was appalled by her mother's gall. "How dare she come into the home I share with my husband and act as if I were a teenager who needed to be taught about decorating?" she exclaimed to us.

Francesca, who had always been intimidated by her mother's controlling nature, told us that being married gave her the strength and confidence to speak up to her mother for the first time. "My mother has always been the type to take over. But seeing her try to run the show now that I'm married really emphasized to me the extent to which she is controlling." While her mother seemed a little hurt when Francesca told her off, the message did get through. During subsequent visits to Francesca's home, her mother behaved more as a guest.

Unfortunately, some people don't find it easy to speak up to parents or in-laws when they feel them butting in.

Alice, a 31-year-old architect, told us she was having a particularly hard time with her mother, whose phone calls she had come to dread.

My husband is just starting out in business and my mother wants to make sure her daughter is well taken care of. Whenever she speaks to me she asks me, "How is Barry's business going? Is he attracting many new customers?" She gets me crazy, because she stirs up all of my own doubts. When I get off the phone I become furious with Barry for not being more successful. My mother touches upon what is a sensitive issue for me and makes it worse.

Because Alice was used to her mother's being a strong, controlling force in her life, it took her time to realize that what her mother was presenting as loving concern was actually none of her business. Yet even after coming to the realization, Alice found herself hesitant to inform her mother of these feelings.

Alice's solution has been to see and speak to her mother less frequently. "I find that when I speak to my mother less, I think less pessimistically about Barry's career," she explained.

An alternative that Alice might have considered is to have shared her feelings with her mother—in an open, rather than an attacking, manner. It is doubtful her mom would have been insulted had Alice said something like, "Mom, please don't constantly ask me about Barry's business. If there is any news, of course we'll tell you. We know it's going to take a few years for things to get off the ground, but we're both confident that he'll be successful. When you keep questioning me, though, it puts doubts in my mind and I take them out on Barry. I'm sure you want what's best for our marriage—so please don't make us more anxious than we already are."

Though Alice hasn't chosen to be so open, her strategy does serve the dual purpose of strengthening her commitment to her husband and loosening her from the grip of her mother.

Often the challenge newlyweds face is one of altering their parents' expectations.

A 27-year-old groom, for instance, told us he was informed by his parents shortly after he married that they expected him and his wife to visit them every Sunday, as they themselves had done with their own parents when they had first married. At his wife's insistence, he explained to his parents that he and his wife needed weekends to spend with each other, since both worked all week.

The fact is that my parents don't want to recognize that I have other obligations now. All the demands they make on me are really denials on their part that there has been a major change in my life.

In-Law Intrusiveness

It's hard enough when your own relatives intrude on your marriage—and even more difficult when your in-laws try to become a dominating force. Brenda, married just a year, asserted:

My in-laws automatically started treating me the way they treat their own kids. It's one thing when they impose their opinions on their own children—*their* children love them. But *I don't!* I resent their interference enormously. I moved hundreds of miles away from my hometown to escape my family, and now I end up living ten miles from my in-laws. It's awful.

One newlywed woman complained about her sister-in-law, who suddenly expected her to spend every weekend shopping or going to the movies with her. "We have very little in common, but my sister-in-law has this picture of the way a family is supposed to be. And to her it doesn't matter that we are really two very different types of people."

Of course, what you see as intrusiveness on the part of your in-laws may not be interpreted as such by your spouse.

Short, plump, blue-eyed Stella, now married ten years, told us that her marriage almost broke up during her newlywed year because of her husband's close relationship with his mother.

My husband, Danny, was nine when his father died, and so he was extremely close to his mother. His mother felt left out from the two of us when we got married. But I also felt left out from the two of them. She used to call up and only want to speak with Danny. And it was never enough if he just told her we were going out. She always wanted to know where and with whom. It drove me crazy.

Stella's rivalry with her mother-in-law came to a head during a two-week vacation in Florida they all took together.

I wanted to have one day just to spend with Danny alone, and she insisted on coming with us. Danny took

her side. He didn't think that she should be alone. I
started screaming at her and crying. That incident made
me decide to see a psychotherapist.

Stella said that in therapy she came to realize that her anger
at her mother-in-law's intrusiveness stemmed, in large part,
from her own needs. Having been left by her father when she
was three years old, Stella realized that she had been looking
for the unconditional love of a man and was furious at Danny's
mother for taking Danny away from her. Stella now admitted:

Danny's mother *was* intrusive, but I was also a child. I
wasn't able to see her side of things—that she had lost
her companion and was lonely. Because I was raised
by my mother I feel more comfortable with women,
and so I vented my anger at my mother-in-law more
than at Danny.

Fortunately Stella and her mother-in-law did reconcile. But
even then, she regretted the toll the conflict took on the early
years of her marriage. "Danny and I used to have incredible
fights about his mother. It would have been nice if all that
energy could have been channeled in a positive way," she said
wistfully.

The Stepchild Situation

If you and/or your spouse have children from a previous
marriage, then you may have harbored all sorts of fantasies
about the terrific rapport that will develop between all of you
as you become a new family. But the reality is often very different. The lingering anger children may feel about their parents' divorce or a parent's death, the sense of loss and jealousy
they may experience now that their parent is remarrying, all
may intrude upon any romantic newlywed phase you had hoped
for.

If marriage presents you or your spouse with a first-time
experience of having children in the house, then one of you
may suffer a particularly rude awakening on discovering just
how demanding children can be. Not only may they impinge
on your privacy, not only may they be disobedient and test your
disciplinary skills, but they may pit you and your spouse against
each other, turning you into opposing players rather than a

team. Children have a great way of making themselves the focus so that you and your spouse are left competing with them for attention, nurturance, support.

It's not that new marriages in which children are involved are less happy—but rather that they are often forced to confront certain challenges. Our study findings, although based on a small sample of newlyweds with children or stepchildren, suggest this phenomenon. We found:

- There is *no* relationship between happiness in marriage and whether or not newlyweds have children from a previous marriage.[5]

If you're a newlywed with children, then you and your spouse must address not only marital issues, but also parenting tasks —meaning that values, religious differences, and the time demands of your job all take on even greater importance.[6]

If your stepchildren are themselves adults, you may be surprised to discover that despite being grown up, they can intervene in your new marriage in ways you hadn't anticipated.

Sandra, a 36-year-old artist married for five years to a man who is twenty years her senior, recalled,

Calvin's four sons are in their twenties. We never had anything to do with his kids before marriage, so I was struck by surprise when we married and they suddenly became a big part of our lives. Being older, they had much more to say about our getting married than they would have if they were a lot younger. They didn't want him to remarry, and what I've finally realized is that it didn't matter who I was—they *didn't* want him to remarry. They treat me pretty poorly. One of his children said to my husband in front of me, "You don't have to be too intelligent to be a painter."

In retrospect Sandra regretted having allowed her husband's sons to cause her as much anguish as they did.

I let his kids walk all over me the first year. I wish I'd been harder with them. It was very rough at the beginning. I thought that maybe I had bitten off more than I could chew. I was testing my husband a lot to see whose side he was on. For a long time he didn't really understand what I was going through. He finally admitted that his sons were being extremely hostile to me.

The Ex-Spouse Scenario

If you are marrying someone who has been wed before, then you may find that your predecessor—your spouse's "ex" —pops into the picture. This may especially be the case if your mate's spouse is still in love with your spouse, or if the two of them have a child in common. Whether the reasons your spouse's "ex" keeps in touch with your mate are legitimate or not, the situation can be very hard to accept and handle. After all, when you're trying to establish a marriage of your own it is painful to be reminded that your spouse went through the process once before.

Carol, a 38-year-old woman now married three years, told us that the most difficult aspect of her newlywed year was that her husband's ex-wife ("one of the angriest ex-wives imaginable," says Carol), who lived nearby, became like a third person in her marriage. According to Carol, when Laura, her 13-year-old stepdaughter, came for dinner she'd inevitably talk about what her mother was doing.

> Sometimes she'd repeat horrible things that her mother said about me. And I knew that her mother asked her lots of questions when she went home. I felt like I was being spied on. I never knew what was going to be repeated to her mother. My husband's ex-wife pops messages into Laura's schoolbag for me like: "To the maid"—that's me—"Make sure Laura's school uniform is ironed." Once after I taught Laura to play solitaire, her mother sent me an accusatory letter saying how dare I teach a child to play cards by herself. I followed the advice of a friend and sent her letter back with the English corrected. I was trying to show that I couldn't take her seriously. It helped—she never sent me a letter again.

Although Carol stated that having a stepdaughter had enriched her life, she also confessed that at first it was hard not to resent her. As a noncustodial parent, she said:

> My husband and I had our own life, because she wasn't living with us. But every time she came over, the boat was getting rocked. Her mother was getting all this attention in our house. I also felt let down by Mike. I

didn't feel that he was being a husband, because he wasn't protecting me from his ex-wife. She would call up and he'd stay on the phone listening to a torrent of abuse for two hours. I used to say to him, "I feel like the three of you are allied against me."

The situation eventually improved, according to Carol. Gradually her husband overcame his guilt about leaving his former wife and was able to ignore her and avoid long-winded, anguished phone conversations. Also, as Laura got older and realized that she was hurting Carol by repeating her mother's insults, she tried her best to keep her two worlds separate. Finally, Carol had changed her own attitude.

I'm much more open about my own feelings with Laura. Now, if she brings up her mother at the dinner table, I'll say lightly, "Oh, can't we get her out of the house?" I wouldn't have felt that comfortable with her several years ago. But Laura knows that I love her and I think she loves me. We're trying to support each other in our situations.

TORN BETWEEN LOYALTIES

The reason that the intrusiveness of relatives can feel so threatening to newlyweds is that in the first year of marriage, often there is still a certain tenuousness to the marriage bond. Attachments to one's parents or children or siblings can seem much stronger than one's attachment to one's spouse. There's an old saying that there are at least six people in a marriage—the bride, the groom, and the two parents of each. Even when one's parents are no longer living, a person may feel torn between wanting to do things "my family's way" and "your family's way." And if you're bringing to your marriage children from a previous relationship, it's inevitable that at times you will struggle to balance your allegiance to your children with your loyalty to your spouse.

Achieving, as a couple, an identity separate from your family is a major task in marriage.[7] That's not to say that you should alienate yourselves from your parents—and certainly not from your children. But it does mean that you should focus on establishing a strong primary bond with your mate. Close family relationships are enriching for both your life and your marriage—but only once you've developed a solid marital partnership. If you start your marriage by focusing most of your energies on the welfare of your parents, siblings, or children, then essentially you are stating that they are your priority. You need to build a marriage foundation before you can let other concerns take center stage from time to time. Sure, if you have children it's natural to care deeply about how they are adjusting to your new marriage. But the fact is that they won't thrive in the new stepfamily situation until you and your spouse are yourselves comfortable in your marital relationship.

The problem is that it's not always easy to loosen the grip on one's family ties. One groom recounted to us that at a certain point during his wedding reception, he found himself being swept up amid a swarm of his wife's relatives to sing a cousin's club song. Feeling overwhelmed, he thought to himself, "Oh, my God. What did I get myself into?"

The new presence in your life of your spouse's family is in many ways a reminder that you are letting go—at least to some extent—of your own family. Much of the in-law resentment that is so common among newlyweds and their families is rooted in this anxiety about leaving one's family of origin. It's common, for instance, for people who are very enmeshed in their own families to avoid becoming close with their spouse's family, fearing that to do so would be disloyal, or be perceived by their own parents or siblings as disloyal. And criticism of in-laws is often, in reality, a displacement of one's own frustration and anger at one's own family. If you're feeling torn between your parents and your spouse, you may lash out at your in-laws in an effort to deny your feelings of attachment to your family.

If you and your mate are very involved with family members—whether in positive or conflictual relationships—you should consider the role these attachments play in your marriage. For instance, you and your mate may "gang up" against one or both sets of parents—which has the effect not only of unifying yourselves against them, but also, possibly, of disguising certain unresolved issues that may exist between the two of you. Therapist Murray Bowen describes the process of "triangulation"[8]—which is the involvement of a third party in a relationship as a way of relieving some of the pressure and tension between a couple. Family ties can serve both a healthy and a hazardous function in this regard.

INTEGRATING FAMILY AND
MARRIAGE

Despite the difficulties we've described, you *can* resolve family issues in a positive manner so that family relationships nourish rather than hinder your new marriage. In fact, of the newlyweds we surveyed:

- 51 percent reported that their relationship with their parents had *improved* since their wedding.
- 54 percent reported that their relationship with their spouse's family had *improved* since their wedding.

Although getting married represents separating from your parents, it also signifies a reconciliation with them. By assuming the role of husband or wife, you are emulating your parents—and relating to them as peer, as adult, as equal. Once you've established your independence by getting married, you may feel less threatened by your parents' attempts at intervention in your life; or you may feel more secure in asserting yourself to them. One recent bride told us:

> When I was living on my own I *never* told my mother anything. I never told her who I was dating or where I was going. I knew she'd always have a comment that I wouldn't want to hear. Now I'm much closer with her. On my days off we sometimes go shopping or to exercise class. She still tends to lecture. She can't help but meddle. But I find myself laughing about it, not getting angry the way I would have a year ago.

Getting married may offer you a more objective view of your parents—especially if your spouse helps you gain a balanced perspective. One woman we interviewed, the daughter of an alcoholic father and a mentally disturbed mother, was encouraged by her husband to join Al-Anon, an organization for the relatives of alcoholics, which, she said, helped her put the focus back on herself. Having always played the "caretaker" role in her family, this woman, with her husband's support, discovered that she was able to "let go" of her family so that she could focus her energies on her present life and her marriage. She still feels close to her parents, but in a much healthier way.

Marriage may not only benefit your relationship with your

family but also reward you by making you part of a new family.[9] Until now, we've emphasized the problems that may stem from becoming part of your spouse's family. But there are advantages.

Having in-laws offers you the opportunity to re-create family relationships the way you want them, to rewrite scripts that were problematic in your own family. Having a mother-in-law or father-in-law offers you a chance to forge a relationship with an older adult that is free of the mistakes, guilt, and unresolved conflicts that you may have experienced with your own parents. Gaining a sister-in-law, brother-in-law, or stepchild may afford you the possibility of enjoying the sister, brother, or child you never had. One groom noted that he took special pleasure in his weekly tennis games with his father-in-law because he had always regretted that his father had never played ball with him. Another man told us that he was able to share intellectual ideas with his father-in-law in a way he could never do with his own father. Grasp this opportunity with your new family to make up for past needs unfulfilled.

WORKSHOP: ESTABLISHING HEALTHY FAMILY RELATIONSHIPS

It's natural to have many feelings about your changing family relationships. But how you handle your and your spouse's feelings about family will make all the difference in whether family relationships enhance or hinder your marriage.

As we interviewed couples, we found that certain approaches best promise success in dealing with families. Here, based on those conclusions, are our guidelines:

1. Share your feelings about your families respectfully. In chapter 5, on communication, we'll consider *how* to talk with your spouse, focusing on the importance of time and place and tone. But here we place special emphasis on one factor—SENSITIVITY! Remember that your spouse probably loves his or her family dearly. Any of your observations about your in-laws may be perceived as an attack demanding an equivalent defense.

The key to preventing your spouse from feeling threatened

is to focus on *your* feelings rather than on what your spouse or their family is doing "wrong." If you think your mate stands aloof from your family, don't attack your spouse for being distant, but share your feelings about how you wish your mate and your family were closer to one another. If you feel excluded from your spouse's family, don't complain that they are snobbish, but explain that you would love to get to know your new family better. Rather than attack your mate for not understanding you and your family, confide the nitty-gritty details about family feuds or rituals that will help illuminate your family dynamics.

As an outer-circle member of your spouse's family, you will inevitably see certain aspects of your adopted family with some objectivity. Your observations, in some cases, can be helpful to your spouse if you present them as we've just suggested. For instance, one woman we spoke with told her husband that she felt uncomfortable when he was with his parents because he seemed to become almost childlike in their presence. By putting the focus on her discomfort rather than on his behavior, she was able to make her husband aware of his demeanor without being accusatory. He, in turn, was able to acknowledge that he did behave differently with his parents and that he should probably try to act more adult with them.

We should note that it may not always be advisable to share with your mate your feelings about your spouse's family. If you despise your in-laws, then it's best to keep mum. There is probably nothing constructive that will emerge from your hateful comments.

On the other hand, there may be some family issues that you should be certain to discuss before marriage. If you plan on living near or with any relatives—perhaps your elderly parents—then be sure to discuss such arrangements *before* the wedding. You may harbor opposing ideas about what close family life entails and should clarify those ideas early on.

Throughout your marriage—depending on circumstances, such as the health of your relatives—family will at times play a major part in your life together, and at other times have less importance. The purpose of sharing your feelings is to understand each other's view of family roles and family life. By learning what the other feels and wants, you will be equipped to support, rather than undermine, one another in your family roles.

2. Show your families you care about them. The major fear of relatives when you get married is that you've abandoned them in favor of each other. Calm their fears by reassuring them they still have an important place in your life—send them postcards when you're on your honeymoon, remember family birthdays and occasions, keep in touch regularly. If your family misses time alone with you, then be sure to arrange for some private time with them. If you live far from your parents, having occasional private phone conversations with them (you might call when your spouse isn't home) can reassure them that your bond is still strong. And don't be insulted if your spouse also wants to spend time alone with a parent or brother or sister.

As excited as you may be about making a marital commitment, remember that family attachments can help nourish and sustain your marital bond. Although now you may want your spouse to confide in you alone about work or personal problems, several years from now you may appreciate your mate's being able to gain support also from loving relatives, thereby reducing the pressure on you. Don't cut yourselves off, even though your primary attachment is to each other. Make it clear—through words and actions—that family members are still important in your lives.

3. Try to cultivate a positive relationship with new relatives. Get off to a good start with in-laws by giving them time and attention. Show them you are interested in who they are, what they have to say—maybe by asking to see old family photo albums, or inquiring about the family tree. Try to find some common meeting ground, whether it's art, theatre, bowling, or baseball. You may find that you have few joint interests, or that you'll never be good friends. But at least you can feel that you've made an effort and that nobody can fault you for being cold and uncaring about your mate's family.

4. Always consider alternative solutions and try to compromise. For any disagreement having to do with family, examine the options with your spouse and try to work out some compromise. For instance, if you're debating whose family to spend a holiday with, consider the possibilities. You might ask one family to invite the other as well, so that you can all be together; or you might invite both sets of relatives over to your home for the holiday; or you might accept either invitation, with the understanding that you'll visit the other's family for the next holiday.

To be successful at compromising, you need the flexibility to allow each other to get some of your needs met. One woman, married six months, complained that she and her husband visited his parents more often than she liked. They eventually worked it out that she sees her girlfriends one night a week while her husband goes to visit his parents for dinner.

> I think my husband is too tied in with his family, but I don't think I can change that. So I see them a lot during the summer because they live on the beach, but during the rest of the year he often goes alone to see them. They might have been a little insulted at the beginning, but I speak to them on the phone a few times a week and see them every couple of weeks.

5. Demonstrate to relatives the relationship you want with them. If you two look forward to having a very close relationship with relatives, then encourage them to drop by without notice. But if you want to preserve your privacy—which generally isn't a bad idea—then occasionally invite them over for dinner or brunch or coffee at a specific time so that they get the idea that you cherish your time alone together, and may not wish to relinquish it on a moment's notice. One newlywed woman we spoke with, whose mother-in-law is the dominating force in her husband's family, said she made it a point to invite her in-laws over for her husband's birthday instead of letting her mother-in-law plan his birthday party, as had been usual. "I wanted to establish that *I'm* running the show," she explained.

If your mother-in-law wants you to call her Mom but you aren't comfortable doing so, respond warmly by saying or showing that you appreciate being made to feel so welcome, but gently refuse the invitation. You might say (especially if it happens to be the truth) that your relationship with your own mother is, or was, so special that she alone is Mom to you. Most

spousal mothers ought to appreciate that attitude in a daughter-
or son-in-law. If a sister- or brother-in-law wants to become
very chummy, plan occasional outings together, but don't let
them clutter up your calendar with activities. You can communicate the relationship you want with your families by how
you behave.

6. Don't take everything relatives say at face value. Remember that everyone's nerves get ruffled when there is a change
in the family, so don't harp on insults that may have been made
by relatives in the heat of the moment. Try to empathize with
family members rather than be too harsh on them.

7. Present a united front. The key to not letting pressures
exerted by family members come between you two is to act as
a couple. If your relatives are excessively controlling, then fend
them off politely but firmly. When they try to impose advice,
assert that you make decisions with your mate.

One woman, married over 30 years, told us that when she
and her husband returned from their honeymoon, they found
a note from her mother specifying everything she expected
from them now that they were married—including how often
they should visit and how religious they should be. In response
to such intrusiveness, a couple should face relatives and clearly
state their intent to create their own life together. Respect for
your family is important, but so is standing up for yourselves
as a married couple. Only by your demonstrating your commitment to each other will others respect that commitment. If
your relatives talk behind your spouse's back to you, then make
it clear that the person being berated is your marriage partner,
and must be respected as such. Relatives may be jealous of your
marrying—but that is their problem, not yours. You have to
make the message clear that your spouse comes first.

When Kids Are in the Picture

If children are involved in your new marriage, then there
are some added steps you should take to prevent and to cope
with stepfamily conflicts:

**1. Discuss custodial and child care arrangements before mar-
rying.** Before your wedding, you and your mate should sit down

and talk about exactly how involved you each will be in child care. You might be very upset should you, as a newlywed, suddenly discover that you're expected to entertain your stepchildren every weekend. On the other hand, if you, as a stepparent, want to be very much involved in their care, that wish too should be expressed in advance.

2. Give your children time to adjust to the idea of your new marriage. Young children who have experienced a divorce or the death of a parent have already been put through quite an ordeal, so don't shock them with sudden news of your impending marriage. Instead, allow them time to get to know the new parent before announcing your wedding plans. Try to include the children in your wedding ceremony or other plans so that they won't feel left out in the cold.

3. Discuss your feelings about raising children with your mate. Ideally, you and your spouse should agree on parental attitudes and strategies. If, in talking, you discover that you are a disciplinarian and your spouse is far more lenient, decide how you will handle your differences. Express to your mate how you would like to be supported in your parenting role.

4. Make sure that the children have private time with their natural parent. One of the fears of stepchildren—of any age— is that rather than gaining a new parent they are losing their natural parent. By seeing to it that they spend time with their natural parent, you are assuring them that they are not losing that unique parent–child bond.

5. Develop a special stepparent/stepchild relationship. Stepparents need to devote time and attention to showing that they care. With young stepchildren, sit down and help with homework, go shopping together, share in their special interests. With adult stepchildren, try to find some common meeting ground—maybe by visiting an art museum, attending the theatre, going bowling, playing tennis. It's important to demonstrate to your stepchildren that you're not trying to replace their primary parent; that you want to establish a new and independent relationship.

6. Encourage the children to talk about their feelings. Gaining a stepparent can trigger very complex emotional reactions in children. Even those who like their new stepparent may feel guilty that by doing so they are betraying their primary parent. Don't let fears, anger, resentments fester. Try to get things out in the open. Respond to children's thoughts and feelings with understanding; part of what they need is to feel understood.

7. Make sure you have the support of your mate. It can be especially difficult for remarried parents to form a united front with a new spouse,[10] out of guilt that their children experienced a divorce or the death of their other natural parent. As a result, such parents may feel an extra measure of devotion and loyalty toward their children. It's important to be alert to how you may be resisting forming a solid couple identity, and to focus on making solidarity a priority.

8. Don't expect too much too soon. Don't anticipate that your children or stepchildren will immediately accept your new stepfamily situation. Relationships need to evolve. They can't be forced. It's only by developing a shared history that the members of your new stepfamily can attain a meaningful bond.

PART 3

CONFLICT

Conflict creates the fire of affects and emotions, and like every fire it has two aspects: that of burning and that of giving light.

C. G. Jung,
Psychological Reflections

IN LOVE BUT NOT ALIKE

Differences in Personality, Lifestyle, and Values

Barbara Dobbs appeared to be someone whose life was in perfect order. Tall, thin, and blond, the 30-year-old accountant from Boston was as pretty as any young model and carried herself with the composure of a seasoned executive. The first time we met Barbara, she was dressed elegantly in a black pleated skirt, white silk blouse, and black cardigan sweater, with a string of pearls around her neck. She greeted us with a wide smile and a gracious handshake, and after chatting for a moment with some of her male colleagues in the hallway, she led us to her office. To all appearances she was the epitome of the successful corporate woman.

Yet as Barbara began to talk, it quickly became apparent that beneath her careful, studied demeanor she was sizzling with inner turmoil and confusion. Her honeymoon in Italy several weeks before had been a great disappointment for her, and she expressed her unhappiness over all the bickering that had gone on there between her and her new husband, Ned. She was convinced that going to Italy on her honeymoon had been a mistake.

> It was awful. We didn't know the language and so we needed a dictionary to go shopping, to find a restaurant, to ask directions. It was too much thrown at us after a big wedding. We fought much more than I expected—over what the signs meant, which way to go. It was very upsetting. It was almost a relief to come home and go back to work.

As our conversation together continued, Barbara delved further, admitting that it wasn't just Italy, but also Ned's behavior in Italy, that upset her. As she spoke, she still sounded exasperated by the memory.

Ned planned the honeymoon, did all the research. Well, that was fine—except when we got there, I didn't want him to make all the decisions. But he was totally compulsive. He had it in his mind to do all his leather shopping—he had to buy a leather coat for this one, a leather jacket for that one. We missed all the major sights in Florence because Ned wanted to buy gifts. Finally, we arranged that in the morning we'd split up. He'd shop and I'd explore. But my feelings were hurt that we weren't together.

I'm discovering how nervous Ned is. He always seemed so relaxed before we got married. We hadn't lived together, but I still don't know how I didn't see his nervousness. *Now* I see his nervousness, and it carries over into everything he does. He'll push back his hair with his hand when he is nervous. He talks with his hands to illustrate a point. His arms are like sandpaper, because when he is in his office and is nervous, he bites the hair on his arm. Seeing these things makes *me* nervous. I didn't see these things before marriage, because I didn't spend as much time with him. Maybe I saw the clues but I missed them.

THERE IS NO PERFECT MATCH

Barbara Dobbs's exasperation is not uncommon. Every couple about to be married harbors dreams of a life together filled with shared interests, common goals and values, mutual cares and concerns. Many newlyweds reported to us how *lucky* they felt on their wedding day—to have met someone who understood them, who shared their likes and dislikes, who was so compatible with them and so "right" for them.

Yet, no matter how ideally suited they are, at some point every husband and wife realize that theirs is *not* a perfect match. They become aware that they do not always agree, that they do not think, feel, and behave in exactly the same manner, that merging their two personalities and preferences and backgrounds is a lot harder than they ever expected. Like Barbara Dobbs, recent brides and grooms may be shocked or devastated to discover that their bubble has burst, that their idyllic vision of their spouse isn't quite accurate, that marital bliss may be more difficult to achieve than they realized.

For Barbara, the reality that Ned was far from perfect first struck her when she became aware of his nervous habits on their honeymoon. But in contacting newlyweds throughout the country, we found that there were endless variations on what triggers irritation toward a new spouse. Although such differences between husband and wife may seem superficial or mundane, actually they can be quite frustrating—and can seriously affect a relationship. For many, small annoyances trigger big fears that their spouse in no way resembles the person they thought they married.

You can probably divide the differences that exist between you and your spouse into two types. The first type encompasses those differences that can't be helped—things that have to do with the accident of birth, like contrasts in age, race, cultural background, height, looks—differences whose ramifications you may or may not have anticipated before marriage. The second type includes those differences that may seem to be more readily resolvable—for instance, you like to wake up early and your spouse tends to sleep late, or you enjoy dancing all night and your spouse prefers to stay home and watch television. Such personality differences you may not have recognized or given much attention to before your marriage.

Later in this chapter we will discuss why seemingly minor differences may lead to big blowups, and why sometimes major, tangible differences between a man and woman are easily tolerated. Throughout this book we explore in detail specific areas in which spouses often have major differences—money management, household responsibilities, sex, intimacy, friendships, etc. Here we just want to give a quick sampling of the kinds of surprising, and sometimes difficult, discoveries made by newlyweds despite their assumption that they knew everything about each other before their wedding.

Lifestyle Clashes

It's the little things that I find the hardest to get used to. I like to sleep with the bedcovers tucked in, and she likes them left loose. I like all the bureau doors closed, she leaves them opened. My wife is perfectly happy with a bowl of spaghetti for dinner. When I come home I want a decent meal. She acts like I'm expecting something fancy. I'm not. I'd just like a regular dinner.

> —a 34-year-old newlywed who works as a dentist

On our honeymoon, my spouse was disappointed to find I wasn't an outdoorswoman, didn't want to hike in the rain, and I wasn't a good map reader. I was disappointed that my spouse was irritable. We traveled for two weeks and had many arguments.

> —a 37-year-old who had lived with her husband for two years before they married

During our honeymoon I discovered that I am a lot more reserved than my husband. I was self-conscious of dancing. My husband is not at all self-conscious and could not understand my fears. I never realized that we had such different attitudes and acted so differently in public.

> —a 21-year-old secretary who honeymooned at a Poconos resort

Religious Rifts

I didn't know my husband was religious before I married him. I didn't come from a religious background, and we didn't discuss religion much before our wedding. He asked me if I would keep kosher, and I said, "It's a big deal, but okay, I'll do it." All of a sudden we get married and he tells me he was a yeshiva boy in Israel. Then he tells me he wants me to observe Sabbath. For six weeks I tried. I thought I was being punished. I couldn't talk to my friends on the phone. I couldn't shop. Well, it's gotten to the point where I work on Saturday and he stays at home and goes to the synagogue. I do my own thing. But I do resent it enormously. And I know that it's a very big compromise for him too. It turns out that when I met him it was just a nonreligious phase he was going through. He really does want to be a religious person.

> —an American Jew married to an Israeli

My wife and I are both lapsed Catholics, and so religion was never an issue before we got married. But now we're planning to have a child, and I want our child to have religious schooling. Every time we discuss it, one of us always ends up storming out of the room.

> —a Boston physician

Political Powwows

I have a conservative philosophy, and my wife is more of a liberal. The difference in our views really came home to me during this presidential election. It was very important to me that my wife vote Republican. I worked hard to get where I am. I'm not sympathetic about people on welfare. It was a matter of her understanding where I came from.

> —a businessman newly married to an artist 12 years his junior

Communication Conflicts

I never knew my husband could get so angry. We never lived together before marriage. I was shocked by his anger. It was scary. I was brought up in a large family of eight kids. Sharing was a must. He sort of dominates a lot. The first year has been lots of bickering and fighting.

> —a 24-year-old Caribbean woman living in New York

Varied Values

I like going out to eat whenever I can and trying different foods. My wife gets real uptight about spending money when we can save money by eating at home. I like to buy new clothing. She's satisfied wearing dresses from two to three years ago. I'm more of a "live for the moment" person. My wife is more concerned about the future.

—an electrical engineer from Syracuse

Divergent Goals

My husband claims that I never told him before we got married that I wanted to move back to Japan. He is annoyed because he feels that I sprung the news on him after our wedding. It's really hard for me to believe that something so major slipped my mind, but maybe it did.

—a Japanese woman who met her Japanese husband in the United States when they were both in graduate school

LOVE IS BLIND BUT MARRIAGE ISN'T

In an age when so many people live together, have sex together, and travel together before marriage, it may seem amazing that newlyweds find any surprises in store. Surely, we think, anyone who marries, at least in the Western world, believes that they know the person they are marrying.

Yet, as the saying goes, love is blind, or at least partially so.

Idealization

Of course, it's not always that we *do not* see certain qualities in our spouse before marriage, but rather that we *do not want* to see those qualities. Lovers swept up in a surge of passion often do not want to focus on anything but the positive in each other. Men and women alike—eager to find a partner who shares their goals and outlook—are frequently drawn to the person they marry because of what they have in common, and only notice their differences once they have made their relationship permanent.

Barbara Dobbs, described in the opening of this chapter, told us that it was the interests she shared with Ned—skiing, traveling, antiquing, running, enjoying trips to cider mills and country inns—that first drew them together. Barbara was eager to respond to those qualities in Ned that fit in with her life plans and expectations. She didn't choose to be bothered by certain obsessive qualities in Ned, even though, she later admitted, the clues had been there. In fact, Barbara confessed to us that she relied upon and cherished Ned's finickiness—the very quality that now bothered her so—during their engagement period, when he was so helpful in organizing their wedding.

The truth is that people not only *don't want* to see the faults of their loved ones, but probably *are not supposed* to notice the flaws in their partner during the infatuation stage of their relationship. Under the hypnotic trance of romance, we tend to attribute to a lover the traits we *wish* we had ourselves, or the qualities we have and want to see also in our partner.

Psychoanalysts explain this idealized phase, which helps bring two individuals together in marriage, as a rekindling of the longed-for "perfect love object" of childhood—in other words, it evokes in the adult the yearning from youth for the perfect, all-loving relationship with Mommy, or whoever was the primary caretaker. Freud[1] described the process of idealization—which he called a "falsification"—as a bestowing onto the lover the power to instill in us feelings of omnipotence, self-approval, love, protectedness—feelings that hearken back to the childhood sense of one's own or one's parents' omnipotence. Just as our parents made us feel wonderful with their approving gaze, so can a lover.

Psychoanalytic theorist Melanie Klein[2] attributed idealization to the early "splitting" that a child does between the "good," loving caretaker and the "bad," frustrating caretaker. Klein notes that a child struggles to get rid of the negative image of their parents by projecting those images outward—onto another person, a stuffed animal, a storybook character. While all children and adults resort to idealizing people from time to time, doing so in excess results in harboring markedly distorted views of others—that they're either "all good" or "all bad."[3]

The Disappointment Phase

Idealizing any individual—especially one whom you've chosen to live your life with—is bound to lead to disappointment. People joke that marriage kills the romance in a relationship, and to some extent that's true. Romance is a very unreal and dreamy relationship; marriage is a very real, very intimate bond in which people come to know each other in ways they've never known another person before. Romance may be founded on minimum knowledge of another person, but marriage involves a complex intertwining of two lives. During the courtship phase—when there is still the challenge of "winning" the lover—there's no time to focus on foibles. But when you've "hitched" the man or woman of your choice—and begin to rest in the knowledge that they're yours—suddenly you can take off your rose-colored glasses and start seeing your spouse more realistically. Sure, it was easy to tolerate your loved one's quirky habits when you saw him or her only several times a week or when you regarded your relationship as a day-by-day affair. But when you realize that you may have to live with those eccentricities day in, day out, for the rest of your life, being tolerant is not as easy. Our statistical findings illustrate this phenomenon:

- 37 percent of the newlyweds we surveyed stated that since their wedding they have become *more critical* of their mate.
- Only 14 percent of the newlyweds we surveyed said they have become less critical of their partner.
- 39 percent of the newlyweds we surveyed reported feeling that their mate had become *more* critical of them since they had gotten married.
- Only 12 percent of the newlyweds we surveyed felt that their spouse has been less critical since their wedding.

Since, as a married couple, you have to make daily decisions and plan for the future, differences are taken much more seriously and personally—they cannot be easily glossed over or pooh-poohed. Even among those people who marry "with their eyes wide open"—who marry not because they are swept up in passion but because of realistic considerations, such as money, social status, good looks—disappointment may come after the wedding when they realize that, despite the tangible benefits of their union, an essential quality—love—is missing.[4]

The period that follows soon after the wedding is a vulnerable time for many people. Newlyweds often describe it as "coming down from cloud nine." Once the excitement of the wedding is over, there's a sense of disappointment about returning to reality. Without all the distractions of planning the wedding down to the last detail, newlyweds can finally focus on their mate—and bring previously unnoticed qualities into the glaring limelight.

Doreen Wolf, a pixieish 35-year-old married 12 years, still remembers the crash after the high of her wedding.

My first year of marriage was *terrible!* Why? Because my husband was nothing like my father. Before we got married, my husband thought everything I did was wonderful, and after we got married, he thought that everything about me was awful. He didn't like my clothes, he didn't like my posture, he didn't like how I wore my hair, he didn't like my cooking. He used to tell me not to take his criticisms personally. But I'm his wife. How was I supposed to take it? His whole family is very blunt and tactless with their criticisms. My father was just the opposite. He thought everything I did was wonderful. But we've worked it out.

Gail Saunders, a pretty 30-year-old, noticed the change in her own disposition almost immediately, on her honeymoon. Although she greatly enjoyed their trip to Europe, she told us, she became annoyed with her husband because he stopped at every ice cream stand they passed—and fattening indulgences were not something she thought his physique could afford.

Gail's husband had been overweight for months, yet it was *only* once they got married that his plumpness bothered her and she began nagging him. "I feel embarrassed by his paunch," she told us. Interestingly, Gail hadn't mentioned her mate's being overweight when we interviewed her before her wedding.

Like many people, Gail became a harsher critic of her mate once she married him because she started viewing him as an extension and reflection of herself. She began to feel more of a connection with her partner and so became more self-conscious of his annoying habits.

Before marriage, Gail may have rebelled against identifying with her parents, whom she sees as demanding, and so controlled her critical impulses; but after her wedding she found herself acting more like her mother, whom she described as "a nag." Also, because marriage required her to give up the fantasy that she could always meet someone else, she began to have very detailed expectations of her husband. Suddenly it seemed that everything in her life—all her wishes and dreams—hinged upon him.

"I wish he would lose weight," Gail told us. "It may be tied to the fact that my father died of a heart attack and my husband has the same kind of build. I think there is an internal fear that he is going to die and abandon me." Gail became more critical and demanding of her husbnd since getting married because her emotional investment in him had greatly intensified.

WHY PEOPLE CHANGE AFTER MARRIAGE

As we mentioned earlier, it's not just that people see each other differently after marriage; they actually change as a result of being married. An early nineteenth-century wit put it this way: "It doesn't much signify whom one marries, for one is sure to find next morning that it was someone else."[5]

In the case of Gail, discussed above, it may be not just that she was viewing her husband more critically but also that her husband, although he was always plump, actually began eating more since they were married.

Letting Your Hair Down

Many newlyweds, feeling secure in the knowledge that now they are legally "tied," breathe a sigh of relief and let down their guard.[6] They do not feel the need to be quite so polite, well groomed, and agreeable with their mate as they did when they were dating and even living together. Many of the newlyweds we surveyed told us that since their wedding they had gained weight. Feeling less pressure to impress or woo their lover, they became less strict with themselves about diet and exercise. Some men who lived with their mates before marriage admitted to us that afterward they became sloppier at home. When they lived with their partners, they were on good behavior. Later their attitude was: Now that I'm married, I can relax.

It's also common, within the safety and comfort of marriage, for people to "regress"[7] and exhibit the more childlike aspects of their personality—sometimes becoming more playful, sometimes expressing dependency more openly. Reactions to such changes in one's mate are varied. Some women may be delighted, and others repulsed, to find that the strong businessman they thought they married can suddenly turn into a silly, sensitive, vulnerable little boy at home. The same mix of reactions is common among men who find that the well-controlled, "together" woman they proposed to can fall apart after a bad day at the office or can suddenly adopt the role of a complete incompetent.

What's Really Important to Me?

Secret beliefs, deep values, inner hopes and needs also emerge as you ease into the coziness of marriage. The woman who earlier expressed surprise that her Jewish husband wanted to resume a religious way of life was responding to a common newlywed experience. Getting married often pushes people to reexamine their value and belief systems. It's quite possible that the man didn't mention to his wife before marriage that he wanted to be observant *because he didn't himself realize* that religion would be important to him as a married man. He quickly discovered, however, that for him marriage and family were vitally connected with Judaism.

As the noted marital therapist Dr. Clifford Sager points out, people have conscious and unconscious expectations of marriage. According to Sager, some of these expectations a person is aware of and expresses to their mate, some they are aware of but do not express, and some they are not consciously aware of.[8] Each person has associations, needs, and wishes connected with marriage and, once married, acts different from the way they did when single. A Canadian woman, now married five years, told us,

> The funny thing is that Spencer isn't the person I married. When we were dating, he was the *bon vivant* about town. We used to go to clubs every night and get home at two or three in the morning. Now he likes to read books and is very home-loving. He never likes to go anywhere. Marriage to him means gardening and cooking. I like him better this way, but I didn't know him this way before I married him.

Help! My Spouse Isn't the Person I Married!

The stress of making the transition to marriage also brings out certain traits. Barbara Dobbs complained of Ned's nervousness and wondered how she failed to see his nervous habits before she married him. It is quite possible that Ned began *acting more nervous* once he married. Aside from the obvious reasons for such nervousness—the immensity of taking the "big step" after 39 years of bachelorhood, uncertainty about whether he married the right woman—there are other psychological stressors that he, or any newlywed, might feel.

Freud noted that it's inevitable for certain issues (he termed them "oedipal") to be triggered in marriage, because by marrying we symbolically step into the shoes of our parent of the same sex and symbolically "win" our parent of the opposite sex. The effect is twofold. On one hand, although our spouse is modeled on the idealized images of the mommy or daddy we knew when we were children, inevitably our spouse does not "fit the bill." There is no adult who can fulfill our needs and adore us in the same unflagging way our parents did, or we wish they had done. So no sooner do we take a mate—because of the resemblance we perceive—than our disappointment, perhaps anger, at the failed resemblance sets in[9] (as we discussed earlier from the perspective of Klein's "idealization").

Also, although the desire to have a mate of our own (one like our mom or dad had) is part of what drives us to marry, fears are also associated with this triumphant acquisition. Freud noted that gaining a mate revives the conflict experienced by every four-year-old child, who typically wants to possess their parent of the opposite sex. To want Mom or Dad is, in the mind of the child, to do battle with the other parent.

Ned may have become more nervous since getting married because he felt guilty that he was "not supposed to have a woman." His wife, Barbara, blamed herself for not seeing Ned's nervousness before marriage, though in fact that trait may have been highly accentuated as a result of Ned's getting married.

In many cases, of course, people change for the better after marriage. Some newlyweds, no longer anxious about their future, are more relaxed, feel more giving toward others. Marriage has the potential for bringing out people's strengths. Forty-seven percent of the newlyweds we surveyed said that their feelings of self-confidence had increased since their wedding.[10] As your marriage blossoms, so too may you and your partner feel rewarded in your growing ability to love and feel loved.

THE DYNAMICS OF MARRIAGE

The dynamics that are established between you and your spouse once you marry may change each of you. For instance, it's natural for roles to become somewhat concretized in a relationship—one mate becomes the social planner, the other goes along with those plans; one partner is always late, the other is always angry about the lateness. A polarization takes place so that certain behaviors or attitudes get emphasized in each spouse's personality.

Anthropologist Gregory Bateson observed such a polarization process, which he termed *schizmogenesis,* operating between individuals.[11] In it, behavior of person A leads to a complementary—that is, opposite—behavior in person B. For instance, dominance in A leads to submissiveness in B. Likewise, B's submissiveness leads to A's assertiveness. A progressive escalation leads to a polarization of positions—schizmogenesis. This process can be seen operating quite often between spouses. For example, two partners may feel ambivalent about getting married. One vocalizes the urgent desire to get married, while the other expresses hesitation and doubt. In analytic terms we could say that each partner is projecting some of their own ambivalence onto their partner—A is projecting his or her fears about marrying onto B, and B is projecting some of his or her own desire to marry onto A. The result is that A and B have induced a polarized and paralyzing situation.

Psychologists have described other polarization processes, one of which is called *projection* or *projective identification.*[12] In projection, you "project" a disliked part of yourself onto your spouse. You might, for instance, project your own self-critical aspect (termed "superego" by Freudian psychotherapists, the "parental self" by transactional analysts)[13] onto your spouse, in which case your spouse is seen as constantly critical and is essentially acting like your own conscience. In projective identification, you not only project a quality of yours onto your spouse, but you identify with that quality and react to it. For example, you not only experience your spouse as critical but criticize that trait and insist that your mate should change. Or you project your own "childlike self," with which you may feel uncomfortable, onto your partner and then accuse your mate of being self-indulgent, irresponsible, self-centered.

Many clinicians[14] have noted the tendency for people to find spouses who possess traits similar to the ones they themselves have and want to get rid of. One groom we interviewed, for example, told us he was annoyed because his wife went on shopping sprees with her mother, in which her mother paid for all her clothes. In our conversation, it emerged that this man occasionally borrowed money from his parents to meet his payments. Uncomfortable with taking money from his own parents, he blamed his wife for exactly the same behavior. This man found it easier to accuse his spouse for what he disliked in himself than to recognize his displeasure with himself for relying on his parents for money.

Projection may actually serve as one of the powerful *functions* of marital coupling. That is, it offers each partner psychic relief. Some people are attracted to each other specifically because of their complementary needs. For instance, you may have the need to project your demanding, childlike self onto your mate, who enjoys that role and prefers to allow you to be serious and responsible. Therein often lies the reason that "opposites attract."

Projective identification, however, can also be problematic —and potentially lock a couple in conflict—depending on how intensely you need to ward off a disliked trait in yourself by attacking it in your spouse.

Cuing[15] is another process that may influence you to think your spouse has changed since the wedding day. Cuing is similar to projective identification, but in this case you actually *trigger* your spouse to exhibit the trait you don't like in yourself so that you can criticize your mate for it. Maybe, for instance, you're very uncomfortable with displaying anger and tend to bottle it up. You may unconsciously egg on your spouse until he or she blows up. Then, you may accuse your mate of changing now that you're married—of becoming hysterical, unreasonable, furious—when, in fact, you are stirring up that behavior in your spouse. Temporarily such an argument may leave you feeling more comfortable with yourself. Your mate has become the angry, hostile person—not you. The tendency to use such a mechanism, unfortunately, may lead you to sacrifice the happiness of your marriage to your own neurotic need to appease your inner anxiety.

Splitting,[16] a third mechanism (which we introduced earlier), occurs when at one moment in your marriage you feel that everything about your spouse is wonderful and at another moment, usually in a fit of rage, you feel that everything about your mate is awful. Psychoanalyst Melanie Klein[17] felt that this phenomenon relates to early childhood, when a child splits the image of the mother (or primary caretaker) into two: the good, gratifying mother versus the bad, frustrating mother. Klein believed that this mechanism protects against depression—that is, by splitting you can feel that you're not angry at that wonderful person you love (which would make you feel guilty), but rather at that "bad" person. If you feel your spouse has changed since marriage, that might be because you are splitting their image in your mind. You are refusing to see at once their good side and their bad side—refusing to see them for the full person they are. "Splitting" may be particularly intense in the early months of marriage, when combining your two lifestyles may stir up the first intense conflicts in your relationship.[18] Ideally, with time, a couple comes to terms with the "split"—with periods of anger buffered by the knowledge that one's spouse can't be all bad, since they have, after all, so many good traits.

CHECKUP:
HOW CRITICAL ARE YOU?

Splitting, projective identification, and cuing may be difficult psychological mechanisms to note about oneself. On the other hand, powerful feelings of anger, criticism, or resentment at feeling criticized are all too palpable. Before we explore further the reasons why differences can be aggravated and become problematic in marriage, we think it is time for you, the reader, to think about your own attitudes toward the differences that exist between you and your mate. The following is a list of statements beside which you should place a check in the appropriate column, "Yes" or "No."

		Yes	No
1.	I feel critical toward my spouse three times a week or more.	☐	☐
2.	I feel critical toward my spouse for how they look.	☐	☐
3.	I feel critical toward my spouse for how they talk.	☐	☐
4.	I feel critical toward my spouse for how they relate to others.	☐	☐
5.	I feel critical toward my spouse for their values.	☐	☐
6.	I feel critical toward my spouse for their household habits.	☐	☐
7.	I wish my spouse were more like me.	☐	☐
8.	I think my spouse is capable of changing in the ways that I want.	☐	☐
9.	I think my spouse behaves in certain ways *just* to annoy me.	☐	☐
10.	I find it hard to forgive my spouse for not living up to all of my expectations.	☐	☐
11.	I find it hard to accept the ways in which my spouse is different from me.	☐	☐
12.	My parents often criticized me when I was a child.	☐	☐
13.	My spouse often accuses me of being a nag.	☐	☐
14.	I wish I were more accepting of my spouse.	☐	☐
15.	One (or both) of my parents often criticized the other.	☐	☐

Now, count up the number of checks you placed in the "Yes" column. Then find which of the following categories you belong to:

If you checked "Yes" for three or fewer statements, you are **cool as a cucumber.** Whatever may bother you about your spouse you usually let roll off your back. You probably prefer to focus on the positive aspects, rather than the weaknesses, of your mate. It may be that you have a strong sense of yourself and don't feel personally threatened by the differences that exist between you and your spouse.[19] Or it may be that you retain a bit of distance from your relationship—which prevents you from feeling overconcerned by certain traits you dislike in your mate. At times your mate may accuse you of being indifferent. And it could be you're a bit of a cold fish. What criticisms you do have, you tend to keep to yourself.

If you checked "Yes" for more than three but less than eight statements, you are **a casual complainer.** Specific things about your mate bother you, and they surface in your thoughts or in conversation with your spouse again and again. When these touchy issues don't arise, you feel mostly positive about your spouse. But when they do, you feel annoyed by what you perceive to be your spouse's flaws.

If you checked "Yes" for eight or more statements, you are **a constant critic.** If you're not complaining about one thing, then you're complaining about another. No matter what your spouse does, it seems that you always feel let down, betrayed, disappointed. Your spouse may have learned to tune you out, finding it too hurtful to listen to all of your criticisms. You yourself may be sick of hearing yourself complain about your mate. In fact, your tendency to criticize may feel almost involuntary. It's not that you want to be critical; you just can't help yourself. Perhaps you were totally starry-eyed and married in haste—and are now feeling devastatingly disappointed. To change your attitude you need to reexamine your expectations.

WHAT MAKES THE DIFFERENCE IN HOW YOU ADJUST TO DIFFERENCES?

Since it's natural that differences exist between husband and wife, why do some people get so upset by them?

According to psychologist Erich Fromm, people become disturbed about differences between themselves and their loved ones because recognizing those differences forces them to realize that they are essentially separate and alone. "The deepest need of man, then, is the need to overcome his separateness, to leave the prison of his aloneness."[20]

Sure, we may feel the deep desire for a total union with our loved one, and certainly we feel the temptation to try to transform our spouse into the person we want them to be.[21] But the fact is that some marriages thrive despite major differences between husband and wife. For instance, in our study[22] we compared those newlyweds who married mates of a different religion with those who married mates of the same religion. This finding may surprise you:

- Newlyweds in interfaith marriages were 10 percent *more* likely to report that marriage was easier than they had expected it to be.

On the other hand, distinct differences between spouses can lead to distinct problems. Although in our study the percentage of respondents who married interracially is very small—4.9 percent (only 1.3 percent of all married couples in the United States are interracial couples, according to the U.S. Census Bureau)—our findings hinted that they may encounter considerable obstacles.

- 25 percent of newlyweds in interracial marriages reported that marriage was *much harder* than they had expected.
- 47 percent of newlyweds in interracial marriages reported that marriage was a difficult adjustment.

In contrast:

- Only 8 percent of newlyweds married to someone of the same race reported that marriage was much harder than they had expected.
- Only 17 percent of newlyweds married to someone of the same race reported that marriage was a difficult adjustment.

In our idealization and disappointment sections, we covered individual psychological issues that contribute to the experience and adjustment to the marital experience. The following are some additional components that help explain why differences between husband and wife may be problematic in some marriages but not in others.

Marital Expectations

Marital therapist Clifford J. Sager, M.D.,[23] whom we mentioned earlier, reasons that each person brings into marriage very specific ideas about what they expect from their spouse and what they themselves are willing to give. When one's spouse doesn't live up to one's expectations, essentially there exists a breach of the *unwritten* marriage contract. Some of these expectations are conscious and verbalized ("I'd like you to help me with the dishes"; "I think we should pool our salaries and pay for expenses jointly"; "I'd prefer socializing together with our friends"). Many of the expectations people have, however, remain unarticulated. Often, such expectations may fail to emerge clearly even in one's *own* awareness.

For instance, using our earlier example, perhaps Barbara Dobbs found Ned's nervous habits irksome partly because she expected her spouse to be a strong, protective figure for her. Despite her usual air of calm control, she herself was a nervous person and wanted a mate who would provide reassurance, rather than someone who would make her feel more anxious. She became angry at Ned because he wasn't fulfilling his end of the bargain.

Let's say that in your marriage you criticize your spouse for always being late, while you're always prompt. The reason you may feel hurt, angry, and betrayed by your different styles is that your expectation of your marriage partner is that he or she will be reliable and considerate.

Or maybe you're perplexed because your spouse is over-critical about how you handle situations with your boss. It may be that one of your spouse's (possibly unstated) expectations of marriage is an enhanced status in society. Your spouse seems annoyed if you don't handle a job problem well, because he or she assumed that being successful is one of your functions in marriage.

Where do your expectations come from?

As noted throughout this chapter, the expectations that we bring to marriage are rooted in our yearning to re-create the love and closeness and nurturance that we experienced or *wished* we had experienced in our first love relationship, with our mother (or original caretaker). Our disappointment that our mate is not perfect is our disappointment at being deprived of the longed-for, imagined perfect relationship with Mother.

It was only after talking with Barbara Dobbs for two hours that we learned she had experienced a major, dramatic rejection during her childhood. When Barbara was two years old, her mother walked out on her family for good. Not until Barbara was ten years old and her father remarried did Barbara enjoy again a mother–daughter relationship. It is likely that at some level Barbara's desire for her new marriage to be perfect is related to her early longing for a close, loving relationship with a protecting mother. On the other hand, it is also possible that in her choice of mate she found or even needed someone toward whom anger would be evoked or could be expressed without their disappearing, as her mother did. Marriage, the closest adult equivalent to the parent–child relationship, evoked in Barbara deep wishes relating to her youth.

Areas in which you and your spouse are different but have *no* conflict are areas that are probably not embedded with your expectations, or that involve shared expectations. For instance, the reason that being of different faiths may not be problematic for some newlyweds (as our findings suggested) is that people who enter interfaith marriages may not have the expectation that they will share religious values with their mates. It may be that religion doesn't play an important role in their lives, and so it isn't part of their marriage "contract." Or it may be that as a result of planning their wedding together, they have already come to terms with many of their religious differences and so have moved toward a single "contract" that results from understanding and sharing each other's expectations.

Later in this chapter we'll help you identify what you and your spouse's expectations are for yourselves and each other. In thinking about what you want from your mate, you may be surprised to discover that you have contradictory wishes. On one hand, you may expect your spouse to give you the freedom to enjoy friendships and time and interests on your own; on the other, you may expect your spouse to protect you and take care of you. It's common for people to harbor contradictory expectations. But you should be aware of any conflicting desires you have and how they may be affecting the demands you make on your spouse.

If your spouse can do nothing right by you, or you can't seem to do anything right according to your spouse, it may be that you have contradictory expectations of each other that create a double-bind, no-win situation. On the other hand, if either of you expects too little from the other, then little may be given or gained in your marriage.[24]

Having expectations is not the problem. It's just that the more you and your spouse's expectations for yourselves and each other are geared to reality, the greater the likelihood that you will fulfill them.

Family Patterns

How you respond to differences between you and your spouse may result not just from the expectations you have of your spouse but also from how you and members of your family respond to differences with one another.

One newlywed woman we interviewed (a "constant critic") complained to us that her husband "isn't charismatic, isn't the life of the party, isn't funny or a scintillating conversationalist."

For this woman, the problem was not just that she expected her husband to be extremely sociable, although that was undoubtedly part of her unwritten marriage contract; it was also that she was constantly criticized by her mother when she was growing up, and later identified with her mother by perpetuating her critical tendencies. This woman had always felt guilty and disappointed that she wasn't pleasing her mother, and now she was making her husband feel the way she did while she was growing up. Never having felt accepted, she now had trouble accepting her spouse for who he was.

If you've grown up among people who had difficulty accepting the ways in which others are different, then you may need consciously to focus on the harm such attitudes can bring and deliberately try new modes of response—which we will present at the end of this chapter.

The Marital Mesh

Part of how you respond to the ways in which your spouse is different from you will depend on why you married your mate in the first place. The old saying "Opposites attract" is based on the phenomenon that many individuals are drawn to people who complement them—who are good at things that they are not, who complete them in some way.[25]

It may please you that your spouse is sociable while you are more reserved, or that your mate is cultured and enjoys the opera even though you prefer "B" movies.

Despite your differences, you and your spouse may share

deeper, more important similarities. If a couple shares a certain attitude toward life—whether that attitude is optimistic, pessimistic, cynical, intellectual, impulsive, or morally superior—it can unite them in a very important and binding way.[26] A 27-year-old female banker who met her husband in graduate school told us:

> I'm from a Jewish background and my husband is a WASP. *But there was something about him that immediately drew me to him.* I think we basically view life very similarly. We both work hard, but we don't kill ourselves for our jobs. We both value our home life and the arts. We both want a balanced life. The interesting thing about my husband is that *I was immediately comfortable with him.* There wasn't the usual silly talk when you start dating someone. We immediately skipped the first ten steps of getting to know each other. I knew exactly what I was looking for because I waited a long time before I got married. *Everyone I had gone out with before I was 25 was much too superficial.* Then it was either power or money that attracted me.

A man and woman are drawn together because they suit each other's deep psychological needs. And so whatever has drawn them together is often enough to keep them together, no matter what differences lie between them. In fact, those couples who fight fiercely over their differences yet are inseparable from each other may be satisfying deep needs, and so in a strange way be well suited to each other. In their case, a calm, peaceful, harmonious marriage would not satisfy.

Since differences exist in every marriage, it may be that a certain *number* of differences are tolerable between spouses; too many, however, may be destructive. For example, if spouses differ not only in their leisure interests and personality styles but also in their socioeconomic class and family backgrounds, it may be difficult for their relationship to sustain the tension that results from so many disparities.[27]

Life Stages

Different things are important at different life stages. Some spouses can tolerate the differences between them because at that point in their lives, those differences just aren't important.

For instance, many of the intermarried newlyweds we interviewed admitted that although religion was not a subject of conflict for them, they anticipated that it might become an area of disagreement when they had children. Conversely, areas in which a couple may disagree vehemently at the beginning of marriage may later become unimportant. You may have married your spouse at a stage in which establishing your own job identity is crucial. Your spouse, however, may be closer to the period that Erikson calls "generativity,"[28] a stage at which one is already established, and is more focused on passing something along to the next generation. Your spouse may want a baby; you may not. Once you feel more secure as a working person, however, you too may feel that pull toward parenthood, and so you and your spouse will be more in sync regarding your future goals.

NEWLYWED SILHOUETTES
REVISITED

At the end of this chapter we offer some suggestions for developing a constructive attitude about differences. Keep in mind that, to a large extent, your ability to tolerate disappointment about the differences that exist between you and your mate will determine how you adjust to marriage—in other words, whether you are an "Inseparable Sweetheart," "Ho-Hum Honeymooner," "Fearful Fleer," "Disappointed Dreamer," or "Realistic Romantic" (all of which we described in chapter 1).

"Inseparable Sweethearts" attempt to hold on to idealization, denying any disappointment they feel toward their spouse—but often at the expense of viewing their mate in any but a superficial way that denies any aggressive components. Anger may emerge in vague feelings of depression that aren't connected to any source and are often misplaced focuses of aggression. That's not to say that the relationship won't or can't last—but that it may suffer from a lack of depth.

"Ho-Hum Honeymooners" use denial to mitigate disappointment. These people may project their feelings of dissatisfaction outward. For instance, one couple complained to us: "Why is it that our families are making such a big fuss about our wedding? It's not a big deal to us." But of course, at least at some level, it had to be a turning point in this couple's lives.

"Fearful Fleers" see their spouses as the harbingers of everything that makes them feel lousy, and imagine they'll be much happier if they escape the marriage. Indeed, they often feel enormous relief at ending the relationship—but the feeling is almost always short-lived. It is the projection of their demanding desire that they experience coming from their spouse and which they attempt to flee.

The "Disappointed Dreamers" seem to be those that theorist Melanie Klein might regard as stuck in the depressive position. They are able to integrate the "good" and "bad" images of their partner but unable to accept them. Klein believed that caretaking gestures and gratitude are important ways to overcome the guilty, angry, destructive feelings felt toward a loved one. Genuine, deep gratitude, however, seems to escape "Disappointed Dreamers."

"Realistic Romantics" are those who *do* have the ability to overcome the "depressive" position described by Klein. They go on to experience both their mate and themselves in depth —the "good" and "bad" aspects—without feeling depression. They are capable of experiencing genuine joy and gratitude and appreciation.

While it's natural to react in a variety of ways to the realization that one's spouse isn't perfect, it is in the process of dealing with these disappointments—in an accepting and realistic way—that a marriage deepens and matures.

WORKSHOP: IDENTIFYING AND DEALING WITH DIFFERENCES

It's important to look at what differences exist between the two of you, to become aware of your attitudes toward them, and to find ways to deal with these differences so that they enhance rather than hinder your relationship.

An Example of Coping

For Barbara Dobbs, who was beset with anxieties about her husband's irritating habits, a turning point came six months after her wedding, when she decided to speak to her minister. Having the opportunity to unburden her marital disappointments to an objective third party was in itself a tremendous help, says Barbara. Following that meeting, Barbara suggested to Ned that they both visit the minister as a "six-month checkup." That meeting was positive for both of them. Ned told us: "I'm trying to be more aware of my compulsive habits and do less of them. But the minister also told Barbara not to be so hard on me." Since they saw the minister, said Barbara, "there's been a definite improvement. I've developed more of a sense of humor about Ned's compulsiveness. And I'm realizing that a lot of his nervousness is due to his unhappiness at work."

By sharing her feelings about her marriage with her minister, Barbara realized that her disappointments since marriage weren't unusual. Feeling understood and supported by her minister, she felt less anxious about her discovery that not everything about Ned was "perfect." She also learned that, while Ned could certainly work on changing certain qualities in himself, she too would have to change her attitude so that she could be more accepting of the person she married.

In many ways, the approach that Barbara and Ned took in dealing with the differences that became problematic in their relationship was ideal:

- Barbara ventilated some of her feelings about Ned's not being the "perfect" spouse by sharing her feelings with an outside party.
- She communicated to Ned what she found irritating.
- Ned agreed to work on changing what habits he felt he could. (More important than his actual changes was Barbara's feeling that her concerns were understood and appreciated.)
- Barbara developed a different perspective on Ned's behavior. She became more accepting and adopted a sense of humor about certain traits of Ned's that she could not change.

Questions to Help You Focus

How can *you* handle the differences that have caused problems between you and your spouse? At the end of all the following chapters, we offer precise guidelines for coping with specific issues. Here, however, is a *general* framework that can help you resolve whatever rifts exist between you and your mate. Write your answers in the space provided, or on a separate piece of paper if you need more space. Answer each question as fully as you can. You may want to do this exercise at the same time as your spouse, in which case you should give each other privacy while working on your answers.

1a. What bothers you the most about your spouse? (Example: What bothers me is that I am very neat and my spouse is very sloppy.)

_____

_____

1b. What is your expectation of your spouse that is not being met? (Example: My expectation is that my spouse will keep things as neatly as I and that everything in our marriage, including the housework, will be shared.)

_____

_____

1c. What is an underlying reason that this issue bothers you so much? (Example: I get irritated by my spouse's sloppiness because it reminds me that I have to share my space with another person.)

_____

_____

1d. What are other, perhaps even _deeper_ reasons that you feel so uncomfortable and annoyed by this trait or behavior of your spouse? (Example: Secretly I think my spouse's messiness makes me anxious because I would really like to be that way too but wouldn't dare.)

_____

_____

2. About your complaint in 1, above, what could your spouse do that would make you happier? (Example: My spouse could put dirty socks in the hamper, and cook and do the dishes for a few meals during the week.)

_____

(Note: Your spouse may be able to do certain things that will relieve superficial problems, but be aware that it may be impossible for your mate's actions alone to relieve the inner anxiety related to your comments in 1c and 1d. For instance: Even if my mate becomes neater, I may still become angered that the very presence of another person affects how *my* living space is arranged. Or: I may still have a deep need to rebel against being "good" and "neat," and if I can't blame my mate for this behavior, then I'll find another outlet for ventilation.)

3. What do you do that may prevent your spouse from doing those things that you want? Or more specifically, in what ways may you *induce* the negative behavior in your mate that annoys you? (Example: I yell and scream, which makes my spouse angry and resistant. Or: I ask my spouse so indirectly that my spouse either doesn't get my message or, possibly resenting my unwillingness to be direct, does not feel impelled to change.)

4. What could you do to be more effective in getting your spouse to do what you want? (Example: I could ask in a more pleasant tone. I could be more explicit and firm about what I want. I could do something my spouse wants in exchange for my spouse's doing what I want.)

5a. What bothers your spouse most about you? Be honest! (Example: My spouse wishes I were more careful about the way I dress.)

5b. What is your spouse's expectation of you that is not being met? (Example: My spouse's expectation is that I be someone to be proud of in public.)

_____

_____

_____

5c.   What is an underlying reason that this bothers your spouse so much? (Example: My spouse is somewhat insecure and wants to rely on my powerful presentation to boost self-esteem.)

_____

_____

5d.   What is another, perhaps even *deeper,* reason that your spouse is so bothered and annoyed by your behavior? (Example: My not dressing well highlights my mate's own unsophisticated taste and lack of flair for fashion.)

_____

_____

6.   Regarding the above complaints, what things could you do that would make your spouse happier? (Example: I could dress better, especially on occasions that are important to my mate.)

_____

_____

(Note: Be aware that even if you accommodate your spouse's wishes, certain things may not change. For instance, even if you dress well, your spouse may still feel insecure and blame you for it in other ways.)

7.   What is your spouse doing that is keeping you from making those accommodations? (Example: My spouse becomes insistent, at which point I withdraw or resist even more.)

_____

_____

8.   How could your spouse be more effective in getting you to modify your behavior? (Example: My spouse could reassure me that I am loved for who I am, which would make me less resistant to my mate's suggestions.)

_____

_____

9. What are possible exchanges that you and your spouse might make? (Example: I could dress more to my spouse's liking if my spouse agreed to help out more with housework; I would agree to sleep with the window open if my spouse agreed to watch television in the living room rather than the bedroom when I go to bed early.)

    a. I could: _____

    _____

    My spouse could: _____

    _____

    b. I could: _____

    _____

    My spouse could: _____

    _____

    c. I could: _____

    _____

    My spouse could: _____

    _____

10. Which of your expectations of your spouse are unrealistic or even impossible for your spouse to accomplish? (Example: I cannot expect that my spouse will exactly share my attitude toward our living space, or that I can live exactly as I did when I was single.)

_____

_____

11. Which of your spouse's expectations of you are unrealistic or even impossible for you to accomplish? (Example: It is unrealistic for my spouse to expect me to become a fashion plate when I couldn't care less about clothing.)

_____

_____

12.   Plan to set aside some time in the future to go back and answer the above questions in regard to other traits and behaviors that bother you and your spouse about each other. But not today—you deserve a breather! Enjoy feeling good about yourselves for the knowledge you've gained and the progress you've just made together.

The purpose of the exercise above is to help you focus on the expectations you and your spouse have of each other and how you might be more successful at getting those expectations fulfilled. As question 11 acknowledges, however, there will undoubtedly be issues on which you and your mate will have difficulty agreeing. There will be areas where you won't want to compromise or negotiate or give in. What can you do then?

It's All in the Right Attitude

1. Try to empathize with your spouse. There are certain things you do that you would never think of changing, and so, you must admit, it makes sense that there is certain behavior your spouse does not want to change. Try to stand in your spouse's shoes; consider things from the other side of the story.

2. Don't take your spouse's behavior too personally. You'll find it much easier to accept your mate's behavior once you realize that it isn't entirely a personal reflection on you. The more confident you feel about yourself, the better able you will be to realize that your spouse is separate from you and that his or her actions or looks don't take away from who *you* are.

3. Focus on what you two share. At some points in your marriage the differences between you and your spouse will stand out more than your similarities; at other times the reverse will apply. But let's face it—you must have shared some interests or goals or values to have been drawn together in the first place. Emphasize in your marriage the ways in which you are similar. For instance, if you both like old films, make it a point to see more of them. If you both like classical music, plan evenings at concerts or listen together at home to recordings.

4. Agree to disagree. It's not always possible to agree or compromise, and so at times it's best just to disagree. He is religious, you are not: If neither of you is going to change, you might as well accept the situation as best you can. This entails realizing, accepting, and respecting that you are separate people with individual needs and desires. Adopting an accepting attitude is not always easy, *but it is a matter of habit*. Make a conscious effort to stop nagging your spouse to change, and gradually you won't feel such a strong impulse to criticize. Your marriage is bound to improve when neither of you feels pressured to change for the other.

5. *Appreciate the differences between you and your spouse.* Remember that there is a positive way of looking at most things. If your husband is a night owl, perhaps he's better at parties than you are, and that can be a boon to both your social life and your career. If your wife is tactless, chances are she's also probably very honest and can be trusted to give you a fair and true opinion. Try to recall what originally attracted you to that certain someone who is different from you. Perhaps you initially found your mate's differences appealingly exotic; perhaps they represented a means of rebelling against the way you were brought up. Keep in mind that if you and your spouse were too similar, you might be more competitive with each other. Instead of feeling threatened by the different ways in which your spouse thinks, feels, and acts, look at those differences in wonder and amazement and interest and think about how they enrich you as a person and as a couple. Heraclitus said, "From different tones comes the fairest tune." And as the French say, "Vive la différence!"

6. *Develop constructive ways of fighting.* This brings us to chapters 4 and 5.

THE BALANCE OF POWER

Establishing Decision-Making Patterns

It doesn't take long after choosing whom to marry to realize that the decision-making process has just begun. Soon you're swept up in questions of when to marry, and where, and whom to invite, and what wedding invitations and flowers and menu to choose, and which dress and tuxedo to wear, and what to do for a honeymoon, and where to live once you're married, and what gifts to register for, and what style of furniture to buy, and on and on and on and on.

Some of the decisions, like which style of thank-you notes to buy, are pretty minor. Others, like choosing where to live and how to arrange finances, are more significant. But the impact of having to make all these decisions—both major and minor ones—is that you realize that besides being a romantic attachment, yours is a business partnership—that in being married you will frequently have to make decisions together in order to get on with the business of life. Decisions you may have found easy to make as a single person—things as simple as where and what to eat—suddenly, you realize, become much more confused and belabored when two people have opinions in making those choices. And because you're likely to become more open about your differing needs and desires once you're married, the potential for conflict is greater than before. In fact, 29 percent of the newlyweds we surveyed reported that their number of arguments increased since their wedding.

Of course, once you are married your investment in *resolving* conflict also increases. Studies have shown that couples who find ways to compromise rate themselves as happier in their marriages than those who are not able to come to a common agreement.[1] And among the newlyweds we surveyed, those couples who fought less frequently rated themselves as happier in their marriages.[2] It's not that happily married newlyweds don't have problems, but rather that they are more confident about working out their problems.[3]

Being able to make decisions that acknowledge the sometimes differing needs of both of you is an important goal to work toward in marriage. It necessitates your being strong enough to assert your own needs and wishes, caring enough to take into account your spouse's needs and wishes, and flexible enough to sometimes be in control and sometimes give up control. In other words, it has to do with being truly comfortable with the divisions of power in your relationship, and with fluctuations within that division.

POWER PLAY

When we interviewed newlyweds about their problems involved in making decisions with their spouses, most of them complained about the differences between what "he needs" and "she needs," what "he wants" and "she wants," what "he expects" and "she expects." In speaking about the subject, rarely did anyone mention the phrase *power struggle*. Yet when we asked our interviewees if they thought that underlying their decision-making problems lay a power struggle, they inevitably said, "Sure," or "Of course!"

What became clear from those interviews is that power is a very difficult thing to talk about. Newlyweds readily acknowledge that power is an issue in their marriage, yet they find it hard to verbalize what *they mean* when they say that. The phenomenon has partly to do with the fact that often spouses are comfortable with the power roles they have assumed more or less unconsciously—be they assertive or passive—and so they don't give the matter much thought. But also, it frequently takes couples a long time to realize that certain power patterns are being set up—and so it isn't until several years down the line that they wake up to find that the decisions being made in the marriage aren't meeting their needs. And finally, part of it has to do with the fact that even when people aren't satisfied with the power they hold in their marriage, they may focus on a specific, tangible issue of disagreement—such as money or house cleaning—and bypass the more subtle, complex, and pervasive problem of power. Because surface issues are easier to look at, basic, underlying power issues are often ignored. Frequently it is not until conflicts escalate to a point where spouses are totally frustrated in their marriage that they finally recognize that their problem is not just a matter of disagreement over a present issue but an acting out of a gigantic power struggle.

WHAT IS POWER?

Most broadly defined, power is the ability to achieve an end. In human relationships that usually means effecting something that will satisfy one's perceived needs or desires. Just as a baby cries, at first instinctively, then premeditatively, to get its hunger satiated, so too do adults learn ways to fulfill their physical and emotional needs to ensure their survival. Alfred Adler, an early psychoanalyst, asserted that the drive for power is fundamental to human beings. (His firm conviction in this caused him to break away from his colleague Freud, who maintained early in his career that the sex drive is the primary human drive.)

It's true that in any relationship—whether between boss and employee, say, or parent and child—people attempt to satisfy their needs. But in a relationship as intimate and important as marriage, fulfilling one's needs is especially crucial. In every decision that gets made in marriage, there is a tacit negotiation between one spouse's needs and wishes and the other spouse's needs and wishes. When both partners' needs get met, the making of the decision is conflict free. When the needs of one or both partners are left unmet, the ground is laid for a power struggle.

Psychoanalyst Alfred Adler[4] has been quoted as saying, "Most married couples conduct themselves as if each party were afraid that the other one could see that it was the weaker." It's certainly true, especially in the early stages of marriage, that most people want to make sure to stand their ground—to protect their sense of self and security. Psychiatrist Martin Goldberg notes that most power struggles develop *not* because of a desire to control the other, but because each spouse is afraid of *being controlled*.[5]

But the need to feel in control is not always demonstrated in an obvious manner. Sometimes it's the quiet, low-key spouse who is really running the show, or the agreeable, obliging marital partner who eventually lashes out in anger and frustration.

Martin Goldberg comments that passive maneuvers can be just as aggressive (and sometimes even more effective) weapons than overt behavior in making claims for dominance.[6]

The question of how power gets distributed in a marriage used to be dictated by society.[7] The husband was expected to make all the money *and* all the decisions about how it should be spent or saved. He was the one who was supposed to make all the political decisions for the family and to determine when and how he and his wife had sex. He was acknowledged to be the king in his own home. The wife also had reign—but usually in matters of home and family. She was in charge of cleaning and decorating the house, raising the children, feeding the family. If she did exert power in other areas, then it was subtly and secretly. She might be "wearing the pants in the family," but if that was so, it was rarely acknowledged openly even between the two of them. It was the wife's role to make her husband feel confident that it was he who was boss.

Nowadays the contract is more complicated. The women's movement, feminist expectations, changing and not-so-changing male conceptions of familial and work roles have all been influential in challenging newly married couples in ways that a generation ago few could have foreseen. With the blurring of social roles today, there are no clear domains for what a husband should decide and what a wife should decide. It is acceptable for women to take part in traditional male arenas of decision making, and vice versa. Marriage researchers[8] have described what happens when roles traditionally determined for husband and wife are suddenly up for grabs. They refer to conventional, role-determined marriages as "closed structures." In such closed structures the bride and groom come to marriage with agreed-upon expectations regarding their roles —maybe she cooks and he mows the lawn—and little discussion is required. However, as structures become more *open*—and there are no clear definitions as to male–female roles—the decision-making terrain may be rife with misunderstanding, conflict, and power struggles.[9]

OVERSTEPPING BOUNDARIES

Nancy and Eddie Stilton bought a weekend home several hours away from their downtown Chicago apartment several months after their wedding. Getting away for weekends had become a cherished habit for each of them, and they looked forward to spending time in their dream house.

Soon after buying the house, however, they found that their weekends away together were tense and filled with conflict rather than romantic and relaxing. The problems all flowed from determining how they would spent their precious leisure time. Nancy's idea of a fun weekend was to spend time gardening, playing softball with a neighborhood team, jogging, and riding her bike. Eddie's attitude was that he worked hard all week and on the weekend he just wanted to relax quietly with Nancy. He found himself resenting Nancy's getting out of bed to run outdoors before 10 A.M., when he wanted them to linger in bed and snuggle. His plans for weekend activities at the house always included Nancy. Unfortunately, the plans he made were not the ones Nancy envisioned for herself. So they fought.

According to Nancy, what bothered her was not that she and Eddie differed in how they wanted to spend their free time, but that Eddie thought to *impose* his ideas upon her. When she'd been married eight months, she told us:

> Eddie has a controlling aspect to his personality. I have an inordinate aversion to being told what to do. His personality is very strong and dominating. I can feel overwhelmed by him. He plans way in advance. When we went out to the house last weekend with friends, he began talking to them about all the things *we* would do together. I had things in mind *I* wanted to do. I feel stifled because he talks about *what* we're going to do and *when* we're going to do it. I feel overwhelmed by his manic enthusiasm. I have to doubly assert myself to be heard. Before marriage I took his controlling nature as strength and decisiveness. Now I feel like I'm choking.

On the surface Nancy and Eddie have a difference of opinion regarding weekend activities. Underneath, however, is a no-holds-barred battle for who controls a certain area of decision making in the couple's life. We don't know why it was so important for Eddie to control his wife's free time, but we do know that he was trying to impose his will in an area of Nancy's life that she saw cordoned off as her own.

Why was Nancy feeling so threatened by Eddie's infringing on her "space"? Essentially, we all grow up and leave home to have autonomy over our life, and it can be a frightening reminder of childhood powerlessness to have that gain suddenly, abruptly, or rudely diminished by our partner. Nancy wanted to be married, but she didn't want to give up her independence. She was, in essence, making a statement: "I don't want to give up who I am and who I want to be." Like many other women today, Nancy felt she had made such valuable strides in creating her own life—developing her own career and interests—that she found it difficult to adapt her ways to her new husband's wishes. Implied in Nancy's conversation with us seemed to be the feeling, "Goddamn it, I had to work so hard to be independent, to take care of myself, and now I'm being asked to give up what I've gained!"

Partners come into marriage with a rather well formed, though rarely articulated sense of "domain": As marriage partners you have an unconscious but vitally important sense of what areas of decision making you feel are yours, which are your spouse's, and which you both share. Your ideas about domain are probably influenced by a number of factors:

- the balance of power you observed in your parents' home: You may want to emulate that model; you may want to rebel against it.
- whatever expertise you or your spouse may have:[10] If, say, your spouse is a bookkeeper or an accountant, it is likely that he or she will be the one to manage finances.
- your own sense of dependence or desire for independence

Overstepping those bounds, as *inevitably* happens in at least the early stages of marriage, leads to conflict.

This sense of having one's "space" intruded upon can result from the subtlest of behaviors. For instance, one newlywed woman complained to us that when she cooked dinner her husband came into the kitchen and did things like spice the spaghetti sauce. She recounted that numerous arguments had arisen because she got angry that her husband was such a "busybody," always "into everything" and "always fussing and in the way." She lamented to us that often on the way home from work he would pick up groceries despite knowing she went grocery shopping, and then ended up buying duplicates of products she purchased. As we discussed with this woman her anger at her husband she began to realize how strongly she felt the need to be in control of "her" kitchen, how tied up her sense of being a woman and wife was with providing the food for her family. While her husband saw his involvement as being helpful and nurturing, his wife felt his actions implied that she was a failure, that she couldn't meet her husband's food needs.

For this couple, mealtime was a struggle because they had different notions about whose territory the kitchen was. The wife wanted the kitchen to be her domain, but her husband also wanted to participate there. Rather than focus on the nit-picking details of what spice her husband might throw into the spaghetti sauce, the couple needed to address their feelings about what roles they saw for themselves and each other in domestic life.

OTHER TIFFS ABOUT TURF

Overstepping boundaries is a problem, and its flip side—not sharing in responsibilities in a given area—can also cause conflict.

Carla Newman, of Detroit, complained to us that her husband didn't help out enough in areas she thought he should. Shortly after marrying and settling into their new apartment, Carla suggested to Craig that they start shopping for furniture and fixtures. He agreed. Yet, whenever Carla mentioned a specific time to meet at a department store, Craig begged off, saying he had to study for business classes he was taking at night. He advised her to go alone. "Don't worry, I know I'll like whatever you like," he assured her.

Carla fumed over Craig's lack of interest. She'd scour the stores in her free time, but whenever she saw something that she seriously considered buying she'd go home and tell Craig to come with her to check it out. He would hem and haw and one way or another put it off, until he refused outright and accused her of being wishy-washy.

"Why can't you just make up your mind!" he shouted at her.

"Why don't you care about our home?" she yelled back.

Time passed, and Carla wouldn't order the furniture. The subject of decorating their home became more and more heated.

Carla and Craig were involved in a not-so-funny game of Carla testing Craig to see if she could get him to come shopping with her, and Craig resisting getting involved in an area he had no interest in. Accusations and insults began to fly. After one particularly angry argument, Carla threw herself on their bed crying. Things had hit rock bottom over this seemingly inconsequential issue, and so, hesitatingly and with much residual anger, they began to talk. Their conversation, according to Carla, went something like this:

> "Why can't you help me? Why can't you come with me shopping?" Carla asked. "Why don't you want to do this together?"
>
> "Give me a break!" Craig responded. "I trust your taste. I know nothing about furniture. I don't like it. I do other things about the house! How could I possibly help you anyway?"
>
> "You're my husband. We're supposed to do these things together!" she answered. "I want this to be *our* house, not *my* house."
>
> "My father never did things like that. My mother was able to handle all the decorating decisions herself. He'd like whatever she brought home. I feel the same way."
>
> "But don't you want to be part of this house? Don't you want to feel like you had something to do with the way it looks, with helping to create it?"
>
> "I do feel that way. But I don't need to pick the pillows to feel that way."

Carla viewed decorating as an area of decision making that was important to share with her husband. She was unhappy having full control in that area. For other wives, the complaint might be: You don't want to help me with the dishes . . . laundry . . . child care . . .

Like Craig, most spouses resist demands that run against their male or female inclinations. In fact, if you think about some of the difficulties you're having making decisions with your mate, you'll probably see that many problems have to do with this sex-linked notion of domain.

For example, it's quite common for the question of who *initiates* sex to be of key concern to each spouse. The man may need to feel that he decides, but secretly wishes to have his wife decide. The wife, likewise, may long to be "taken" by her husband, but resist giving up control. In each case the question of who makes the decision is linked to deeper issues of expectations of male–female roles and feelings about being dependent and independent. Lingering dissatisfactions, resentments, and discontent can result from this common but rarely spoken about struggle of who takes charge of different domains.

UNCONSCIOUS CONFLICTS

Complicating the issue of domain are usually very ambivalent feelings that a person has toward being dependent and being independent, being in control versus being taken care of.

For instance, Nancy, who felt stifled by Eddie's emphatic desire to schedule her weekends according to his wishes, *specifically* chose to marry somebody who would be strong enough for her to lean on, strong enough to "save" her from her dominating mother. She herself realized the irony of wanting a husband who was powerful, but resenting his power. In fact, not surprisingly, her struggle had many elements in common with the struggle she had always had with her mother.

And Carla Newman, in much the same way, may have married somebody who needed her and depended on her—but then felt overwhelmed by the responsibilities of having to make decisions alone. One man told us that he basically liked being married to a successful corporate woman, but was beginning to feel unsure of his "manliness" because his wife had strong opinions and expressed them in a very forceful way.[12] And another recent groom admitted that, while he liked the fact that his wife let him be the "man of the house," he was starting to get annoyed that she waited for him to pay all the bills and to make all their social plans. Part of him felt it was his role to be the "in-charge macho husband," but a more pragmatic part of him felt extremely time-pressured and overburdened.

The fact is, people are often confused about how much power they want in their marriage. Deeply inherent in many power struggles is not just a struggle between two people but an internal conflict within one or both partners. Deep needs that have gone unmet may cause a husband or wife to be extremely aggressive in seeking to get those needs met in marriage. Outwardly, a person may seem to need to be in control but inwardly may yearn to be taken care of and nurtured. Or, a lack of self-esteem may make someone afraid to assert their wishes, yet leave them feeling frustrated, deprived, and angry. Some of these feelings might be called "preconscious," since one becomes aware of such needs only upon experiencing a particular frustration. Others remain "unconscious" (not in our awareness) but can fuel arguments by adding to feelings of deprivation and anger.

When seemingly inconsequential issues suddenly erupt into major arguments, it's likely that one of those pockets of anger has been tapped into. In fact, the key to recognizing an unconscious conflict is noting when an issue is being blown way out of proportion. If you become uncontrollably angry when your spouse chooses the movie for both of you to see, it is more than likely that something is going on beyond the actual decision being negotiated and might not even be related to it at all.

Because marriage is such an intimate relationship, deep feelings are constantly being touched upon—and depending on how lively an unconscious issue is to you or your spouse, all can go smoothly or smolderingly. Needless to say, people who have many pockets of such anger will have difficulty maintaining relations with other than the most compliant of spouses.

The following are stories of two couples. The first exemplifies how potentially destructive it can be to a relationship when a spouse is totally confused about how much power they want in their marriage. The second story demonstrates how unconscious conflicts can be manifested in even the most trivial interactions and circumstances.

Jacki and Earl

For Jacki and Earl, whom we introduced in chapter 2, decision-making problems about the wedding got so out of hand that they spent their wedding night apart.

In her initial interview with us, several days before her wedding, Jacki revealed that she and Earl were facing some problems.

It's going to be an old-fashioned church wedding. There'll be about two hundred guests, with music for the reception. I've never been married before. I mean I *have* to have a big wedding. Earl was married before. He wanted it to be very simple. I think if it was up to him he would have preferred it if we'd take off somewhere and get married. He went along with my idea though, and together we saved money to pay for the wedding.

But now he's yelling at me that I am spending too much on the wedding. He said he's beginning to feel that I'm not talking to him enough about certain details. At the beginning, he used to tell me to go ahead and do what I had to do! He seems to just go back and forth. Yesterday morning he was screaming and he walked out of our apartment. He called me later at work and argued about it some more.

I'm tired of this. Earl wants me to get arrangements done because he has a tendency of laying back for a while and assuming that, you know, "Oh, she's going to take care of it." Now he's angry that I'm taking care of things. His attitude bothers me. He should take the initiative and do something first. I think he sort of got used to the idea that I'm the administrator.

While Jacki was aware of Earl's anger in the days before the wedding, nothing quite prepared her for his outburst on their wedding day. Several weeks after her wedding, she told us:

He was very uptight at the reception. He yelled at a lot of people. At the end of the wedding he got angry with me because guests were giving me envelopes with checks in them. He thought it should be his role to take the gift envelopes. But people were giving them to me. What could I do? I was angry at his attitude.

We were supposed to go to a hotel on our wedding night. First we took our gifts home. And as soon we got home we had an argument about my taking the money. He didn't stay at home that night. I guess he was out drinking with the boys. I was beyond the point of shock. It was a tremendous disappointment. It will take me a long time to get over this.

Obviously something had gone dramatically wrong for Jacki and Earl. For five years they lived together, relatively harmoniously. In fact, Jacki told us during our first interview with her that it was their ability to *communicate* that had initially drawn her and Earl together. But in the weeks before their wedding a conflict erupted that created tremendous strain. Jacki was hurt and disappointed. Earl was angry. Neither of them seemed to have a clue to what was going on.

But if we look at the story Jacki told us, we can see that Earl had very mixed feelings about how involved he wanted to be in the wedding planning. First he went along with Jacki's plans for a big wedding and agreed to let her "run the show." But as the wedding approached he became nervous—probably to some extent about losing his independence as a bachelor—and began attacking Jacki for taking charge and not consulting him. As we mentioned before, you can always tell that there is an underlying, unconscious conflict if a spouse overreacts to a given situation. Clearly Earl was upset about more than just wedding details and expenses. He was so filled with rage—and fear of being "swallowed up" in marriage and by his new wife—that he ruined his wedding day and night.

Judging from the contradiction between what he was saying and doing, Earl was obviously ambivalent. On the one hand, he seemed to want Jacki to take care of him. He let her decide how much money they should save, how much money they should spend, and how to deal with the caterer and musicians and handle other wedding details. On the other hand, he said he felt controlled and resented it. Earl experienced certain dependency needs—as we all do—but he also felt as though he *should* be independent. He was flip-flopping between these two needs.

It's interesting to note that, according to Jacki, Earl became angry with her only after his mother came to stay with them in the weeks before the wedding. As we said, unconscious conflicts usually have to do with deep, unmet childhood needs. His mother's visit seems to have triggered some unresolved issues from his early life. Perhaps he felt overwhelmed by his dominating mother and was now transferring those feelings onto his new wife, Jacki. Or perhaps he felt his mother, his first caretaker, was inconsistent or inadequate or unavailable to him and so he was, in the recesses of his soul, angry—so that when he got closer to Jacki as the wedding approached, a danger signal went off—he attacked and ran away. It may be that for him, getting close had itself become a danger signal.

Since Earl never came for an interview—he was never able to fit an interview into his schedule, or at least that's what he told us—we don't know exactly what set off his rage. It remains clear, however, on the basis of what Jacki told us, that he was torn between wanting to be taken care of by Jacki and needing to see himself as strong and independent. He was so conflicted that when guests bestowed their wedding gifts upon his wife, he became fearful and paranoid that he was losing control in his marriage, that she was taking over his "masculine" role. Because Earl didn't recognize his internal conflict—and thought that his anger had to do only with practical matters relating to the wedding—he had no handle on his emotions. He "acted out" to the detriment of his marriage and to the anguish of his wife.

Amanda and Phil

Unconscious conflicts don't always have such dramatic and extreme consequences.

Phil and Amanda Diamond stumbled upon a major bone of contention several months into their marriage. Phil was furious with Amanda because she had not submitted a number of insurance forms for her weekly visits to her allergist. Meticulous about paperwork, he was angered at what he viewed as Amanda's laziness, as well as about the reimbursements they were losing as a result of it. He offered to fill out the forms for Amanda, but she refused. She explained to us:

> The hardest thing is for me to admit that I'm wrong. I'm so used to being self-sufficient that I'll go to the nth degree to do things by myself. I'm really awful about filling out forms, but instead of saying, "This is hard for me—please help me with this," I put it off. When Phil constantly asks me about the forms I get furious that he's treating me like a child.

Amanda, who grew up as an eldest child and had helped raise her younger siblings, was accustomed to being the responsible partner in previous relationships. Part of Phil's appeal for her, she acknowledged, was that he was predictable, conscientious, and able to nurture her—qualities her parents lacked. "It's nice to have somebody take care of me for a change. After a while you get sick of always having to take care of other people," she said.

But the power struggle that arose over the insurance forms clearly demonstrates how ambivalent Amanda was between wanting to be in control and wanting to be taken care of. She was drawn to Phil because he was strong and protective, but she was also fearful of letting herself become too helpless and dependent. Her determination not to let her husband fill out her insurance forms—though she would have loved to be free of the task—was an attempt to show herself and her husband that she was in charge, as she had always felt in her past.

Amanda did eventually fill out the insurance forms, convinced by Phil's argument that she was wasting money they could be saving. But from the experience, she told us, she realized that despite her cherishing Phil's nurturance, she has a strong need to do things her way. "While it is tempting for me to let Phil take charge of things for me, I need to hold on to my self-sufficiency," she told us. "Phil will just have to learn to relax—to let me be in control of things that relate to me—and let me do things in my own time."

Because Amanda was able to step back and look at the reasons why she was in conflict with her husband over the insurance forms, she helped prevent the issue from becoming more explosive.

POWER PATTERNS

So far, we've addressed two issues relating to power: The importance of being aware of how the decision-making terrain is divided or shared in your marriage; and the benefits of recognizing how you may feel torn between wanting to be in control of certain areas in your marriage, but wanting also to be taken care of by your spouse.

Now we want to focus on the power style you project to others, especially your spouse. For the way you feel about the two issues mentioned above—how powerful or unpowerful you feel, how powerful or unpowerful you want to be, how comfortable or uncomfortable you are with power—is inevitably exhibited in your personality.

There is a wide spectrum of power patterns, and the following categories are just meant to offer a range of choices from which you can consider where you fit in. As you look over the following choices, think about how you and your spouse try to achieve your goals. Do you both use the same strategies, or do you use differing strategies? Be aware that you each may approach different areas of decision making with different power attitudes.

Passive-Submissive

If you fall into this pattern, you usually follow your spouse's lead. You may not mind if your mate makes the decisions. In fact, you may be relieved not to have to be burdened with problem solving, since you aren't comfortable being "in charge." If you are passive-submissive in many areas of your marriage, you're likely to be very dependent, a trait your spouse may primarily enjoy or may primarily perceive as burdensome. Most people, except those who are overly controlling, are passive-submissive in some decision-making areas, usually those in which they have no great investment or interest.

Passive-Aggressive

If you're a passive-aggressive type, you are not comfortable with any outward shows of power, but you excel at indirect manipulation. You often go along with your mate's decisions, but inwardly resent that you are doing so. Often you will subtly resist, and sometimes sabotage, your spouse's plans. For example: You may agree to spend an evening with friends of your spouse whom you do not like, but then ruin the night by embarrassing your spouse in front of their friends—leaving your mate to regret the evening. The reasons you don't come right out and present what you want can vary. You may be fearful of seeming pushy, or afraid of rejection or disappointment. Despite your indirectness about what you want, you often end up getting your way. You don't think of yourself as powerful, but you are.

Passive-Suffering

If you fit into this category, you go along with your spouse's decisions but then suffer as a result. Your suffering is not as selfless as it may seem, because it may be intended to induce guilt in your spouse. For instance: You may agree to visit your spouse's family but then act miserable during your entire stay there. You may feel righteous and sacrificing because you are following your mate's decision, but actually you are exerting power by getting back at your spouse through your suffering. Your response, termed "masochistic" in psychological literature, can be extremely frustrating and punishing to your spouse.

Assertive-Compromising

If you can assert your needs to your spouse, but also compromise after listening to your mate's side of the story, then your attitude toward power and approach to decision making is ideal. It means you feel comfortable exhibiting power, but also comfortable relinquishing power. Your spouse knows where you stand on issues, but also feels reassured that their needs are being taken into account. You are able to determine what is important to you and what isn't. You consider your spouse's opinions. Sometimes you go along with them; other times you don't.

Assertive-Controlling

If you assert your needs and find it difficult to compromise when compromise is required, you fit into this category. You usually insist that you get your way. You are afraid of being vulnerable and of not being in charge. "Winning" for you means forcing your mate to be submissive. You may not always feel rewarded when you get your way, since you may do so at your spouse's expense. Often it is just the *point* of getting your way that is important. You are terrified of feeling powerless, perhaps because that is the way your parents made you feel.

As you've read through the above categories, we're sure you remembered times when both you and your spouse were "passive-submissive" because neither of you cared to make a decision, conflicts that emerged when one or both of you behaved in an "assertive-controlling" manner, instances when you and your mate sabotaged each other's plans by being "passive-aggressive." While it is natural to call into use all of these strategies at one time or another, it can greatly benefit your marriage to be aware of how you are manipulating or relinquishing power in your relationship.

CHECKUP:
HOW POWERFUL ARE YOU?

The exercise below is designed to help you focus on specific areas in your marriage and determine how you feel about the way decisions are made in those areas. By considering a variety of decisions that get made by you and your spouse, you should gain a clearer idea of which are the areas in which you feel powerful and which you feel powerless.

Scan the following list of five statements, *a–e*:

> *a.* I like my spouse to take the lead and make decisions in this area.
>
> *b.* I let my spouse make decisions in this area, but often resent it and subtly resist it.
>
> *c.* My spouse makes decisions in this area. I go along with them, but oftentimes suffer and feel that I'm sacrificing.
>
> *d.* I am pretty good at asserting my needs in this area, but I can compromise.
>
> *e.* I assert my needs in this area, but have a difficult time when compromise is required.

Below is a list of decisions that commonly get made in marriages. Next to each decision, place the letter corresponding to the statement above that is most suited to how you feel about the way the decision gets made in your marriage.

- ☐ choosing what leisure activity to do together
- ☐ deciding how often we clean our home
- ☐ making major purchases for our home, like furniture, a dishwasher . . .
- ☐ making major purchases for outside our home, like a car, a lawn mower . . .
- ☐ deciding who initiates sex
- ☐ deciding how often to see family
- ☐ deciding how much money we save
- ☐ deciding how often to entertain friends and family
- ☐ deciding where to live
- ☐ deciding how to celebrate occasions, like birthdays . . .
- ☐ choosing cards and gifts for family members
- ☐ deciding how committed we are to our jobs

☐ deciding where to go on vacation
☐ deciding what to have for dinner

Once you've completed the above list, we'd like you to examine it carefully in order to identify those areas in which you and your spouse do and do not have problems relating to power. Where you feel satisfied by the way the decision is handled in your marriage, place a *check* next to it on the list. *Circle* each decision not being handled to your satisfaction.

As you may have guessed, the letters next to the statements above correspond to the five categories we listed earlier. The letter *a* corresponds to being "Passive-Submissive," the letter *b* to "Passive-Aggressive," the letter *c* to "Passive-Suffering," the letter *d* to "Assertive-Compromising," and the letter *e* to "Assertive-Controlling."

It would be impossible for us to determine which of the issues listed above are problematic for you based on which letter you placed next to them. Only *you,* as a couple, can decide when the balance of power in your relationship is a problem for your marriage.

For instance, if you placed a letter *a* next to "deciding who initiates sex," you may be satisfied that you leave that decision up to your spouse. But your mate may be very frustrated that you don't take more of a sexual initiative and so find it a problem that you aren't more assertive in this area. In another marriage, however, it may work very well that one partner is "passive-submissive" in the bedroom, if the other mate enjoys being "assertive-controlling."

As you go through the above list, observe whether in your responses you tended to think of yourself as more passive or more assertive. In thinking about your answers, you may find that in some areas being passive-submissive or assertive-controlling may be a problem, and in other areas not.

WORKSHOP: STRIKING
THE RIGHT BALANCE

The important thing to remember is that power is not equal in a relationship all the time, nor is it necessarily desirable that power be equal. You don't always need two chiefs in a relationship. Differences in power between you and your spouse may suit your needs. For instance, your spouse may like your being "assertive-controlling" because he or she feels very taken care of by your being the boss. Your spouse may even benefit from your being a "passive-sufferer," if he or she is the type who needs to feel guilty.

It's unrealistic to expect that every decision will be resolved by the two of you together. Decision making would be tedious and prolonged if you negotiated every issue in unison. Being too concerned that everything in your marriage be "fifty-fifty" would force you to focus too much attention on how much you are "giving" and "getting" from your spouse. It is inevitable that during your marriage there will be times when you're giving 80 percent and getting only 20 percent, and other times when it's just the reverse.

You should work on changing the power balance in your marriage only in areas where you or your spouse feel frustrated that you aren't getting your needs met. If on the above list you jotted down a lot of letters *b* and *c,* then you are clearly having trouble asserting your needs to your mate and as a result do not feel powerful enough in your marriage. If you found that you put down many letters *e,* then it's likely that your spouse feels frustrated that you are overstepping bounds and trampling on their own wishes and expectations.

To help you focus even more precisely on what changes you might make regarding the power balance in your marriage, here are some questions to answer in the space provided. Be as specific as possible in your answers.

• Which areas of decision making do you want to be *more* involved in? (Examples: planning weekends, household decorating, budgeting . . .) _____

_____

• Which areas of decision making does *your spouse want to be more* involved in? (If you don't know, ask.)

_____

_____

• Which areas of decision making would *you like your spouse to be more* involved in? _____

_____

_____

• Which areas of decision making does *your spouse want you to be more* involved in? (If you don't know, ask.)

_____

_____

• Which areas of decision making would *you like your spouse to be less* involved in? _____

_____

_____

• Which areas of decision making would *your spouse like you to be less* involved in? (If you don't know, ask.)

_____

_____

To a large extent, how successful you and your spouse will be in carrying out the changes you've just listed will depend on your communication skills—a topic we'll delve into in the next chapter. We'll offer guidelines for how to express yourself more effectively so that you can get your needs understood by your mate, and how to listen more carefully as to make sure that you take your spouse's needs into account. As you read the communication chapter, it will be important to pay close attention to how your style of communication may be shifting the power balance in ways that ultimately harm your relationship.

For now, however, there are several steps you can take to make some changes:

1. Be alert to whatever dissatisfactions you each have about the way power is distributed in your marriage. If possible, have your spouse answer the six questions listed above on a separate piece of paper. Even if they are interested in examining their own feelings about the power balance in your marriage, share with your mate what you have discovered through the exercises above. Tell your mate what areas of decision making you'd like to be more or less involved in. (For example: "I'd really like to go along when you pick out your office furniture. I know they are purchases for your business, but they are expensive items and I think I should have some say in the matter." Or, "I really wish you'd take a more active role in deciding where to go on vacations.") Informing your spouse of these feelings won't necessarily alter the way decisions get made, but it will introduce the notion that changes may be forthcoming. Just vocalizing your thoughts may trigger you both to think twice the next time you make a decision, about how that decision is getting made. And you'll feel you can stop holding your breath (out of trepidation); you've expressed your feelings.

If your spouse is open to negotiation, try to work out trades that are agreeable to both of you. Agree to let your spouse be more involved in an area of decision making that is important to him or her with the understanding that you then can be more involved in an area of decision making significant to you.

In your discussion with your spouse, you also may want to talk about any third parties who get drawn into power struggles in your marriage. In some marriages, both spouses are comfortable calling upon relatives or friends to help them make marital decisions. For others, seeking the advice of a third party complicates the family "system"[13] and becomes a bone of contention. You may relish your friends' suggestions while your spouse resents such "interference." Be aware of any tensions that may be mounting due to differing attitudes about who should have power in your marriage.

2. *Look at your behavior*. Consider what you may be doing that is hampering the power balance in your marriage. For example: You may be taking on certain decision responsibilities and then feeling overburdened and angry, while your spouse feels annoyed at being left with feelings of powerlessness. Or, you may be bolstering your own power in your marriage by arguing that your mother, sister, and boss agree with you, while your spouse is left feeling powerless in the face of such strong opposition. You may take advantage of your spouse who's slow to know his or her own mind, by acting on your wishes without giving your mate a chance to offer an opinion. Or you may be afraid of asserting yourself to your mate because of some secret fear that if you do so your mate will feel hurt. *Be honest with yourself*. Do you give in to your spouse just to maintain harmony in your marriage? Do you insist on doing things your way even when the issue itself isn't especially important to you?

If you have difficulty pinpointing how you may contribute to power problems in your marriage, get your spouse's opinions.

Your husband or wife is bound to come up with at least a few power ploys you use to get, however indirectly, your own way. Remember to be nonconfrontational in manner in these frank discussions, and be prepared to accept your spouse's comments as well as express your own.

3. Examine what is influencing your attitude about power. You've already identified whether or not you are passive or controlling, and how you might like to be different. But it's also important to question the motivation for your behavior. If you'd like to be more assertive than you are, think about what might be preventing you from being more forthright about your needs and wishes. Were you punished as a child when you were too outspoken? Do you have a fear of being rejected or disappointed by your spouse? Evaluate how realistic those fears are. In the past your parents may have been very disapproving, or like many children you *perceived* them as disapproving at least some of the time. In your current life, however, your spouse may be very accepting and interested in meeting your needs, a reality that you need to integrate in your mind.

On the other hand, if you are overinsistent about getting your way, consider why you are so fearful of compromising. Did you feel that your needs were discounted when you were growing up and that you now have to make up for those years of deprivation?

Understanding what influences your attitudes about power is an important step toward changing.

4. Take responsibility for the power balance in your marriage. You can't count on an assertive, aggressive, or noisy spouse to tone down without your exerting some influence. You must eventually own up to the role you play in *allowing* them to control you, and your *responsibility* in reining them in. This may be difficult, and loaded with childhood issues like fears of speaking up to dominating parents, identifying with a meek parent, guilt at being more assertive than a submissive parent.

Make your spouse aware of their power style by reflecting it back to them, calmly rather than accusingly. Comments such as: "Darling, are you aware of how controlling you can be sometimes?" or "I don't think you hear how angry and controlling you can seem" offer your spouse the chance to understand how you perceive their actions. It may be the *first* time anyone told them what effect they have.

5. Keep in mind the marital advantages of having a comfortable balance of power. Being effective in getting your needs met can take time and determination, and the process may seem awkward at first. Initially your spouse may react with displeasure at your newfound assertiveness, since it is not easy to give up power if you're the type who likes to dominate. But you should expect that you and your spouse will ultimately react more positively to changes in each other's power attitudes as you work through to a new balance between you. And there can be no question that creating a marriage in which both you and your spouse are satisfied with the way power is handled is a worthwhile, even crucial, goal.

Ultimately, you and your mate should feel that the important decisions in your marriage get made with the needs and wishes of both of you taken into account. Deep down you should both feel that you are treated in your marriage as valued adults possessing valued thoughts and emotions that are recognized and appreciated. You should both feel *empowered* in the areas in your marriage that are important to each of you.

As one man told us after the first year of his second marriage:

> I'm so used to having an opinion. I'm convinced that I'm smart, that I know a lot and have a lot of the answers. But my wife is a lot stronger than she first appeared. Since I've remarried there's been a realization that now there are two people involved and making decisions has become a different process. Actually it's fun. It's really much more exciting to create something together than to just make commands about how you want things done.

A marriage in which spouses strive for a balance of power that suits them both is a relationship in which husband and wife respect and appreciate each other's thoughts and feelings and needs.

COMMUNICATION

How to Say What You Want to Say

It was once said, "In the right key one can say anything, in the wrong key, nothing: the only delicate part of the job is the establishment of the key."

That communicating well is vital to the success of your marriage cannot be overstated.[1] Communicating successfully means being able to express yourself in a way that can be heard by your mate and listening carefully enough to interpret what your mate is trying to get across to you. Communicating well is a matter of paying attention not just to how you and your spouse converse, but also to how you relate nonverbally. It means making as much effort as possible to understand and be understood.

Considering that you and your spouse have spent your entire lives interacting with others, it may seem odd that in this chapter we will emphasize the need to be conscious of how you communicate. But communicating effectively is not necessarily something that comes naturally. Communication style, along with household tasks, was rated by newlyweds in our survey as the third major cause of marital arguments,[2] after money and family. According to our findings, newlyweds fight about the way they talk—or don't talk—with each other more frequently than they fight about sex, friends, religion, values, job obligations, and finding time for each other.[3] Of those newlyweds who said they feel unhappy or only "fair" about their marriages, 52 percent said they have significant problems regarding communication styles. In contrast, among those who described themselves as "pretty happy," "very happy," or "I couldn't be happier," only 9 percent reported having significant problems with communication styles. Difficulties with communication do not forebode well for marital satisfaction.

All of the power issues we described in our previous chapter are manifested in how you communicate with each other. If you're the outgoing, outspoken type, you may end up making most marital decisions just because your style is the more aggressive one. If you tend to be shy about expressing what's on your mind, you may be swept along because of your mate's more dominating oratorical abilities. If you're both likely to mouth off, with each of you trying to get in the last word, then every decision may turn into a major battle over who is in control.

The way you communicate can aggravate any problems you already have. If you or your spouse expresses yourself in ways that make it difficult to be heard accurately, or if either of you bottles up your feelings so that the other feels insulted or confused, making decisions will be not only belabored but also painful and destructive. It's a matter of not just the issue at hand—for instance, whose family to visit for the holidays—but how you deal with the issue. Do you attack each other? avoid talking about it? go along meekly and then become infuriated with yourself and your spouse?

Communicating well does not guarantee a peaceful, conflict-free marriage. In fact, there is nothing wrong or abnormal or unhealthy about conflict. A good, old-fashioned argument can clear the air, bring you and your spouse back in touch with each other, ease the way toward the tender opportunity for you to "make up." Psychologist Israel W. Charny criticizes marital treatments that aim at eliminating fighting rather than helping and teaching people to experience the positive effects of fighting. Charny writes that "the business of marriage is inherently a disturbing one—no less than the state of being a human being is inherently troubling and difficult. . . . For a marriage to be reasonably productive a couple needs to arrive at a balance of love *and* hate, honor *and* dishonor, obedience *and* disobedience. . . . The goal of marriage counseling should be to teach people how to be strong enough to be honestly loving *and* hating, how to extend themselves enough to support *and* confront each other, not to be volatile and violent but *how* to fight."[4]

The point is: There are ways of communicating that are beneficial and there are ways of communicating that are harmful. Our goal in this chapter is to help you find ways of better connecting with each other, of feeling closer, of becoming more understanding and better understood.

CHECKUP: COMMUNICATIONS

Before we examine the issues that affect how you and your mate communicate in your marriage, we thought we'd stir your thoughts about the *way* you communicate, by providing the following questions for you to answer. Except where noted, put a check in the box beside the response that *best* applies to you.

1. How often do you two have fights?
- ☐ every day
- ☐ two to three times a week
- ☐ once a week
- ☐ once or twice a month
- ☐ once every several months
- ☐ once a year
- ☐ never

2. On average, how long do your fights last?
- ☐ minutes   ☐ hours   ☐ days   ☐ weeks

3. How do you two handle your big conflicts? (Check the boxes beside *all* those that apply.)
- ☐ We discuss things calmly.
- ☐ We suffer silently, bottling up our feelings.
- ☐ One or both of us usually start screaming.
- ☐ One of us storms out of the house.
- ☐ One or both of us throw things.
- ☐ One or both of us pound walls.
- ☐ One or both of us hit the other.

4. When hurt or threatened, I tend to:
- ☐ withdraw from my spouse
- ☐ verbally attack my spouse (scream, yell, hurl insults)
- ☐ withdraw from and then verbally attack my spouse
- ☐ express my feelings calmly to my spouse
- ☐ hide my feelings from my spouse

5. When hurt or threatened, my spouse tends to:
- ☐ withdraw from me
- ☐ verbally attack me (scream, yell, hurl insults)
- ☐ withdraw from me and then verbally attack me
- ☐ express his or her feelings calmly to me
- ☐ hide his or her feelings from me

6. How do your fights usually end?
- [ ] They drag on until we gradually forget about them.
- [ ] One of us takes responsibility for "making up."
- [ ] We share the responsibility for "making up."
- [ ] One or both of us tend to harbor grudges.

7. When my spouse and I have an argument, I'm usually left feeling:
- [ ] hurt
- [ ] frustrated because we never seem to get anywhere
- [ ] closer because we understand each other better

8. The major problems in how my spouse and I communicate are that (check *all* that apply):
- [ ] I am too withdrawn
- [ ] my spouse is too withdrawn
- [ ] I am too emotional
- [ ] my spouse is too emotional
- [ ] I am not a good listener
- [ ] my spouse is not a good listener
- [ ] we don't devote enough time to talking with each other
- [ ] one or both of us harbor grudges
- [ ] one or both of us escalate minor disagreements into major assaults
- [ ] other (Explain: _____)

COMMUNICATION QUESTION MARKS

There are no right or wrong answers to the questions listed above. There is no guide we can provide that can tell you whether the way you and your spouse communicate is a "good" way or a "bad" way. You may be a couple who are revitalized by frequent blowups or devastated by any displays of anger. The point of our questions above is to make you aware of how you and your spouse relate to each other so that as you read through this chapter, you'll know where you fit in and where your trouble spots lie. Review your responses, to get a clearer idea of how combative you are, how you handle conflict, how you resolve or don't resolve disagreements, and how satisfied you are with your mode of communicating.

The first three questions listed above were also asked of

newlyweds in our survey. To get an idea of how your responses compared to those of our survey respondents, here are our findings:*

When we asked newlyweds, *How often do you two have fights?*:
- 4 percent reported fighting daily
- 15 percent reported fighting 2–3 times a week
- 20 percent reported fighting once a week
- 29 percent reported fighting once or twice a month
- 21 percent reported fighting once every several months
- 2 percent reported fighting once a year
- 10 percent reported that they never fight

When we asked newlyweds, *On average, how long do your fights last?*:
- 63 percent said minutes
- 34 percent said hours
- 4 percent said days

When we asked newlyweds, *How do you two handle your big conflicts?* (with the request that they "circle all those that apply"):
- 41 percent said, "We suffer silently, bottling up our feelings."
- 47 percent said, "One or both of us usually start screaming."
- 15 percent said, "One of us storms out of the house."
- 8 percent said, "One or both of us throw things."
- 8 percent said, "One or both of us pound walls."
- 4 percent said, "One or both of us hit the other."
- 59 percent said, "We discuss things calmly." (Judging from our interviews, it seems that often this discussion comes after some of the other behaviors listed above.)

As suggested in the choices above, there are different ways of getting your point across, both verbally and nonverbally. Your verbal communication style and your spouse's may range from being overexpressive to withdrawn and unexpressive. Often, two spouses in a marriage have different styles of communicating—one being expressive, the other less so. And it's not surprising that a shrinking violet and a loudmouth are frequently attracted to each other. If you're soft-spoken, it can be

---

*Totals of percentages in this and other tables may equal 101% due to rounding out of percentages to the nearest whole percent.

nice to have somebody serve as your mouthpiece. And if you're gregarious, it can be convenient to have a partner who lets you do all the ventilating.

It's natural that some people are more verbal or articulate and others less so. But in some marriages, communication styles become accentuated and serious problems result. Here we will focus on the extreme ends of the spectrum—the communication styles that can be extremely destructive to relationships. If you and your spouse have difficulty communicating, consider whether either of you fits into one of the following two categories:

The Overexpressive Mate

If you can't just say why you're angry, but always need to yell and shout to express your anger, if you aren't content with stating your thoughts and opinions but need to rant and rave about what you believe in, if you don't just feel happy but need to let everyone know how happy you feel, then you are someone with what psychiatrists call "histrionic" traits. You tend to live in a whirlwind of emotional frenzy and feel anxious when things become quiet and calm.

The Underexpressive Mate

If you are quiet, uncomfortable with expressing feelings, rational rather than impulsive, then, in psychiatric terms, you may have "obsessional" traits. You keep your feelings in, never really saying what's on your mind. You often leave your spouse wondering what you are thinking.

COMMUNICATION
COMBINATIONS

Being either overexpressive or withdrawn does not necessarily have to create problems in your relationship. The impact of your communication styles upon your marriage depends on the chemistry between the two of you. What matters is not just how you *act* toward each other, but how you *react*. In most marriages, a typical pattern of communicating gets set up between mates. The following are the most common combinations:

The Mixed Match

The pairing of a verbal, expressive person with a quiet, reserved mate is a common match, and often a very successful one. Ideally the styles and needs of each partner complement the other.[5] The more outgoing mate draws out the quiet one, the reserved spouse calms the more emotional partner. One woman wrote on her questionnaire:

> When I'm upset I get quiet and stop talking. He [her husband] recognizes that when I'm quiet he needs to find out what's bothering me.

Another woman wrote:

> Throughout our relationship my husband has gradually encouraged me to overcome my tendency to "keep things in." He's very good at recognizing when something is bothering me. Now we talk about our problems. I vent my feelings more and discuss possible solutions.

The coupling of the expressive and withdrawn mate becomes frustrating when the former wants to talk and "get things out" and the latter resists talking and acts indifferent. One woman, married eight months, complained:

> When I'm upset I rant, I rave, I put all my cards on the table. My husband bottles everything up. I never know what's going on in his mind.

Sometimes an unexpressive mate may *want* to be more open but, unaccustomed to verbalizing thoughts and emotions, finds the process difficult. Said a banker trying to make the adjustment from longtime bachelorhood to marriage:

> My biggest problem since being married is learning to take 34 years of keeping everything to myself and letting my wife be part of my inner feelings.

However, the biggest difficulties that result from a marriage between an expressive person and an unexpressive one arise when each feels threatened by the other's communication style.[6] If you're quiet and withdrawn, you may derive a vicarious outlet for your feelings from being married to an expressive individual. But the emotional frenzy of your spouse may also stir up conflict inside you. You may benefit in some way from your spouse's ventilating all the anger that you fear articulating, but that anger may also scare you and make you even more restrained. If you're outgoing, with "histrionic" tendencies, you may enjoy the orderliness and stability that your reserved mate provides, but you also may find your partner's rational and calm approach to life boring and stodgy.

Oftentimes spouses use their personal style of arguing as a power tool. If you scream and yell, you may be trying to scare your mate into giving in to you. If you tend to withdraw, you may be using your silence to make your mate feel anxious or guilty. If your style is highly exaggerated—if you're either very withdrawn or overemotional in your communication style—that exaggeration may reflect a deeper personality problem. You may wield your temper or keep your feelings to yourself because of fears of underlying emotions, some of which may stem from low self-esteem.

Generally, if your styles clash you know it—for instead of being able to come to mutual decisions and successfully resolving conflicts, you spend your time together attacking each other for how you communicate—like this 35-year-old teacher and her husband, a computer analyst.

> How do my husband and I resolve problems? I initiate discussion, get no response, yell, then have my husband say we can never discuss anything because I shout rather than talk.

The "Let It All Hang Out" Couple

> We don't have an easygoing relationship. We fight quite often—over what restaurant to go to, how to get there. We've been sort of appalled by how much we fight— we storm around, slam doors. She directs her anger at exactly what makes her angry. I probably channel my anger at other things—like why isn't the laundry done. We fight less since we're married, because we feel there's a control imposed upon us. We realized we had to behave better.
>
> > —a 26-year-old artist who recently married the woman he lived with for five years

If you and your spouse are both expressive, you may have a very open, calm, sharing marriage or a very aggressive, competitive relationship—all depending on how you express yourselves. If you both present your feelings calmly and respectfully then you probably have a very strong, healthy relationship. If you express your feelings through screaming, yelling, throwing things at each other, then your need to assert yourselves may stem from insecurity—from a fear of being swallowed up by each other, a fear of being vulnerable or passive.

There is no great virtue in expressing what's on your mind if it's done in a way that is hurtful. Not all sharing of one's thoughts is done as an attempt to be closer. If you voice your most angry and hostile thoughts to your spouse it may be that you're secretly afraid of intimacy and are assuring yourself of distance under the guise of "opening up" to your mate. Or, it may be that you aren't comfortable conversing in a calm, gentle, tender manner and use fighting as a way to feel closer, as a way of connecting.

If you are an expressive, "let it all hang out" couple, consider whether your open sharing of feelings is done with sensitivity and empathy or with attacks, barbs, and taunts.

The Silent Duo

Had we spoken with Anne Wyte, a 32-year-old nurse from New York City, in her first year of marriage, chances are she would have told us they were both very happy, for they had few arguments. But after seven years of marriage and in the midst of considering a divorce, Ann reflected:

> Looking back on my newlywed year I can see that I felt angry and helpless at times. My husband experiences bouts of depression, and I tried to "baby" him. I often felt like my needs weren't getting met, but we had little overt conflict. If I had to do it over again I would have learned to *argue* that first year. But my parents had never argued either. My father was also often depressed and my mother had always tried to cheer my dad up! The problem is that now my husband and I have long periods of not talking to each other. Neither of us are fighters, and we both withdraw from each other.

Indeed, probably the only thing worse than when a couple fights all the time is when a couple never airs their needs, wishes or discontent. If you're a silent sufferer, you may feel that it is not your *right* to voice your concerns. Anne Wyte, for instance, put her husband's needs ahead of her own at the start of her marriage, which eventually took its toll. Perhaps, having watched her mother suffer with a depressed father, Anne might have unconsciously felt guilty if she'd married a man who could take care of her, rather than the other way around. If her mother suffered, then Anne may have felt she didn't deserve to do any different. She seems to have identified with her mother, both in her choice of mate and the marital role she assumed.

One man we spoke with told us he was upset because he paid all the household and entertainment bills and thought that his wife, who earns a sizeable salary, should take responsibility for some of their expenses. Yet when we asked him what his wife did with her money—did she put it into a savings account? did she spend it on herself?—he didn't know. He never had asked his wife what she did with her money, thinking it wasn't his "right" to "pry" into his wife's financial affairs. He was harboring resentments against his wife, yet had made no attempt even to find out any facts about the issue that had so upset him.

Being silent when communication is clearly called for may result from a fear of rejection, disappointment, humiliation. A reserved person is often thought to have an easygoing personality. And it's true that sometimes a quiet spouse wants to avoid conflict by having their mate take control. But silence may also be a power ploy. There is power in holding back, in leaving your mate to wonder what is going on in your mind. Perhaps the man we just mentioned wanted to feel angry, and self-righteous. Maybe eventually he would explode with anger and "get back" at his wife by attacking her for being selfish with her money.

Early in marriage, some people back away from being too forceful about what they want because they are afraid of strife and fearful of bursting their newlywed bubble. If you are a silent duo, you may take pride in the fact that your marriage is free of overt conflict. Yet, as we discussed in our previous chapter, because there are so many decisions that need to get made in marriage, you must be direct about your wishes and expectations in order to reap marital and individual fulfillment.

If you are too withdrawn about what you want from your spouse and your marriage, inevitably your needs won't get met and underlying resentments will fester. Silence is not always golden.

VICIOUS CYCLES

Whatever your communication styles, at some point you and your spouse are bound to become embroiled in a major argument that leaves you both feeling incensed at each other and hopeless that you'll ever come to a resolution. Such fights may be characterized by screaming and yelling or by "the silent treatment." But during these vicious cycles[7]—these arguments that continue to snowball rather than end—you probably feel highly frustrated about how you and your mate communicate with each other. You seem to spin circles around each other.

Here's how a vicious cycle works: You have a disagreement that leads one of you to feeling attacked, threatened, hurt, uncared for, unloved, or berated—which leads the injured party (let's say it's you) to counterattack—which sets the vicious cycle in motion. Following a disagreement the injured party may also withdraw—which sets up a *different* negative pattern, involving grudge-holding, delayed explosion, tit-for-tat, and inducement of guilt. But that process, though destructive, does not lead to the immediate, malignant cycle we're describing here. (See Diagram I for an illustration.)

During these embittered, "vicious cycle" arguments you may be frightened not only by your spouse's response but also by your own. One woman told us, "I didn't even know I was capable of such anger. Since I'm married, sometimes I find that I'm scared by my own rage."

Being conscious of the process that gets set off can help you have some control over those big fights. Before reading the following story of a couple we met who experienced a long, drawn-out "vicious cycle," take a look at the diagram that illustrates how a "vicious cycle" works.

To demonstrate how you, as a couple, may get caught up in this bind, we give you the story of two newlyweds, Patti and Dave Lazar, who unwittingly became engaged in a vicious cycle they found hard to break.

Six months after their wedding, Dave's company transferred him from Cincinnati to New York. Because of the high

Resolution

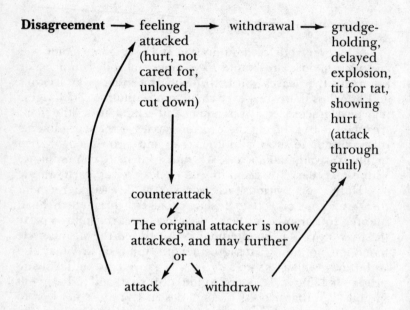

VICIOUS CYCLE

rents in Manhattan, Patti and Dave resigned themselves to rent-ing a one-bedroom apartment, which was considerably smaller than the spacious two-bedroom apartment they had shared in Ohio. Both Patti and Dave were nervous about the move. She was worried about how their oversized oak antique furniture would fit into their cramped new living room. Dave was con-cerned about where he would put his desk and file cabinets that in Cincinnati had been kept in his study.

Beginning weeks before the move, Dave would bring up the subject of his desk to Patti: Should he buy a smaller desk that would fit into their new living room? Or maybe it would be better to keep the desk he had now and put it in their bedroom? They would be walking down a street heading toward a friend's house, and out of the blue he would enthusiastically suggest to Patti various angles at which they might position his desk so they could get maximum use of their space.

Dave needed to talk about his desk for just two minutes before Patti would blow up. "Would you stop worrying about your desk! We'll worry about it when we move in! We have to see first how our furniture looks in the apartment before we can decide what to do with your desk!" Dave, accustomed to Patti's emotional reactions, pursued his line of thinking: "Come on, just tell me what your opinion is." Occasionally he would pull out a photo of a desk advertised in a newspaper and show it to Patti. The more he persisted, the angrier Patti became. "Just leave me alone," she would shout. "Oh, you're impossible," he responded angrily.

Before long they would both be exploding—she yelling that he was driving her crazy with his obsession about his desk; he accusing her of being impossible to talk to. Suddenly the issue of decorating wasn't even discussed. Instead, they were immersed in a battle of wills, a shower of accusations, a torrent of threats about leaving each other and getting divorced.

The problem for Patti and Dave was not just that they didn't know what to do about Dave's desk, but also that they hadn't found a way to discuss it so that they could *hear* each other's concerns.[8] Dave opened a discussion, Patti became upset and escalated into anger, Dave became frustrated by what he described as Patti's "cannonball attacks," and soon also turned angry. Both, of course, had their sides to the story. Dave thought his concern about his desk was legitimate since he was accustomed to using it for job-related matters as well as for taking care of household bills. It was his feeling that if he knew where he'd be able to work in their new apartment, he'd feel more relaxed about their move. Patti hated Dave's desk, couldn't stand the thought of its "ruining" their living room or bedroom, and felt it ridiculous to think about decorating until they'd moved their furniture into their new apartment and could see how things shaped up.

For our present purpose, it doesn't matter how valid each of their concerns were; the key problem was that Patti and Dave had set up a pattern that made it impossible for them to air their feelings and *feel understood*. Their style of making decisions—Dave's persistence at a time when Patti was on edge, the charged nature of Patti's response when she could have reacted more calmly—had gotten in the way so that no decision could be reached. The fact underlying their arguments was that Patti and Dave alike were troubled and anxious about moving. But the destructiveness of their pattern of taking out their anxiety on each other becomes obvious in the feelings of hopelessness about their relationship that both experienced following their bouts of arguing.

Breaking a Vicious Cycle

If you care about your marriage, you cannot take for granted your recovery from vicious cycles. You both need to make a special effort to break them when they occur. Couples do vary in their level of tolerance for how much pain they can bear from these prolonged struggles. But even though your marriage may seem able to sustain the hurts and insults being hurled back and forth, we assure you that if vicious cycles develop frequently, it will become harder and harder for you to break the patterns of hurt and anger, and channels of communication will break down.

The following considerations must be weighed and acted upon in order to break a vicious cycle:

1. Recognize when the level of your anger and your spouse's is escalating.

2. Recognize how your spouse may have been unintentionally—or intentionally—hurt by something you said or did, or didn't say or do. Question if their anger may result from their feeling unloved or unappreciated by you.

3. In seeking to end the cycle of hurt, recognize that you may not be able to "win" the argument, even though your temptation to get in the last word may be very strong.

4. After your anger has cooled, either initiate an apology or acknowledge the hurt your spouse may have felt during the argument. Empathizing with your spouse helps defuse hurt and anger and moves you both toward a resolution.

5. Beware of any tendencies you and your spouse may have to get into big arguments (vicious cycles) that may be followed by loving sessions of "making up."

If you and your mate find yourselves locked into arguments frequently, one or both of you may have an unconscious need to suffer before you experience pleasure and tenderness from each other. In the clinical literature, this tendency to have to pay a price for pleasure, or to seek to increase pleasure by first heightening emotion through pain, is referred to as masochism or sadomasochism. Be alert to such tendencies in yourself and your spouse, and be careful about getting drawn into malignant cycles, or drawing your partner in.

COMMUNICATION AGGRAVATORS

Inevitably, certain things that you and your spouse do will aggravate communication between you and draw you into conflict with one another. The following behaviors that people commonly use may escalate conflict in their marriage by inducing combative responses.[9] All of these communication techniques are normal and are called into use by everybody at some time or another. And at many times they may be effective. But even if a ploy "wins" the present argument for you, your mate's resentment may mean a worsening relationship, and you should be aware of this potential.

1. Coercing is an attempt to crowbar your mate into submission or agreement, by using verbal commands, threats regarding the future, or physical force. Your spouse may go along with your wishes passively, but secretly be embittered; agree to go along with your wishes but sabotage your plans by dragging their feet in the execution of the agreement; or defy your efforts outright.

2. Coaxing is a more subtle form of persuasion. You promise, beg, and tempt your spouse in order to have them agree with you. You may try to convince your mate that doing things your way is for their benefit. Your spouse may be annoyed by what they perceive as your manipulative efforts and, as a result, not only refuse your wishes but also become hostile.

3. Evaluating is a common technique, characterized as "pseudo-understanding." The effect is an undermining of your spouse's position. An example: "I think you're really angry at your boss, not at me," a woman tells her husband, trying to deflect his anger from her and discount that he might be upset with her for not having dinner ready when he arrived home from work. This woman's interpretation of her husband's anger makes him even more annoyed than he was originally, because it's a denial of what he is really feeling.

4. *Masking* is often thought of as "white lies" or "white-washing." It involves holding back or distorting certain infor-mation. It can elicit counterefforts by your spouse to unmask and reveal the truth. "I was late at work tonight," a husband tells his wife, trying to disguise the fact that he feared coming home to a continuation of an argument from the day before. But his explanation lacks conviction and suggests that he wants his wife to know that he was irritated with her. He is essentially inviting her to challenge his thinly veiled excuse.

5. *Postponing* is a technique that can be used as an angry, passive-aggressive maneuver and frequently causes a spouse to be provoked. "Can you tell me when we can go out with my friends from work?" a husband asks his wife. "I'll check my schedule in the morning," she responds, rolling over in bed, hoping her husband will forget about making social plans with his work colleagues if she delays her answer. Her husband, picking up his wife's unenthusiastic reaction, accuses her of not making any effort to share in his friendships and work life.

6. *Blaming*,[10] one of the most common mechanisms for starting or fueling an argument, occurs when one spouse is angry but doesn't know why, and so looks for a target for that anger in order to channel it in a seemingly justifiable way. Patti and Dave, whom we described earlier as being caught in a vicious cycle, blame each other for, in turn, their overconcern and lack of concern about Dave's desk because they are inwardly extremely anxious about moving. It is easier to fight about a desk than to face all of their worries about rerooting themselves in a new city and new jobs.

As we discussed in chapter 3, it's also possible that you and your spouse blame each other for traits for which you secretly hold yourselves in reproach. For instance, if you blame your partner for flirting, it may be that you feel secretly guilty about your own flirtatious thoughts or acts.

For some people there is a special pleasure in seeing another suffer. If you were frequently blamed by your parents while you were growing up, you may have adopted this blaming behavior and derive a special pleasure in seeing your spouse suffer as you once did. People sometimes try to overcome the pain of their childhood by "identifying with the aggressor" and so take on the role of "blamer." Perhaps you chose a mate who, already suffering from masochism or dependency or a depressed condition, accepts the unjustified blame you heap on them.

Unfortunately, the euphoria that can accompany relieving one's sense of guilt by shifting blame to another only works while the blaming is going on. If you get caught in a repetitive cycle of blame and resolution, you'll find it draining and burdensome to your relationship. The temptation to blame lies in our wish that the answer to our problems be simple: "If only my spouse would change, everything would be all right." But, ultimately, blaming is unproductive, unsatisfying, and highly destructive to the blossoming of any warm, close, loving feelings between spouses.

It's important to think about those behaviors, how you use them, and the impact they have on your marital relationship. It may be that you tend to be coercive in how you communicate, but your spouse, a submissive, dependent individual, doesn't mind. On the other hand, it may be your coercive behavior that sparks most of your marital arguments.

All of the behaviors we've just described have the potential for starting vicious cycles if they result in your mate's feeling hurt and then attacking in return. Even if vicious cycles don't occur, but your spouse withdraws in response to your communication style, you are preventing fruitful interaction from ensuing.[11] In the following section we present alternatives— strategies to follow for positive communication.

WORKSHOP: PRACTICING
GOOD COMMUNICATION

We are both very straightforward about things that bug us. We try to say how important something is before anger gets heavy.
                    —a 25-year-old woman from Colorado

We talk and say, "Hey, I'm upset. We need to discuss this.

>   —a 34-year-old man from Seattle

When we're trying to resolve arguments, we putz around the house, give each other time to think, and then sit down and talk together.

>   —a 28-year-old male physician from Buffalo

With my first husband I used to yell and scream. Sometimes I hit him. In this marriage I will not sink to that level. It's too destructive. I'm hoping my husband will realize it takes two to fight. When he screams, I back off, because nobody wins when you let your tempers get out of hand.

>   —a 43-year-old woman who divorced her first husband and had recently married a 55-year-old man

When speaking to couples who say (convincingly) that they communicate well and make decisions to their mutual satisfaction, we consistently find that in their marriages each spouse *respects* the other and takes personal *responsibility* for how they communicate with one another. These are people who are aware that good communication is an essential part of a healthy marriage, and they are willing to work at it.

The following are the key principles of good marital communication. Whether or not you implement these guidelines in your marriage can make the difference between feeling listened to and appreciated or feeling hurt and neglected.[12] All of them involve making an active effort.

1. Don't expect your spouse to read your mind. If you think that because your spouse loves you they should know what you want, what you think, and what you expect, you are dead wrong! It is unfair and unrealistic to expect someone else to read your mind. It is your *responsibility* to express your thoughts and feelings to your mate. That's important, because putting into words as best you can what is bothering you can prevent, or at least diminish, the risk of anger being "bottled up," and thus lessens the chances of one or both of you "acting out" in ways that are destructive to yourselves and your relationship.

2. *Take time to talk and listen to your spouse.* Make communication a priority in your marriage by setting aside time for casual conversations as well as in-depth, intimate discussions. Many couples complain of not being able to communicate with each other, when the fact is that they plan absolutely no time devoted exclusively to their being alone and talking with each other. Build time into your daily schedule for keeping in close touch. But be sure that you agree on what times are the best to talk. One woman we interviewed was upset because she came home eager to share her day's activities with her husband, but he preferred to unwind in private after a full day on the job. They came to an agreement that the first hour at home would be quiet time. If she does have something she wants to discuss, the wife asks her husband, "Can you hear it now?"

Here are some ideas to consider for keeping the communication channels open and functioning at their best:

• If your weeknights are busy because of work, make sure that you spend at least one weekend night totally alone with one another, or make it a point to share a cup of coffee or tea at 10 P.M. for catching up on the day's activities. Don't allow friends or family to intervene during these special times.

• If your job allows, phone each other for quick "how are you doing?" conversations several times a day to keep your close connection.

• Be sensitive to when your spouse needs to talk, not just when you need to talk. Develop ways to alert each other to when something is on your minds.

• Don't bring up a touchy subject when you're both exhausted or under stress.

• Choose an appropriate place to talk. If you both tend to be more polite and listen to each other better while eating at a restaurant than while at home, then the restaurant may be the better place for certain discussions. Be aware that you may differ in your ideas about when or where is a good time to talk. One of you may have no compunctions about arguing while walking down the street; the other might feel terribly embarrassed by any public display of emotion. Be considerate of each other's feelings on this matter.

3. *Present your thoughts and feelings in a way that can be heard by your mate.* As you've read this chapter, you should

have become aware of your communication style—whether expressive and emotional or quiet and withdrawn. Be conscious of that style and its impact on your spouse. If you tend to yell or be sarcastic, work on expressing your feelings in a way that is less offensive and less likely to provoke and cause conflict. One study found that people are more polite to strangers than they are to their spouses.[13] Humiliating, embarrassing, or criticizing your spouse only lessens the chance that what you say will be heard by your mate.

Be aware that there is no benefit to your spouse's feeling attacked. So instead of saying "You acted just horribly today," say, "I felt very hurt today when you spent all your time with the guys. I felt ignored." Own up to your own feelings, rather than attack your spouse for their behavior.

If your tendency is to bottle up your feelings, you must work on airing your dissatisfactions—in a constructive way— even though expressiveness does not come naturally to you. If your spouse ignores your comments when you do speak up, make it a point of saying that you need to be heard.

If you're unhappy with the way you and your spouse communicate with each other—if you feel there is too much criticism, complaining, and berating and not enough open, positive interaction—suggest to your spouse that you make it a point of devoting a certain amount of time each day to sharing your thoughts and feelings *only* in a calm, respectful, positive manner. In the time you set aside, stay away from any touchy marital issues and just focus on how the job's going, whom you spoke with today, what you did for lunch—in other words, day-to-day details that tighten your connection with each other but are nonexplosive. Make an agreement that this special time is not when problems about dirty laundry and annoying in-laws should be brought out in the open. Use this "sharing time" to practice positive communication skills:

- Reflect your mate's feelings back to them so that they feel understood. ("You sound very angry at your boss today.")
- Be encouraging and reinforcing to your spouse with positive statements. ("When I was at lunch I thought about how much I would have enjoyed your being there.")

If you and your spouse seem to find it impossible to talk about your problems without fighting, you might try a more structured exercise, one advocated by behavioral therapists:[14] Together select a 15-minute period that you can spend each day in talking with each other. During that time take your telephone off the hook, turn your radio and television off, and leave all distractions aside. Sit down opposite each other with your knees touching, hold hands, and look into each other's eyes. Take turns asking the other three open-ended questions that cannot be answered with a mere "yes" or "no." (Don't ask, "Should we spend more time together?" but "How would it be if we spent more time together?") Try to ask nonthreatening questions and give nonoffensive, nonaccusatory answers.

Although such an exercise may seem contrived, it will set you to thinking about how you phrase your ideas and how you respond to each other. It can foster positive habits by making you aware of how to speak in a positive, constructive manner.

4. State what the goal of your conversation is. There are times when you just want to air your feelings, times when you want to arrive at a solution to a problem, times when you need most to feel supported. Let your spouse know your needs of the moment so that you won't be disappointed and angered by what you find to be an inappropriate or inadequate response.

5. Listen fully and try to understand your spouse. That's often difficult to do, especially if you are highly invested in winning a point. But being able to understand what your mate is saying and making them feel understood is an important way to defuse conflict and to resolve strife. Ask yourself:

- Do I truly understand what is bothering my spouse?
- Am I really giving my mate a chance to express their viewpoint?
- What is he/she really saying? Does it make sense?
- Do I need to help my spouse clarify what's bothering them (for their own sake and mine)?
- Can I empathize? That is, can I put myself in my mate's place and understand what's bothering them?
- Is the issue we're discussing really the problem, or is something else going on?
- Are we really having a fight about whose *right* it is to make this decision?

You both must try to be aware of all the possible multiple levels that may be getting activated by the issues being dealt with. For instance, if your spouse is intensely angered by your tendency to take charge, it may be that such strong feelings are stirred because of unresolved childhood experiences with authority figures. Or it may be that the argument triggers feelings of not being loved by you. Or it may be that the argument got started because you're both on vacation and your spouse, a workaholic type, feels guilty and uncomfortable about not working and so is looking for an outlet for his or her anxiety. Perhaps your spouse was recently treated as an infant by overbearing parents. Finding it hard to stand up to them, your mate may have adopted that parental role, and vented frustration on you.

If you become aware that unconscious conflicts are being stimulated in your spouse, that may not, of course, mean that you necessarily want to concede the point now under discussion. Nevertheless, your increased sensitivity may soften your position; or if not that, it may enhance your ability to behave in an understanding manner that will help you both prevent a malignant cycle from occurring.

Even if you don't agree with your mate, try to make him or her feel understood. The goal of communication is really understanding, not necessarily agreement.

6. *Learn to understand your spouse's language.* Your spouse may speak a different language from you, and if you are to be content in your marriage, you must learn to understand that language. Rather than using words to convey love or anger, your spouse may employ touching to convey care, affection, sensuality, aggression.[15] Your spouse may never be the person to say "I love you," but instead may bring you home flowers as a surprise, or cuddle up to you while you're watching TV, or nurse you back to health when you're sick. Demanding words of love, when love is being conveyed in so many other ways, may make your spouse feel that their efforts at loving are futile.

Also, don't take everything your spouse says at face value. If your mate comes from a family who were all blunt about their feelings and you came from a family whose members were tentative with their requests, you may feel unduly insulted and criticized by your spouse's remarks, and your spouse may feel that you are entirely too noncommittal about your opinions. You each need to learn to hear what the other is really saying.[16]

7. *End an argument before it becomes destructive.* You must each take responsibility for ending a heated argument at a certain point despite its being unresolved. The longer an angry, hurtful argument goes on, the uglier and more destructive it will be. Stopping a fight—even though you may not feel you have expressed all your feelings and don't feel understood by your mate—will allow you to cool off, giving you each time to think quietly about both sides of your argument. Being able to laugh at yourselves and each other is a sign that you've managed to obtain some distance from your intense conflict.[17] It also marks your ability to hold your sense of yourselves as a couple as more important than "winning" an argument as individuals.[18] If you have a great deal of trouble coming to any resolution, you might want to seek the advice of a third person[19]—a friend or relative or professional counselor—who might help you out of your bind.

8. *Find other outlets.* There are some times when it's just best *not* to communicate.[20] You've had a hard day at the office—don't take it out on your spouse! He or she need *not* be the dumping ground for all of your worries and anxieties. Instead, go jogging, watch a movie, "let off steam" to another friend for a change. Also, be alert to areas of your life where you may feel you're not adequately assertive—for instance with your parents, or with colleagues in the workplace. Rather than communicate all that frustration to your mate, focus on releasing your feelings to the people for whom they are meant. Don't seek to relieve all your pressures at home.

SETTING UP HOUSE

Negotiating Roles and Tasks

Six months after her wedding, Sally Santini laughed as she recalled,

> What impressed me most about Rick when I first met him is that he made dinner for me on our third date. He had a strong idea of what home life is like, and that really appealed to me.

Sally's laugh was tinged with irony. Rick's domestic streak, originally so attractive to her, was now driving her crazy. She and her husband had just spent an hour talking with us about their household problems—problems that had so far been the biggest bone of contention in their marriage.

Who waits for the TV repairman? Who scrubs the bathtub? Who changes the light bulb? Who cooks dinner? Who buys the toilet paper? Who *changes* the roll of toilet paper? Who puts away the laundry? Who takes out the garbage?

Seemingly simple questions, some of them downright petty, right?

Wrong! The answers to those questions are far from obvious to anyone married since the 1960s, when Betty Friedan's book *The Feminine Mystique*[1] threw all previous assumptions about marital life into bold relief for reexamination.

Traditionally it was the hardworking husbands who were supposed to come home to find dinner waiting on the table and a house that was tended to by their domesticized wives. Today many of those wives (or their daughters) are working, and they are just as likely to want their husbands to cook dinner or pick up take-out food for supper as vice versa.

Yet although most women work, most also still bear almost all the responsibility for housework, according to researchers.[2] Nevertheless, the rules about who does what around the home are no longer set in stone. Many wives no longer accept as a given that it is their task to do all the cooking and cleaning. And many husbands can no longer relax guilt-free in front of the television set while their wives do the dinner dishes every night. Either their wives—or their own consciences—demand that they help out. What the "woman's job" is inside the home is no longer defined by society, and so each couple must decide for themselves what, in their own marriage, is to be the "wife's job" and the "husband's job."

The pettiness, the nit-pickiness of household arguments are astonishing, and often embarrassing, to couples. It seems ridiculous, when you think rationally about it, that you went to sleep not talking to your husband last night because he doesn't put down the toilet seat after he goes to the bathroom. And are you, a liberated man, going to complain to your friends that your wife doesn't have dinner on the table when you come home—even though that's what you gripe about to her? Probably not. How shameful to be so demanding, so petty.

Whether it's embarrassing or not, the fact is that the trivial, day-to-day household arguments can become terribly annoying, grating, and destructive to the marital relationship. According to our survey results, household tasks tie for third place (with communication styles)[3] as the third major cause of arguments among newlyweds. And in *Behind Closed Doors,*[4] sociologist Murray Straus and his coauthors reported that in their nationwide random sampling of families, one out of three American couples say that they *always* disagree about cooking and cleaning. Though housework may be a mundane subject, how couples deal with household strife does make a difference. One study[5] found that spouses who perceive that the housework is fairly divided are more satisfied with marriage than are those who are dissatisfied with the distribution of housework.

It makes sense that many couples have battles on the domestic front. In dual-career marriages, in which both spouses suffer from a lack of time and energy, the burden of household responsibilities can seem overwhelming and relentless. And even if you and your spouse agree on *who* does which chores around the house, you may not agree on *how* to do household chores. You may think: My mess doesn't seem so bad—in fact to me it isn't a mess at all, since I know where everything is in that pile on my desk. But your partner may find that *your* mess is impossible to live with.

How you and your spouse share your mutual space will inevitably bring up not only practical housekeeping issues of cleanliness and organization, but also strong feelings regarding intimacy, privacy, and other expectations you each have regarding home life. Whatever the differences between you in those attitudes, they're bound to crop up again and again. Your home is your base, your security, the foundation for your day-to-day life. Conflicts about your domestic life must be faced, because they cannot be ignored. They are too obvious.

You and your spouse each bring to marriage your own vision of what a married home life should be like. The key for you as a couple is to find a comfortable balance between your two visions.

THE ODD COUPLE SYNDROME

Sally and Rick Santini, introduced at the opening of this chapter, didn't take long in plunging into their household problems. The subject was clearly on their minds.

According to Sally, Rick was too routinized about household work. While other wives might complain that their husbands never help out, Sally lamented that Rick, although willing and even eager to take part, wanted her to follow his ideas about their shared housekeeping:

> Rick likes to do the laundry *every* Thursday, and he wants us to sort the laundry *together*. It's not unusual for him to suggest, "Why don't we take next Saturday and plan to really clean the bedroom and do the windows?" I would never make that suggestion or choose to spend a weekend that way.

Sally and Rick, who live in a cozy ground-floor brownstone apartment filled with plants and pottery, had one of their worst fights about housework during Sally's two-week break between changing jobs. Explained Sally:

> Rick had an agenda that he wanted me to carry out on my vacation, but he didn't tell me. He wanted me to pay parking tickets, clean off my desk, and clean our bedroom. But he didn't *say* anything. Instead I spent the week reading, baking pumpkin pies, which

he likes, and making nice dinners. One night that week
while we were both reading in bed, Rick said, "I'd like
to talk to you about your vacation. I feel like you're
being lazy." I was stunned. I thought I was doing nice
things for him by baking and cooking. There had been
a lot of stress at my former job and I worked long
hours. I feel like I deserve to enjoy my free time.

The housework issue was at least as frustrating to Rick as
to Sally.

I know that I'm much too demanding of Sally. But I
feel she is very messy and disrupts the routine. I accuse
her of being lazy and then she feels demanded of,
insulted, and often acquiesces. During Sally's vacation
I hoped that she would clean the house without my
saying anything. I wish she were more like me—and
just took care of things without being asked.

You see, home is the main point of my life. If I get
home early I clean the bathroom and make dinner. I
expect her to do the same things, but she just doesn't
care about housework as much as I do.

In chapter 4 we discussed the sense of domain that each
spouse brings to marriage. But in Rick and Sally's marriage the
issue was not one of domain—both agreed that each mate should
be involved in household chores. Instead, theirs was a question
of style. In our previous chapter, about communication, we
discussed the impact of styles. But here too, in the realm of the
household, we see how different styles affect a relationship. If
we look at Rick and Sally's backgrounds, we're able to understand the root of their differences.

Sally, a blond, soft-spoken New Englander, was raised in
an Irish family by an emotionally unstable mother who had
been hospitalized periodically for depression. Sally's father was
an alcoholic. For as long as she could remember, her parents'
marriage had been an unhappy one. As the oldest child, Sally
raised her younger sister and brother. A lot of the housekeeping
fell to her, since neither her mother nor her father was able to
handle those responsibilities.

Rick, a native New Yorker, grew up in a close-knit Italian
family. His father helped his mother cook, clean, and raise the

children. In Rick's family *everyone*—mother, father, and all five sons—grocery-shopped and did household chores *together*. His family were all fanatical about cleanliness and orderliness, and among them he was probably the most relaxed member.

It's easy to see why Sally and Rick were attracted to one another. Sally, burdened by responsibility from a very young age, saw in Rick someone who could take charge of some of the duties she felt had unfairly weighed upon her during her neglected childhood. She liked feeling that Rick nurtured her —and by cooking and cleaning for her, he gave her that sense. In many ways, Sally had shifted roles since being married. In her family, where everyone else was sloppy and irresponsible, she was the efficient, orderly one. Now that she was married, she switched to being the more carefree family member—rather as though she were tacitly saying, "Now, it's my turn to be nurtured."

Rick had also changed since being married. Perhaps because in his family he was the least obsessive about cleanliness, he unconsciously sought out a wife who would *not* be so persistent and organized a housekeeper as everyone in his family. While he had adopted his family's meticulous ways, somewhere inside him he must also have felt that the finickiness with which his family regarded household matters was too controlling. It probably wasn't by accident that he married someone with a more laissez-faire attitude—someone who didn't worry if the dishes weren't done the second dinner was over, someone who exhibited his messy side. It may be that the disapproval he showed toward Sally for her sloppiness was the disapproval he experienced from his parents when he was sloppy. As the most relaxed member of his family, he probably always felt, in a secret corner of himself, a desire to slack off—but didn't give in to it. Sally lived out that side of Rick—that side he tried to deny and repress.

Understanding why you and your spouse have different housekeeping habits and why you each may actually gain something from your conflicting styles can be enlightening. But unfortunately, that comprehension won't necessarily solve the day-to-day problems that arise in your home. Rick realized that Sally's mother hadn't acted as a positive role model—but that alone didn't help him accept what he saw as Sally's neglect of their apartment.

COPING WITH THE BIG ISSUE

As we mentioned in chapter 1, for every couple there is a different *big issue* that becomes an ongoing metaphor for their evolving relationship. In the case of Sally and Rick, their contrasting styles initially served to unify them—both were attracted to someone unlike themselves. After their wedding, their differences became a divisive factor as they examined each other in a closer, more glaring light. Sally and Rick recognized in each other a part of themselves that they rejected—leading to strife and conflict. Anxieties related to marital intimacy, sex, and aggression were expressed for Rick in his compulsiveness and for Sally in her messiness.

Looking at how Sally and Rick's domestic conflict evolved over the year yields a prime example of how dealing with a specific problem area is a continuous process. Like Sally and Rick, most newlyweds who find themselves confronting the same problems over and over discover that there is no quick, easy solution. Instead, successful couples come to see that the resolution is integrally bound up in the maturing of the relationship. As their relationship grows, their approach to their problem subtly changes. Sometimes they flare up, but sometimes they are better able to talk about their differences. Ideally, they come to tire of bickering and see compromise as a better alternative to continued strife.

During the first few months of marriage, Rick tended to nag and criticize Sally a lot. Sally withdrew. "It's difficult for me to yell," she told us. "When Rick gets annoyed I cry and leave the room. In Rick's family they always yelled and fought. In my family everyone was quiet and stoic."

Rick's approach was successful in that he did get his message across—Sally *knew* that Rick was upset with her about not doing enough housework. But Sally didn't change. So Rick tried a different technique—he didn't say anything, but hoped that Sally would clean the house without his prodding. That wasn't successful either, since Sally could not read Rick's mind—and felt hurt the time she found that he had harbored a secret agenda and then showed annoyance at her for not having carried it out. Nevertheless, it was the argument that ensued on that day that turned things around for the couple. Instead of withdrawing in anger, Sally told Rick that she felt she *had* been helping out, and thought she worked hard and deserved to unwind in her free time. Rick also made his needs known. They got through to each other enough for Sally to make a list of things that Rick and she agreed she should do during the rest of her vacation. But now Rick, more sensitive to Sally's viewpoint, advised, "Don't do so much to pressure yourself. And give yourself time to sleep late." They had reached an *understanding* and a *compromise*. It was a beginning.

Several months later we met with Rick and Sally and discovered that two developments had taken place. Sally had changed jobs and was working very close to home. Because she no longer had a long commute and her job was much easier, she felt less stressed than she had earlier in her marriage and more capable of devoting energy to her home. Second, she and Rick had rearranged their living room/dining room area—a change that left Sally feeling that she wasn't just living in Rick's old apartment (to which she had moved six months before marriage), but now it was *their* home.

While Sally acknowledged feeling a lot more invested in "keeping house," Rick seemed more comfortable accepting Sally "as is." He told us:

> I appreciate that Sally is trying harder. But I think I'm coming to accept that she doesn't care as much as me. We came home this past Saturday at 4:00 P.M. We had company coming for dinner at seven that evening. As we walked in the door Sally said she was going to take a nap. All I could think about was all we had to do before company came. Later on that night, right before our guests came, she said, "Don't worry about doing the dishes afterward. I'll do them." I said, "Fine." Well, for her that meant leaving the dishes in the sink overnight and doing them the next morning. She just has a much higher tolerance for messiness than I do.

Since household issues had become a common motif during our meetings with Sally and Rick, when we met with the couple again, shortly before their first anniversary, we were surprised that they made no mention of anything relating to their home. We brought the subject up. Sally explained that housework wasn't such a big issue anymore:

I work nearby, so I have more time to do things at home, and Rick is less compulsive. We joke about his compulsiveness now. I make the bed in the morning. I now feel that this is *our* place. It used to be that doing things for the house was doing things for him. A few weeks ago I went on a cleaning rampage and Rick was stunned. Part of it is related to feeling more in control of my life. I have a greater sense of order. I was very fragmented when I was doing a lot of commuting. Now there's a regularity to things I never felt before. Anyway, I just don't take Rick's compulsiveness as seriously as I did before. I don't get insulted. I know that's just his own nuttiness.

Rick also seemed more relaxed. He explained to us:

Now, rather than focus on the specifics of who cleans, we realize that it's my rigidity or structure versus Sally's laissez-faire style. We've kind of worked out compromises. I don't bug her like I used to. I have more of an appreciation that for her unpacking the laundry isn't an important thing. She doesn't have the same need that I do for getting things done. I used to talk to her about the need for structure in her life and the importance of getting up early. I saw her attitude as a weakness in character. I recognize a change in me, that I'm more relaxed. Sally is helping me understand my need for order. I'm becoming less compulsive.

For Rick, developing a more relaxed attitude about household cleanliness and order wasn't just a compromise he made to suit Sally, but one that developed internally as he gained greater control of his compulsive anxiety. Having talked with Sally about his need for order—and having felt understood and accepted by her—he started to feel more comfortable with her contrasting style and, ultimately, with himself.

THE PULL BETWEEN
TRADITIONAL AND MODERN
ROLES

How a couple comes to terms with their different styles is an age-old problem. But the conflict having to do with traditional versus nontraditional roles is very much a problem of our times.

The dilemma for most of you who are marrying today is that you live in an age when one set of ideals is espoused, yet you grew up in a time when another set of ideas was valued.

If you're a woman who works, you're likely to hold the feminist belief that men should share in household chores. Yet you also may be influenced by the social environment in which you grew up—an environment where women may have been expected to sit at home, nurturing and catering to the needs of their family. Even though you may work nine-to-five, just as your husband does, inwardly you may feel that by not taking full responsibility for your home, you are failing to live up to your wifely duty. That inner conflict may be difficult to acknowledge or admit, since rationally it makes so much sense that your mate should assume equal responsibility. But the images of male–female roles that we grow up with remain powerful.

If you're a husband, you also may feel conflicted. You are aware that your wife works hard, and know it would be fair to share the burden of household work, but find it hard not to think back to all that your mother did for you and your father. If your mother picked up your socks and cooked your dinner when you were growing up, why shouldn't your wife assume those "female" duties as well? Your mother never seemed unhappy, you tell yourself, so why does your wife complain so much? Even Rick Santini, who grew up in an unconventional family where his father, his brother, and he himself took an active role in doing domestic chores, found that once he got married he wanted his wife to take on more responsibility for their home. Having lived in his own apartment for several years before marrying, Rick had been used to doing his own housekeeping. Yet after marrying, he didn't want to be *the* one in charge of the house. Sure, he would help out a lot. But wasn't his wife supposed to take an active role in domesticity?

The values we learn while growing up reverberate in our minds forever. That's not to say that people don't change with the times. But there are subtle expectations and assumptions that we all hold on to.

Faith Goldstein, 24, married just over a year, personifies the conflict of the modern woman influenced by the conventional values imprinted on her in childhood. Having given up her job in New York City to move to Philadelphia, where her husband, Adam, 34, is in medical school, Faith told us:

> I resent being thrust into a traditional woman's role—moving to Philadelphia to be with "my man," giving up my life in New York. The first few months after I came to Philadelphia I didn't have a job. For some reason I felt some compulsion to be like Adam's mother, who is very neat and always has dinner on the table, so I turned into "Suzy Homemaker." Adam doesn't know how to cook. Even though now I have a job and I travel an hour twice a day to and from work, I always end up making dinner. It makes me furious.

Adam, looking from his wife to us, quickly came to his own defense. "I do know how to cook! I always cooked for myself before I got married. It's just that Faith wants control of the kitchen."

"The problem is he doesn't take over and cook a whole meal," Faith interrupted. "He likes to do one dish or help out by slicing an onion. That's not my idea of cooking."

"You see what I mean? She's controlling," said Adam.

In even this short snippet of conversation, Faith's ambivalence about her role as wife and woman comes shining through. Faith talked about resenting living out the "traditional woman's role," yet it was she who ultimately decided to marry Adam, to give up her apartment and job in New York, and to move to Philadelphia. And it was she who made the decision to cook dinner for Adam every night. But there was an incongruence between her actions and feelings. On the one hand, she wanted to be married and be wherever Adam was; yet she also felt uncomfortable conforming to anything she saw as fitting the picture of the dependent, home-based wife. The competition she felt with her mother-in-law, a supposedly perfect housekeeper, underlines her confusion about her role. A part of her felt she *should* have dinner on the table for her husband, she *should* have a perfectly neat and organized house—as his mother had and Faith's own mother had—but she also disliked feeling that way. After all, a truly liberated woman wouldn't be worried about whether the beds were made every morning.

Another sign of Faith's ambivalence was that she said she

resented having to cook dinner every night, yet, according to Adam, he was willing to assume responsibilities in the kitchen. Apparently some of the domestic pressure that Faith experienced was self-imposed, because she felt uncomfortable letting Adam take part in the dinner-making ritual. Inwardly she felt that the kitchen should be her area of competence and control, her terrain. Yet by assuming so much responsibility, Faith was setting herself up to be unhappy. She not only resented the chore of making dinner, but also was left feeling unnourished and uncared for. A part of Faith wanted Adam to dote on her. But because she took charge of the kitchen, she was left feeling deprived and angry.

The stress experienced by Faith Goldstein is not unusual for married women. Numerous studies[6] have shown that married women seek help for physical and emotional problems more often than married men. One of the reasons cited for this disparity is that a woman usually modifies her life more than a man when she gets married.[7] Since she is almost always the one who does the housekeeping, she often bears the double burden of working inside and outside the home.[8] Despite our age of liberation, a wife is more likely than a husband to alter career patterns in order to have more time to devote to home life. There are few rewards to doing monotonous housework, and many women feel depressed and overwhelmed by domestic responsibilities.

As we mentioned, however, it's not just women who feel ambivalent in today's society. Thirty-one-year-old George Harmon readily admitted to us that housework was the major source of problems in his eight-month marriage:

> My wife wants me to take more responsibility. I'm basically lazy and sloppy. I try and do some stuff and clean up a little bit. In a sense I know she's right. I'm a slob. If she yells at me I'll be more conscientious for a few days and then I'll slip back. It's hard. At home, my mom would do everything. She'd do laundry, cook, do dishes. It's not that I think it's a wifely duty. It's just that it's what I'm used to. I think it's more my nature. I'm not particularly neat and it doesn't bother me.

George didn't sound like a man in particular conflict: Basically, he said, he was never used to doing housework and it was just not in his personality. It sounds simple enough.

But think a little further about what George said. He made it sound as though his actions were involuntary—as though he had no choice about being neat or messy, as though he'd been born with a special gene, over which he had no control, that made him "a slob."

Obviously, George *did* have some control over his behavior. He may not have been greatly bothered by his own mess, but he surely knew that his mess would trigger fights with his wife. He claimed to agree with his wife's belief that since they both worked, he should help out in the house. Yet, like Faith Goldstein, he was holding on to the childhood vision he had of male–female roles. Having watched his mother do all the household work, George couldn't see himself, as a man, taking on the responsibilities of household work.

GENDER IDENTITY

From a psychological standpoint, a part of both Faith's and George's ambivalence, described above, has to do with their *gender identity*—which is to be distinguished from sexual identity.

Sexual identity is strictly related to whether one sees oneself as male or female. Gender identity, on the other hand, has to do with all the accompanying behaviors that one feels are part of, or required of, the sexual role. Boys and girls know their sexual identity (the difference between male and female) at a very early age. Virtually everyone maintains this sexual affiliation throughout life as a core feature of personality. (Transsexuals, who want to be the opposite sex, are the notable exceptions.)

Gender identity, however, is not fully established until after age five or six. At that point the little boy begins strongly identifying with his father and the little girl with her mother. This ability to take on the characteristics of one's same-sex parent and to prepare oneself to eventually find a mate of the opposite sex is an essential part of an individual's development.

Despite this identification with the same-sex parent, children are also strongly influenced by their parent of the opposite sex. Little boys spend much of their early lives with their mothers and identify somewhat with her feminine roles. Little girls play with their fathers and identify with some of his "masculine" traits. Freud felt "bisexuality" was part of our constitutional inheritance.[9] In the typical nuclear family, boys and girls are exposed to masculine and feminine role models and both have the capacity for masculine and feminine gender identifications. Usually the same-sex identification predominates, although remnants of the other remain. As a result, a little boy may grow up and leave child care tasks predominantly to his wife but still have a great need for taking part in raising his children, and may reap great enjoyment in doing so. Similarly, women may not only be absorbed in domestic roles during their childbearing years but also compete as men are generally expected to do in the business world.

Problems crop up when having masculine or feminine traits is conflictual for a man or woman. A man who doesn't feel comfortable with his female identifications—whose passive qualities feel womanly to him and instill in him intense homosexual fears—often overcompensates by becoming a "macho" type. For such men, expressing any soft, emotional, nurturing, or needy feelings would trigger intense anxiety. Clearly, a marriage in which a woman longs to find certain of these aspects in her mate will have difficulty if she's selected such a man as just described.

George Harmon had trouble assuming household responsibilities because he saw them as "woman's work." Household chores were what a woman did—what his mother did—and to take on such tasks wouldn't fit in with how he saw himself as a man. He identified with his father, the male who worked outside the home but got taken care of inside, and he felt threatened by deviating from that model. He knew he was being unfair to his wife, and he felt somewhat guilty—yet his sense of gender identity was so strong that he did little to change his habits. Research has demonstrated that the happiest marriages are those in which husbands feel that they are men in the same way their fathers were, and in which their wives also think that their husbands live up to how they (the wives) saw their own fathers.[10] George was trying to emulate his father's model, but that didn't meet with the satisfaction of his wife (whose father may have been more involved in housekeeping). Their conflict revolved around how each saw the man's role at home. Their notions of male and female roles didn't mesh.

Faith Goldstein's problem was much the same as George Harmon's, but in reverse. Her gender identity, shaped and molded in her childhood, inwardly whispered to her that it was her wifely duty to keep a nice home for her husband. Yet, her feminist ideals cried out to her that she should strive to create an egalitarian marriage. She was in a bind. If she let her husband cook dinner she felt she was failing as a wife. If she refused to let him help her and did everything herself, she felt exhausted, resentful, and unnurtured. She didn't know how to integrate the two aspects of her womanhood.

Marriage can function in a very wonderful way by working as a "releaser" of gender identity roles that were prevented from emerging before marriage. For instance, if you are a male who was afraid of showing your tender, nurturing side before marriage because you harbored fears of being weak, you may experience marriage as a validation of your heterosexuality and thus become more comfortable being gentle, loving, and appreciative of home life.[11] This is the well-known "domestic streak" that men discover after marriage. Likewise, if you're a woman who was afraid of asserting her ambitions and competitive goals because you were afraid of appearing too masculine and aggressive, once married you may feel more secure in your femininity and feel less inhibited about being forthright. For many people, marriage confirms their sexual identity and so broadens their view of gender identity roles.

THE NESTING INSTINCT

While the household differences we've discussed can arise between any two people who live together, they can seem especially intense and irritating early in marriage because, for many newlyweds, their home is a particularly important symbol of marital unity. In our survey, 51 percent of newlyweds noted that their desire for a clean, attractive home had *increased* since their wedding.

No matter how many years you've lived on your own, if you're like many other newlyweds, you may find that once you marry, your living environment becomes more important to you. For one thing, friends and relatives will probably bestow upon you gifts for your married home, giving you the sense that by getting married you should be changing (or rather, improving) your lifestyle. Suddenly you may find yourself making room for china and crystal in your cabinets, when before you couldn't even piece together a matching place setting.

You and your spouse probably also have certain expectations about what your married home should be like. It may not have been important to you to have "real" furniture when you were single or living together, but as a husband or wife you may feel a desire to be more "established."

Household issues take on an exaggerated significance for newlyweds, because how you handle issues regarding your home is symbolic of your overall relationship. Your home is your statement of how you see yourselves as a couple and as individuals. Conflicts over housekeeping, decorating, and how much privacy you have at home may touch upon how you each want to live and how you want to appear to the rest of the world. You may discover that setting up your married home revives feelings about your childhood home. You may aim to re-create the sense of safety and security your family home offered, or, if you felt deprived of love and comfort while growing up, you may attempt to make sure your married home is different.

This emphasis on home was expressed to us even by couples who lived together before marrying. Some rearranged their old furniture to create a new feeling in their homes. Others changed residences to demarcate that their relationship was different— more committed and permanent—from what it had been while they were living together as singles.

One couple who had cohabited for five years before their wedding moved shortly before their first anniversary. Besides being delighted about having more space, the 25-year-old wife boasted, "We're bringing up all this wonderful furniture from my grandfather's house. I'm feeling very adult."

Getting married is an "adult" thing to do, and establishing a home as a married couple is a further major step in that direction. Some couples associate getting married with buying a home and setting down permanent roots for the future. But even for couples who live in rented or temporary spaces, just the act of decorating evokes many feelings regarding the commitment they have made. In fact, decorating their home is significant for many newlyweds because it is their first joint creation together. And merging your possessions with your spouse's has to do not just with what looks good but with how you feel about each other. Being surrounded by your mate's possessions can feel either very reassuring or very threatening. It may evoke a warm sense of togetherness or a choking, stifling sensation.

For many newlyweds, the very idea of sharing and using space together is threatening, especially because so many people who marry today have lived on their own before and have developed habits that are hard to break. When one mate moves into the space where the other had lived alone, the issue of sharing can be particularly sensitive. One woman we interviewed told us that the week before her wedding she started clearing out space for her husband's belongings. "My first feeling about being married is feeling cluttered," she said, laughing but sounding a little annoyed that her husband was intruding on the space that had been so suitable for her as a single person.

Another woman, who gave up her apartment just before her wedding to move in with her husband, recalled being offended because he wanted her to move all of her "extra stuff" to her (now their) weekend home in the country. When she suggested that he also deposit there the train set he had bought twenty years ago for his daughter by a previous marriage, he seemed taken aback. "What? It cost me a lot of money!" The combination of feeling crowded by his wife's moving in and feeling protective toward his daughter now that he was remarrying, led this man to horde his space, which in turn made his wife feel excluded.

Whenever one mate moves into the home of another, it's important to try to balance the newcomer's desire to feel at home with the need of the original "tenant" to preserve what was already there. For couples who marry where there are stepchildren involved, there is the added challenge of creating a home that suits the needs and vision of those children. One woman who moved with her two daughters into her husband's house, where he lived with his two sons, discovered that home became a battleground between the two families—her husband's sons claimed the sofas and television sets were "theirs," and complained that her daughters spoke too loudly and "screeched." She felt intimidated by the pictures she found of her husband's dead former wife. Her husband found himself uncomfortably reminded of his former wife by seeing his new wife run his home.

It is often recommended that people who remarry move into a new, "neutral" space—one not tainted by memories of former spouses, one in which one spouse (with or without children) isn't made to feel like an intruder. But that isn't always economically or circumstantially possible—and so when it isn't, you have to expect that it will take time for *everyone* to feel at home.

Whatever your situation—whether or not you were married before, whether or not you lived together before—you should be patient about having your home reflect all of your needs, styles, and tastes. It's true that how comfortable you feel in your home is an indication of how comfortable you feel together. But resolving issues over household chores and decorating dilemmas inevitably challenges all of your communication abilities, controlling tendencies, and fears and desires about intimacy. As you become accustomed to being married and as your relationship deepens, you will probably have an easier time merging your two visions of home life. You'll know that the payoff to resolving all of those petty household problems was worth it when at last you are secure in the feeling that "There's no place like home."

CHECKUP:
HANDLING HOUSEHOLD
CHORES

Few things are more basic to marriage than setting up house together. And there is no better time to create the home life you want than right from the start. Your home is where you probably spend most of your time together, it is where you entertain your friends and family, it is your central connection from which you go off—and to which you return—to live your lives. Feeling positive about the way in which you live together gives your marriage a strong foundation.

To help you clarify how household responsibilities are being handled now and how you might like them to change, try the following exercise. Below is a list of household chores. In the first column, write down who is currently responsible for taking care of the task. Then, in the second column, write down who you think *should be* responsible for the chore (whether it's you, your spouse, both of you, a housekeeper, or no one). As you fill in your answers, think about what's reflected in your reasoning. Is it a desire for more equality in your household? Do you each have certain areas of expertise that could be used to better advantage?

HOUSEHOLD CHORE:	WHO IS CURRENTLY RESPONSIBLE?	WHOM WOULD YOU LIKE RESPONSIBLE?
preparing breakfast	_____	_____
preparing dinner	_____	_____
washing dishes	_____	_____
drying dishes	_____	_____
washing laundry	_____	_____
ironing	_____	_____
taking out the garbage	_____	_____
cleaning the bathtub	_____	_____
sweeping	_____	_____
vacuuming	_____	_____
buying food/groceries	_____	_____
making the bed	_____	_____
changing a light bulb	_____	_____
watering the plants	_____	_____
calling repairmen	_____	_____
selecting furniture to buy	_____	_____
hanging paintings or posters	_____	_____
arranging decorative items	_____	_____

This is just a sample list of chores. On a separate piece of paper, add any other household tasks that come to mind.

When you've completed your answers, review the list to see what kind of distribution of answers you have. Ask your spouse to look over your list with you and comment on the results. Together you might discuss questions like: Is one of you taking on the entire burden of household work? Are both of you trying to do everything together, leading to mutual exhaustion and strain? Does work remain undone, with neither of you picking up the slack?

As you look over your list, think about how you feel regarding the current state of affairs. The following workshop is geared to helping you make whatever changes you think would improve household matters at home.

WORKSHOP: CREATING THE HOME LIFE YOU WANT

1. Pinpoint at least five very specific household issues that you consider problematic. (Example: I'd like my spouse to initiate washing the dishes after dinner rather than wait to be asked. . . .)

_____

_____

_____

_____

_____

_____

2. Review your above list, paying attention to what is realistic and what may reflect your ambivalence. Do you have conflicting or unrealistic desires that set you up to be disappointed and angry? For instance:

• Do you want your mate to be a wonderful housekeeper but also to be out making a fabulous living for you?

• Are you a fanatical housekeeper who expects your spouse to keep to the same meticulous standards?

• Are you trying to be a successful career person *and* a perfect homemaker, so that at times you find yourself feeling like a failure at both?

• Do you assume that your spouse will take charge of housekeeping because everything was always taken care of for you at home while you were growing up?

Think about how you view your own household role and your spouse's household role: Are you being fair? realistic? taking upon yourself too much or too little responsibility?

3. Divide tasks to maximize both parties' acceptance of their lot. Reduce occasions of domestic strife by apportioning jobs according to which fit you best. If one of you has a talent for gardening, and the other is great at fixing appliances, then you have a natural division of labor right there. If your spouse can't stand coming home to an unmade bed and you don't mind in the least, then suggest that your mate make the bed in the mornings and derive satisfaction from the result. If you're a night owl and your spouse falls asleep at the stroke of 9:00 P.M., offer to do the dinner dishes so your spouse can relax before bedtime, if he or she agrees to prepare dinner.

It's not always possible to divide chores equitably or to both mates' satisfaction, but it's a good start to split up as many tasks as possible in this way.

4. Don't nag your spouse. Try to involve your mate in household work by making it seem like an activity to do together. Put on old, favorite records while you're dusting the living room, or share some of the best tidbits of the day while you're doing the dishes together. Once you get your spouse in the habit of taking part in household chores, they'll be more likely to assume responsibilities on their own. Constant complaining, on the other hand, will just irritate your spouse and make him or her less eager to take charge of household responsibilities.

5. In general, avoid criticizing your spouse for how they do housework. Cleaning up the bathroom or making the bed may mean completely different things to each of you. But don't discourage your spouse's housekeeping efforts by berating them, or they will just respond with: "If you don't like it, do it yourself!" Express appreciation when they show an effort to help out, and demonstrate that their sharing in responsibilities makes you feel more loving toward them.

6. If disagreements about household chores persist, examine the possible causes.
• Are you direct and consistent with your requests to your spouse? If you say that you'd like your spouse to cook dinner that night, but don an apron the second you come home from work, you mix your messages, and succeed only in conveying that you want to be in charge of the kitchen.

• Compare your ideas and your spouse's about the division of labor. Is one of you more traditional than the other? Are you afraid of appearing less manly (or less womanly) if you partake in certain responsibilities? Are you torn between traditional and modern notions of how a husband and a wife should act?

• Look at your family backgrounds. If you recognize that your husband is adamant about having an organized home because his mother died when he was young and he felt deprived of a secure environment, then you can at least understand where his attitude comes from. Or if you acknowledge that your spouse came from a poor family, you may be able to appreciate why decorating a home expertly may not be something they know how to do.

Trying to apprehend the underlying reasons for your disagreements may help you to become more compassionate and accepting, which may eventually lead to compromise.

7. *Be flexible.* If one arrangement for dividing chores doesn't satisfy you, try another. Keep an open mind, and don't get hung up with sexist stereotypes—as in thinking, He's a man, so it should be his job to take care of car repairs. Be sensitive to any resentments that build up due to chores that don't get done or that take too long—and consider alternatives. One woman got so fed up with picking up after her husband that she told us she finally stopped. After about two weeks her husband began to notice the mountain of dirty laundry that was growing near his side of the bed. Embarrassed, he admitted that he was a bit of a slob and began making more of an effort to pick up after himself.

8. *Make sure you have enough time to enjoy yourselves.* Is household work weighing you both down? Are the two of you too meticulous or too focused on fixing up your new home— at the expense of just having a good time with each other the way you used to? Limit the amount of time you spend devoted to your home—maybe an hour each day, or just weekend mornings. Don't burden yourselves with unnecessary "shoulds" (your house *should* always be neat, you *should* always have a hot meal on the table, etc.). At a certain point, it is crucial that you just be able to relax at home.

9. *Face the fact that you now* share *your home, and make the best of it.* You may not ever agree with your mate's decorating taste or see the point of collecting old magazines or matchbooks, but at some point you will have to accept that your spouse has certain ways in which he or she wants to live. The trick is not to take your mate's household habits personally. Your spouse isn't being sloppy to make you miserable. By all means, try to communicate your feelings about how your spouse's living habits affect you. But the sooner you recognize that your mate is entitled to have the home you share reflect some of their needs—as well as your own—the sooner you both will more richly enjoy living together as husband and wife.

MONEY

Realities and Expectations

"Money is the most important thing in the world," wrote the eminently quotable George Bernard Shaw.[1] Whether or not that is the case, money definitely matters in marriage. Historically it was the reason people got married. Occasionally it is the reason people break up their marriages. Often it is the reason for strife within marriage. According to our survey:

- Money is the leading cause of argument among newlyweds—with almost one out of four newlyweds saying they argue most about money.[2]
- 63 percent of newlyweds report having some marital problems relating to money; half of them describe those money problems as significant.[3]

It's been found that the less money people have, the more arguments they have about money.[4] But rich or poor, every newlywed couple must decide multiple money issues—how much money to spend, how much money to save, how much money to pool, how much money to keep individually, what kinds of bank accounts to set up, what purchases and investments to make, what financial goals to work toward, what money experts to consult. . . .

Because partners come to marriage with mutually differing spending habits, financial backgrounds, and expectations about their social status and lifestyle, money matters can lead to heated arguments, hurt feelings, and frustrating disappointments. It can take months or years to work out a financial arrangement that satisfies both spouses. One study focusing on the length of time it takes to adjust to marriage found that the spending of family income was felt to be the second most difficult area in which to achieve adjustment. In fact, 10 percent of the one thousand couples studied said they had *never* made a satisfactory adjustment regarding finances in their marriage.[5]

Complicating money matters nowadays is the fact that men

and women are marrying at an older age, have worked on their own prior to marriage, and are used to spending their own salaries as they see fit. Merging finances, setting joint priorities, aspiring toward mutual goals can be difficult if you've long been accustomed to making your own money decisions. Today, money conflicts may also be exacerbated for young couples in particular, because they may be shouldering a greater financial burden than their predecessors. Public-policy analysts Frank Levy and Richard Michel[6] found that in 1983 the average 30-year-old working male earned, in effect, a fourth less than he would have a decade before. In 1973 the average 30-year-old male covered his typical mortgage on his house with 21 percent of his paycheck, but ten years later he needed to use 44 percent of his paycheck to cover his house mortgage.

The variety of options you can choose from, especially if you're a two-income family, also confuses the issue of how to handle money in marriage. We found it interesting that even couples who had lived together prior to marriage—and who had settled upon a workable money scheme—often decided after marrying to change their financial routine. Feeling closer and more committed to each other as husband and wife, they said marriage had made them regard each other's finances differently. In some cases they felt more of a right to say how their spouse "should" be spending their money; in other cases they felt more of a desire to share, and so decided to merge their salaries rather than keep everything separate. Some newlyweds admitted to us that they felt more comfortable arguing about money and making certain financial demands now that they were married. Also, with marriage there often comes the decision to make major purchases—such as a house or an apartment or a car. As you make joint acquisitions, your feelings, expectations, and thinking about how to handle money change.

YOURS, MINE, OR OURS?
METHODS OF MONEY
MANAGEMENT

The following are four of the most common ways in which couples handle their finances. In deciding which will work best for you as a couple, consider the personality and needs of both you and your spouse. Be prepared to undergo a period of trial and error before you land on just the right arrangement. And take into account the pros and cons of each method listed here:

Pooled Money

This is the most traditional arrangement, with spouses combining their earnings and having equal access to a joint account. Many people perceive this arrangement as a sign of unity and trust—and assume that it reflects marriage "the way it should be." Such a plan demands that newlyweds take care to communicate and cooperate about their finances, since they are depositing and withdrawing money from the same account. It also necessitates that partners respect each other enough so that they don't question each and every purchase that is made.

This arrangement works well when couples agree, for the most part, on how money should be spent and on how much should be saved. It also eliminates having to pay fees on lots of bank accounts. Problems, however, can arise from a number of situations: (1) if there is a big difference in income between you and your partner, tending toward inequality in decision-making power; (2) if you and your spouse have very different ways of spending money and resent seeing "your" money spent on things you don't support; (3) if logistics make things difficult—for instance, if you and your mate work fifty miles apart and you both need to have a bank near your jobs; or (4) if one or both of you feel stifled by financial "togetherness" and prefer functioning autonomously regarding money.

Separate Accounts, Joint Payments

Some couples keep separate bank accounts but split common expenses. Both pay from their individual accounts for half of joint expenses—such as rent, electricity, food, laundry bills, restaurant bills, and vacations. Or, rather than split everything down the middle, you may decide that one spouse pays for certain expenses (for example, rent, gas, electricity) and the other for other expenses (telephone, laundry, dry cleaning, movies, dinners out). After paying for mutual expenses, whatever is left in the spouses' accounts is used for your individual purposes.

The advantage to this arrangement is that if you've worked and lived on your own for many years prior to marriage, you can continue to function much the same as before. Having your own account, you may feel more independent, and won't have to worry about what your mate will say about your each and every purchase.

There are potential drawbacks to this separatist arrangement: (1) it doesn't necessitate that you communicate with each other about how you are each spending your money, and so it may delay or prevent your developing a joint financial plan; (2) if one of you earns much more than the other, the higher wage earner may end up having a lot of money to keep, while the mate with a lower salary is left with nothing after paying bills. This situation might be avoided if you each contribute money for expenses in proportion to earnings. In other words, if you earn one third of your spouse's salary, then you pay one third of all the bills.

Joint and Separate Accounts

You might consider this compromise arrangement, which calls for each spouse keeping money in both joint and separate accounts. The joint account is usually used for joint expenses —such as rent, electricity, furniture purchases, and vacations —while the individual accounts are for personal expenditures. Sometimes couples use their individual accounts for bill paying, but open a joint savings account or money market fund so that together they can save toward mutual goals.

The advantage of this method is that it allows you to function independently as well as *inter*dependently. The disadvantage is that the more accounts you have, the more difficult and time consuming it may be to keep track of budgeting and bookkeeping.

Separate But Not Equal Finances

In this arrangement you keep your finances separate but do not attempt to pay for expenses equally. You might live off one salary and save the other, which can be a very simple and effective way of saving money. It is not suitable for everyone, however, because you need to have one salary that is substantial enough to support all your needs. If you do follow this plan, you need to make certain that you both are in agreement about it. One potential disadvantage is that a spouse may resent not being able to spend any of their own salary; another is that the other partner may become angered and feel pressured that their paycheck is relied upon to meet both mates' needs.

The other scenario for this arrangement is that of a very wealthy couple living off one mate's—traditionally the husband's—account. The wife is then free to use her salary for her personal expenditures. While this setup may seem ideal from the woman's perspective, the disadvantage for her is that she usually has little knowledge regarding her husband's salary, assets, bookkeeping, or financial decisions—all distinct drawbacks if he should become ill or they should divorce. Also, whenever one mate makes all the financial decisions, the other might easily come to feel controlled and resentful, hardly a base for a strong, loving marriage.

There are some people who claim that keeping finances separate makes for fewer financial feuds in marriage. Others believe that a couple aren't truly entwined—or married—unless they share their finances in a joint account. The important thing to keep in mind is that *there is no one "right" solution that applies for everybody*. How you feel about money and act with money is very individual. Whatever financial arrangement you settle upon has to be appropriate for your monetary situation and your practical concerns. And, as we shall see, it must meet and respect your deeper needs and your spouse's.

MONEY TALKS: THE UNSPOKEN MESSAGES

Although the practical aspects of managing money can be difficult and burdensome to a newlywed couple, it is the *emotional significance* attached to money that makes it such a highly charged issue in marriage. The questions are not just "How much should we spend? How much should we save? What kind of accounts should we keep?" What is really being asked is: "How much can I trust you? Do you trust me? Do we work together well?"

Money has enormous psychological significance for each of us. It is one of the primary ways we relate to others and think about ourselves. It represents a giving of ourselves and a taking from others. It is a "currency" of interpersonal negotiation. People often don't like to talk frankly about money and what it means to them, because they fear being considered rude or crude or greedy. But the fact is that money is so interwoven in the fabric of our lives that it inevitably becomes weighted with a myriad of meanings. When you, as a couple, fight over money, your intensity doesn't have to do with just the ten dollars or hundred dollars or thousand dollars in question—it has to do with feeling taken care of or feeling cheated, feeling secure or insecure, feeling dependent or independent. It has to do with how you felt about your financial situation during childhood and what lifestyle you hope for in the future. People often talk about the value of money—but the value of money for each of us is ultimately tied up with what it means in our lives. Money often functions as a metaphor for a variety of other issues.

It is our guess that the reason almost one quarter of our survey respondents said they argue more often about money than any other issue is that it is easier to quarrel about money than about other deeper, more sensitive topics. Most people feel less threatened by pointing to money as a problem than by speaking about an absence of trust or nurturance in their love relationship.

Money means a lot of things to people, and so differences over money usually have multileveled meanings. Unless you are keyed in to the possible presence of those unspoken messages—which you are both giving and receiving—your marital arguments about money may escalate, because you aren't addressing the underlying issues.

CHECKUP: WHAT DOES MONEY MEAN IN YOUR MARRIAGE?

Before we examine the various ways that money may function in marriage to reflect the inner needs and wishes of each spouse, we'd like you to go through the following checklist to prod your thinking about what money may mean for you and your mate and how that thinking may influence your individual approaches to the subject.

For each of the four questions below, place a check beside *every* statement that applies.

1. Which of these describes how you felt about money as you were growing up?

- ☐ I always felt secure that there would be enough money for whatever I needed and wanted.
- ☐ I never felt certain my parents would have enough money to give me what I wanted or needed.
- ☐ I always felt that I had less than my friends had.
- ☐ I felt the people around me placed too much importance on money.
- ☐ I was embarrassed by being seen as a "rich kid."
- ☐ I knew I wanted to grow up to have a lot of money.
- ☐ Other_____

2. Which of these describes how you think your spouse felt about money as he or she was growing up?

- ☐ My spouse always felt secure that there would be enough money to cover needs and wants.
- ☐ My spouse never felt certain that there would be enough money to meet needs and wants.
- ☐ My spouse always felt that he or she had less money than friends had.
- ☐ My spouse felt that the people around him or her placed too much importance on money.
- ☐ My spouse was embarrassed by being seen as a "rich kid."
- ☐ My spouse knew he or she wanted to grow up to have a lot of money.
- ☐ Other_____

3. Most times when my spouse and I argue about money, our disagreement starts because:

- ☐ I think my spouse spends too much money.
- ☐ My spouse thinks I spend too much money.
- ☐ I think my spouse is cheap.
- ☐ My spouse thinks I am cheap.
- ☐ I feel my spouse doesn't consult me enough about money decisions.
- ☐ My spouse feels I don't consult him or her enough about money decisions.
- ☐ My spouse and I disagree over what things to spend money on.
- ☐ Other_____

4. Underlying many of our marital arguments about money are such thoughts as:

- ☐ I don't trust my mate with money.
- ☐ My spouse doesn't trust me with money.
- ☐ I don't feel sufficiently taken care of by my spouse.
- ☐ My spouse doesn't feel sufficiently taken care of by me.
- ☐ I resent my spouse's dependence on me.
- ☐ My spouse resents my dependence on him or her.
- ☐ I feel threatened by losing control over my money.
- ☐ My spouse feels threatened by losing control over his or her money.
- ☐ Other_____

Whatever you may have checked off above, the statements suggest the complexity that may lie behind financial decision making and thinking in your marriage.

In the following sections we will explore the various meanings of money:

- money as a symbol of trust and security
- money as a means of control
- money and the conflict between wanting to be dependent and wanting to be independent
- money as a sign of nurturance
- money as a source of status and esteem

Although we delineate each "meaning" of money as though it were separate unto itself, in reality all those meanings usually come into play within a person's psyche. In fact, they actually exist on a continuum and often overlap. In other words, you may relate to money in your marriage as a way of feeling cared for (by letting your spouse handle it), which can make you feel dependent, and eventually lead you to feeling submissive and dominated. Or you may like to handle money independently, but as a result you sometimes feel uncared for. Or you may like to take care of your spouse by handling financial responsibilities, but you have to be careful that you don't become controlling, and in the process prevent yourself from feeling cared for by your mate.

In any marital conflict about money there are numerous, complex emotions at work. It is only for the sake of understanding the deep significance that money holds for each of us that we turn now to examining each meaning individually.

MONEY AS A SYMBOL OF
TRUST AND SECURITY

Sean Linden, 32 years old, recounted for us the terror he
felt when he and his new wife, Lynn, were shopping in a department store shortly after being married and were approached by a representative of the store who asked them if
they'd like to open an account there. Having just paid for a suit
in the store by check, Sean said, "Sure," and began filling out
a form. When he finished, the representative asked if he'd like
to make it a joint account with his wife. Lynn instantly stretched
out her hand to add her signature to the account. Sean told us:

> I became a wreck. I guess I thought because Lynn also
> works, that getting married wouldn't really affect me
> financially. I expected we'd pretty much pay for every-
> thing separately. The idea of having her name on my
> account terrified me. Suddenly I fantasized that Lynn
> was going to start buying everything in the store and
> that I'd go broke. I felt so vulnerable. I wondered if
> I could really trust her.

For Sean, as for many people, money was an intimate extension of himself—it had to do with how powerful he felt and
how independent he believed himself to be. He was afraid to
let his wife meddle with his money, afraid she would take something important away from him.

People who have felt let down by others in the past—emotionally or financially—may have a particularly difficult time
being trusting. If in your childhood you had trouble counting
on caretakers for love and sustenance, you may have come to
rely solely on yourself. Money may have taken on the meaning
of how you care for yourself. Sharing your money may touch
upon your fear of becoming depleted—of having everything
taken from you.[7]

One of the essential ingredients in your being able to share
your funds with your mate is your ability to trust that you will
not be either emotionally or financially depleted.

You and your spouse may have very different attitudes
toward money because one of you trusts that it will always be
there and the other is always worried about there not being
enough. Of course, there is usually some element of reality

involved in one's sense of security regarding money. Perhaps one of you grew up in a much more financially comfortable home than the other. Or maybe one of you has a much higher salary than the other and therefore is more carefree about how money is spent in your marriage. But the truth is that how much money it takes to make a person feel safe and secure is really "all relative"—relative to attitude. One woman who answered our survey wrote that she and her husband jointly earn $450,000, yet they have significant problems related to money. Another newlywed wrote that he and his wife together earn $13,000, yet they have no problems regarding money.

It's not just early childhood experiences that influence your ability to feel secure about money. If you've been "burnt" in the more recent past, you may also have obstacles to overcome.

Helen Miller, who married at age 28, recalled several years later how she'd insisted when she and her husband Steve got married that they share a joint-signature checking account. Helen had been engaged once before, and her former fiancé ran off with all the money in their joint account when they broke up. She wanted to make certain that wouldn't happen again.

After a few months it became clear that the Millers' arrangement would not work. Recalled Steve:

> It became so terribly unwieldy. I'd have to chase after Helen to sign the checks. I found it impossible to deal with. It finally got to a point that Helen recognized that it made no sense in terms of taking care of everyday financial responsibilities.

When Helen and Steve switched to a one-signature joint account during their second year of marriage, "that demonstrated a growing trust in our relationship," says Steve.

In this age of divorce it's not surprising that so many couples start out in marriage afraid to trust each other completely. Emotionally they may be scared to "lay it all on the line," and financially they may feel the same way. Certainly the increasing number of American couples who are consulting lawyers *before* they get married, to draw up prenuptial agreements—which usually stipulate which assets go to which mate in case of divorce—vouches for the skepticism with which people today approach marriage. Nevertheless, being able to trust and knowing that you are trusted are necessary ingredients in a satisfying marriage.

What can you do if a lack of trust surfaces in regard to money? First, give yourselves time. As you become more secure in your marriage and more confident in the future of your relationship, your feelings of trust toward your mate will probably grow. For many couples there is a blossoming sense of "what's good for you is good for me." Eventually that feeling permeates their financial attitudes, so that there is more open sharing, less fear of financial risk and mistrust. But it may take months or even years for you to arrive at that point.

Until then, if lack of trust seems to be reflected in your marital conflicts about money, follow these suggestions:

• If you're the one being accused of not knowing how to handle money or of being selfish about money, rather than charge your mate with not being trusting enough, demonstrate that you are worthy of trust—whether that means saving money, working out a budget and adhering to it, or keeping good financial records.

• Recognize that what it takes for your spouse to feel secure about money may be very different from what it takes for you. In an understanding way, acknowledge your spouse's concerns. Say something like: "I know you're worried that I'm going to blow all our money," or "I know you're concerned that we won't have enough to get by." If your spouse feels understood, some of his or her anxiety will automatically be relieved.

• If you're the mate who isn't being trusting, force yourself to give your partner the benefit of the doubt. Rather than berate your mate for not being able to save or handle money, consider that your spouse may have never before been required to adhere to a budget, or may hold to a different philosophy about money.

• Try to arrange it so that you each have at least a small amount of "extra" purchasing money to spend as you wish and for which you are not accountable. That way even if you have very different views about spending money, you each have an outlet that should relieve some of the tension and anxiety.

• Share your feelings of mistrust or insecurity in a loving way so that your spouse can better understand your concerns.

Telling your mate something like, "My parents could never save a dime and I'm scared that if I trust anyone with my money they will also mess up" is more helpful than just exploding every time your spouse tells you they bought themselves an article of clothing. Speaking with each other in a respectful way will draw you closer and help give you both confidence that your marriage is a mutually cherished partnership.

MONEY AS A MEANS OF CONTROL

Historically the husband has been the breadwinner *and* the boss in the family. Power and purse strings are still strongly correlated with each other. In their nationwide survey for their book *American Couples,*[8] sociologists Pepper Schwartz and Philip Blumstein found that the amount of money a person earns, in comparison with their partner's income, establishes relative power in their relationship. Their study showed that wives with high incomes had greater freedom to spend money as they wanted and were more likely to have personal savings accounts to which their husbands had no access.

Despite the persisting correlation between money and power, that it's the husband who has both is no longer accepted as a given. In many marriages today, both husband and wife earn similar salaries, making it harder for one mate to claim greater power based on greater income. Even if you're a woman and your husband earns more money than you, you may not be willing to accept that as a basis for his exerting power over you. And if the woman in your marriage earns more than the man, then power and financial issues may be particularly sensitive, since your situation is opposite that of the traditional marriage model.

The question of who is in charge of finances—who has the final word on how much is saved, how much is spent, what to buy, and what not to buy—is a potentially explosive issue in many marriages. There are multiple guises under which a person may try to use money as a power tool. Often the mate who attempts to control with money does so by acting as though that control is merely an extension of his or her love or a natural consequence of his or her financial skills. But usually beneath the desire to take control over monetary issues in marriage is a vulnerability—a fear that to share control is to become powerless.

Stanley Sage, an artist wed to a newspaper editor, insisted upon getting married that he and his wife, Audrey, who earn similar salaries, open a joint checking account. Several months later Audrey complained that the arrangement wasn't working. She suggested they keep their joint checking account to pay rent and utilities, but open individual accounts from which to make individual purchases. Stanley reluctantly agreed, though frequently he became annoyed with Audrey for buying expensive clothing and for keeping a balance in her credit card accounts. Audrey reacted with anger and indignation. The tension about money matters mounted, and one night the couple had an argument that became so heated that Audrey threw off her wedding ring. She explained her frustration to us this way:

> Stanley's a saver. He will pass up buying nice shirts or a book he'd like, but then he'll go out and buy a video unit or a car. He expects me to have the same priorities. When he yelled at me about the balance on my credit cards it was too much. Somebody dictating to me was just more than I can deal with. He had this vision that after we married we'd go off into the sunset together and everything would be perfect between us. He doesn't like it when I don't agree with him. There's just something that clicks off in him—it's like some sort of betrayal. He becomes indignant that I should disagree. I'm just asking him to acknowledge my way.

From an objective viewpoint, money should have been no problem in Stanley and Audrey's marriage. They seemed to make enough money to dress well, live comfortably, and enjoy their leisure time. Yet money had become the focus of a power struggle in the Sages' marriage. Stanley wanted more control of how Audrey spent her money; Audrey wanted total freedom in how she used her money and paid her bills. Stanley grew up feeling powerless in his family. His mother was a dominant, almost tyrannical figure, and now he wanted to make sure his wife didn't adopt the same dominating traits. But, Audrey lamented, "He does to me exactly what his mother does to him."

Audrey, on the other hand, was raised in a home where she was given a great deal of autonomy. "No one has ever had the nerve to tell me what to do like Stanley does," she complained.

Both Audrey and Stanley felt nervous that marriage was going to make them powerless. Each tried to exert power over the other—Audrey in an attempt to hold on to her autonomy, Stanley in an effort to have greater power over Audrey. The problem was that by using money as a power tool, they were aggravating their problem rather than resolving it. By flying off the handle because Audrey bought a lot of clothes and didn't always pay back her credit card expenses immediately, Stanley was making her feel even *more* threatened that he was encroaching on her life and taking away her autonomy. By becoming infuriated with Stanley because he commented about her handling of money, Audrey made Stanley even more afraid that she was financially impulsive and unpredictable. Audrey knew about but didn't empathize with the childhood experiences that influenced Stanley's attitude as an adult. And Stanley hadn't yet accepted that Audrey had worked on her own and managed her own money as a single woman for a long time. He hadn't yet accepted that she wasn't ready instantly to do things his way.

What can you do if you and your spouse become enmeshed in power struggles whenever you have a disagreement about money?

• Try to appreciate why you or your spouse may be so worried about being rendered financially powerless. Have you each been in control of your own pocketbook for so long that it is difficult to share? Have you just begun to earn your own money and so find it tough to share in financial matters because you're excited about having some money of your own? Did you feel powerless when you were a child and find you have an exceptional need as an adult to feel powerful? Share your feelings in a sensitive way so that you can each understand and feel understood.

• Pinpoint those financial issues upon which you do agree. For instance, if you both agree that saving money is important, open a joint savings account to which you both contribute. The more secure you each feel that you are working toward mutual goals, the less likely you will be to engage in power struggles.

• Work out a financial arrangement by which you each have some money to save, spend, or invest on your own. If one or both of you tends to be controlling and as a result the other feels bothered, you might agree not to talk about or question how that extra money is handled.

• Pose some alternative ideas for ways you might compromise. (Example: I'll go along with saving a quarter of my salary if you'll agree to let me spend the money I have left after paying household bills for whatever I want.)

MONEY AND THE CONFLICT:
DO I WANT TO BE
DEPENDENT OR
INDEPENDENT?

Money allows some people to be independent, and the lack of it forces some people to be dependent. Money can bind people together, for instance in the case of a wife who stays married because she wants or needs the money her husband provides. Money can also be a way of maintaining one's self-sufficiency—when, for example, a husband or wife has enough of their own money that they can buy exactly what they choose without having to answer to their mate.

For any newlywed there is inevitably a pull between wanting to lean on one's mate and wanting to go and do exactly as one pleases. And there is inevitably a conflict between wanting to be leaned on—depended on—and wanting to be left alone.[9] These dichotomous feelings—between wanting to be dependent and wanting to be autonomous—are almost always manifested in a couple's money situation. Ideally the type of bank account you set up should reflect your feelings about how jointly and how separately you and your mate would like to operate. If you both agree on functioning either independently or together in regard to finances, there is no problem. But if you have different notions about how a married couple should operate financially, conflict will probably arise.

Janet Leifer's father died three years before she met and then married Scott, 15 years her senior. Janet recalled during her first interview with us that she had felt frustrated because her parents hadn't done any financial planning while she was growing up. She straightforwardly said that one of the things that attracted her to Scott was his success as a businessman. As she put it, "The idea of someone who had more financial resources than I had was attractive." Janet felt she could depend on Scott for money—a factor that was very important to her.

Interestingly, Scott's feelings about Janet were not dissimilar. At age 46, he came to marriage after living as a divorcé for 12 years. His previous wife, whom he married right after college, had never worked, and he had experienced her dependency as a burden. When he met Janet, she had recently completed a movie editing job. He felt assured by the fact that Janet had her own career and could earn her own living. Shortly before their wedding, Scott told us:

> I don't want to take care of Janet. I'm pleased that she has a career, that she gets paid for it, that she gets things done—like getting phones and stationery ordered. When I was married before, I had to do everything.

Though Scott was earning a lucrative salary by the time he met Janet, he had grown up poor and had not gotten over the insecurity of his impoverished childhood. He acknowledged being deeply affected by having had a mother who was medically handicapped and mentally troubled. Part of Scott's attraction to Janet, he said, was that he saw her as someone who could function on her own.

Given the contrasting attitudes brought to marriage by Scott and Janet, it's not surprising that they found themselves embroiled in financial conflicts—even before they walked down the aisle to the altar.

The first inkling Janet had that she could not be as financially dependent upon Scott as she had hoped was several weeks before their wedding. She expressed to us her frustration.

> He says, "Trust me. I'll share." I said, "I don't want to trust you. I want an arrangement." I explained to him why I didn't want to be in the position of having to ask for money. He couldn't understand why I just couldn't rely on his generosity. I think he has to trust me that I'm not just going to go buy a diamond necklace. I don't want to have to ask him for money. I want to feel that I have the license to spend what I need. It would lead to resentment otherwise.

With the wedding quickly approaching, the issue of how money would be handled in their marriage became increasingly tense. In the back of Janet's mind was an image of what an engagement should be—and the fights she and Scott were having did not fit into that rosy picture. Scott was unhappy enough about the situation to finally speak to a married friend, who it turned out shared a joint account with his wife. As a result of that conversation, Scott came up with the suggestion of pooling some, but not all, of their money in a joint account. Both Scott and Janet agreed to put their salaries into a joint account but to also keep separate accounts—he for his bonuses from work, she for money from her trust fund. "It's a good arrangement," Janet told us after being married several months. "It satisfies my need that I won't feel like I'm scraping. And he'll feel that he'll have enough control and independence."

But the Leifers confronted other money problems in their newlywed year. Janet, who wanted to decorate their home, criticized Scott for being cheap and controlling. He accused her of being nagging and demanding. "When Janet gets argumentative and says, 'I want to buy that lamp,' I get angry," says Scott. "I feel like she has it pretty good. How dare she ask for more."

Scott's unwillingness to let Janet totally depend on him to pay for all her purchases forced her to take responsibility for her own expenditures. Eight months after her wedding Janet told us, "I've had to realize that I get overly excited about the future and I'm not always sensitive to Scott's fears about money. When he feels tight about money, I spend my own."

Janet's willingness to spend her own money made an impact upon Scott. Several months after their wedding, the couple decided to buy a house. Janet found one she loved, but Scott complained that it was too expensive. Convinced that this was their perfect house, Janet offered to be responsible for half of the down payment. Scott commented to us:

> The minute she made that offer, I said, "Don't worry about it." It meant a lot to me. My mother had always been dependent on me and my ex-wife was a troubled, nongiving person. Janet's desire to contribute made the house a joint venture.

As Scott began to trust Janet more, his need to prove his independence within marriage—and in regard to money

matters—diminished. He started to adopt Janet's more confident attitude toward money, which, he acknowledged, was a
liberating experience for him.

> I've been dogged all my life by a fear of success. I've
> always been afraid to spend money, afraid it would
> evaporate. My income radically increased in the last
> several years, and I still don't quite believe that I have
> as much money as I do. We've had a lot of arguments
> where I've felt Janet was spending too much money.
> She was really spending a reasonable amount of
> money—she wanted to buy nice cushions for the bed-
> room, for both of us—not just for her. Janet has had
> an effect on me. All of a sudden you realize what the
> hell? What is the net personal value of money sitting
> in the bank? Janet is much more prone to spend money
> on joint things than she was a year ago, and so am I.

Despite these developments, the process of Scott giving up
or rather sharing financial control wasn't easy. After nine months
of marriage Janet complained to us that she still wasn't as involved in money matters as she would like.

> I have to ask Scott for checks from our joint accounts.
> And he is the one who decides when to spend money
> on what. He makes most of the financial decisions, with
> the priority system being devised by him. I resent that.

Janet, who had wanted Scott to take care of her, to fulfill
the powerful role that her father had not, discovered that she
resented Scott when he took control. Again and again she suggested to Scott that she become more involved in money matters. Eventually he agreed.
According to Scott:

> When Janet first suggested she work on finances, I was
> threatened. Then I said, "Do it." At one point I had
> considered hiring a bookkeeper. I was backed up on
> bills. And I realized if Janet wanted to be involved it
> could be a tremendous help. Recently Janet gave me
> two thousand dollars to help pay bills. I'm realizing
> more and more that she really wants to contribute and
> work together. And I feel much more confident about

our relationship. I'm finding I enjoy doing things and being involved in things together.

Scott and Janet have grown together in marriage, and as a result they have softened in their attitudes. Janet has become more understanding of Scott's anxieties about money and has realized that Scott's unwillingness to let her be totally dependent on him for money was not an abandonment of her. She has realized she can rely on him to be there for her, but she must also draw on her own strengths and resources. Scott has become less threatened by Janet's dependence on him and come to lean on her—for both financial assistance and moral support. As their marriage has blossomed, the issues of dependence and independence have become less important. And, as a result, money arguments have become less frequent and more easily resolved.

What can you do if you and your spouse have different ideas about how dependent or independent you both should be in regard to money?

• You must communicate—and *don't stop* until you get your message across. Janet didn't ease up on Scott until she made him understand that their marriage couldn't work unless she felt more a part of financial decision making.

• Acknowledge any conflicting feelings you have. Perhaps you want to be taken care of financially but at the same time resent being controlled. Or maybe you wish your spouse was financially independent, but you also want your mate to obediently follow your financial planning. It is only after you each recognize your own mixed feelings that you will be able to find the right balance of dependence and independence by reaching a compromise solution about how intertwined your finances and financial decision making should be.

• Remember that for almost everyone there is at times a certain temptation to be dependent. But to allow yourself or your mate to be completely financially (or emotionally) dependent is to shortchange both of you. A person who is totally dependent—not only for money, but also regarding all financial decision making—is being prevented from drawing on their own strengths and from gaining the self-confidence and capability to share in the responsibilities of marriage. Even if only one of you earns a paycheck, make sure that there is some distribution of financial responsibilities—maybe the nonemployed spouse can be the one to write checks—so that you both see your marriage as an adult partnership.

MONEY AS A SIGN OF NURTURANCE

For many people the idea of "taking care of" and "being taken care of" has to do with money. Traditionally men have seen it as their role to provide for their wives—to "bring home the bacon"—to make enough money so that their wives could keep a nice home and take care of themselves and their children. As long as they gave their wives a weekly allowance, provided them with the lives they expected, they rested assured that they were demonstrating their love and concern in the appropriate male way.

On the flip side, women traditionally sought men who were "good providers"—men who could offer them stability, safety, security. Since women were not encouraged to support themselves, they depended upon a man to do that for them—and so being supported became the equivalent of feeling loved.

Because both husband and wife often work nowadays, it might seem that couples would no longer regard money as a sign of nurturance; after all, if both earn an income they can each nurture themselves—at least, financially. Yet that isn't the case. Providing money for one's mate—whether that involves paying the rent or buying lavish gifts—is a way of demonstrating affection. Both husband and wife inevitably want to feel cared for—and many marital arguments about money have to do with the fact that the financial situation discourages them from feeling loved and cared for.

Melissa Brown met with us several hours after she had blown up at her husband Jeremy when he announced to her that he was going to give a forty-dollar Christmas gift to the superintendent of their apartment building. She was still fuming as she told us about the incident.

> I am furious. What right does he have to be so generous to our super—who does nothing for us—when I can barely get by to pay our butcher and dry cleaning bills?

As she went on venting her frustration, it became clear that she was angry about something else.

Early in their marriage, Melissa and Jeremy had agreed to keep separate checking accounts. Melissa earned considerably less than Jeremy, but Jeremy promised to pay for rent and utilities to compensate for Melissa's lower income. Yet after paying the food, dry cleaning, laundry, and her clothing bills, Melissa often found herself left with no money. As she shared her feelings with us, Melissa realized that it wasn't how Jeremy was treating the super that bothered her, but how he was treating *her*.

> I think the reason I ranted and raved this morning is because I felt Jeremy was taking care of our super, but he isn't taking care of me. I feel like it's left up to me to make ends meet—I don't feel like he's helping me as much as he should.

Once she understood her anger, Melissa felt relieved. She said she planned to go home and speak to Jeremy about making a different financial arrangement. "I know he cares about me, but I need for our money situation to reflect that."

Couples who lived together before marriage often change their financial arrangement after their wedding because of an increase in nurturing feelings. Gina Littoni, who lived with her husband Tony for five years before marrying, told us:

> Before we got married I never asked Tony for money, though he makes so much more money than I do. Now that we're married he offers me money. It makes me feel very much married. Before, I felt guilty if I took money from him.

Tony adds:

> I want her to feel that what I make is hers, even though Gina likes to think that she can support herself. My father was an immigrant painter and worked hard for his kids. I worked hard to establish myself professionally and financially before I got married. I feel very happy and proud to be able to provide Gina with a nice life.

Some newlyweds become upset if they feel they are not making sufficient money to be as nurturing toward their spouse as they would like. Said one 26-year-old man married six months:

> I eat my insides out about financial things—buying a co-op, moving expenses. . . . I feel I bear the financial brunt. Even though we don't have a totally traditional household, I hold traditional values—and I see it as my job to take care of my wife.

There is something expansive about marriage when it works well—you open up emotionally, become willing to be more vulnerable, begin to see the world anew. There's an opening up of the heart that affects not only how you feel toward your spouse, but how you act in matters involving them. The desire to be more generous to your spouse, to buy him or her small gifts, to make joint purchases, like a house or car, demonstrates a loving, nurturing feeling. Sometimes those feelings filter outward to others in a couple's lives as well.

Scott Leifer, whom we introduced earlier in this chapter, found that during his newlywed year he became not only less resistant to spending money on things his wife wanted but also more giving and generous toward his daughters from a previous marriage.

> I realized at some point that I was anxious about letting Janet spend money extravagantly because it triggered guilt feelings and regrets about how I had treated my daughters. When they were growing up I didn't—and couldn't—give my kids lots of things. I didn't have much money then and I was also stingy. As I went along I became more giving. I'm lavishing a lot on Janet and I find now that I want to be fair to my kids.

By being more generous toward his wife and daughters, Scott is trying to reassure all involved in his new marriage that they will be taken care of.

What can you do if problems arise in your marriage because one or both spouses feel that they are not being taken care of financially, and thus emotionally?

• If you're feeling unloved, you need both to express that

for you money is an important symbol of feeling loved and to offer specific suggestions about how money matters might be handled differently. Perhaps you'd feel more "taken care of" if you shared your bank accounts with your mate; maybe all you need is to be remembered with a gift on your birthday instead of just the card your mate has until now routinely opted for.

• If it's your mate who wants to be pampered more, take opportunities to bestow your loved one with a small gift, a card, a box of chocolates, a rose—for no reason at all other than to demonstrate that you care enough to spend a little extra for an impractical but romantic remembrance. For some spouses, those small but generous gestures can make all the difference in feeling appreciated.

• Set an example of how you want to be treated by treating your spouse that way. You wish your mate would be more generous with gifts to your family? Present lovely, thoughtful gifts to your in-laws so that your mate can appreciate the importance you place on such gift giving. You'd like to be taken out occasionally for dinner, but your mate prefers to split the bill with you as you did while dating? Graciously treating your spouse to several dinners out may be a way of conveying your idea, although it may not be a substitute for talking the issue through.

• If you or your mate has an enormous need to feel taken care of financially and/or emotionally, you may have a deeper problem that needs to be addressed. If you dream about never having to work and having your spouse totally provide for you, you may be harboring fantasies that don't fit your financial situation. If no matter how generous your mate is, you are always left feeling unnurtured, your sense of deprivation may stem from experiences that occurred long before you married. In marriage you must always question if your expectations are realistic.

MONEY AS A SOURCE OF STATUS AND ESTEEM

For some people, money is mostly a means to an end—a necessity for survival. For some others, money is to a great extent an end in itself—a cherished goal for the status it represents and for the luxuries it can buy. When someone from the former group marries someone from the latter group, a conflict of values usually results. The practical-minded spouse is most likely to spend money on the basics—food, durable clothing, transportation, housing. The prestige-minded will want to splurge on extravagances—furs, jewelry, fashionable vacations—anything that spells success. One spouse wants to own the house that is the best buy, the other wants the choicest house he or she can afford, the one that his or her friends will envy.

While the above are descriptions of two extreme attitudes, there are many reasons one might perceive money as an extension of self-esteem. It may be that you grew up poor in a community of predominantly wealthy people and never felt accepted. Money may represent a quest for acceptance, from others as well as from yourself. Or it may be that your parents always equated someone's wealth with their worth, and you adopted that attitude. Or perhaps you have a drive to be competitive, a need to be envied, or a need not to envy others. Money and its materialistic manifestations may also compensate for other areas in which you feel inadequate.

Whatever the reason, when you regard money very highly and pursue it because of the psychological confidence that it offers, or you believe it will offer, it's important that your spouse understand and appreciate the reasons for your attitude. It's counterproductive for one mate to accuse another, "Oh, you're money hungry," or "You just want to keep up with the Joneses." If one of you is a "big spender" and the other is perfectly happy with a simple lifestyle, you each need to respect the other's preference and find some comfortable middle path.

The story of Susan and Carl, both successful accountants, is an example of how conflicting attitudes get acted out in a marriage. Susan's complaint about her husband Carl was highly unusual: He liked to buy her expensive presents. A few weeks before our interview with Susan, Carl bought her a $300 bracelet and, "on a whim," a $90 running suit. Susan was annoyed. She told us she'd rather he'd just saved the money toward a house. Carl's viewpoint was that they saved 60 percent of their salaries and they deserved to splurge on whatever was left after paying expenses. Carl enjoyed buying nice clothes for himself and liked to see his wife look good. He grew up in a family where gift giving was very common. Susan grew up with a mother who was very practical—who bought things she *needed* rather than things she dreamt of. Susan wasn't comfortable being showy. She made a lot of money, but no one would guess it from the way she dressed. Carl too was successful—and liked to look it and live like it.

Yet despite their contrasting attitudes, Susan and Carl had a positive influence on each other. Susan, practical like her parents, hadn't allowed herself to indulge in luxuries. Carl's generosity and occasional impulsiveness demonstrated to her that it was all right to enjoy her money, not just use it to make more money. By buying her expensive gifts to wear, he was stating to the world that he could afford to dress his wife nicely—but he was also introducing Susan to a possible new image of herself, one that wasn't necessarily all bad.

Susan, on the other hand, had confidence in herself—without needing any boost from frivolous spending. She curbed Carl's spending habit and reminded him that stylish clothes and extravagant purchases were not all there was to life.

What can you do if you and your spouse value money differently?

• Make sure you have a good system for paying routine monthly expenses. Maybe sit down together on the first of each month and write out checks for the basics—rent, utilities, loan expenses. This way if one of you is frivolous about money, at least the priority expenses will get paid.

• If possible, keep at least some money separate, so that neither of you feels completely confined by the other's ideas about how to spend money.

• If one of you is admittedly "dizzy" about money and is building up a big debt, deposit all paychecks in the bank and dole out a certain amount of cash each week—just enough to meet reasonable expenses. Don't carry checks or credit cards with you, and use just your weekly cash allotments. In this way, you'll be imposing a limit on your purchases.

• Acknowledge your priorities. Don't feel guilty about them, and don't hide them from your mate. If you'd rather give money to charity than buy a new coat, you might talk with your mate about your desire to be philanthropic, or discuss the work of your favorite charity. On the other hand, if you're salivating about buying a luxurious coat, point out ones you'd love to buy. You're each individuals, and there is no point in hiding your attitudes and opinions.

• Do not impose your financial views on each other. Flaunting money may be distasteful to you, but that doesn't mean your spouse can't indulge in fanciful, eye-catching clothes if they enjoy showing off as a fashion plate. Try to reach compromises to bridge your differences, but don't attempt to "make over" each other.

WORKSHOP: MONEY DOS AND DON'TS

To grow ever more comfortable with each other and secure in your relationship, you will need to be sensitive to both the financial and the emotional factors that underlie whatever money conflicts you have.

Here are some steps to start addressing money issues in your marriage.

DO

1. DO discuss your basic financial situation as early as possible—even before the wedding. Together write down:
    • how much you each earn
    • what bank accounts you each have
    • what outstanding debts or loans you each have
    • what investments you each have
    • what assets you each have
    • what trust funds you each have
2. DO work out a budget based on your earnings and expenses. Write as detailed a list of your expenses as you can. If money seems to just fly out of your fingers, keep a daily record for one month of all your purchases—including how much you spend on newspapers, gum, candies, transportation, cigarettes, gifts, and such other incidentals.
3. DO be open about your feelings about money and financial togetherness. Ask yourselves:
    • How much money do we each feel we need to save in order to feel secure about money?

- How important is it to each of us to have a lot of money or make expensive purchases, or in general to achieve a luxurious lifestyle?
- What goals do we agree on?
- What goals do we disagree on?
- What sacrifices or compromises can we make in areas where we disagree?
- How do we each feel about pooling money?
- How would we each feel about being financially accountable to each other about every purchase?
- How do we each feel about having our own financial accounts?

4. DO devise a financial plan—one that takes into account your earnings, your expenses, and your feelings about financial togetherness. If you are very strapped for money, for instance, it may be most practical to keep just one joint account in order to minimize bank fees. If one of you has little free time, perhaps the other mate should be the one to pay bills and keep financial records.

5. DO be honest with your spouse about money. If you are having financial problems or think that your mate is being extravagant, explain why you don't want him or her to buy a certain item. Explain your reasoning when you discourage a purchase—that for the price of one expensive sweater you can buy two or three less expensive ones, or that a black dress may lend itself to more uses than a hot-pink dress.

6. DO set aside specific blocks of time to discuss money-related issues. You may want to meet weekly to talk about bills and budgeting; or if you keep almost all of your finances separate, once a month may be sufficient. Either way, your regularly scheduled sessions will enable you to clarify money problems and reevaluate your financial goals (both short-term and long-term)—and keep finances separate from the romantic aspects of your marriage.

7. DO try to make a distinction between financial dependence and emotional dependence. If one of you relies on the other for money, or both of you are being financially supported by parents, make a determined effort not to let the monetary dependence lead to childlike submission or other regressive behavior. Marriage is an adult relationship, and it's important to act as adults. Marital and family resentments will build if you

feel that you are always kowtowing to the person holding the purse strings.

DON'T

1. DON'T bring up money problems at the end of a long day when your spouse is tired and prone to be irritable. Instead, find a time when he or she is relaxed and in a receptive mood for offering empathy or advice.

2. DON'T automatically assume that your mate's anger about how you handle money is due to insensitivity. It's quite likely that he or she is ignorant about what money means to you and how it was handled in your home while you were growing up. Inform your spouse about how money was dealt with and valued when you were a child, so that he or she can better understand your actions and attitudes.

3. DON'T be overconcerned if you and your spouse have very different attitudes about money. There may be benefits to your contrasting views. Each of you may balance the other so that while one of you makes sure the basics get taken care of and money is saved for the future, the other of you adds excitement by bringing home fun, impulsive items that prevent your relationship from becoming too predictable and staid.

WORK AND MARRIAGE

Juggling Competing Loyalties

A fortnight after returning from her honeymoon in Spain, Marian Lee, a 31-year-old advertising executive, told us:

> I haven't been very enthusiastic about my job since we came home from our vacation. This week my agency is sending me on a business trip and I wish I didn't have to go. I want to stay home and be married to John. I don't feel the same involvement with my work that I used to. John is more of a priority. For years all I wanted was for my firm to give me more responsibility. I would have died to go on a business trip. Now that I'm in that stage I feel a reversal—that I need to take care of our home and our life together. I wonder if other career women fall into more traditional patterns once they get married? You know, the first night I worked late after we got back from our honeymoon, I cried. It was a Friday evening and John and I had planned on having dinner together. When I walked into our apartment at 10:00 P.M. I felt like I had failed him—I hadn't made our time together enough of a priority. I'm afraid if I become too involved in my work my marriage will suffer. And I worry if I'm too involved with John my work will suffer. It's a conflict. It's definitely a conflict.

Marian's husband, John, a 30-year-old real-estate broker, painted a totally different picture when he described his feelings to us. He declared happily:

> I am feeling more motivated about my work than before. I was so involved with all the details of the wedding before we got married that I was distracted. Now I can think clearly about my work. I'm thinking about purchasing some new properties. I feel more directed

because I've got definite goals now—like buying a co-op apartment and taking some nice vacations together. I feel more focused and determined than I've felt in a long time.

THE LOVE–WORK CONNECTION

People's attitudes about work often change once they marry, as our survey confirmed[1]:

- 11 percent of newlyweds reported that their work ambitions *greatly increased* following their wedding.
- Another 30 percent of newlyweds reported that their work ambitions *somewhat increased* after marrying.
- 17 percent of newlyweds reported their work ambitions had *decreased* after their wedding.

It makes sense that feelings about work change once you marry. Love and work are two of the major aspects of life. In fact, Freud believed that achieving success in those two realms constitutes maturity and good mental health. Because people invest so much energy and feeling into their personal lives, it's inevitable that what happens in their love relationship will affect their attitude toward work. And how one feels about one's job also affects one's personal life, since most of us spend more waking hours at work than at leisure.[2]

Also, most people today regard their work as more than just a means to an end. They expect it to be a source of satisfaction. Some people spend years training for careers, hoping they'll be both monetarily rewarding and personally fulfilling. In *American Couples*,[3] Philip Blumstein and Pepper Schwartz report that the happier employed wives are with their jobs, the happier they are with their marriages. This finding seems logical, since so much of one's self-esteem and sense of self-worth is connected to one's work.

Nevertheless, being successful at your job does not necessarily mean being successful at your marriage. If, say, you are successful at work but your mate is not, resentment may build between you. Or perhaps the pleasure and confidence you derive from your job emphasizes any discontentment you have about your domestic situation. Psychiatrist Jay B. Rohrlich, M.D.[4] goes so far as to maintain that the qualities that make one good at work are totally opposite from the qualities that make one able to love. While work is a goal-directed, achievement-oriented activity, he points out, love is something experienced in the here and now—its rewards are intangible. Work has to do with the setting up of boundaries—it necessitates being structured and organized. Love, on the other hand, entails a loss of boundaries, a union, an ability to be sufficiently relaxed, even at times passive, so that you are able to drop your defenses and bask in the joy and sensuousness of the feeling of the moment.

To merge work and love successfully, you must find the right balance between the two. While it's difficult for any individual or couple to combine the best of both worlds, attaining a balance when you are newlyweds can be particularly problematic, since you are at a stage when emotions about work and love run high. If you are in your twenties or thirties, your focus on work may be especially intense, because you are likely to be at the most active, upwardly mobile stage of your careers. Among the people we interviewed—especially those in their twenties —an enormous number, eager to climb up the career ladder, changed jobs during their first year of marriage. From what we found, the excitement and intensity that those newlyweds experience in their work and love lives can be exhilarating but also stressful. On one hand, they are committed to building the best marriage they can. On the other hand, they are determined to get as far as possible in their careers. The desire and attempt to "have it all" is exhausting.

CHECKUP: HOW DOES WORK FIT INTO YOUR MARRIAGE?

No matter what your employment situation—whether you both work, only one of you earns a paycheck, you both are students, or one of you was recently laid off from your job— you're bound to have lots of feelings about how work meshes with your love life. Place a check next to each of the following statements that relates to how you or your spouse feels about your job—marriage situation.

- ☐ I think my spouse spends too much time working.
- ☐ My spouse thinks I spend too much time working.
- ☐ I wish my spouse were *more* committed to their work.

☐ My spouse wishes I were *more* committed to my work.

☐ I wish my spouse were more interested in hearing about my work.

☐ My spouse wishes I were more interested in hearing about their work.

☐ I wish my spouse would talk more about what goes on at their workplace.

☐ My spouse wishes I would talk more about what goes on at my workplace.

☐ My spouse and I are very competitive with each other about our work.

☐ I view work as something that interferes with our marriage.

☐ I view work as being compatible with our marriage.

☐ I sometimes work late to avoid coming home to my spouse.

☐ I think my spouse sometimes works late to avoid coming home to me.

Review the statements you just checked off. As you read the following sections, be extra aware of those issues that you and your spouse find particularly challenging in your attempts to combine job and marriage.

MARITAL VERSUS JOB RESPONSIBILITIES

A 1945 *Fortune* magazine poll showed that *63 percent* of Americans surveyed thought that married women should stay at home if their husbands could earn a living. Women with ambitions usually channeled them by prodding their husbands and sons on to achievement. (Or, to borrow an old witticism: "The road to success is filled with women pushing their husbands along."[5]) Typical complaints from stay-at-home wives were that their husbands didn't have enough time for them. Stereotypical henpecked husbands complained that their wives nagged them for attention.

Today's situation is different. A 1984 report published by the United States Census Bureau found that only 29 percent of families have a single breadwinner. And a 1985 poll conducted by the Roper Organization showed that 51 percent of women would choose career over family if they could not have both. This transformation necessitates an adjustment if you are a husband or wife who was brought up with traditional assumptions about married life. For one thing, there are tangible challenges to coordinating two careers in a marriage. If both you and your spouse feel the pressure of job demands and responsibilities, you each may come home tired from work, with little energy left to do routine chores, let alone create romantic moments. In your marriage it may be the husband who complains that the wife doesn't have enough time for him, and the wife who feels torn by competing loyalties to work and love. And it takes added effort to synchronize schedules, vacations, career moves, and marital decisions (like when to have a baby) so that your jobs are not jeopardized by your personal lives. And if your parents did not work while you were growing up, you may suffer from not having had a model on which you might pattern your dual-career marriage.

You and your spouse may respond differently to the challenge of juggling work and marriage. Marian Lee, whom we introduced at the outset of this chapter, felt conflicted between her marital and job roles because of expectations, formed in her childhood, based on her mother's fulfillment of traditional wifely duties. For her husband, however, performing well at work was consistent with being a good marriage partner. Even though his wife worked—and earned *more* than he—John viewed himself as the one who would eventually be the main breadwinner in the family. He hoped that at some point his wife would take off time to have a baby. For John, being a good husband entailed being a good provider—a role he patterned on his father's model. His marital and personal goals were in sync.

In some relationships it's not the wives who are troubled by juggling work and marriage, but the husbands who have difficulty accepting their wives' dual responsibilities. Despite our age of "liberation," it's not uncommon for men to resent their wives' job obligations. According to one study,[6] husbands of working wives feel less adequate as family breadwinners than do men whose wives work only as homemakers. In fact, the study found that a wife's employment had a negative effect on her husband's mental health, regardless of the husband's age, income bracket, or educational level. One explanation offered by researchers in that study is that when husbands and wives both work, total income rises, and so, usually, do expenses. With time a husband may begin to feel that he could not support his family on his income alone if his wife were to stop working. Brought up with the expectation that as husbands they are to be the providers for their families, men can find it hard to appreciate their wives as working women.

The potential benefits of combining work and marriage are many. But first you need to address the practical and psychological demands of integrating both in your lives.

"THERE'S NEVER ENOUGH TIME!"

The type of work you're each pursuing before you marry should indicate what work hours you'll keep after the wedding. Professionals—doctors, lawyers, doctoral students—are infamous for burning the midnight oil. Some self-employed businessmen tend to be preoccupied with their work for the majority of their waking hours, even to the point of using leisure time for socializing with business contacts. Teachers may have regular job hours, but they still need time to do preparatory work at home. And artists and "creative types" may keep irregular hours, but feel unable to tear themselves away from their workplace when inspiration hits them.

Ideally, before you marry you should sit down with your mate and discuss your individual attitudes toward work.

- Is work your prime source of fulfillment, or something you see as secondary to family life?
- Do you plan on committing extra time to your work now in order to have greater independence and flexibility in your job at a later stage?
- Will your job always demand long hours, even though you'd prefer to spend more time at home?

If your job demands more than the usual nine-to-five schedule, be open about the hours you'll be devoting to your work and explain why so great a time commitment is necessary.

Nevertheless, no matter how well prepared you feel before marriage to face the demands of your job or your spouse's, it is inevitable that the more time your jobs entail, the more difficult it will probably be for you two to balance your work and love lives.

Ian Green, a newly married medical intern, calculates that—because of his on-call night schedule—he is, effectively, "on the job" 110 hours a week. He admits:

> I feel under tremendous pressure to perform well at the hospital and as a husband. It's been a very difficult, tense, exhausting year in terms of the medicine I'm doing. While my wife understands, it's hard for her to accept that I'm frequently unable to attend family functions and that I often want to spend my free time sleeping rather than going out. I try to make up for my schedule by calling her several times during the day, buying her flowers on the weekend, and reminding her I love her. I think she's gradually recognizing that my working hard doesn't mean I don't love her. Ultimately I feel I'm working for her and the family we hope to have.

Linda, Ian's wife, who works at a bank as a computer programmer, acknowledged to us that, at first, it was difficult for her not to feel neglected by Ian's being away so much.

> Of course I knew that a doctor would have long hours—but what that meant didn't really hit me until we got married and he started staying at the hospital every third night. At first, I tried to make Ian feel guilty. I'd make nice dinners and be angry when he walked in the door at nine-thirty. Then I realized, "Hey, he's not any happier about working these hours than I am." Now I don't cook elaborate meals unless I know he'll get off early. That way I don't feel neglected and he doesn't feel guilty. I think I'm adjusting to our situation better—I'm not trying to turn us into the romantic honeymoon couple that lazes over candlelit dinners for hours. That just can't be.

Several months later we spoke with Linda again. She told us that she no longer minded Ian's schedule so much because she was also working evenings—doing computer programming at home.

At some point I just had enough of spending nights watching TV and talking with friends on the phone. I have a friend who does freelance work and she convinced me to buy a computer and try to start a business on the side. So far it seems like it might take off. It's funny—by Ian working so hard it's pushing me a lot farther in my career. I'll probably end up being more successful than I would have been if he kept normal hours.

How preoccupied you or your spouse are with your job may relate to how far along you are in your career. For Linda Green, adjusting to Ian's schedule involved reconciling herself to the fact that he was in the early phases of his training. Eventually, as Ian rose within his profession, he would have more choice regarding how much time to devote to his work. Meanwhile, he was doing his best to maintain the closeness and connection he felt with Linda by calling her throughout his long workday and making loving gestures. Linda altered her expectations of Ian, bringing them more in line with what he can realistically fulfill, and found a productive use for her time by starting a side business.

If you and your spouse are at the same stage in your careers—and especially if you are in the same field of work—there is a greater likelihood that you will understand the job pressures each experiences. One couple we met have a "weekend marriage," living and working in different cities, and they commute on weekends to see each other. Because both are very much involved in their own careers, they can appreciate each other's professional commitments. Rather than resent not having weeknights together, they see living apart as an advantage.[7] The wife told us:

Even if we did live together we wouldn't have much time together anyway. I'd end up feeling guilty that I stay so late at the office. This way the time we spend with each other is set aside to devote to us.

If you and your spouse are at different levels of your careers, however, you may find it difficult to handle the discrepancies in your schedules.

Gilbert Scaali, a 34-year-old businessman, complained to

us during his first few months of marriage that his wife, Doris, a lawyer with a large New York firm, didn't arrive home from work until nine o'clock—three hours after he walked in the door. Gilbert had entered his family's business right after college and had established himself in his field years before marrying. He worked hard and loved it, but came home, as he said, "at a normal hour ready to have dinner and spend time with my wife."

Doris also seemed distressed by the situation. "I just don't think my marriage can thrive when I come home from work totally drained after a 13-hour day."

Though she felt excited and challenged by her job, after several months of being married, Doris concluded that she did not want law to be her whole life. She acknowledged that despite her feminist ideals, she wants a semblance of a traditional marriage, with her and her husband eating dinner and spending their evenings together. She decided to interview to see if she could find a law job with more regular hours, and within weeks had accepted a job she was offered in the district attorney's office. "Though in the long run I may not make as much money at this job," she told us, "the work is challenging and it allows me time with my husband. It's working out much better for us."

Doris's solution is not for everyone. Most people don't have the luxury of leaving their job because it is too time consuming. And many people would never even consider giving up a prestigious or lucrative position, no matter how much the job might interfere with their marriage.

But there are ways to find time to be with your spouse. Remember, a successful marriage—like anything else that blossoms—needs nurturing. The following are "rules" that couples have found useful in preserving time together in their busy lives:

1. Set aside at least one weeknight to be together. Treat it as a date and plan something special, either at home or outside the house. Try activities that are fun and different, whether that means visiting new restaurants, buying tickets for the circus, taking dance lessons, or going bowling. Make an effort to keep the energy, excitement, and wonder in your relationship by making your time together stimulating and interesting.

2. Make a list of each other's favorite activities. Do those things together as often as you can. Even if you have different leisure styles (one of you likes to spend Sundays at museums, while the other prefers attending a baseball game), chances are there are some activities you both enjoy—reading, listening to records, hopping in the car to visit a new neighborhood. Your favorite activity together may be just lying next to each other and watching your favorite old movie. The point is to make it a habit of doing together things you *both* enjoy.

3. Don't let others interfere with time set aside for you and your spouse. Stand up to your parents, friends, or whoever else doesn't think that your being with your mate is sufficient reason for them not to take up your time. Explain to them nicely that you'll see them or speak to them another time.

4. Specify to your mate exactly when you feel you need him or her to be available for you, your mutual friends, and family functions. Remember that your spouse can't read your mind. Give him or her advance notice about any birthday or anniversary celebrations you want them to be around for. And let your spouse know when you've been having a particularly hard week and need some extra tender loving care and rest and relaxation. If you feel your spouse isn't home enough or doesn't celebrate occasions as you'd like, you may not be sufficiently forceful in making your needs known.

5. When you and your spouse have leisure time together, try to leave your work behind. Or if that's impossible, then convey your feelings about work—but don't take out your job frustrations on your spouse. There's a difference between expressing your feelings and acting them out.

6. Arrange your time together around your job schedules if necessary. If one of you finds it especially difficult to leave work at a reasonable hour, arrange to meet at that spouse's office or a nearby restaurant in the evening and have a late dinner together, or plan to meet for lunch occasionally. Or you both might enjoy getting together for a five o'clock break. Then, if one of you has to go back to the office to work late, at least you'll have seized the chance to be together and chat during the day.

THE WORKAHOLIC'S
MARRIAGE

We've talked about balancing your work and love lives—but balance is *not* what everyone wants. Some people are obsessed with their work to the extent that, though they may love their spouse, their marriage is secondary to their job.

If you and your mate both share a passion for work, you may rarely argue about the long hours at the office or your shortage of time for each other. As one man, a TV sportscaster who works nights and weekends and is married to a medical student, told us,

> I think my wife and I would get bored with each other if we had a normal relationship. I find my wife more refreshing when I don't see her every night. But we also feel a certain pressure to do something out of the ordinary when we have time together. And our conflicting schedules do add pressure to sex. I get home late and my wife goes to bed early. But I guess I don't mind our arrangement that much because my parents also never spent a lot of time together. My dad goes to sleep at 9:00 P.M. and wakes at 4:00 A.M. and my mother stays up until midnight and wakes late. They say that having the free time to themselves has helped their marriage. Sometimes I ask myself: Am I working so I don't have to go home? But the answer is always negative. I love to go home—but I still work late.

There is generally diminished understanding between spouses when one takes an involvement in work to great lengths and the other does not. The latter is planning cozy evenings at home, Sunday movie matinees, dinner invitations to friends, while the former stays late at the office, spends "free" weekends thinking about work, and has difficulty relaxing on a vacation. It's natural for the mate of the workaholic to feel frustrated, angry, and depressed.

Mary Ann Hall, an occupational therapist, married Douglas Silver when he was just finishing graduate school and starting out with an accounting firm. She had never seen Douglas in a job environment—and had no idea that he would be the type to work until eleven at night. Mary Ann divorced Douglas after two years of marriage.

I became so depressed and insecure because all Douglas ever talked or thought about was work. I like my job too—but I leave it when I leave my office. Even when Douglas got home early he'd bring work with him. Our sex life fizzled down to nothing. I wanted to feel loved and desired as a wife.

Because Mary Ann cared nothing about accounting, her lack of interest made it even more difficult for her to understand Douglas's job preoccupations. She told us she couldn't bring herself to share her husband's enthusiasm in his work, and so the gap between them grew larger. With little shared leisure time, Mary Ann and Douglas did little to cultivate those qualities in their relationship that had drawn them together in the first place.

Often work-absorbed spouses defend their long work hours to their mate with statements like "I'm doing it all for you—so that we can have a future" or "If I didn't work the hours I do, I would be kicked out of my company in a minute." It's hard to argue with a spouse already exhausted from hours of dedicated work put in on the job, especially when they claim it is for the benefit of their family.

It's important to distinguish, however, between dedication to work and obsession to work. The latter almost inevitably constitutes an avoidance of aspects of one's life. Chances are that if you're irritated by a spouse's workaholism, you are reacting even more to something else—something that goes unstated and may be difficult to pinpoint. People who are workaholics often use their work to maintain a distance from other people. Being at work is a way of *not* being home—of *not* expressing oneself toward one spouse or of *not* allowing one's spouse to open up about their emotions. It may also be a way of avoiding pleasure, perhaps sex—as it seemed to have been in Douglas's case. It's possible that Douglas felt threatened by too much closeness and used work as an excuse in order not to have to be intimate.

If there is dissatisfaction between you and your spouse over the number of hours one or both of you put into your jobs, you should:

1. Discuss the pressures, challenges, and feelings you each experience. Talk about the hours you put into your jobs—whether at the office, at home, in socializing—and how you feel about those time demands. One of you may feel comfortable with your present situation while the other harbors gripes about feeling ignored or excluded. Get your feelings out in the open and pinpoint the areas you'd like to change. Some questions to bring up:

- Will you always put in long work hours, or are your job preoccupations temporary?
- How is this phase of your career different from what will be in the future?
- Why do you spend so much time working? Is it necessary (because of pressure from a boss), or is it something you do because you love your job?
- Are there certain times of the year when you will always be busier than at other times?
- What are your job goals?

If you're the one working late, explain the reasons to your spouse. Don't just say "I have to," but offer details about the necessity of meeting certain deadlines, or whatever other reasons there are for the urgency of working.

2. *Confront yourselves and each other about whether staying at work late is being caused by problems at home.* Go beyond the possibilities connected with the job itself, and ask yourself or your mate these questions:

- Do you sometimes stay late at your job even though you could finish your work the next day?
- Is staying late at work your response to being angry at or irritated with your spouse?
- Are you happier on the job than you are at home with your mate?

Be honest with yourselves, and discuss what one or even both of you may be doing that encourages the workaholic mate to seek refuge in their work.

If either of you answered "yes" to any of the above questions, you need to confront the issues in your marriage that are being dealt with by throwing yourselves into work. In your case, working too hard or too long is really a cover-up for other marital problems.

PROFESSIONAL RIVALRIES

When both husband and wife work, their talents and abilities are tested on outside soil. Ideally you and your spouse support each other's work efforts, bolster each other in times of trouble, triumph in each other's successes. But marriage is never altogether ideal. Whether you work in the same area of interest or in different fields, you may find yourselves competing in your work achievements and envious of each other's successes.

A recently wed male cardiologist found that he resented hearing people address his wife as "doctor." His attitude was: I worked all those years to become a physician, and now that I have a wife who is also a doctor, my achievement is made less special. His feelings became so troubling that he entered short-term therapy to address the issue.

Jacki and Earl Robbins, whom we introduced in chapter 2, also experienced conflict as a result of the wife's rising stature in the work world.

Jacki and Earl met while working at a social agency—she as a secretary, he as an electrical engineer. They'd both been working at their jobs for about seven years when they married, and were both restless for a job change. Their plan was for Jacki to look for a new job first, and then, once she was settled, Earl would also look for a position elsewhere.

Two months after their wedding, Jacki found a job working for a financial firm, where it was her task to quickly learn about and research the stock market. Her job was fast-paced, challenging, and demanding. At her previous job, if Jacki worked late Earl waited for her so they could go home together. And because he worked in the same building, he always knew where she was.

Jacki's new job often required her to work late. Almost immediately Earl showed signs of mistrust.

He gets home by 7:00 P.M. If I'm not home before he is, his mind starts racing. He asks me if someone is taking me out to lunch. He accuses me of having affairs. It bothers me that he's insecure. Work is very pressurized. When I come home I want to relax. He starts arguments that I really don't want to get into.

Earl began accusing Jacki of changing, she told us—and of not loving him anymore.

> When I started my new job I felt very insecure about it. But I'm growing into it and Earl's attacking me for it. I'm developing much more of a sense of myself. My feelings aren't changing for Earl except when he harasses me and is vindictive. He's admitted that he has a tendency to be jealous—maybe because his ex-wife cheated on him or maybe it's cultural. The women in his family didn't work, they just catered to men, and he'd probably like me to be that way.

> I'm annoyed because Earl's not following our plan. He's intimidated—he hasn't started looking for a new job. I feel he should get off his butt and move on. Financially he can do better. Right now I'm making more money. He helped me get a job. I feel he's not practicing what he preaches.

A job that could be richly rewarding, not only to Jacki but also to her relationship with her husband, had turned sour for Jacki and Earl. Jacki's new and demanding position had become a trigger for deep-seated feelings. Meeting the challenges of her new job had increased her self-confidence and made her realize how ambitious she really was—more ambitious, in fact, than Earl. Gaining a sense of her own self-worth had touched off a desire within Jacki to discover herself.

> I'm realizing now that I never had a chance to be on my own or to have my own apartment. I went from my mother's house to moving in with Earl at age 21. Maybe it's too late to think about this, but I am thinking about it.

For Earl, Jacki's job had triggered feelings of insecurity and incompetence. He was resentful of Jacki's abilities and success, and fearful that she was surpassing him and would leave him for a more exciting life.

When a couple's relationship is threatened by a strong sense of competition, as in Jacki and Earl's case, the problem can be difficult for them to resolve by themselves, because that rivalry emerged from deeply unhappy and insecure feelings tucked in the recesses of their psyches. Earl's sudden suspicion that Jacki was having an affair when she moved to a demanding, higher-level job was clearly an overreaction. The intensity of his response, however, reflected the intensity of his fears about getting left, about being topped. And Jacki's sudden awareness of her talents and capabilities also served to point up the level of insecurity that, until then, she had been operating under.

It would be a shame for Jacki and Earl to end their marriage because those feelings had arisen. For five years they had lived and worked together with no major conflicts. Jacki's new job had brought a new stress to their relationship, one they needed to acknowledge and attempt to cope with.

If competition is an issue in your marriage, you need to approach the problem from both an emotional and a practical viewpoint.

1. Try to understand your feelings of competitiveness. Place a check next to any of the following statements that describe why you feel threatened by your spouse's job achievements:

- ☐ I am secretly afraid my spouse will leave me if he or she is very successful in the work world.
- ☐ I feel my work is less impressive if my spouse is also successful.
- ☐ I think my spouse will value me more if they realize how successful I am in my work.
- ☐ Other

2. Consider practical steps you can take that may minimize your competitiveness with your spouse. Here are some suggestions:

• Make yourself happier in your own work situation so that you aren't irritated by your mate's job achievements. That may mean changing jobs, working toward a promotion, or becoming friendlier with your work colleagues so that you feel better about your own job environment.

• Be sensitive in how you talk about your work. Don't emphasize how well you're doing at work or gloat about your new raise, if such a remark will tend to provoke your spouse to jealousy.

• Appreciate the benefits of your spouse's job success. Rather than regard your partner as your competitor, adopt the attitude that you and your mate are team players. If you didn't get a promotion but your spouse did, then consider the advantages of the added income rather than resent your mate for "one-upping" you.

•   Remember that you're each going to have ups and downs in your jobs, and although one of you may be much more successful at the moment, the situation may be reversed at another time. Treat your spouse with the consideration and support that you hope to get in return throughout your married work life.

JOB STRESS AND YOUR MARRIAGE

Stress in any job is a given. Deadlines, demanding bosses, long work hours are all a normal part of work life. How you and your mate handle the pressures of your jobs once you are home—and how you both respond to each other's work concerns—will have a lot to do with how successfully you juggle your two worlds.

Different people have different ways of handling job stress at home.

Jim, a salesman, told us, "I don't like to dwell on work once I get home. Work is so consuming anyway that it's nice to forget it for a while." His wife, however, claimed that she could tell when Jim was upset about work, and she said she knew when to keep away.

> I know not to ask Jim anything about money before Chirstmas, because he is so nervous about what his bonus will be that he gets very edgy. Also, if he comes home and starts yelling about his socks having shrunk in the wash, or the sofa being lumpy, or something stupid—I know he's anxious about work and I just leave him alone for a while.

Others want to talk about what's happening in their work lives and become frustrated if their spouse doesn't understand that need. Gwen, a third-year law student married to a store owner, said:

> Right now I'm looking for a job and it's very scary. Sometimes I get very depressed. I think Dan should empathize more. I think he should understand my

position better than he does. He doesn't seem to share my nervousness. But I'm a worrier and he's not.

One newly married man told us that he was so preoccupied with his own unhappiness on his job that he found it difficult to concentrate on what his wife was telling him about her work. She became annoyed that he was not tuned into her work situation and took his distraction to mean that he just didn't care.

Timing is crucial when it comes to sharing your work woes. If you unburden yourself when your mate is unable to listen —either because they are so absorbed in their own job dilemmas or because they want to relax for the moment without any worries—conflict, misunderstandings, and hurt feelings can escalate. But while it's important to be sensitive to when your spouse can hear what you want to say, it's also crucial that your spouse recognize when you need to be heard.

There is probably no time when those sensitivities are more challenged than when a spouse is fired or can't find work. Unemployment can be grueling in the newlywed year, because of monetary concerns and because the newlywed has been dealt a severe blow to the ego. Just at a time when they should feel hopeful about the future and confident about their potential, the out-of-work newlywed is likely to suffer from feelings of depression, rejection, embarrassment, helplessness, failure. While the loss or lack of a job is never pleasant, it can be particularly stressful for those in a new and still somewhat fragile marriage.

Newlywed Tom Delray, a native Caribbean who moved to New York to be with his wife and now had a job in a steel plant, recalled:

> I wasn't working the first few months of this year because I didn't have my working papers. My wife was studying nursing during the days and working as a chef in a restaurant at night. I had a lot of time on my hands and resented that she had no time for me. Not being able to contribute financially was also a real problem for me.

Phyllis and Rex Singer, who met in graduate school, also went through a tense time when they moved to Boston one month after their wedding because of Rex's new job. Phyllis hoped to find a position in Boston, but her hopes dimmed as her determined job search led nowhere. Married just a year and a half, Phyllis said:

> I was extremely depressed during our first year because I couldn't find a job. My family lives in California, and in Boston I was left alone a lot. Rex had to travel for his job and was gone most of the week. I felt neglected and resented not getting a job. Rex was supportive, but he didn't understand. He thought I was doing something wrong . . . that I wasn't conducting my job search well. We argued about where I should look for a job and how I should go about getting one. It took him a long time to realize that there are a lot of qualified people looking for jobs in Boston.

According to Phyllis, her marriage nearly broke up because of the stress her unemployment put on her marriage.

> Finally we both realized that Boston wasn't working for us, and we decided to look for jobs in New York —that's when we began working toward a common goal.

Now living and working in New York with her husband, Phyllis said:

> One of the problems was that we were used to being in school together, and once Rex started working I couldn't get used to having no time together. It was like everything came down on us at once—I was out of a job, Rex was never home, we were fighting whereas we had never fought before.

There is no question that when a spouse wants to work and cannot find work, the strength of a marriage is tested. But despite the strain that a job loss puts on a marriage, there are couples who find that going through that difficult experience together solidifies their relationship.

Joan Lindy, whose husband, Gene, was put on job probation six months after their wedding, said that until that happened she hadn't realized how invested she felt in her husband's welfare and how much she was willing to do for him. For months her husband had trouble sleeping, and suffered from diminished sex drive and loss of self-confidence. Mustering all of her inner strength, that wife cared for her husband physically—making sure he ate and didn't neglect his body, bolstering his ego, minimizing their social schedule (since he was not in the mood to face people), offering him suggestions for restoring his boss's confidence in him, and knowing when to leave him alone. In those months the couple turned from happy honeymooners to struggling survivors.

Fortunately for that couple, the husband proved himself to his boss and was taken off job probation by their first anniversary. Nevertheless, he said, the experience had a lasting impact.

> When I was put on probation I was devastated and petrified to go home and tell my wife. But she was astoundingly calm about it—and stood by me the whole time in a way I never expected. Going through that together made me realize that we are really in this together. It was something that we just kept between us—we didn't tell our family or friends what was happening. I realized how much I could depend on her and I feel immensely grateful.

It won't last forever: That's the important thing to remember when one of you is faced with a particularly difficult period in connection with work. Rather than harp on the negative, it helps for you both to focus on the positive, productive steps that can be taken to remedy the situation. Both of you need to handle the situation sensitively—or feelings of anger and rejection will explode. Much of the support you offer will be in the way you communicate with and listen to your partner. Here are some recommendations for successful communication:

1. Consider each of your needs regarding how you would like job-related issues to be discussed at home. Ask yourself:
- To what extent do I want to share my job concerns with my mate?
- When do I prefer to talk with my mate about work?
- How satisfied am I with the way my spouse listens to my job concerns?
- How involved do I want to be in my spouse's work world?

Now, have your spouse answer these questions. Compare your responses.

- Do you both agree or disagree on when is the best time to share news of the trials and tribulations of your job?
- Do you both feel comfortable with how much you impart to each other about your jobs?

2. If your needs are different, experiment with alternative solutions. Does your spouse need to unwind by forgetting about the work day? Don't bring up the subject of your job until after dinner, when they've relaxed. Does your spouse always want to know how your day went, while you prefer to forget about the job you hate? Satisfy your spouse by sharing the highlights of your day as soon as you come home, then tell your mate to let you relax for the rest of the evening.

3. Consider possible underlying reasons for your difficulties in communicating about work. If you never want to listen to your mate's job concerns or your spouse never wants to share the day's activities, think about what tensions may exist between you both that could be preventing good communication.

WORKSHOP: ATTAINING THE BEST OF BOTH WORLDS

Despite all the problems we've outlined, there are many advantages—financial as well as emotional—to merging work and love in your relationship.

If you and your spouse work, you bring outside experiences, knowledge, and contacts to your marriage that have the potential to enrich you each individually as well as to nourish your relationship. By working, you provide yourselves with additional sources of gratification, stimulation, and fulfillment—so that you don't need to be dependent upon each other to satisfy all of your needs. When things don't go well at home, you'll probably find it's nice to have a job to run to—to distract you from domestic troubles. And when the boss comes down too hard on you, you'll appreciate having a spouse who is comforting and nurturing.

Rather than detract from one another, work and love can support and enhance each other. It can be especially rewarding

for you if you both understand and share in each other's enthusiasm about work. You also may find that the synergy of
working and being married can bring out the best in you. One
woman, a psychiatric nurse, told us as she neared her first
anniversary that being married had greatly bolstered her job
confidence.

> I'm being more assertive on the job and at home. Now
> I feel like I need more of a challenge, to do more
> conceptual work—not just be on the front lines. I think
> marriage has really given me a better sense of
> myself—my strengths have come out. I feel safer now
> about changing jobs.

You may find that being married offers you a helpful perspective on your work. One female journalist told us,

> I'm still excited by my work, but I'm not as driven.
> Right now my paper is very shaky and I could lose my
> job at any moment—but I'm not consumed by fear. I
> look at the people around me in the newsroom and I
> feel sorry for them. Their lives are so narrow—they're
> so absorbed in their jobs. Life is more rounded since
> I'm married.

One man noted that if he didn't get the teaching position
he wanted in the coming semester, he wouldn't be devastated,
as he might have been if he were still single. "Work is just one
half of my life now," he explained.

And a female freelance book editor told us:

> I've gotten less anxious about my work—a lot of the
> pressure is off. I always felt I had to have six projects
> going at once. I felt financial pressure which translated
> into emotional pressure. I was more eager to be a suc-
> cess. This period has been one of settling into marriage
> and not pushing myself careerwise. I don't feel com-
> pelled in the way that I used to. I came from a family
> that's very achievement-oriented. It's a big relief to give
> up that self-imposed pressure. It's nice to feel that I
> don't have to be on that treadmill. Of course, I still
> have two voices within me. One voice is saying work,
> but also relax and have a good time. The other voice

is the part of me that's always been ambitious. The goal is to coordinate those two—to decide how far to strive.

The excitement that you each may derive from each other's work can also add to your relationship. A lawyer married to a well-known writer told us:

I'm very proud of what my wife does. It's an ego trip for me. She works nights and weekends but I don't feel like she's neglecting me. I'm tremendously interested in what she does. That has been a very strong point for us.

The above sentiments express the rewards that can be reaped when there is the right blend of work and love, and when a couple have reached an understanding of the role that their jobs play in their marriage.

Throughout this chapter we've listed suggestions for aiding you and your spouse in your attempt to deal with the tensions and challenges that may arise as you try to balance your two commitments. Several points are worth summarizing—and pondering:

1. Review whether you understand each other's work obligations and attitudes.

2. Review whether you're communicating about work in a way that suits the needs of both partners in marriage.

3. Review the extent of your need, and your spouse's need, to find time to spend together no matter how great your commitment to work.

4. If you're dissatisfied with how your job fits into your marriage, explore all your options for compromise, but don't make any rash decisons or moves. There are always alternatives to consider, whatever your employment or marital situation. If, say, you're torn between your desire to share equally in the responsibilities of marriage and your obligations to your job, here are just a number of possibilities available to you:

• You can change to a job that would be less demanding

of your time, or closer to home so that you'd have less commuting time.

- You can find ways to use your time at work more effectively so that you need not stay late at your job.
- You can bring work home with you instead of staying late at the office.
- You and your spouse can lower your expectations about cooking and housekeeping so that you both feel less pressured.
- You can invest some of your salary in hiring outside help so that there is a third person who can help bear the burden of household responsibilities.
- You can arrange to do more housekeeping over the weekends if your spouse is able to do more housework during the weekdays.

Always *think about the long-term impact of any decision you may make*. Right now it may be worthwhile to invest more time in your career than you'd like—if it means that in several years you'll probably be in a position to benefit from a lot more money, prestige, flexibility, or free time. On the other hand, consider the effect that working longer hours or traveling more frequently for your job would have on your marriage *now:* Would it jeopardize your relationship? It has been suggested that newly married couples have more difficulty coping with separation than longer-married couples who share a backlog of marital experiences.[8] So it's important to weigh the advantages and disadvantages of any job decision you make.

One woman we know fell in love with a man, married him, and quit her sales job—all within four months—so she could have time with her husband at breakfast, meet him for lunch, and have dinner on the table when he came home. That lovebird feeling of wanting to spend every minute together lasted a few months, and then the woman began to feel isolated and in need of some outside stimulation. By that time her husband had gotten used to hot dinners waiting for him when he got home. And so going back to work ended up being much more difficult for her, and for him, than had she just continued working.

As a newlywed, your feelings about work may fluctuate for a few months, because the challenge of merging your job commitments with your marriage is new. Be open to alternatives that may ease the pressures you are feeling, but hold yourself back from making any impulsive decisions.

5. Face the fact that work is a part of your lives and adopt a positive attitude about your work and your spouse's. The truth is: There is no magical solution to making it easy to combine job and marriage. You may dream about the days when you won't have to work or when your job hours will be fewer, but depending on financial circumstances, it's possible those days will never come. So the sooner you adjust to the reality that you must deal with the challenges of your jobs, the better.

Make the most of your situation. If your spouse's job demands long work hours, recognize that their not being home is not a rejection or an abandonment of you. Create a life for yourself by developing outside interests, a social life with your friends, a part-time career or hobby. If you enjoy rather than resent the time you have without your spouse, your attitude will benefit your relationship enormously.

Rather than have your jobs seem a divisive factor, think about how you might involve each other in your work lives so that you don't feel distanced from each other. If you find that you each tend to become very absorbed in your relationships at the workplace, socialize as a couple with work colleagues so that you both have an opportunity to benefit from those relationships. Drop by each other's offices occasionally so you can see for yourself some of the office politics that you describe to each other at home. When you get a raise or a promotion at work, celebrate with your mate and express your appreciation for their support. And give your mate a small gift when they're blue about their job or have finally achieved the praise they've long waited for at work.

The more you feel that "we're both in this together," the easier it will be to make your merging of job and marriage harmonious.

PART 4

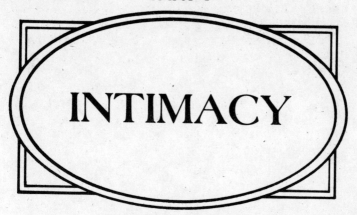

INTIMACY

And I said to myself, This is love.
It is saying, You are the only one,
it could not possibly be any other.

Mary Gordon
Final Payments

SEX

Fears, Fantasies, Frustrations, Fun

For centuries, sex and marriage were synonymous. Sex was *the* reason people got married. Traditionally, marriage was the only context within which the release of sexual feelings was socially permissible and sanctioned. As George Bernard Shaw once wrote: "Marriage is popular because it combines the maximum of temptation with the maximum of opportunity."[1] And in earlier times, sex in marriage also served a utilitarian function. People depended upon children as a necessary source of cheap labor.

Passion, lust, and romance, of course, have always been associated with sex. The wild and wonderful ways in which a man woos his woman and a woman her man are an integral component of ancient literature, poetry, and life. It's true that most poets—from Chaucer and Shakespeare on down the line—focused on the love and physical desire that *draw* lovers together, not on the intimacy and sexual relationship that *keep* them together through years of marriage. For, until recently, married sex was *not* something to be spoken about. It was considered too boring, too private, too sacrosanct, or too taboo.

Attitudes about marital sex, however, have dramatically changed. Couples today don't automatically subscribe to the "love-marriage-baby carriage" philosophy. Many married couples postpone having children or intend to stay childless forever. And others, who want to become parents, have the freedom of bearing children without getting married.

Years ago people married so they could have sex, but today many people feel that by marrying they are *giving up* their sexual freedom. With the widespread social acceptance of premarital or nonmarital sex, it's quite common to lead an active sex life without benefit of a marriage certificate. According to a report by the National Center for Health Statistics,[2] more than three quarters of American women have sexual intercourse before they marry. In our survey the percentage was even higher:

- *85 percent* of our respondents made love with their mate before marriage.
- *54 percent* lived together before marriage.

Given the sexual familiarity with which men and women approach marriage nowadays, it would seem that the sexual aspect of marriage might be less important to them. Yet our findings suggest that contemporary newlyweds are acutely aware of the importance of sex in marriage:

- 40 percent of newlyweds stated that they consider sex to be *very* important in marriage.
- Another 57 percent said they believed sex to be somewhat important in marriage.

Because there is so much publicity in the media and so much emphasis by sex experts on the mutual satisfaction of both sex partners, sex may be on the minds of married couples more than ever before. In fact, one of the legacies of the so-called sexual revolution of the 1960s is that people's standards for sexual satisfaction are probably higher than they once were. In the days when a person's spouse was their first and only sexual partner and nobody revealed what was going on inside their bedroom, no comparisons could be made. But because many newlyweds today have had previous sexual experience— involving both their present and former partners—and have read about the sex exploits of others, they can rate their marital sexual experience with some discrimination. Even brides and grooms who come to marriage as virgins feel the need to live up to certain sexual standards. There is so much talk—on television, on radio, in the movies, and in the streets—about how important sex is, that almost everyone feels *entitled* to a fulfilling sex life.

Believing that sex is highly important in marriage can be a very positive factor in making *your* marriage successful. Sex may add fun, excitement, and closeness to your relationship, and the very awareness of its potential to yield those rewards can lead you to strive to attain them.

The drawback to placing such a great emphasis on sex and to having lots of sex information available, however, is that you may evaluate your sex life against so many criteria—technique, emotional quality, frequency, previous experiences, what other people and the media say about sex—that you may find it difficult not to feel, Maybe we should be doing better than we are.

Twenty-five percent of the newlyweds we surveyed noted that they have sexual problems in their marriage, a remarkably large proportion considering that 85 percent of those surveyed had engaged in intercourse before marriage—and so, we assume, had time to evaluate and adjust to each other sexually. Our guess is that the high expectations people cherish about sex—as well as marriage—are partially responsible for this striking statistic.

Many couples who've engaged in sex before their wedding are also taken aback when they discover that marriage changes their sex life. In our study we found that how often a couple makes love before marriage is no indication of how often they will have sex in their newlywed year.[3] And having sexual problems in marriage has *nothing* to do with whether or not a newlywed lived with their mate before marriage.[4]

Despite the romanticized myth of the newlywed year—that it's filled with sex, sex, sex—many newly married couples find that sex is neither as frequent nor as romantically honeymoon-like as they'd anticipated. Because sex merges the physical and the emotional, it is, for most couples, an extension of their relationship rather than just a separate aspect of it. And so because you will probably experience many emotional changes as you adjust to being a married couple, it's natural that your sexual relationship will reflect some of those vicissitudes of emotion. At times sex may be intensely loving and passionate; at other times you may feel less desire and excitement.

Patterns of who initiates sex, how free or inhibited your sex life is, and how frequently you engage in sex may all be set in your newlywed year. In fact, a study has shown that the best predictor of how often a couple has sex in the second to sixth year of their marriage is how often they had sex in their first year of marriage.[5] We say this not to make you feel pressured, but to motivate you to try early on to understand and resolve sexual anxieties and problems that you may experience, so that you can make sex a fun, fulfilling, comfortable, and enriching part of your marriage—for now and for the years to come.

THE WEDDING NIGHT

Throughout history the wedding night has taken on an almost mythic importance. Traditionally it has represented a rite of passage[6]—at least for the female, for whom the marriage consummation was assumed to mean loss of virginity. It has been laden with ancient symbols, fertility rituals, images of fear, horror, pride, and jubilation.[7]

Many of the people who responded to our survey about looking back on the first year of marriage vividly recalled the anticipation and excitement with which they, as virgins, approached their wedding night. A 63-year-old woman married in 1943 wrote on her questionnaire:

> We had a small wedding and spent our wedding night at the Waldorf-Astoria. Our first real intimate contact was taking a bath together at night—and it was such a thrill to be able to spend the night together! Sleeping together was thrilling enough for the first night! We saved the BIG DEAL for the second night.

The fear and trepidation of having intercourse for the first time were also described by many. One woman revealed that she locked herself in the bathroom and cried for her mother after the wedding. Another wrote:

> We were both inexperienced. My husband was more nervous and maybe not very ready. The first night we tried but nothing happened. After the first few nights I went to the doctor to check if all was okay with me because the marriage had not been consummated. My husband was only 21 years old and was afraid to hurt me. It was very unpleasant for me to go to the doctor. After a while we enjoyed our sex life very much and had no problems.

And a 62-year-old man wrote,

> Our wedding night was our first experience with sex. It was not earth-shattering as in the books. This took time but improved with experience.

Given that the majority of couples sleep together before their wedding, you might think that the buildup to the wedding night generally would be less than momentous. Indeed, for some people it *is* "just more of the same." A 42-year-old psychotherapist who lived with her husband before marriage wrote: "On my wedding night I just felt tired. Sex was the same. I was more relieved than nervous." And a 26-year-old groom, who had lived with his bride for six months before marriage, recalled:

> We got to our hotel room and started counting the checks we were given at the wedding. By the time I finished, she had fallen asleep. It was no big deal.

This blasé attitude, however, does not hold true for most couples:

- *53 percent* of our respondents said they were very or somewhat anxious about their wedding night.

While sex may not be new to them, brides and grooms still want their wedding night to be memorable and special. And for many it is wonderful:

- *44 percent* of newlyweds said that they were *very satisfied* with sex on their wedding night.
- Another *40 percent* said they were *satisfied* with sex on their wedding night.

Apparently, being sexually experienced before marriage enables many brides and grooms to enjoy their wedding night without the terror, panic, and pain suffered by those of previous generations. "Sex was great and definitely different in ways it's hard to explain—more open and intense," commented a 23-year-old suburban woman. And a 29-year-old flight attendant noted that wedding night sex "was the best we'd ever had."

When their wedding night does not meet their magical expectations, people feel hurt, disappointed, and sometimes resentful. One groom, six months after marriage, told us he was still upset because he and his bride spent three hours after their wedding at her parents' house rehashing wedding details. They never got around to making love that night in their hotel room. Even though they had lived together before marrying, he had anticipated that making love on their wedding night would have a special significance.

One bride was so upset that she and her husband had fallen asleep after their wedding without making love, that the next morning, as her husband began to dress for a brunch being held in their honor, she insisted that they *had* to have sex. She reminisced to us:

> With everyone waiting downstairs for us in our hotel it was hardly the best conditions for romance. But I would have felt devastated if we hadn't made love. Even though sex wasn't new to us, it just seemed that as a newly married couple there would be something wrong if we didn't have sex.

Those couples who find that exhaustion and stress prevent wedding night sex from being as wonderful as it is built up to be should not feel upset. In fact, it can be a good idea, especially for couples who have not had sexual intercourse prior to marriage, to wait until they are more relaxed and refreshed. And those who don't engage in intercourse on their wedding night should not feel like failures or oddballs. *Twenty-two percent*—almost a quarter—of those surveyed said they didn't have sexual intercourse on their wedding night. It takes some couples weeks before they actually have intercourse. If you were a virgin before your wedding, don't be surprised if intercourse is disappointing at the beginning. Most people need time to become comfortable with another's sexual needs and desires.

Rather than focus on the sexual experience, you should appreciate the wedding night as your first evening spent as husband and wife. A 25-year-old magazine writer wrote in her questionnaire:

> On our wedding night I felt closer to my husband than ever before. We stayed up for a few hours talking, laughing, going over the day's events, and sipping champagne. We stayed at a very quiet inn in a separate cottage overlooking the water. It was extremely romantic.

What is most important in creating a memorable wedding night is not the sexual act in itself, but sharing your feelings of closeness as you embark on your married life together.

HONEYMOON HOPES AND REALITIES

Originally, the wedding trip was conceived as a time for a couple to be alone—away from family and friends—so that they

could get to know each other and begin their sexual life together. And even today, for brides and grooms who have made
love, vacationed, and lived together previously, the honeymoon
is generally assumed to be a time chiefly for lovemaking. Ten
percent of those who answered our survey said they felt pressured to live up to the traditional image of the romantic honeymoon couple. Many newlyweds did tell us that sex was more
intense, closer, had more a feeling of "oneness" during their
honeymoon than before. Yet others expressed disappointment
that their honeymoon did not live up to their idyllic expectations.

Arnold, a 30-year-old computer programmer, said:

> It's true that my wife and I had dated and slept to-
> gether for three years before our wedding. But I was
> still surprised that my wife jumped out of bed at 7:00
> A.M. each day while we were in Hawaii to go jogging
> on the beach. I wanted her to lounge around with me
> in bed—but she wasn't feeling as romantic as I. I'm
> sure she's as happy to be married as I am, but I wanted
> to play the romantic honeymoon image up more.

Arnold's wife complained to us that she felt guilty on her
honeymoon about wanting to do other activities, besides making
love.

> I felt compelled at some point each day to go back to
> our hotel room to have sex. It just seemed like we
> couldn't have a normal vacation—where some days
> you have sex and other days you don't.

One woman we spoke with, who at age 42 married for the
second time, had delayed her honeymoon for several months
because of business pressures weighing upon her and her 56-
year-old husband. She described their belated trip to Canada
as a "fiasco."

> I had dreams of having romantic interludes in the
> middle of the day. He wasn't up to it. He was worried
> about being away from the business and not having
> any money come in. Every time he feels pressed to
> perform—financially or sexually—he can't do it. If I
> say "Don't worry about it" he gets angrier. I wanted a
> honeymoon, but I should not have pushed it.

The extent to which newlyweds may harbor unrealistic expectations was epitomized by one female nurse who, upon returning from her honeymoon, confided in her gynecologist friend that she and her new husband were having sexual problems. "What's the trouble?" asked her doctor friend with concern. The woman explained that on her honeymoon she and her husband had sex only once a day. The married doctor friend was baffled. "So *what* is the trouble?" he asked again. Well, it seems that before their marriage the newlywed couple had snuck away from their strict parents for one weekend, during which they made love three or four times a day. The woman assumed that that was the pace they would continue after marriage. The doctor explained to her that if she and her husband contined to have sex once a day throughout their marriage, they'd be in *excellent* shape.

As for the newlyweds who hadn't made love with their mates before marriage, we heard a variety of honeymoon recollections. Some were happy to make up for lost time by engaging in as much honeymoon lovemaking as they could find time for. Others felt uncomfortably pressured. A 24-year-old Ohio woman said:

> It's taken me some time to enjoy having sex. My husband and I had both agreed to wait until we married to have intercourse. But once the wedding was over he was gung-ho every second. I tried to slow him down a little.

How you relate sexually during your honeymoon may set a tone for the months to come. In our study we found that newlyweds who reported having a great time on their honeymoon were more likely to feel happy about their marriage in general.[8] It's likely that those honeymooners who enjoy themselves are those who have realistic rather than overly romantic expectations.

Getting off to a good sexual start in marriage involves some practical planning and psychological preparation. Here are some guidelines to keep in mind:

1. Think ahead about what you each expect from your honeymoon, and make plans that suit you mutually. Share your individual fantasies about how you envision your honeymoon.

Talk about where you would like to go, what kind of activities you would like to do, how much time you want to be alone with each other or with other people. You may remember Barbara Dobbs from chapter 3, who thought it was the groom's role to plan the honeymoon but later complained that their trip to Italy was not as she had hoped. Had she and her groom consulted one another about their needs, their honeymoon might have fulfilled the expectations of them both. One bride we interviewed had dreamed of a warm, sunny honeymoon; her groom looked forward to camping with his new wife. They compromised by camping out in the Caribbean.

2. Plan time for relaxation and romance. No matter how eager you may be to go sightseeing or be active in sports on your honeymoon, make sure to schedule free time, to be filled in any way you'd like—whether by lying on the beach, savoring a cocktail in a local bar, or lounging around your hotel room cuddling and reading. Newlyweds who overextended themselves during trips heavy on touring complained to us that they did so much sightseeing that they weren't able to recover from the exhaustion and stress leading up to their wedding.

3. Don't put sexual pressure on yourselves. If you expect nothing but great sex, and lots of it, throughout your honeymoon, you may be setting yourselves up for disappointment. You may feel tired from your wedding or anxious about being married, and putting too much emphasis on honeymoon sex will add stress. You might mention to your mate that sometimes you'd prefer to just hug in bed and talk, rather than engage in lovemaking. Let your spouse know they needn't "perform" to live up to some honeymoon fantasy.

4. Time your honeymoon well. Postpone your honeymoon for another time if the weeks after your wedding are an inconvenient time for you to go away. Why create pressure where there needn't be any?

5. Enjoy your trip. Remember that this is a special vacation, aimed entirely at giving you pleasure. Try to avoid bringing up subjects that are bound to stir conflict—such as the angry feelings you have toward your in-laws. Make an extra effort to defuse conflict by calming your mate or letting a hurtful remark slide off your shoulders rather than respond to it with attack. Remember, you have just one honeymoon together. You'll probably regret it if you use this special time to engage in argument instead of creating happy memories to look back on.

THE SEXUAL DROP-OFF

The first few weeks—and sometimes months—after the honeymoon are often highly sexually charged. The excitement that many couples feel about having made a public commitment of love often carries over and invigorates their sexual bond. The assumption that newlyweds are *supposed* to have frequent sex also prompts some recent brides and grooms to engage in lovemaking more than they otherwise might.

Yet, despite this initial increase in sex, by their first anniversary many newlyweds reported to us a decrease in sexual frequency. In fact, a 1981 study reported that sexual activity is reduced by 50 percent by the end of the first year of marriage for the average American couple.[9] And 46 percent of newlyweds we surveyed noted that they don't have sex as often as they would like.

The facts are that a decrease in sexual frequency is normal and that the sexual high at the beginning of marriage is, if anything, abnormal. Nevertheless, even when both mates are satisfied with the decreased frequency with which they have sex, they're likely to experience underlying doubts about why they are not living up to some imagined sex standard. Such feelings are especially emphasized when there is a discrepancy in sexual desire between spouses. If you have less desire for sex than your spouse, you're likely to feel guilty, confused, inadequate, while your partner feels rejected and concerned that your marriage is going stale.

Bob Mitchell, married for the first time at age 39, voiced his concern to us about the drop-off in his sexual desire. Five months after his wedding he told us:

When I was single there was a fairly constant sexual urge. Now that urgency's gone. If my wife and I had lived together before marriage the same thing would have probably happened. We hug a lot, we cuddle.

While sex is not as important to me as it was, I'm concerned that it's dropped to the level it has—we make love once a week, sometimes less. I'm concerned not for me, but for my wife Molly. I know she needs me to initiate it more. I'm wondering why I'm so content, that I'm not having the urge to jump her like I did.

As Bob continued talking, he cast about for reasons to explain the waning of his sexual drive.

Part of it might be her fault. I'd like her to be a little more sexy. I'll buy her lingerie. She gets a kick out of it, but doesn't wear it much. She usually goes to bed in an old nightgown. Have I mentioned to her that this bothers me? No. I think she would be a little disappointed that she would have to wear sexy lingerie to arouse me. My wife is a gorgeous woman. She's probably the most beautiful woman I've ever seen in my life. Yet she's not a sexpot. She's so wholesome. . . . Much as I hate to admit it, part of the sexual urge when I was single was the challenge. . . . Also, my wife's a little too serious in her lovemaking. I'd like her to laugh more. . . . My unhappiness at work is also gnawing at me. I think that affects my sex drive a lot.

Bob's wife, Molly, in a separate interview, told us that she too was concerned.

Last week I brought it up—that I'd like sex more often. He said that, to his way of thinking, before a man gets married he is lonely, and sex is a substitute for emotional closeness. He says that now he feels calmer, more relaxed in general, as well as about sex. I understand that. And it's not that we're really that far apart in how often we'd like it. It's just that I'd like it once a week in addition to weekend sex. I've spoken with a friend and with two people at work about the frequency of sex in their marriages. They also said that they had sex less often since getting married. I'm worried because I see sex as a very important component in marriage. It brings us closer. It is a special sharing.

Veronica, 25, who had made love with Hank, the man who is now her husband, since they were in high school, confided to us that she felt rejected when Hank wasn't in the mood for sex.

> I worry about him not wanting me. I worry that there is something wrong if he rolls over and goes to sleep. I'm worried that because we know each other for so long that sex will become stale. He hasn't been that responsive lately. I've been concerned when he doesn't want sex. Sex isn't as frequent as I want it. I'm worried about married sex slowing down. I've been sleeping with him since I was seventeen. The longer you know someone— I mean, I can't expect the constant sex that we had in college. Sex is more important to me than to him. I don't think it's been his main concern. He's less aggressive, experimental, adventurous than I am. He gets annoyed if I talk about it. Each time it becomes an issue. Sex is better when we're on vacations.

She attributed what she viewed as her husband's lack of interest in sex to the twenty pounds she'd gained since her wedding.

> If I looked better and felt better about myself, we'd have sex more often, I think. I'd initiate it more and he'd be more attracted. I try to tell him in an inoffensive way that I'd like sex more frequently. When we first lived together we had sex more often. Basically, he's not as interested. I don't mind, really, as long as I know it's not a reflection of me.

It's natural to worry when your sex life becomes less frequent after your wedding. After all, we've been told over and over by experts that a couple's sexual relationship is a barometer of their emotional relationship. In their book *American Couples,*[10] sociologists Pepper Schwartz and Philip Blumstein report that married couples who said they have sex with their spouse infrequently tend to be dissatisfied with their marriages in general. They think, if sex is so important, there must be something wrong if we don't keep up a certain pace.

Yet, as we've already mentioned, a decrease in sexual frequency after marriage is normal. As people feel increasingly secure in marriage, it's common for them to take their mates a little for granted, or to feel more comfortable about refusing sex when they aren't in the mood. After the wedding, some feel less need to prove to their spouses—via sex—that they care about them. They assume that the proof of their love lies in their having married their mate, and in their expressing their devotion in other ways from day to day.

Even gaining weight soon after the wedding, as Veronica did, was not uncommon among our interviewees. An eagerness to settle into domestic life often prompts newlyweds to prepare home-cooked meals or invite friends for dinners, a style that may differ from their fast-food, eat-and-run days as singles. Many people also feel less pressured to diet and keep trim once they are "hitched." As one newly married woman said to us, "The weight that I find acceptable for me now is five pounds more than it was when I was single." Part of this increased self-indulgence may be due to the relief of no longer having to "win" a mate. Some people also assume that once they are married they don't need to be sexy anymore. After all, if your role models for marriage were your parents and you didn't view them as sexy, then your image of your "husband" or "wife" role may not include being or feeling sexy.

One woman noted almost immediately after her wedding a change in her husband's attitude:

> When we dated he always wore bikini underwear. Now he wears boxer shorts, which I find a turnoff. He doesn't seem to care anymore about projecting to me a sexy image. Now he expects me to accept him no matter how he is because he's my husband.

Infatuation does not last forever, and many couples who've lived together undergo this sexual drop-off *before marriage*. Cohabitating couples who have experienced such a change sometimes expect marriage to give them a sexual boost, but disappointedly discover that once the "honeymoon high" is over, their sexual activity has dropped again. Research[11] has shown that unmarried couples who live together have more sex than those who marry, and so getting married to spark one's sex life does not reflect a very realistic expectation.

THE LOSS OF PASSION

According to our survey:

- 22.4 percent of newlywed wives suffer from a lack of sexual desire.
- 11.3 percent of newlywed husbands suffer from a lack of sexual desire.

These findings may seem astounding, since they are of *newlyweds* married on the average *six* months. Whatever happened to those romantic honeymooners who just wanted to spend all day in bed?

The fact is that marriage makes sex more routine. Just think about it. When you dated, you set aside special times to see each other. Before those dates you primped and fussed in preparation. During those dates you probably focused exclusively on each other. And even if you lived together before marriage and the frequency with which you had sex decreased with time, sex may still have had an excitement that dissipated once you made your relationship "legal."

In some cultures, sex is regarded as a duty in marriage. (Remember the famously stoic Victorian advice about sex—"Lie back and think of England"?) But whether or not you consider sex an obligation, once you're married and know that you can make love with your mate anytime, sex may seem less tempting. You tell yourself, "If not today, tomorrow." There is no great urgency.

Accepting that your spouse will be your sole sexual partner for the rest of your life can also feel imprisoning and frightening, especially if you've had many sexual partners before marrying. And if you've been in and out of a series of relationships and are used to intense sexual highs, the loss of novelty and the fading of passion can be particularly depressing and upsetting.

The responsibility that marriage brings also affects sex. In some ways marriage is like a business—it entails innumerable household, financial, and familial responsibilities, any of which can easily infringe on a couple's time together. As you attend to mundane household chores and negotiate domestic decisions—from who does the dishes to where to buy a house —you may find that tensions, conflict, and exhaustion dissipate feelings of infatuation that may have existed before marriage. The day-to-day contact may make you feel closer, more inextricably connected—yet it can also diminish erotic desire. And, as our interviewee Bob Mitchell pointed out earlier, the challenge isn't the same once you're married. You may, like him, feel relieved that "the game is over"—that you no longer have to worry about finding someone with whom to share your life. But with the loss of conquest there is also a dwindling of excitement; with the loss of anxiety, a loss of sexual tension and unpredictability.

According to Denis de Rougemont,[12] author of *Love in the Western World*, a major work on the vicissitudes of passion, passion is antithetical to marriage *precisely because* marriage provides security and stability, while passion thrives on suffering. *"Romance is by its very nature incompatible with marriage even if the one has led to the other, for it is the very essence of romance to thrive on obstacles, delays, separation, and dreams, whereas it is the basic function of marriage daily to reduce and obliterate these obstacles,"* de Rougemont explains.[13] According to his theory, Romeo and Juliet, Heloise and Abelard, Scarlett O'Hara and Rhett Butler —and all other historic and literary lovers separated from each other because of external obstacles—loved so deeply and passionately precisely *because* of their separation. Had those partners been able to live long lives together, he believes, their passion would not have lasted.

Freud offers another interpretation for the loss of sexual passion among spouses. He believed that since every love object reminds us at deeper psychological levels of our parents, a spouse stimulates in us unconscious incest fears, childhood guilt about displacing our parent of the same sex, and fear of retaliation for taking on that parent's role. The mind's "defense" to avoid all that conflict is to diminish one's sexual drive toward those for whom we have affection.[14] In addition, if you suspect that your parents did not have a satisfactory sex life, then you may feel especially guilty or fearful about enjoying sex in your own marriage. You may unconsciously equate your enjoyment with outdoing your parents—which may lead you to feel anxious about stirring their competitive ire, their vengeful desire, or their vulnerability.

As a couple become closer and feel more loving toward

each other, it's not uncommon for them to become uncomfortable with the more aggressive aspects of sex.[15] Bruce, a college teacher married nine months, confided:

> I once made up to my wife Jill after a fight just because I was horny and I wanted to have sex. I felt like such a shit and I didn't enjoy making love. It seemed like such an angry act. I was so disturbed by it that later on I brought it up to Jill. I said, "It's funny that sex can be such an aggressive act." She said, "What do you mean?" I told her what I had done. She was understanding about it. Her niceness is part of why it's so hard for me to be aggressive sexually. But it's true about the classic division—men want their women to be virgins and whores. I'm disappointed in myself that I think that way. Both images are unreal.

The "classic" division Bruce spoke of is often referred to as "the madonna/whore complex." The theory is that men want their women to be loving, caring, virginal, *motherly*—yet they also want them to be sexy, sensual, and showy-looking. Many men, as they become closer emotionally to their wives, find it hard to integrate those two images—just as they may have found it difficult to accept the sexual side of their mothers. Freud felt that sexual desire would therefore flow toward "debased" sexual objects, people with whom one isn't close and upon whom it is easier and safer to project one's sexual fantasies. As he explained it, "Man almost always feels his respect for a woman acting as a restriction on his sexual activity."[16]

As your affectionate love for your spouse deepens, it may become more difficult for you to experience raw sexual passion. Sex with your spouse may have less allure for you because you know him or her so well. If you've had sexual relationships in the past with people you didn't know that well, you may have been able to project onto them exciting fantasies of how you thought they were or how you wanted them to be. But you know your mate's weaknesses as well as their strengths, their annoying habits as well as their best traits. As we'll soon see, there are many benefits to such intimate sexual communication. Nevertheless, it does not have the dramatic and suspenseful quality of sex with a stranger.

THE DEEPER JOYS
OF MARRIED SEX

Despite all the reasons we've noted for the diminution of passion, the closeness, love, and intimacy that marriage bring can easily make up in quality for what is lost in quantity. Although you may no longer feel breathless infatuation toward each other once you're married, the deepening of your bond can enhance your lovemaking. You may discover you have less anxiety, guilt, or insecurity associated with marital sex and therefore feel freer, warmer, and more open about sex. The safety and security that you feel within your marriage can enable you to get in touch with sexual feelings, desires, and fantasies that had been untapped. Sleeping with someone who is almost a stranger may be erotically exciting, even thrilling, but it can leave you feeling lonely and embarrassed in the morning. The wonderful thing about sex with your spouse when you really know each other is that it can be fulfilling on the deepest, most basic, heartfelt level.[17] It can leave you feeling loved, attractive, competent, and happy about yourselves and each other.

A man, married almost a year, commented to us:

> I'm attracted to my wife now with a much greater knowledge of what makes her tick. I'm not deadened to the existence of other women but I'm not looking at them. I'm enjoying sex a lot. It's much more relaxed than before we were married. Sex follows what's going on in the relationship, it doesn't lead. I've had sexual difficulties in the past with other women because of other things that were going on in the relationship. I was saying "I love you" to a woman I didn't love. The love I feel now is making sex better. My wife's much more aggressive sexually. I like her sexual aggressiveness. I'm now responding in kind.

A newlywed woman, who lived with her mate for six months before they married, told us:

> I'm much more able to ask for what I need sexually since we're married. That was very scary to me before. My husband loves newness and discovery. He really *wants* to please me. It's wonderful. I feel much more

satisfied than I did before. We're freer with each other.
His attraction to me makes me more comfortable. I
feel better about my body. I've always felt self-conscious that I need to lose weight. But his desire for me
has made me less unhappy with my weight.

An impressive *58 percent* of newlyweds we surveyed reported that their feelings of sexual attraction toward their spouse
increased since marriage. But even among those whose feelings
of physical attraction toward their spouse lessened, we found
that their growing appreciation and acceptance of their mate
since marriage enabled them to enjoy sex to a greater degree.
Tall, thin, 30-year-old Sybil Stevens is a prime example.
She is married to a man 15 years older than she, who, with his
paunchy physique, is a far cry from the fit, lean men she used
to date.

Physical appearance used to be a big thing for me. My
attitude toward sex was very caught up with that.
Sometimes I still look at my husband and wish he'd
lose twenty pounds. On the other hand, when we're
together there's a real nice communion of thoughts
and feelings. I think there's more concern now. Sex
takes on a different dimension. I think he's more considerate of me for the most part and I don't think I
nag him as much as I did about losing weight. I call
him "Bronto" and express it more playfully. Having
seen him when he weighed a lot less, I know he attracted me more then. I hope he does something about
his weight, but more for his health than for any other
reason. I don't feel that self-conscious about his stom-
ach the way I used to.

In the beginning I'd compare my husband to other
lovers who were more athletic. Now I feel that the
sexual experiences I had before marriage probably
helped me see sex in a different light—it's not all-
important, center stage as if I had no experience. My
previous experience also helped me put a lot of the
guilt and tension about sex away, which my mother
had laid on me.

There is no doubt that when you're married there's less of a sense of mystery. The lack of mystery about him bothers me a little bit because there's nothing like feeling smitten and out of your mind in love. There isn't this gushing sense and that makes me a little sad. It's not the otherworldly excitement that was stirred up in the past. With other people I went out with, their image from across the street excited me more. But now that we're married my husband seems to be more relaxed about being affectionate. He'll just throw his arms around me and say how much he loves me. We have a very nice full sex life because there's a real emotional bond. Sex is an important part now of a larger relationship. He seems to really care that I am sexually satisfied. Occasionally, while we're having sex, it washes over me that this is my husband. There's a lot more tenderness now. We're more playful.

Otto Kernberg, an eminent psychoanalyst,[18] believes that even in long-term relationships people are able to maintain a sense of mystery and excitement. He notes that periodically a person may want to use their spouse *strictly* as an instrument for sexual excitement. "Using" and "being used" by one's spouse sexually, he believes, can lead to periods of maximal sexual excitement. This ability to understand, accept, and collude with your spouse's desire in this regard, he says, is one mark of a strong relationship. Just as occasional attacks of anger and rejection can be tolerated within a strong relationship, so can these sexual excursions be contained within a larger, loving relationship. Like periods of mutual contemplation and discussion, sexual adventurousness can add to the richness of a marriage.

A 27-year-old groom who was a virgin before he married articulated the enrichment that may be reaped from such sexual escapades:

The nice thing is that I feel comfortable trying different things with my wife. She is somebody I could carry out my fantasies with. We saw a movie—*Crimes of Passion*—in which there were a couple of scenes with anal sex. I said to her, "Do you ever think you'd be interested in doing that?" She said, "Yeah, maybe we'll try it sometime."

A major benefit of married sex is that you become comfortable enough with one another to frankly compare your needs and desires, and you care enough to try to fulfill some of each other's wishes. But, as we'll see, there are numerous practical issues that you'll need to address as you adapt your sex life to meet your needs and goals as husband and wife.

CHECKUP: HOW SATISFIED WITH SEX ARE YOU?

In the movie *Annie Hall,* the lovers portrayed by Woody Allen and Diane Keaton are shown on a split screen as they talk to their individual therapists about how often they have sex. She laments, "He wants sex all the time. At least four times a week." He complains that they practically never have sex— "four times a week at most."

How satisfied are you with the frequency with which you and your spouse have sex? who initiates sex? the quality of your sex life? The following questions are aimed at helping you focus on the reasons for any sexual dissatisfaction you may have. For each question, place a check in the "yes" or "no" column, depending which answer is appropriate.

		Yes	No
1.	Do you have sex as often as you'd like? (Be honest. Don't evaluate your sexual desire according to what you think it's *supposed* to be.)	___	___
2.	Are you satisfied with *when* you have sex? (In other words, if you have sex at night, would you really prefer it in the mornings? Would you find it more exciting to have sex a couple of times during the week rather than just on weekends, when it's "too predictable"?)	___	___
3.	Are you happy with the pattern of *who* initiates sex in your marriage?	___	___
4.	Do you feel comfortable approaching your spouse about sex?	___	___

5. Does your spouse initiate sex when he or she is in the mood? —— ——

6. Are you and your spouse comfortable refusing sex when you don't want it? —— ——

7. Are you content with the *way* sex is initiated? (For example, would you prefer it to be more unexpected and spontaneous, or would you like it to be more planned so that you could plan and prepare for it?) —— ——

8. Are you satisfied with the means of birth-control you use? (Is it leaving you feeling nervous about having an unwanted pregnancy? Is it interfering with spontaneous sex?) —— ——

9. Are you satisfied with sex when you have it? —— ——

10. Do you feel confident that you and your mate are setting aside the right amount of time to be alone with each other sexually? —— ——

Now, add up the number of checks you placed in the "yes" column. Then add up the number of checks you placed in the "no" column. The more checks you placed in the "no" column, the more unhappy you probably are about your marital sex relationship. But even if you just checked off one or two "no"s, it's possible that you're very discontented sexually. Sex is a delicate and often vulnerable issue for many people, touching their deepest needs, desires, and expectations. If sex is not living up to your hopes, then you may feel very disappointed.

It would be ideal if you can get your spouse to sit down and answer these questions also. Or if they're not around or don't want to answer "formal" questions, find a time—during a relaxing dinner or over Sunday brunch—when you two can casually discuss your feelings about how your sex schedule is working out. You can start by mentioning that you just read that 46 percent of newlyweds want sex more often. Ask: "Is that something you feel?" Then, find out from your mate how he or she feels about the timing of sex, the *way* sex gets initiated, and *who* initiates sex in your marriage. Remember this is a time to just listen to each other's feelings. Don't attack or accuse each other or be judgmental. Just try to learn what one another's wishes are.

In the following sections we examine the sex problems commonly confronted by couples, focusing on the underlying reasons for those differences and on ways you might find to cope with them.

FINDING TIME FOR SEX

The frequency of sex in marriage is important to some newlyweds[19] because of the expectations they have about how it *should* be. For others it is a matter of actual sexual desire. Regardless of the reason, sexual frequency is a major concern. In our study we found that the more often newlyweds have sex, the happier they feel about their marriage—and the less sex they have, the unhappier they feel about their marriage.

The major reason cited by newlyweds for not having sex as much as they'd like is time—or rather the lack of it. If you and your spouse both work, you may have difficulty fitting sex into your lives together. If you're juggling work schedules, are distracted by job responsibilities, need to attend to household tasks, want to take the time to keep fit, and try to see friends and family—sex may easily get lost among other priorities and become just one more chore.

As one woman explained:

My husband and I work so hard at our jobs. Both of us are distracted by our careers. I'll say, "Gee, it's been three weeks." But it's difficult finding time when we're both relaxed.

Her husband added:

We both have different schedules. She goes to bed earlier and gets up later. I like to read in bed. We're both sort of guilty. When you don't have sex for a while it builds up as work. It feels like it's going to be an effort—with foreplay and everything. Then when we do have sex we rediscover how great it is. Then we say, "Hey, why don't we do this more often?"

If you've lived together before marriage, you may be especially lax about finding time for sex. Said one husband, who'd lived with his wife for four years before they married:

> The novelty wears off after you live together for a while. We see each other more as best friends than as lovers. The former is more important. But lovemaking does add to the intimacy. It's part of why we're together.

The problem of finding time for sex does not get resolved by itself. In February 1983, the *Ladies Home Journal* published the results of a sex survey. Conducted by the magazine, the survey drew the responses of 83,000 women who had been married, for on the average, 12 years. Eighty-three percent of those women said they wished they had more time to make love.

It wasn't until one newlywed woman we interviewed sought the guidance of her minister that she realized her sex life was foundering because she and her husband weren't timing it right.

> I shower at night and by the time I would come out of the shower my husband would be sleeping with all the lights on and a book still in his hand. The minister pointed out to me that it's good for a couple to have a special time for each other and that may mean rearranging our schedule. Now sometimes we have sex after we come home from work—before dinner—rather than right before we go to sleep, when we have no energy left. It's improved immensely. Sex was always good—but now it's better.

It's not just a matter of finding the time for sex, but also *agreeing* with your mate on when is the best time to have sex. One newly married husband related:

> I like to have sex more often than my wife. On occasion when we've gone to bed and I wanted to, she said, "Well, how about in the morning?" I take things literally. I'd wake up at seven and she'd want to sleep. Now when she's not in the mood, she just says, "I really don't feel like it." It doesn't make me happy, but at least I don't anticipate sex and then am disappointed.

When one spouse refuses sex, it's easy for a vicious cycle

to get set up. Let's say a husband initiates sex and his wife refuses. Feeling insulted and rejected, he may stop expressing his sexual desire to his wife, and instead act frustrated and angry. His wife, in turn, becomes irritated by her husband's pouting, insulted by his never initiating sex anymore, and vengefully decides also to hold back from initiating sex. A negative cycle of hurt, withdrawal, irritability, and possibly depression and denial, gets set into motion.[21]

How can you prevent your schedules and other obligations from impinging on your sex life?

Consider the following tactics:

• Schedule sex for prime time. Don't put off having sex until you get into bed after watching late-night television. Your fatigue will make you regard sex as a headache rather than a pleasure. Try making love right when you get home from work, immediately after dinner, in the morning before you leave for your jobs, or even during your lunch break if you can arrange a rendezvous.

• Make appointments to see each other. Some couples find that by circling a "sex date" on their calendars, their sexual anticipation is heightened.

• If you're each the type that doesn't like to feel pinned down, it won't work to plan to have sex every Tuesday night —because that would become a chore and kill the sexual thrill. Instead, just make sure to set aside a special time, or times, each week to devote to each other—time in which you may end up having sex, but you don't have to. Chances are that if you plan for one weeknight as your night for each other—whether to go to a movie, eat dinner out, or cuddle at home in front of the TV—you'll end up feeling closer, more intimate, possibly sexual. The point is that periodically it helps to shut out the rest of the world—so don't talk to friends and family on the phone, don't bring home extra work, don't watch TV alone during that specially reserved time. By focusing exclusively on each other you get back in touch with one another and remember why you fell in love in the first place.

• Make your surroundings conducive for spontaneous sex. If there are certain things that turn you two on, keep them stocked in the house. If you find sex videos provocative, keep some around so you can pop one into the video cassette recorder if the mood strikes. Keep birth control devices and body lotions and creams near the bed so that once sex starts, it doesn't have to be interrupted.

• Be sensitive to the tensions your spouse feels, and discuss with each other when is the best time for *both* of you to have sex. Don't pressure your mate to engage in lovemaking if he or she has other things on their mind. If you feel the need to be close, remember there are other ways of being intimate—hugging, cuddling, holding hands, just being near each other.

• Keep in mind that when you have sex with someone over a long period of time, sex frequency and sex drives have their ups and downs. One study of people married an average of 11 years showed that sexual intercourse had ceased for a definable period—a median of eight weeks—at some point in one third of those eleven-year marriages.[22] So, don't get anxious and unhappy the minute your "sex schedule" isn't as you want. Do, however, try to catch yourselves when you see that you're falling into a rut. When you're going through the "dry" spells, make sure to still keep closely connected to your spouse so that when you're both ready, your lovemaking will be loving, tender, fulfilling.

SEXUAL DYSFUNCTIONS

While lack of time is one reason for a decrease in sexual frequency, another possibility is that you or your spouse are actually avoiding having sex because of problems regarding either sex itself or some other aspect of your relationship.

It can be very difficult sometimes to distinguish the causes of a sexual problem. If you or your spouse, for instance, are experiencing a markedly decreased sexual desire, you may feel very frightened, and at the same time be unaware of the cause of your problem.

Lovemaking is complicated in that it is a physical and emotional interaction. It is intricately bound up with cultural, religious, social, and psychological meanings that can pose obstacles. The fact is that although we often assume that sex is merely a natural, instinctual behavior, it doesn't just happen "naturally" for many people—a fact reflected in our survey, which told us that:

• 25 percent of newlywed wives had difficulty having an orgasm.

- 23 percent of newlywed wives experienced intercourse as painful.
- 13 percent of newlywed husbands suffered from premature ejaculation.
- 5 percent of newlywed husbands had trouble getting an erection.

While those numbers may seem high, they are actually low in comparison to other marriage surveys. For instance, one study of a hundred "happily married couples" reported that 40 percent of those men had either erectile or ejaculatory problems, while 63 percent of the women had either orgasmic or arousal difficulties.[23]

Sexual problems, whether having to do with desire, arousal, or climax, can stem from a number of causes.

Organic disorders can diminish sexual desire and impair sexual performance, and may include:
- a debilitating illness
- a hormonal imbalance
- depression
- medications
- the intake of alcohol or narcotics

Lack of knowledge can lead to unfulfilled sexual needs, through:
- inadequate sexual stimulation
- ignorance of other forms of sexual stimulation besides intercourse
- unfamiliarity with a variety of intercourse positions

Psychological fears or inhibitions may repress a person's sexual needs and desires, and may include:
- fear of sexual failure
- fear of rejection
- guilt about sexual desire
- past sexual trauma (rape, incest)

Marital problems can affect sexual functioning and satisfaction through:
- fear of closeness and intimacy
- marital conflicts and anger
- marital and sexual boredom

Sex experts differentiate between two kinds of sexual difficulties.[24]

Primary sexual problems are those that are clearly sexual and of sufficient severity to cause marital unhappiness. Usually such problems have existed for one or both partners throughout the marriage and often antedate it. In other words, if a husband has always been impotent or always had trouble with premature ejaculation, his condition is considered a primary sexual problem.

Secondary sexual problems are caused by other difficulties in the marital relationship, and usually crop up during a marriage. If a man suddenly becomes impotent or begins to experience premature ejaculation during a marriage, that development is regarded as a secondary sexual problem and is usually assumed to be rooted in other difficulties in the marriage.

According to Harold I. Lief, M.D., and Ellen M. Berman, M.D., of the Marriage Council of Philadelphia, four out of five patients who have sexual problems have them as a consequence of marital conflict, while only one out of five patients has a sex problem that *causes* marital unhappiness.[25]

The way you handle a sexual dysfunction is extremely important for the success of your marriage. A mate who criticizes, compares, or complains about their spouse's sexual dysfunction will increase tensions that can further impair sexual function and lead to emotional problems. Remember, sexual difficulties need not cause marital unhappiness. Twenty-five percent of our respondents noted that they have sexual problems in their marriage, although an overwhelming 92 percent described themselves as feeling happy about their marriages.

Sexual intercourse may be enjoyable and emotionally reassuring even if one or both of you fails to achieve orgasm. Betsey Shaughnessy, a 42-year-old woman we interviewed, whose husband has trouble with premature ejaculation, demonstrated how such a condition need not impinge on a couple's sexual and marriage satisfaction:

> This is my second marriage. I married my first husband when I was very young. I fell in love with his body. He could never relate to the me within, but I thought I could change anything. But I'm a fast-paced, driven woman and he had no desire to make anything of himself. I felt like he was my child, and how can you feel sexual desire for a child. I cared for him, but I never felt the love a woman should feel for a man.

I didn't want him to touch me. I couldn't respond. I didn't know if I was sexual.

After divorcing her first husband, Betsey met her current husband, Kevin, who she says initially was "not my idea of a man physically." Their relationship began as a friendship. "As far as feeling romantic," she recalls, "I felt dead." One night, after a long dinner, they went out to a disco. She leaned over to hear what Kevin said and he kissed her. "He really turned me on," she says. They went to a hotel and started to make love. Kevin was impotent.

They'd been married almost a year when Betsey reported:

Kevin still has problems in that department. He's not able to sustain intercourse. I had to adapt. We had to resort to oral sex. Kevin always satisfies me. He's released inhibitions in me. With my first husband I would never do and be done to the things I do with Kevin.

It's a very comfortable relationship with Kevin. He's not the kind I would have gone for. He's short. Yet this man has the key. There was a matter of looking in each other's eyes and seeing each other's soul.

Kevin worries that he's not giving me enough sex. I try to initiate sex with him every four days, which is a lot by his standards. He says he needs time to recoup. Sure, I would love to make love every night. But with my first husband sex was mechanical. Kevin's made me feel like a full human being—because I know he cares for the real Betsey.

Everyone experiences sexual difficulties on occasion. The severity of a sexual problem has to do with its extent and how it interferes with a marital relationship. The following story demonstrates the danger of not addressing a sexual problem in marriage.

When Camille and Ted Nysinski married, they were both 24 and had known each other for a year. They had met as law students at a Texan university and started sleeping together almost immediately. For months their sex life was passionate, fun, adventurous, and frequent, although when they started living together, four months before their wedding, there was some decrease in frequency and intensity.

But one month into marriage their sex life changed radically. Camille suddenly felt no energy or desire for sex. She began going to bed before or after Ted to avoid a sexual confrontation. Ted tried to talk to Camille about her avoidance, but she shut him off.

> It was so painful I couldn't admit my true feelings. I didn't feel attracted to Ted or want sex anymore, but I didn't know why.

Prior to their wedding Camille and Ted had sex between two and three times a week, but by the fourth month of marriage they were making love about once a month. Although the rest of their relationship seemed pretty much intact—they still enjoyed talking about law and agreed on most household and financial issues—Camille sensed that something was wrong.

> It felt like we were more siblings than lovers. We were good companions, but it didn't feel erotic.

In December, six months after her June wedding, Camille took a job at family court. At her office Christmas party—which Ted could not attend—Camille danced with an attractive, attentive court officer, Mike, with whom she worked. As she was leaving the party, Mike grabbed her and kissed her on the lips. She pulled away and ran toward her car. But for weeks Camille thought back to that arousing kiss and fantasized about being in bed with Mike. She flirted with him at work, while at home she was completely unresponsive with Ted.

Several months passed, and Camille's sex fantasies about Mike continued. She reasoned to herself that if she was not attracted to her husband, yet was turned on by another man, she must have made a mistake by marrying Ted. In April she asked Ted for a separation.

It should be clear from reading Camille and Ted's story that they have a serious sexual problem. An occasional or temporary lack of sexual desire is normal. A total lack of sexual desire is not. Unfortunately, Camille did little to explore the reasons for her problem, choosing instead to just react. Essentially, she sought sexual satisfaction elsewhere and gave up on her marriage to Ted. It was only after leaving Ted and entering therapy that Camille began to understand some of what she had experienced.

She explained to us:

> Sex was always something I had thought of doing with a "forbidden stranger." During most of my college career I had sex with guys I met at parties and really didn't know that well. I always used sex as a way of "getting" a man. When I was going out with Ted I concentrated on pleasing him. But when I married and felt secure in the relationship, I felt I didn't have to please him sexually anymore.

With both Camille and Ted working long hours at their law offices, their sexual problems intensified, since each felt distracted and pressured by work. The fact that as far as she could see, Camille's parents had no sexual relationship as she was growing up—they had been sleeping in separate bedrooms since she was ten years old—also impacted upon her sexual expectations of marriage. "The idea I got from my parents is that marrige is nonsexual and unexciting," she says.

Had Camille chosen to recognize her problem earlier and had she sought professional guidance without delay, she and Ted may very well have worked out their problems. She might have seen that it wasn't Ted she was reacting to, but rather her own unconscious negative feelings about marital sex.

Becoming aware of your problem and understanding the nature of it may sound trivial, but it is not. For many couples any semblance of dissatisfaction with sex may be so disconcerting that they may try to deny that the problem exists. Someone who is dissatisfied sexually may fear that there is something wrong with him or her, or they may fear their spouse's response if they told them how they really felt. Also, if a sex problem is really a manifestation of some other problem in your relationship, you may avoid wanting to confront your underlying difficulty (for instance, anger at your mate).

Also, psychological factors that may inhibit one's sexual drive—for example, guilt over having pleasure—can be easily disguised and difficult to understand. A person may, deep within, be vaguely aware—perhaps only at the time of the sexual act —of feeling dissatisfaction. Because the awareness is only fleeting, by the end of the act he or she may be saying that sex was wonderful.

1. Diagnosis: If you sense there is a problem, try to figure out whether it is:

- technical: having to do with sexual habits, preferences, or knowledge
- individual: having to do with your family history or your spouse's, or with personal attitudes, or hang-ups, about sex
- couple-related: having to do with other emotional conflicts between the two of you

2. Education: The more informed you are about the human body and sex techniques, the more ways you will find to make sex pleasurable. For instance, if intercourse is a problem, you should find out about alternative ways of having sex without penetration. If you feel a lesser sexual desire, you can learn about arousing yourself in advance of lovemaking by reading sexy books, stimulating yourself, or fantasizing.

There are numerous resources to turn to in order to learn about the varied ways you can deal with your sex problems and find out about different pleasuring methods. In many major bookstores you will find a large selection of sex manuals to choose from. Also, the Sex Information and Education Council of the United States is an information service devoted to all topics of human sexuality. They publish a bimonthly journal and consumer pamphlets, and can be contacted by phoning (212) 673-3850 or writing to 715 Broadway, New York, NY 10003.

3. Patience: Be aware that marriage does change a couple's sex life and that any sexual problems arising during the newlywed year may be a normal postmarital syndrome. If you're a woman who is new to sex and having trouble experiencing orgasm, you should try to relax and not put undue pressure on yourself. Talk to your spouse about experimenting with different positions, other forms of lovemaking, using lotions, and enjoying more foreplay. Rather than be upset by your difficulty, why not be adventurous and creative in meeting the challenge?

The same holds true if you're a man who is having trouble getting an erection or who ejaculates prematurely. Try different forms of stimulation, different intercourse positions. Many therapists advise that when a couple is having trouble having intercourse, they should spend two or three weeks not having intercourse at all, and instead concentrate on pleasuring themselves in other ways.

4. *Compassion:* Don't become angry with each other because sex isn't working perfectly. Enjoy sex any way you can. Sex should not be a goal-oriented activity, but rather a physical way of expressing your love. If intercourse is not satisfying or becomes too anxiety-provoking, then just concentrate on pleasuring each other by lying in each other's arms and caressing each other's bodies. Don't worry about what the rest of the newlyweds in the world are supposed to be doing.

5. *Counseling:* If your problem persists and is having a stressful effect on your marriage, then seek help. Your first step should be to go to your medical doctor to see whether there is something physically wrong with you. As we mentioned before, some sexual problems, like chronic impotence, stem from organic disorders and can be treated (for instance, with a penile implant).

Once you find out that there is nothing physically wrong with you, consult a competent sex therapist. (In chapter 12 we enumerate the different approaches of practicing therapists and tell how you can find a well-qualified expert.)

A good sex therapist will evaluate exactly what kind of treatment is appropriate for you. Someone who is consumed by sexual guilt because of childhood prohibitions may discover that support and encouragement by a therapist may be sufficient to relieve their sexual anxiety. A couple experiencing a lack of sexual desire may find that their problem lies in their not allowing themselves enough time for intimacy or foreplay. In the latter case many sex therapists would prescribe what they call "sensate-focus exercises," which entail caressing each other from head to toe without even trying to have intercourse.

William H. Masters and Virginia E. Johnson, pioneers in the field of sex therapy, revolutionized treatment by combining psychotherapy with mechanical techniques. They estimate that cure rates for sexual problems range from 60 to 100 percent, with an average cure rate of 80 percent five years after treatment has ended.[26] Their treatment, however, is more intense than most, since it involves staying in a hotel for the weekend —in St. Louis, where Masters and Johnson work—to practice the communication and sensual exercises without disruption. Most sex therapists see patients on a weekly or biweekly basis for about 15 sessions.

It is essential to find someone well qualified to treat a sex problem. A well-trained therapist will screen potential clients and reject those who have very serious psychiatric problems and those whose marital relationships must be treated before their sexual difficulties are dealt with. Don't think that by "curing" your sexual problems you can banish all other marital and personal troubles.

SEXUAL INCOMPATIBILITIES

You may find that the sexual problems in your marriage have less to do with dysfunction than mere incompatibility. One study found that even among couples who seek sex therapy, more are concerned with interpersonal difficulties than specific sexual dysfunctions.[27]

For many people the sexual act is surprisingly regimented—they like to have it at a certain time of day, in a certain place, using certain positions and certain fantasies. Problems arise when one spouse has even slightly different notions of what the ritual should include. Most couples find compromises, with each spouse trying to meet the other's sexual needs. But when one spouse feels even slightly cheated—giving but not getting—feelings of frustration, hurt, and anger grow. Some people are able to ask for what they want sexually, yet others either don't feel comfortable voicing their sexual needs and desires, voice those needs angrily, or don't think they should have to articulate those feelings. Their attitude is that "my mate should know what I want." The truth is that no one is a mind reader, and so it's unfair to attack your mate for not providing something you never asked for. Nevertheless, in those instances your relationship can quickly deteriorate into a tit-for-tat situation. Before you realize it, your sexual satisfaction and frequency have dropped off and neither of you really knows why.

A great many kinds of sexual incompatibilities can emerge over the newlywed year. In our survey we found that:

- 37 percent of newlyweds said they'd like their sexual relationship to be more open and adventurous.
- 31 percent said they want sex to be more intimate and tender.

A common disagreement is about who should initiate sex. People who feel a need to be in control like to initiate sex; others have the desire to be "taken" by their mate and want to play a more passive role. In *American Couples,* Blumstein and Schwartz report that couples who can initiate and refuse sex with equal ease are more satisfied with their sex life. It makes sense that people who have sex when they want it and don't have sex when they don't want it are more content with their sex life.

A frequent complaint made to us by women was that they want their husbands to devote more time to foreplay. There is a physiological basis to their lament, since because of their biology women need more time to become aroused.

In general, men and women have different attitudes toward sex. Men can come home from work and say, "Let's have sex," while their wives often are eager to talk for a while about the day before they leap into bed. It's quite common for men to use sex to *create* intimacy, and for women to want to *foster* a sense of intimacy—often by sharing their thoughts and feelings with their mate—before engaging in sex.

Some incompatibilities have less to do with the sex act itself than with things surrounding sex. One woman complained to us that she wanted sex to be more spontaneous—she had a vision of her husband sweeping her off her feet at some unexpected moment and carrying her to the bedroom. Instead, they predictably make love every Saturday and Sunday morning. Another woman said:

I get upset because after we make love he holds me but he doesn't say anything. He doesn't say, "Gee that was really nice" or anything like that. He is affectionate, but he doesn't verbalize. That's just the way he is. He says he likes it as a quiet time. I feel cut off and distant from him when he's quiet at that time.

There were husbands who complained to us that they wished their wives were more imaginative in bed, and others who mentioned small details like wanting to have sex with the light on while their mate demanded that the lights be off.

The security and familiarity that comes in marriage may bring out secret sexual wishes, hidden sexual expectations, and surprising sexual idiosyncrasies. In marriage many guards come down—and nowhere is this seen more than in the bedroom. A newlywed who discovers that their spouse wants to tie them up during sex or install mirrors over their bed to enhance love-making may be surprised, elated, or disgusted.[28]

Whatever your sexual differences—and there are bound to be some—you may find yourself fantasizing about a mate with whom sex would be "perfect."

SEXUAL FANTASIES

Fantasizing is normal. Daniel Barlow, director of the Sexuality Research Program at the State University of New York in Albany,[29] reports that the averge person fantasizes six or seven times a day and some people have up to forty sexual fantasies a day.

Among our survey respondents:

- 86 percent of newlyweds reported having sexual fantasies about their spouse.
- 50 percent reported having sexual fantasies about someone other than their spouse.
- Less than 1 percent felt bothered by the sexual fantasies they have about their spouse.
- 25 percent felt bothered by the sexual fantasies they have about people other than their spouse.

Men seem to be more likely than women, or at least admit it more readily, to have fantasies about people other than their mate.[30] But in fact it is highly unlikely that there is any married person who has never had an adulterous thought or a kinky sex fantasy. Unfortunately, however, newlyweds are threatened by their adulterous fantasies—and often mistake them as a sign of trouble in their marriage. A 23-year-old recent bride told us:

> I'm having fantasies about other guys since we're married—about flirting. Once you're married you can't play dilettante as you did when you were single. Sometimes I become entranced with the idea of having a fling—but I know it's not worth it and I would never do it.

The extent to which such fantasies are common is evidenced in research of the Masters and Johnson Institute[31] showing that the most common fantasy among heterosexual men and women involves the replacement of their partners. According to their study, the second most common fantasy among heterosexual men and women involves forced sexual encounters with members of the opposite sex, and the third most frequent one involves observing sexual activity. A quarter of the fantasies of heterosexuals involve sexual variations, such as homosexual, sadomasochistic, or group sex.

Psychoanalytic exploration of fantasies reveals that they are a key to a person's inner drives, wishes, and desires, as well as to their fears and sense of prohibition. They are a compromise between what one wants and what one can allow oneself to have. Sexual fantasies may also represent other issues, such as power or dependency. Having violent sexual fantasies does not necessarily suggest that someone wants to be raped, yet it may indicate that the person has guilt feelings about enjoying sex and can only give themselves permission to enjoy it by creating a coercive element.

There are many roles that fantasy can play in a marriage, many of which are very positive.

Fantasies can bring spouses together. Some couples share their fantasies, carry out fantasies together, laugh about their fantasies. The image of making love in the bathtub enters one spouse's mind, he or she checks it out with their mate, and soon they are both having the time of their lives caressing each other's bodies in the confining space of their bathtub. Fantasies can help sex flourish, yet it often takes a long time before couples feel sufficiently secure and comfortable with each other to release their inhibitions.

Fantasies can be used to increase sexual desire. If you're finding it difficult to become aroused, a fantasy may spark your excitement and then send you back, with a revitalized energy, to focusing on your lovemaking. Sex therapists refer to this technique as using fantasies as a transition.

Fantasies offer clues to a person's sexual needs and desires. They provide hints about what is missing in one's lovemaking or in one's marriage. So if someone fantasizes about making love with someone who is admiring of their body, they may want less criticism and more acceptance from their spouse. A spouse who continually fantasizes about a former lover may be afraid of having too much intimacy in their marriage. They are using their fantasies to create some distance. Or, it may be that their former lover was more adventurous or experimental or tender in bed and they miss that aspect of their previous lovemaking.

What should you do if you find yourself disturbed by your sexual fantasies?

• Remember that there is a difference between fantasy and reality. Thinking about making love with someone else is not tantamount to doing it. Don't automatically think that there is a natural sequence so that what you think today you'll be doing tomorrow.

• Don't worry about your mate's reaction to your fantasies. The only way your spouse will know what your fantasies are is if you reveal them. Most newlyweds told us that they didn't share their sexual fantasies with their mate. As one woman wisely wrote to us:

> I don't tell him my fantasies because no one will ever know all of my thoughts and desires. Fantasies are healthy and what I'm not telling him is of no detriment to our relationship.

Before confiding in your spouse about your fantasy, think about the effect it might have. Would your spouse be hurt or insulted? Fantasies should probably be shared only if they can benefit the relationship.

• Think about what your fantasies signify, rather than rush to the conclusion that you have made the wrong marital choice or that something is wrong with you. Spouses who find themselves having continual sexual fantasies during the day may not be having sex as frequently at home as they really need. A sexual fantasy usually offers a clue to what is missing in your life—it may be that you need sex to be more exotic and thrilling, or you need to feel more loved, or you want to be "taken" rather than be the one in control. Try to learn from your fantasies by implementing those elements that are desirable (avoiding, obviously, any violent and dangerous aspects).

• If you frequently fantasize about having sex with someone other than your spouse, try this exercise: Next time you have a fantasy carry it out to the finish. Don't just stop at the kissing part or the caressing scene, but go through the entire sexual act in your mind until you imagine yourself finished and lying next to that person. Then, see how you feel. Is that really who you'd rather be with? Chances are it's not the *person* that you want—but there's some appealing aspect to that fantasy. Try to figure out what it is.

• What if you have no sexual fantasies? Don't worry. There is nothing wrong with you. Some people fantasize more than others. And if you are busy with work or have other distractions, it's common not to be sexually preoccupied.

If you find yourself needing or wanting to act out your fantasies in a way you think is "perverted" or possibly dangerous, then you should seek the help of a psychotherapist to assist you in expanding your capacities for safe sexual enjoyment.[32]

SEXUAL JEALOUSY

Fantasies about being sexually involved with someone other than one's spouse can be disturbing enough. But having fearful fantasies about one's spouse engaging in sex with other partners is even more unsettling. Most newlyweds we interviewed reported that they did not experience feelings of sexual jealousy. Yet those who did express to us such emotions demonstrated just how heart-wrenching and painful they can be.

Roseanna Harlow, 26, who recently married Jerry after living with him for seven years, said:

When we were in college together, Jerry had affairs and I found out. He hasn't had any since we've been living together in Boston as far as I know. But I worry

more about it since being married. I feel I have more
to lose. Jerry's extremely good-looking. He was once
asked to be a model. I've always felt that we've never
been quite evenly matched. I like it that he's so good-
looking but I'm scared of it. I feel insecure about my
looks anyway. I've always felt, "What is he seeing in
me?" It's probably the worst problem in our marriage
because it's all coming from me. He can't do anything
about it.

I have nightmares about him having affairs all the
time. I wake up very upset. I kick him in the morning
in bed because I dream that I found out he's been
unfaithful. I have these nightmares four or five times
a week. It's the betrayal that I couldn't bear. Marriage
on the one hand is a great protection. On the other
hand, it scares me.

It's been noted in psychiatric literature that spouses who
are jealous—without having any specific reason to be—sometimes had a parent who had been unfaithful to the other parent.[33] As Roseanna talked with us, she related a childhood
memory.

When I was six I heard my parents fight. Somehow I
picked up that my mother thought my father was paying too much attention to another woman, his secretary. Ever since then, I always thought he had an affair
with that secretary. Last week I was at my parents'
house. We were in the kitchen and I asked my mother
if my father had an affair with that woman. Both my
parents laughed. It turns out my father had gotten too
involved with his secretary's personal problems and my
mother was resentful. They were amazed that I remembered the incident. But it's one of the only times
I remember them fighting. They were talking behind
closed doors in the dining room. And I was very protective of my mother because we were very close.

As a child at a vulnerable age, Roseanna had obviously
been deeply affected by the memory of her mother feeling
displaced by another woman. And though now, as an adult, she
has learned from her parents that such cheating had never

actually taken place, it's difficult for Roseanna to nullify the impact that memory has left on her psyche. And it's quite possible that her decision to marry a man who is so attractive—and tempting for other women—may have been an unconscious move to reenact the pattern of betrayal she thought had taken place in her parents' marriage.

Sexual jealousy may also stem from a more recent experience of betrayal. One newly married husband we know has continually accused his wife of cheating on him. In an earlier marriage he'd discovered his wife in bed with another man, and he gets anxious whenever his current wife comes home late from work. Somehow he can't get the idea out of his mind that he can just rely on her—that she is as faithful to him as she says.

Freud noted that a spouse is often jealous because they project onto their mate their own infidelitous thoughts. "It is a matter of everyday experience that fidelity, especially that degree of it required in marriage, is only maintained in the face of continued temptation. Anyone who denies these temptations in himself will nonetheless feel their presence so strongly that he will be glad enough to make use of an unconscious mechanism to alleviate his situation. He can obtain this alleviation and indeed, acquittal by his conscience—if he projects his own impulses to faithlessness onto the partner to whom he owes faith. . . . The subject can justify himself with the reflection that the other is probably not much better than he is himself."[34]

Unfortunately, jealousy can be very difficult to control. For many people it seems almost an involuntary reaction. Even more unfortunately it can have a very harmful, divisive effect on a marriage. According to Jerry, Roseanna's husband:

Roseanna drives me crazy with her jealousy. She just gave me a book, *How to Live the Rest of Your Life Sleeping with the Same Woman*. She calls me a flirt. And I do think about it. I have a hard time being loyal. But I fight it and am proud of myself. I think that if I had an affair with another woman it would destroy our marriage. Her jealousy makes me be secretive about things that I shouldn't be. I have a lot of women friends and she never trusts it. It's easier for me to tell her that I was out for drinks with a guy than with a woman

I work with. I'd rather not have to go through a whole rigmarole to assure her. I can't stand it. If she stopped being jealous it would be a major change in our relationship. I thought getting married would change it— that it would be an affirmation of the commitment I have for her. But it didn't. She says I'm a flirt and that I'll never change. It's true that now that I'm married it's become a challenge for me to see if other women are interested. Where I work there's a macho atmosphere. It's a male-bonding, a street mentality. She knows that's the attitude, and it bothers her about my work.

Frequently as a couple becomes closer and their trust grows stronger, incidents of cheating that took place early on in their relationship are forgotten, or at least forgiven. One woman, who early in her marriage was still upset about an affair her spouse had several years earlier, told us right before her first anniversary that the hurt had faded from memory.

I used to fantasize about all the terrible things I'd tell that woman if I met her on the street. But now I don't feel that way. She's a part of the past. It's my husband and I now. She has no place in our lives.

Flirtation with others may actually serve a purpose in marriage—as a safety valve against infidelity, according to Freud. "Social conventions have wisely taken this universal state of things into account, by granting a certain amount of latitude to the married woman's craving to attract and to the married man's thrust to make conquest in the expectation this inevitable tendency to unfaithfulness will thus find a safety valve and be rendered innocuous," he wrote.[35] By flirting—by playing the role of coquette or playboy—you are essentially testing your ability to attract and trying to enjoy some flattery. Ideally, spouses can accept innocuous attempts at flirtation and, in fact, channel the excitement generated from them into their marriage.

For some people, however, it's extremely difficult to get jealous fantasies out of their mind. Some newlyweds are consumed by thoughts about their spouse's past lovers, others harp on any potential future lovers their mate may find. The reasons why someone suffers feelings of jealousy when there is no direct cause can be very complex. Previous experiences of betrayal, a lack of self-confidence, a fear of abandonment all may contribute. When we spoke with Roseanna, right after she celebrated her first anniversary, she told us she planned on seeing a therapist. She realized that her excessive feelings of jealousy were making her miserable and coming between her and Jerry. If months pass and jealous feelings continue, it's advisable to seek professional guidance.

SEXUAL INFIDELITY

Sometimes, of course, jealous thoughts are founded in reality. Seven people—2 percent of our survey respondents—reported that they have had extramarital affairs since their marriage. The number may sound small, but considering that we surveyed a self-selected group of newlyweds and their incidents of adultery are probably underreported, our findings suggest that sexual infidelity is still an issue even in the earliest, honeymoon stage of marriage. While adultery may be the farthest thing from most newlyweds' minds, research shows that it's not as much of an impossibility in one's marriage as one might like to believe. It was estimated by Kinsey and his colleagues over 25 years ago that half of married men and a quarter of married women had affairs.[36] Much more recently, in her 1981 book entitled *The Cosmo Report*,[37] author Linda Wolfe found that *69 percent* of the 106,000 women she surveyed over the age of 34 had had an affair since being married.

One psychological explanation offered for the tendency of some people toward infidelity is the effect of growing up with more than one love object. For instance, if you're a male who grew up with a mother and a sister as primary love objects, or a female who grew up with several brothers, you may find yourself forever desiring two or more different types of lovers. One married woman who was beginning an affair noted that she always had three or four boyfriends at the same time. Having been the youngest sister of four admired and exciting brothers, she finds herself driven to re-create in her adult love life the male attention and adoration she enjoyed from her brothers in her childhood. Her impulse to run to other men, however, is usually only stirred when she feels unloved or enraged by her husband.

There are various rationalizations an individual may offer for having an affair—"It's purely a sexual thing" and "It doesn't interfere with my marriage" are typical comments. An affair may actually serve to stabilize a marriage.[38] A husband who is bored sexually by his wife but satisfied by his lover may enjoy an adulterous excitement that sustains his marriage, while he unconsciously projects onto his wife his guilt and anger toward his oedipal mother. But infidelity is always a sign of something missing from a marriage.

There are numerous reasons that a person may have an affair.[39] These reasons, we think, are usually related to any of five different issues:

1. A quest for intimacy
   - a fear of intimacy in one's marriage and a desire to create distance from one's spouse
   - a desire for an intimacy missing from one's marriage
2. An outlet of aggression
   - an out-and-out hostile attack on one's partner
   - a desire to talk to someone who is not cast in a critical role (meaning a recipient of one's superego projections)
3. Narcissistic fears
   - a desire to relive one's youth and the excitement of one's days as a single (to ward off fears of aging—the so-called "midlife crisis")
   - a desire for novelty when boredom has set into marriage
   - a yearning to play a new role in a relationship and show another side of one's self[40]
4. Oedipal fears
   - an inability to enjoy a full sexual relationship with one's spouse because of the need to debase one's sexual partner[41]
5. Fears of bisexuality
   - a desire to assert one's manhood or femininity as a way of warding off homosexual fears (seen in the "Don Juan" syndrome in males, and in frequent, usually multiple submissive relationships in females)[42]

If you are having or considering having an extramarital affair, you should step back and take a serious look at what you are doing—to yourself, to your spouse, to your marriage. No matter how harmless you may convince yourself an adulterous affair may be, it is not harmless. It can cause excruciating pain and anguish. If you're engaged in extramarital sex or are thinking about doing so, ask yourself:

- What is missing from my marriage that I'm seeking sex elsewhere?
- Is there something that I can't face about my spouse or myself that I'm trying to deny?
- Am I unconsciously trying to sabotage my marriage?
- Am I uncomfortable with having sex with my mate now that we're married?

It has been written that marital infidelity "is not a sign of liberty and potency but of the opposite."[43] The reasons someone pursues extramarital relationships are psychologically complex and deeply rooted. If you as a newlywed are involved in extramarital affairs, seek professional help before you get so deeply entangled in an extramarital life that it destroys your marriage.

WORKSHOP: INGREDIENTS OF GOOD MARRIED SEX

The goal, of course, is to have such a happy marriage and sex life that sexual infidelity is never an issue. And ultimately the key to a fulfilling sex life is being in a marriage that is loving and open enough to encourage both spouses to express their physical and emotional needs. Nevertheless, there are also practical steps you can take to enhance the role of sex in your marriage:

1. Make sex a priority. Decide that sex is essential to your marriage. Make appointments to meet in bed. Don't put off having sex because other things are more important. You can talk to your friend another time or read that great book tomorrow.

2. Compliment your spouse. Tell them you love them, need them, respect them, can't live without them. Sex flourishes when love and positive feelings are reinforced and secure. Stroking, not stinging, pays dividends. No one objects to being helped to feel sexy, wanted, desirable.

3. Pretend you're still dating. Instead of meeting at home before going out, stop by each other's office and bring flowers. Dress up before meeting, splash on a favorite fragrance. Be considerate of each other the way you used to be. Don't lapse into slothful or otherwise unattractive habits. Remember the way you used to try to impress each other? Do it again.

4. Be romantic. Take a bubble bath together. Prepare a glass of wine or tea before your mate comes home. Buy him or her something sexy to wear to bed. Buy a bouquet of fresh flowers to display in the bedroom. Light a scented candle near your bed. Help build a mood for romance.

5. Communicate—don't complain—about sex. Sex is usually the most difficult subject for couples to talk about, because doing so reveals so much about who we are and how we feel toward our partner, and so can feel very embarrassing. If you say you'd like your spouse to be more aggressive sexually, what you're really saying is that you want to be able to be passive during sex, a desire that is very normal but can feel very frightening to you. Similarly, if you say you want your spouse to be more verbal and affectionate during sex, you're also indicating your own need for reassurance and reinforcement. Talking about sex can be either very harmful or very helpful to a relationship—and it all depends upon how it's done. Here are some pointers to make each other feel comfortable in talking about sex:

- Give positive feedback—before, during, and after sex.
- *Show* your mate what you like, if you think that will be easier and less embarrassing than describing it.
- Listen to your spouse's ideas and convey which ones you'd like to try.
- Don't talk about your sexual dissatisfaction *while* you're having sex. We're all very vulnerable when it comes to our sexual performance.
- Do talk about ways to improve lovemaking only at times when you're both feeling comfortable—not when you're anxious, or pressed for time.
- Use tact, and never make accusations when you suggest changes for your sexual relationship. (Example: Don't shout, "You're always so selfish in bed!")

- Turn suggestions into questions. (Example: "Wouldn't it be fun to spend a half hour just exploring each other's bodies without having intercourse?")
- Don't hammer your point in. Sometimes a mere suggestion or hint is sufficient for your partner to get the idea.
- Be suggestive rather than direct if that is more effective. (Example: Call your mate at work and say, "Let's plan something special for tonight—for just us," to give the idea that you're in the mood for lovemaking.)

6. Break the routine. Change the pace with variety of time, place, technique. Surprise your partner by initiating lovemaking in the living room, by suggesting you set up a tent in your backyard and have sex outside, by reading an erotic story aloud to your partner before going to sleep. If you usually wear pajamas, forgo those pajamas and slip into bed nude. Think of things to do to arouse your partner and enhance your lovemaking.

7. Keep a perspective. Remember that sex is just one part of your relationship. Working to better your relationship in other areas will benefit your sex life also. If you're upset about sexual problems, focus on the positive aspects of your marriage. The closer you both feel to each other, the easier it will be to share your sexual needs and desires.

INTIMACY

Nurturing Hopes of Love and Closeness

More than any other word, *togetherness* captures what marriage is supposed to be about.

Some people come to marriage joyously embracing togetherness, others fearing it. Some can't get enough of it. And others find any amount too much.

Intimacy not only means different things to different people, but it can unleash emotions that may never have been aroused with such intensity. On the one hand, the familiarity that develops between husband and wife offers a sense of comfort, ease, and relief. On the other hand, it brings to the surface feelings of dependency, jealousy, competition, anger, love, and even hate—feelings that are unsettling, frightening, or threatening.

Resolving how far or how close to be from each other is a very subtle but very powerful issue in a couple's life. Different people have different notions about how much closeness marriage should entail. Some have been stung in the past and so erect invisible barriers to protect themselves from getting hurt again; some have never felt loved by anybody and yearn for confirmation that they are lovable; some have felt so suffocated in stifling relationships that they can't tolerate feeling too close with anyone.

Among our survey respondents, 31 percent noted that they would like sex to be more intimate and tender. For many newlyweds, that desire for love and closeness extends beyond the bedroom. But the truth is that distance is inevitable in any relationship. Marriage may be a union—but it is a union of two separate people—not a melting together of two individuals into one. Poet Rainer Maria Rilke noted the beauty that can emerge when a couple appreciates the separation between them. "Once the realization is accepted, that even between the *closest* human beings, infinite distances continue to exist, a wonderful living side by side can grow up, if they succeed in loving the distance between them which makes it possible for each to see the other whole and against a wide sky!"[1]

As we've seen, underlying many of the issues which newly-weds confront—whether having to do with sex, money, power, household, or communication—is a conflict spouses feel between wanting closeness *and* distance, connectedness *and* separation, dependency *and* autonomy. It is only by examining your deepest needs and wishes regarding intimacy that you will be able to come to terms with many of the other issues in your marriage.

INTIMACY ATTITUDES

You may remember Barbara Dobbs, whom we introduced in chapter 3, as the woman who returned from her honeymoon extremely disappointed and annoyed to discover her husband Ned's nervous habits. But when we met with her several months later it was clear her unhappiness extended beyond those concerns. She told us that she was considering getting an annulment. The problem? "I feel like I've never been lonelier," she told us. Ned's view of things? "I feel like I've never been happier," he said. The issue to be resolved: Barbara, 30, and Ned 39, have entirely different expectations, needs, and styles regarding intimacy. Their story, while more dramatic than most, illustrates the contrasting vantage points from which spouses may approach marriage.

In an attempt to describe the reasons for her dissatisfaction, Barbara explained to us during her lunch break:

> Before we were married, Ned used to smile when I talked to him and I thought he was listening. But now I realize that he was in flight—his mind was in space. There are so many things I have to keep repeating because he fades out on me. He's a daydreamer. That's aggravating. It's very important to me to feel that I'm getting through to a friend. But I don't feel that he's with me. And if I nag him about it, that just pushes him back and sends him off on the next flight out.

> We just celebrated our six-month anniversary. We were on vacation and in bed and he said, "Happy Anniversary." I mentioned to him the communication

problem—that I don't feel like I'm with my best friend. I said, "I'm not happy. There's no feedback when I tell you things. I feel like there's a detachment." I said, "I know you love me, but I don't feel like you do." I said, "I don't feel like we share the deep down stuff."

How did Ned respond? Barbara recounted:

What he said is that he's never had a best friend and so he doesn't know how to act to a best friend. And then I realized that he had *chosen* not to have a best friend—that he has a lot of friends but they're more surface acquaintances. That's when I figured out that he's a loner. Before me he never had a girlfriend for longer than eight months. I feel badly because if I was a loner too I wouldn't want him to share so much. But I'm more of an extrovert. I'm expecting a lot. I don't like detachment. *I feel that closeness is when you're able to get inside the other person* and you just want to learn more and more about them. I want to feel that I'm important to Ned. I want him to be excited about what goes on in my life. Right now if somebody asked him what they should buy me as a birthday gift I don't feel like he'd know what I'd want. I'm disappointed. Before we were married I didn't see anything preventing us from getting to be best friends. Our basic values are so similar.

Sometimes I think, "One minute, Barbara—maybe you don't love him. Maybe you're so busy picking at him because you don't really like him." It's scary to think that maybe I made a mistake. The stress is having more of a physical effect on me than I ever thought. I'm having palpitations, tummy rolls, a heaviness in my chest. I have an appointment with the doctor tomorrow for a full physical. Deep down I think things will work out but that it will take time. But it's hard. I feel very strongly that if these things aren't brought out and talked about that it will kill the relationship.

Several weeks later tall, thin, dark-haired Ned gave his side of the story:

I'm not having a hard time being married—Barbara is. Barbara is incredibly supportive, which is one of the problems we're having. I'd been a bachelor for so long that I hadn't had to be supportive of anyone. I'm going through a midlife crisis in my career. I've been consumed in my work problems. Barbara is an extraordinarily good listener. She will absorb every word. I, on the other hand, am not a listener. I tend to daydream. As closely as she listens to me, she wants me to listen to her. She remembers what I said four months ago. She gets upset because I don't remember what she said last week. It can be tough to try to make her understand that not everyone can live up to the high principles that she lives by.

Being married is much more relaxing than being single. When you're single there's always a searching, you're always looking for someone. Now I found someone with whom I feel comfortable. It's like a weight that gets dropped. I don't think Barbara experiences the same degree of relief because she wasn't single as long as I was and didn't experience the same tension. I definitely feel closer to Barbara since I married her. She's much more confrontational than I am. I would let things build up. Women may have certain expectations of marriage that men may not.

How is it possible for one spouse to feel so lonely and the other to feel so personally fulfilled in marriage?

The reasons are numerous. Each individual has different needs, fears, and expectations regarding intimacy in their marriage.

CHECKUP: HOW MUCH INTIMACY DO YOU NEED?

You probably take for granted, as most of us do, that the kind of intimate relationship you want is the type of intimate relationship anyone would want. But the fact is that you and your spouse may have very different ideas about what constitutes a close marriage. To clarify your intimacy attitude, circle *a, b,* or *c,* depending on which is the *most appropriate* answer for each of the following questions:

1. I go to parties by myself:
   (a) never
   (b) sometimes
   (c) always

2. If my spouse and I are at a party together, we spend all our time:
   (a) by each other's side
   (b) socializing together and separately
   (c) circulating separately

3. Ideally, I would like to tell my spouse:
   (a) everything on my mind
   (b) much of what is on my mind
   (c) little of what is on my mind

4. I like to have time at home alone *without* my spouse:
   (a) as little as possible
   (b) occasionally
   (c) as much as possible

5. When my spouse tells me he or she needs time alone, I feel:
   (a) rejected and hurt
   (b) a little insulted, but I understand
   (c) fine, and I completely understand their feelings

6. When I feel I'm becoming very close with my mate, I feel:
   (a) reassured and protected
   (b) comfortable and uncomfortable at the same time
   (c) swallowed up and extremely anxious

7. Regarding how affectionate I like to be with my mate:
   (a) if I could, I would cuddle all day, every day
   (b) I like to hug, cuddle, and hold hands on occasion
   (c) I am not a "touchy-feely" person. I don't like to touch except for while having sex

8. My spouse and I share secrets with each other that we tell no one else:
   (a) often
   (b) on occasion
   (c) never

Now, count the number of *a*'s, *b*'s, and *c*'s you circled. If you chose mostly *a*'s, you're likely to have a strong need for closeness, while if you chose mostly *c*'s you probably prefer greater distance between yourself and other people. If you've chosen mostly b's then you have a need to both be close to your mate, but also to protect your privacy. If you have an equal number of a's, b's, and c's, then you probably vacillate between wanting a very intense, connected, affectionate relationship and wanting your independence.

Ask your spouse to answer the above questions also. If he or she is unwilling, you might answer the questions the way you think your spouse might. Any discrepancies that exist between both your answers probably indicate an area of conflict in your marriage. For instance, if your spouse feels very reassured and protected when you become very close, and you feel swallowed up and threatened, it is inevitable that you will both struggle in order to get your differing needs met.

What influences how you envision your ideal intimate relationship? As we're about to see, attitudes about intimacy are primarily based on six key factors:
- early childhood experiences
- being male or female
- personality type
- role models for intimacy
- experiences in previous relationships
- life cycle stage

THE IMPACT
OF CHILDHOOD HURTS

Whether somebody experiences their marriage as confining, suffocating, a threat to their sense of freedom or as a wonderful protection and comfort, whether a person seeks a lot of nurturance and affection from their mate or is happier with a more distant relationship is dependent to some extent on how they were treated in childhood by close family members.

Barbara Dobbs is a perfect example of how somebody's intimate adult relationships can be influenced by early childhood hurts and rejections.[2] It was toward the end of our interview with her that she casually mentioned that when she was two years old her mother had walked out on her, her ten-month old brother, and her father—for good. Though Barbara spoke about her mother's desertion of the family with calmness and equanimity it is obvious that such a major experience of rejection from her mother at such an early age had to be traumatic.

"From the time I was two to ten, we had ten housekeepers. My brother always got very attached to every housekeeper, but I kept my distance," Barbara recalled.

While it might be a coincidence that Barbara was abandoned by her mother as a toddler and is now complaining of emotional rejection from her husband, it's more likely that there is a very strong connection. Getting married is an attempt to start one's own family, to re-create the sense of closeness and security that one had—or wanted—in childhood. Marriage, therefore, inevitably stirs up one's feelings about one's childhood and family. In fact, many of the tasks of childhood are reworked in marriage. Just as a child must find the right distance between him- or herself and their mother—just as he or she must negotiate between the desire to merge with the mother and the fear of becoming engulfed in the mother—so too does a spouse try to establish a separate identity from their mate, yet reap fulfillment from a close, loving relationship.[3]

When there has been a profound hurt in one's childhood—such as Barbara experienced—it is not unusual for a person to re-create that hurt in their marriage.[4] Barbara has always been very strong, almost courageous, in the way she dealt with her mother's abandonment of her. As the older daughter, she took responsibility for raising her brother; when her father remarried (she was ten) Barbara became close with her stepmother. As an adult Barbara has become a successful businesswoman. Yet marriage seems to have had the effect of permitting Barbara to recognize and voice her own neediness, to express some of her pain and her desire to be taken care of. As she told us, "I've always been aware of a certain insecurity. It's heightened more since I'm married." It may be that having experienced one rejection, Barbara inwardly fears that Ned too will reject her. Or it may be that she has so long hungered to feel loved that she is projecting onto him years of longing and yearning for intimacy.

Mark Taylor, 27, is another newlywed we spoke with whose desire for a strong, intense emotional connection with his wife stems from earlier childhood hurts. Mark, a professional dancer, met Helene, an architect, at their high school reunion and was attracted to her beauty as well as her calm, rational approach to life. Being highly temperamental himself and coming from a volatile family, Mark was drawn by Helene's tendency to discuss rather than yell, to think logically rather than act impulsively. Yet, once married, Mark also finds himself frustrated by Helene's tranquil, and what he sees as distant, manner. Helene, in turn, told us she is exasperated because Mark reads her calmness as being uncaring.

> In Mark's family love was expressed through confrontation and yelling. His mother apparently threw two TV sets at him when he was growing up. He hates her temper but it's very familiar to him.

> I can't understand how he can get so paranoid about some issues. His car got broken into yesterday and he called me up at work to tell me. I said, "What a bummer! What a horrible thing to wake up to." I could tell in his voice that he had an expectation of how he wanted me to react. But I had other things on my mind. I couldn't be all consumed with his car. He wants me to be completely emotionally involved with him. He gets very nervous when he feels any distance between us. That makes me nervous. He starts accusing me of not being supportive, of running away. I know that I love him and I tell him that. I know that in any relationship there are moments of alienation. You can't expect to be connected all the time. When we have children I don't know how I'll cope with his needs. I really resent that he is putting an unfair burden on the relationship and on me. Mark used to scream at me the way his mother used to scream at him. I just wouldn't accept it. As soon as he gets agitated, I respond logically to the question. But he really wants an emotional response.

Both Barbara and Mark are re-creating and reliving in their marriage feelings they experienced while growing up. Barbara, by voicing her need for more of a confirmation of her husband's love, is trying to gain the loving reassurance and security she did not receive as a child from her mother. Mark, who learned in his family to equate intimacy with emotional outbursts, finds that he is desirous of, but also threatened by, his wife's cool, collected disposition.

What hurts/expectations have you brought to marriage which

influence your attitudes about intimacy? Consider which of the following statements may apply for you:

- ☐ I expect my spouse to always be there for me in ways I feel my parents were not.
- ☐ My parents were always very protective of me. I expect my spouse to nurture me in the same way, because I lack the confidence that I am capable of taking care of myself.
- ☐ I think of a close relationship as one in which there is a lot of screaming and yelling, because that's how my family always acted together.
- ☐ I don't want my spouse getting too close to me because my family was very overbearing and I found it stifling.
- ☐ I want a marriage in which my spouse is very independent and capable of having their own life, because when I was growing up everyone depended on me to take care of everything.

There are numerous ways in which your family relationships probably influenced your feelings about close relationships. But the patterns set up in childhood *can* be changed and marriage is a very useful and effective forum for helping you make such changes. As long as you are aware of how you would like your marital relationship to be different from ways in which you were treated as a child, or ways in which your parents treated each other, you have the power to create new and different patterns. Marriage offers you the opportunity to mend many of the hurts and rejections you experienced in childhood. If you are aware of your intimacy needs, marriage can provide the nourishment and security that you didn't receive when you were a child.[5]

MALE/FEMALE APPROACHES TO INTIMACY

Many psychology experts attribute intimacy problems in marriage to the different attitudes that men and women are socialized to have about intimacy. According to psychological theory, boys grow up needing to separate from their mothers in order to develop a masculine identity, while girls do not need to separate from their mothers in order to attain a feminine identity. As a result, men are threatened by intimacy while women are threatened by separation.

Carol Gilligan,[6] a Harvard University professor, conducted a study which supports this theory. When 88 men were shown a picture of a tranquil scene in which a couple were sitting on a bench by a river, more than 21 percent wrote stories about this scene which contained incidents of violence—homicide, suicide, stabbing, kidnapping, or rape. In contrast, *none* of the 50 women in the study projected violence onto the intimate scene. Gilligan concluded from her research that there is violent imagery in men's fantasies of intimate relationships.

Gilligan also reported that women attributed violent explanations to a picture of a man seated alone at his desk—the only picture portraying a person alone. Men, on the other hand, most often saw violence in the only picture with any physical contact—a scene of acrobats on a trapeze. Gilligan suggests that men and women perceive danger in different social situations. Men associate danger more frequently with closeness and intimacy, while women perceive danger in isolation and impersonal achievement situations.[7]

The result of such sex-related differences is that men and women are satisfied with varying degrees of closeness. Like Ned, many men are content by just being with their wives—they don't feel the need to constantly share their thoughts and feelings and affections. And like Barbara, many women want more of a sharing between themselves and their mates—they want to feel more connectedness in order to feel loved and not lonely.

Ted Huston, a psychologist at the University of Texas at Austin, studied 130 couples intensively and found that, "For the wives, intimacy means talking things over, especially talking about the relationship itself. The men, by and large, don't understand what the wives want from them. They say, 'I want to do things with her, and all she wants to do is talk.' " According to Huston, during courtship, men are more willing to spend time talking to women in ways that built their sense of intimacy. After the wedding, however, men devote more time to their work or buddies.[8]

This greater need of women for intimacy may be what

makes them complain more about the state of marriage than husbands do, a finding reported by John Gottman, a psychologist at the University of Illinois.[9] According to Gottman, husbands and wives also have different approaches to conflict. While women want to resolve disagreements so that they feel closer to their husbands, husbands will do anything to avoid a blowup. Men don't see a disagreement as an opportunity to gain greater closeness. In fact, Gottman believes that men have a more physically stressful reaction to marital confrontations than women do. It makes sense then, that, according to Kathleen White, a psychologist at Boston University, the more comfortable a husband is with intimacy, the more satisfied the wife is likely to be with the marriage.[10]

PERSONALITY TYPES
AND INTIMACY

While gender may have a lot to do with how someone feels about intimacy, it clearly is not the determining factor in every case. There are men who yearn for emotional reinforcement —who need for their wives to demonstrate affection or even to start arguments in order to feel reassured of their emotional connection with their mate. And there are women who ward off intimacy, seeking acceptance and approval by excelling and achieving. In chapter 4, we described these problems in our discussion of the "Overexpressive" and the "Underexpressive" mate. As we saw, intimacy problems result[11] when the spouse who craves contact threatens their more obsessional mate with their demands, who in turn withdraws from any tenderness. A vicious cycle gets started as the more histrionic partner reacts by feeling even more rejected, and attacks the passivity of their mate, who in turn responds by withdrawing further. Such a pattern prevents any genuine closeness from developing—a consequence which may or may not serve the deeper, perhaps unconscious needs of each partner. A couple caught up in this cycle cannot help but become focused on this pattern of attack and withdrawal. Such a system locks two spouses into a bind which reassures them of their connection, but prevents any true, loving feelings and genuine pleasure from being generated in their relationship.

ROLE MODELS FOR INTIMACY

Every individual is influenced by the relationships they see around them. Certainly the most influential role models anyone has regarding how to behave in marriage are their own parents.[12] Someone who has witnessed a close, loving, supportive marriage between their mother and father has probably the best education and training as far as how to create such a relationship in their own life. And someone who has observed their parents in a relationship characterized by constant bickering, resentment, distance, and alienation is faced with considerable obstacles in terms of how to go about shaping a marriage that is different from the one they have seen close at hand.

Interestingly, we found that most people who responded to our open-ended questionnaire recognized that their parents did have certain marital problems and noted that they were consciously trying to develop a marriage that would not repeat the same mistakes which they had seen while growing up. Almost all of the newlyweds we heard from stated that they thought that their own marriage was more equal than that of their parents. This ability to be objective about one's parents' marriage —to see the good aspects as well as the negative ones—and the desire to do even better than one's parents in terms of creating a fulfilling home life—is very important to creating a marriage that is suited to one's own needs. Unfortunately, it's not always easy to break away from the marriage models we grew up with. A 48-year-old Colorado woman, recently remarried, wrote to us:

> When I was growing up I often wished my parents would divorce if they could not quit fighting. But the first time I got married, without realizing it I did it their way. This time my marriage is better, much closer, more intimate. I'm doing it my way. We are equals in as many ways as possible—we're each other's best friend.

While there is certainly an advantage to having had parents whose marriage was close and loving, the relationship that you had with your mother and father while growing up seems to be even more important. In other words, the fact that your mother and father divorced when you were younger does not necessarily have to be a detrimental influence in your own marriage, especially if you maintained positive attachments to both of your parents. But if you had a poor relationship with your mother or father, even if they were happy with each other, you may expect negative aspects from your relationship with your parents to emerge in your own marriage. If you never felt good about yourself in your relationship to your parents, it may be difficult to believe that you are truly loved and accepted by your spouse.[13]

Some newlyweds we spoke with expressed concern that they had never seen a marriage that truly worked. One woman, whose parents have an extremely hostile relationship, said that she had made deliberate efforts to become close with an older woman at work whom she knows is happily married. By socializing with that woman and her husband, she says she hopes to get a closer look at how loving spouses treat each other. Occasionally, she consults the older friend for marital advice.

If you feel that you never had the opportunity to observe a successful marriage between your parents, it can be helpful to pay close attention to relatives, friends, or work colleagues who seem to enjoy a loving, fulfilling marriage. Learning about marriage is like learning about anything else—it helps to benefit from others' experiences and guidance.

INTIMACY AND EXPERIENCES
IN PAST RELATIONSHIPS

The experiences you've had in previous relationships may influence your attitudes toward intimacy in marriage. Without thinking about it, you may be repeating in marriage roles you adopted in the past. Or, you may be consciously trying to alter patterns which have frustrated or sabotaged your former relationships.

Especially if you are marrying after having had a number of intense long-term relationships, you may have intentionally looked for certain qualities in your marital partner because you have a strong sense of what suits you and what is important in maintaining an intimate relationship. Having been disappointed in the past by romances gone awry or marriages gone sour, you may be, or at least think you are, a better judge of character. You may see through the gloss more quickly and be less likely to idealize superficial qualities.

Lyle Walker, 33, says that his new wife is a total departure from the women he dated in the past. As a bachelor, Lyle was always attracted to women who were a bit on the outrageous side. They were very impulsive sorts, with a flamboyant style. Inevitably, however, he found himself on an emotional roller coaster. One of the last women he courted told him she loved him madly and then took a vacation in Hawaii where she fell in love with someone else. At that point Lyle took a serious look at his life and decided that it was time to settle down and get married. He wanted a stable and secure relationship and so consciously set out to only date women whom he thought capable of such qualities. His wife, a lawyer, is a loving, down-to-earth woman. The intimacy he has with her, he says, is far more satisfying than the titillating unpredictability of his former girlfriends.

Cynthia Cole, a stunning, 26-year-old fashion coordinator, also noted that her marital choice represented a break from her previous taste in men.

> My husband is much more argumentative than anyone else I ever went out with. But it's also satisfying in ways that all my previous pleasant and easygoing relationships were not. My husband is the first man I met who I can fight with and I realized that I felt comfortable with him in a way I had never experienced with other guys. Our relationship isn't always easy, but it feels real.

Both Lyle and Cynthia altered their view of what kind of intimate relationship they want, based on their past experiences.

If you think back to your past relationships, you will probably be able to see how the spouse you chose either fits in or differs from those people you've dated in the past. Once you are able to distinguish certain patterns in your intimate relationships, it will be easier for you to determine what has and hasn't "worked" for you in the past regarding your romantic attachments.

To help you pinpoint some patterns that may have existed in your intimate relationships, here are some statements. Check off all of those which apply to you.

In past intimate relationships:

☐ I always ended up feeling my mate was too distant and uncaring.

☐ I always went out with people who were very admiring of me.

☐ I always felt too many demands were being made of me.

☐ I was always very demanding.

☐ I was usually the one to do the caretaking.

☐ I was usually the one to do the breaking up.

☐ I was usually the one who felt rejected.

☐ I usually chose partners who made me feel secure.

The above are just a few possibilities. The point is to think about how you would like your marriage to be the same or different from your past intimate relationships. To break certain patterns, you need to think about how you contributed to situations. For instance, if you've always ended up feeling that your mates were too distant or you always felt stifled, perhaps you had unrealistic expectations or were too demanding or focused too many of your needs on your mate, rather than relied on yourself or your friends to fulfill some of your needs.

It *is* possible to change how you act and react in intimate relationships. Being aware of your tendencies and the needs underlying those traits is an important step toward making changes.

INTIMACY AND LIFE CYCLE STAGES

Where you are in the life cycle may have a lot to do with how focused you are on enhancing intimacy in your marriage.[14] If you are in your late teens or early twenties and still very desirous of pleasing your parents, you may find that over-involvement with your family may be a barrier to developing intimacy with your spouse. On the other hand, if you married your mate as a rebellious act against your parents, or are at an age where you lack self-confidence and life experience, you may rely on your mate for their support and be extremely dedicated to cultivating a close, nurturing relationship with your partner.

The career stage you are in will also influence how much

time you will have to devote to building a close, sharing marriage. If you are in your twenties or thirties and trying to establish yourself professionally, as loving as you may feel toward your spouse, you will probably be limited regarding how much time you can spend with him or her. If you've already established your career, however, you may have lots of time and energy to devote toward your personal life.

Needs for intimacy change as you age. During your early career years, mastery at your job may be of prime concern. Eventually, there may be a gradual awareness of "Isn't there more to life than work?" The importance of family and home life usually increase as people get older. One newlywed husband, almost 50, told us he is somewhat amazed by how desirous he is to spend time with his new wife. But, he explained:

> I had a miserable 12 years being single after my divorce
> from my first wife. I lived so long independently that
> I don't attach a great value to it. I don't glorify being
> alone. A very strong dependent quality is coming out
> now.

Intimacy is different at different life stages because the demands made on you are different. If you're a newlywed with children from a previous marriage or your spouse's previous marriage, it is almost inevitable that parenting concerns will impinge on the romanticism of your new marriage.

Or if a wife is pregnant in the newlywed year, the physical strain and emotional anticipation of entering yet a new phase of life adds a special challenge to the task of establishing a marriage that feels stable and secure. Because people are more likely to delay marriage nowadays and are aware of the "biological clock" ticking away, many newlyweds try to conceive soon after their wedding. In our survey:

- 18 percent of newlyweds—almost one in five—reported that they had a wanted pregnancy in their first year of marriage.
- 85 percent of that 18 percent—or 14 percent of our sample—reported that the pregnancy had strengthened their marriage.

While filled with hope and expectation, pregnancy in the newlywed year pushes a couple to deal with a lot in a short amount of time.[15] They need to cultivate an intimate bond that will allow them to prepare for new roles, new tasks, and a new addition to their marital unit.

That being intimate takes on different meanings is especially true when couples go through life crises together. Hard times can do a lot for a marriage—both positively and negatively. It can bind you and your spouse together, or wrench you apart.[16] While every couple who stays together is bound to face traumas of family illness, death, job loss, and other crises, if you face any of these stresses early on in your marriage it can be a particularly excruciating test of your intimacy.

Vivian Fanto, a brown-haired, 38-year-old mother of two, has been married almost 20 years but she still vividly recalls the marital anguish that was set in motion when her father died three weeks after her wedding.

> I was severely depressed. I dove into Sara Lee brownies and cheesecake. I gained twenty pounds in the first six months I got married. My husband Dick was working 'round the clock and I didn't have a job. It took me six months to get out of the house and find a job. We had almost no sex that year. I was feeling very lonely.

With her father's death, Vivian was catapulted into another life stage—one that forced her to grapple with death and mourning and an aging, abandoned mother. At a time when she was dealing with getting married and symbolically breaking away from her family, her father passed away—leaving her confused and angry. Vivian internalized her grief, rather than share it with her husband, Dick. He, in turn, became increasingly involved with his work.

It wasn't until they reached a crisis point—when Vivian almost had an affair with her husband's friend—that they both started exerting the effort to recapture the intimacy they had lost. Vivian recalled:

> At some point, we realized that you have to ventilate, that you just can't let everything stay inside. But Dick also said something to me that was very important. There was a point where I had stopped being polite to Dick. He sat me down and said that no matter how

strongly we disagreed we still had to be polite to each
other. That influenced me a lot because I respect him
a lot. I learned to express myself firmly but politely.

Vivian and Dick began making it a point to spend more
time together, sometimes meeting for late dinners before going
home together. And in their second year of marriage, Dick
started his own company. Vivian pitched in by preparing dinners for Dick and his six partners. It was a stressful time, but
also a fun time. "We were building something together," says
Vivian. "We had learned that you can't retreat from each other
and isolate yourselves. The crisis at the beginning of our marriage tore us apart, but we stuck it out. It took us time for the
two of us to get past it, but we did."

*Whatever your current stage in the life cycle, you need to recognize
the special stresses and impacts that your and your spouse's life stage
has upon your intimacy needs and capabilities.* No matter how pressured you may feel by certain demands—whether related to
your job, aging parents, difficult children, a relative's illness—
it is essential not to bottle up your feelings and build a shell
around yourself. Life brings many obstacles, but if you seek
and accept the love and support of your spouse these will be
easier to overcome. As one newlywed woman, 25, whose husband had just experienced the death of his close friend, told
us:

> When you're able to comfort someone and know that
> they really need you, you realize what you have. My
> husband didn't care about letting his mother know
> about his friend's dying—he turned to me. His friend's
> death evoked feelings of grief in my husband that he
> never worked out about his own father's death 10 years
> ago. He says he felt he was mourning for so many
> things. I think he felt it was all right to cry in front of
> me. I don't feel that there's anything we couldn't really
> cope with now. We've gone through a bad thing and
> I know I could help him through it. His friend's death
> was a trauma, but it drew us closer.

Each stage of life will bring new challenges to maintaining
the intimacy of your relationship. Ideally, as you and your spouse
grow old together, you will both become increasingly capable

and creative in finding ways to express and receive your love and support for one another.

WHAT IS THIS THING CALLED LOVE?

Considering all of the different factors which influence a person's attitudes toward intimacy, it really isn't surprising that love means different things to different individuals. That there are various types of love is obvious in the distinctions between the love people feel for their parents, children, friends, and spouse.[17] But even within your marriage there may be many different types of love you feel toward your mate. Researchers[18] have noted the different kinds of love which may initially draw a man and woman together. They define six bases for loving:

eros—a love style characterized by the search for a beloved whose physical presentation of self embodies an image already held in the mind of the lover.

ludus—playful or gamelike love.

storge—a love style based on a slowly developing affection and companionship.

mania—a love style characterized by obsession, jealousy, and great emotional intensity.

agape—altruistic love, in which the lover views it as his or her duty to love without expectation or reciprocation.

pragma—a practical style involving conscious consideration of the demographic characteristics of the loved one.

(One person we know laughed out loud at the idea that "demographic characteristics" could be the basis of any kind of love. Yet, throughout history a rational assessment of familial and financial backgrounds has been a major—if not *the* major —factor in marital selection.)

In any long-lasting marriage, all different types of love may be called into play. While a couple may initially be drawn together because of their erotic attraction for each other, with time their deep affection for one another may be what truly keeps them together. Or a couple may start their marriage with a pragmatic attitude—"it was time to get married and I just picked the first person who came along"—but then discover that theirs is a very enjoyable, gamelike love. There may be periods in even the most successful marriages in which love is given dutifully rather than passionately, and times when it is more emotionally intense and a focus of one's obsessions.

Intimacy can be cultivated and found in any of the types of love just mentioned. At different times you may find yourselves expressing your intimacy through playfulness, sexuality, companionship, jealousy, self-sacrifice, steadfastness, and loyalty.

The crucial ingredient in any style of loving which makes for intimacy is caring for one's mate. The ability to identify with one's spouse with the same interest and concern that we have for ourselves is expressed by many theorists.[19] Psychologist Rollo May describes care as "a state composed of the recognition of another, a fellow human being like one's self; of identification of one's self with the pain or joy of the other; of guilt, pity, and the awareness that we all stand on the base of a common humanity from which we all stem."[20]

No matter what your and your spouse's needs are for intimacy—no matter how much distance you both may enjoy —creating a marriage in which you are caring and feel cared for is vital to a loving relationship. The key is to find a way for you both to express your caring in a way that suits your mutual needs.

WORKSHOP: HOW TO BE INTIMATE WITHOUT FEELING THREATENED

Determining how close or how far you want to be from each other emotionally is not something that can just be decided by sitting down and coming to an agreement. Intimacy is a highly intangible quality, and it can be achieved only with time.

The struggle between acting as a single entity and as two individuals is replayed in countless decisions made in a marriage:

- Should a wife assume her husband's last name, hyphenate her and his last names, or keep her maiden name?
- Should a couple spend all of their free time together?
- Should a couple socialize with friends only as a twosome?

- Should a couple always visit relatives together, or is it all right if each spouse sometimes goes alone to visit family?

All of these may seem like petty day-to-day concerns, but underlying them is the question of how to strike the right balance between separateness and connectedness.

The key is for you, as newlyweds, to *find the distance that works for you*. Some newlyweds want to spend all their free time together, others find it better for their relationship if each spouse goes off on their own for at least part of their leisure time. Some husbands and wives tend to confide only in each other, others turn to family and friends for support in coping with personal matters.

Inevitably there is a lot of trial and error before you feel comfortable with the amount of intimacy in your relationship. First of all, getting married can immediately trigger certain negative reactions that may taper off over time. Following the wedding, some newlyweds are shocked by the dependent quality that emerges in them, others are frightened by how stifled they feel in marriage. As you adjust to marriage, your attitudes toward and needs for intimacy will change. If you've been burnt in previous relationships and are cautious about demonstrating affection, you may gradually open up and share more feelings with your mate as you become secure in your marriage. If, on the other hand, you demand constant demonstrations of love, you may eventually learn to trust your mate's commitment and need fewer repeated affirmations of affection.

Earlier in this chapter we provided a quiz to help you define your and your spouse's intimacy needs. Compare your responses with your spouse's answers—and see how closely they accord with how you thought he or she would respond. Then share your feelings about what you each want from the other. If you both agree that you each have a great need for closeness or a great need for distance, then you probably have little problem satisfying your intimacy needs. If one or both of you feel you are not getting your needs met, be clear about what it is you need more or less of.

Many couples, when they're talking about intimacy, act as if they're speaking a different language. A husband may assume that if he and his wife have sex three times a week they are being intimate, while she may crave for intimacy in conversation. Or a husband may consider taking his wife fishing an intimate act, while she wonders why they don't make love more often.

Generally people know how to decrease intimacy—they spend less time with their mates, avoid being physical, express directly or otherwise their need to be alone. But many people who say they want to get closer to their spouses, claim they just don't know how to do it. The following behaviors suggest some of the many ways through which you can express your interest and desire in becoming closer.

• *Talk with your spouse.* As novelist George Eliot once said,[21] "I like not only to be loved but also told that I am loved." Words do carry weight, and the expression of loving feelings is reinforcing. But not all intimate talk needs to be about love. Self-disclosure—the sharing of one's feelings—is a fundamental aspect of intimacy. Conversation brings couples closer. The more you share with each other, the more involved you will feel in each other's lives.

• *Be affectionate.* Hand-holding, an arm around the shoulder, a kiss before you leave in the morning—all are physical messages that communicate "I care." You needn't be overly demonstrative to convey affection. Sometimes just looking at your mate directly in the eyes across a restaurant table is enough to communicate loving feelings.

• *Share—and respect secrets imparted to you.* Occasionally sharing secrets with each other[22]—and not telling anyone else —can have a unifying effect. If reaffirms the sense that you're a special unit. It helps create something of a cozy, cocoonlike atmosphere. These secrets may be personal feelings you have, focus on something you know about a relative, friend, or work colleague, or have to do with your own marriage. What you do together sexually is an example of a secret many couples have that can help bind them together.

• *Create romantic rituals.* It's in the small gestures, funny little games, special touches that caring and commitment are often manifested. People have their own ways of showing their feelings—it may be by drawing your spouse a warm bath when he or she comes home from work, running out to buy your mate the newspaper every morning, remembering what kind of cologne your partner likes and buying it when you see it's running out, buying your spouse a special outfit when you go on vacation. Intimate gestures can be very simple but nevertheless meaningful. By continuing to make sentimental gestures, you remind your spouse that you're glad you're married.

•	*Find intimacy in routine activities.* Going horseback riding, sailing, food shopping, or even doing the laundry can be just as "intimate" as having a romantic candlelit dinner. The key to making ordinary activities intimate is to recognize that all your time together can be special if you approach it with a loving, sharing attitude.

•	*Maintain your individuality.* In a healthy relationship, you need not lose your sense of self in order to gain a feeling of togetherness with your mate. In fact, if you lose your individuality, ultimately it will be impossible for you to enjoy a lasting, close relationship, because you will feel as though you have nothing to contribute. Feeling confident that the outside experiences and differing opinions you bring to your marriage make it strong and honest will help you feel good and not fearful about creating an intimate marriage.

•	*Remember that you need not always be intimate.* Appreciating that you and your spouse can't always be on the same wavelength and at times are bound to differ in your need for closeness can help you sustain a loving marriage, free of the hurt of rejection. As Kahlil Gibran advised,[23] "Let there be spaces in your togetherness." Privacy is something to be valued and respected.

FRIENDSHIPS

Altering Your Social Networks

The success of your marriage will be based not just on what happens *in* your relationship, but also on how you and your mate interact with the world. After all, no couple lives in a vacuum. Aside from the honeymoon and other occasional getaways when you can savor your aloneness, you and your spouse will be in constant contact with other people. Just as you need to work out how close and far to be from each other, you'll also need to figure out *how* involved you want your friends to be in your lives and *which* friends you want to be a part of your lives.

THE IMPORTANCE OF
FRIENDSHIPS TO MARRIAGE

Friends can be either a joining or a divisive influence in marriage.[1] You may agree with or, at least, tolerate each other's taste in friends, develop mutual friends, and integrate friends into your life in a way that enhances your marriage. Or you may constantly bicker about how often to socialize and which friends to socialize with, thereby creating deep wells of resentment and frustration.

Establishing a social life that satisfies the needs of both of you is actually a very positive indication of the state of your marriage.[2] It shows that you are sufficiently respectful of each other to recognize the benefit of having outside friends and to appreciate your individual bonds with friends. It also demonstrates that you are mature and secure enough to allow your partner to cultivate relationships with others, without feeling threatened or jealous.

The fact is that friends are necessary. No matter how well

suited you and your mate are to each other, you can't possibly satisfy all of each other's needs. True, one study found that people in happy, long-lasting marriages regard their mates as their best friends.[3] But that doesn't eliminate the need for friends outside of marriage, though it may change the nature of your friendships.

Different people are bound to bring out different sides of your personalities. Having numerous friends can broaden and enrich you as individuals, thereby replenishing and invigorating your marriage. The more interesting people you know, the more varied the experiences you will probably have, the more fulfilled you may feel as people, and the more you will have to contribute to your marriage. Being able to enjoy mutual friends can be an especially important reinforcement for couples. If you enjoy at least some of the same people, you will be able to create a host of happy memories, which will strengthen your connection and sense of camaraderie with each other.

Having friends can also affirm your sense of independence. As we've noted in the previous chapter on intimacy, newlyweds frequently fear becoming engulfed by their partners. Maintaining your bonds with friends can feel very reassuring, especially in the early phase of marriage, if you're concerned about losing your identity. And by being able to turn to others for advice, support, or just a compassionate ear, you may find that some of the tension that builds during difficult times in your marriage can be alleviated.[4]

On the other hand, friendships can pose a threat to a marriage. Being overly involved with friends may endanger the intimacy of your marriage relationship. Time and confidences that are shared with outsiders, instead of with each other, may prevent the development of a unifying marital bond.

Ideally, there is a certain equilibrium established between a couple and their friends. The time they spend with others enriches their tie to each other; the loving and trusting bond they share together enables them to enjoy fruitful relationships with others.

Achieving this balance, however, is not always something that happens easily or instantaneously. For one thing, in crossing the threshold into marriage, you are marking a turning point in your friendships.

CHECKUP: HOW DO FRIENDSHIPS FIT INTO YOUR MARRIAGE?

Chances are you've already noticed some shifts in your relationships with friends as you try to settle into marriage. The following questions are aimed at helping you focus on how you feel about the role friends play in your marriage. For each question listed below, circle *a, b, c, d,* or *e* to correspond to one of the five descriptions shown in the following scale:

(a)	(b)	(c)	(d)	(e)
very satisfied	satisfied	not sure	dissatisfied	very dissatisfied

How do you feel about:
1. the amount of time you have alone with your friends since being married   (a) (b) (c) (d) (e)
2. the amount of time your spouse spends alone with his or her friends   (a) (b) (c) (d) (e)
3. the amount of time you and your spouse socialize as a couple   (a) (b) (c) (d) (e)
4. the number of friends you and your spouse share in common and enjoy together   (a) (b) (c) (d) (e)
5. the way your single friends act toward you since you got married   (a) (b) (c) (d) (e)
6. the way your married friends act with you since you got married   (a) (b) (c) (d) (e)
7. the way your spouse's friends act toward you   (a) (b) (c) (d) (e)
8. the degree to which you confide in friends since being married   (a) (b) (c) (d) (e)

9. the degree to which your spouse confides in friends since being married   **(a)** **(b)** **(c)** **(d)** **(e)**

10. your spouse's choice of friends   **(a)** **(b)** **(c)** **(d)** **(e)**

11. your spouse's opinion of your friends   **(a)** **(b)** **(c)** **(d)** **(e)**

12. your spouse's attitude regarding the role of friends in your marriage   **(a)** **(b)** **(c)** **(d)** **(e)**

13. the way you and your spouse act together in front of friends   **(a)** **(b)** **(c)** **(d)** **(e)**

Obviously the more *d*'s and *e*'s you circled, the more unhappy you are about how questions regarding friends are being resolved in your marriage. And the more *a*'s and *b*'s you circled, the more satisfied you feel with the way friendships fit into your marriage. But even if *you* are satisfied, you need to ask:

- Is my spouse satisfied with how often we each socialize, together and separately?
- Is my spouse satisfied with my attitude toward friendships in general, and toward his or her friends in particular?
- Is there anything we can do to make friends a greater source of enjoyment for both of us?

In different stages of your marriage, friends will play different roles. During your early parenthood years, you may find it tough to find time to get together with others socially; during your retirement years friends may play a more prominent role than ever. But in any stage of life, friends have much to offer, and it's worth thinking about what kind of friendships you'd like to cultivate and what messages you are sending your friends now that you've made a major change in your life.

HOW FRIENDSHIPS CHANGE
WHEN YOU MARRY

Friendships change after you get married—a fact you may find hard to accept, or fail to recognize, until many months after your wedding. At first it may seem that you're just caught up in the hectic pace of wedding and honeymoon planning and that's why things seem to be a little different. With the rush to get wedding arrangements made, with the excitement and nervousness you may feel about the upcoming event, and with the family involvement that gets set in motion by the wedding—it's natural to experience a temporary sense of self-centeredness. Even after the wedding and honeymoon are over, your focus will probably be on setting up a married home life together and on adjusting to your roles as husband and wife. Between juggling domestic concerns and work obligations, it's understandable if you have little time to devote to friends.

But the distancing from friends is not just due to circumstantial factors. Here's what our survey told us:

- Only 2 percent of newlyweds reported to us that their relationships with single friends improved since their wedding

WHILE

- 35 percent reported that their relationship with single friends *worsened* since their wedding

AND

- 48 percent reported that they did not talk with friends—married or single—about their marital doubts or arguments.

In March 1979 *Psychology Today* conducted a poll in which readers were asked to list the thirteen most common reasons that a friendship ended. The tally from forty thousand respondents cited marriage as the fourth and fifth most common causes. Typical explanations given were: "One of us got married" and "My friend became involved with [or married] someone I didn't like."

The fact is that in forming an intimate dyad—by getting married—you are separating yourselves from your surrounding social group. If you are marrying in your thirties or later, your once tight-knit peer group may have already broken up, as members paired off with their own partners or pursued their careers. If, however, you are marrying in your early twenties or at a younger age, it's likely that you have very strong and frequent contact with friends, which makes those close-knit attachments especially difficult to give up.

Friends serve an important purpose, from early childhood on, in helping us to separate from our parents and discover the world. As teenagers, we gain much of our sense of self—how we dress, talk, think—from our peer-group identity. These attachments to friends help us make the transition from our family of origin to a family we create ourselves. It is in these adolescent friendships that we begin to cultivate the qualities that enable us to have intimate adult relationships.[5]

Signs that friendships will change once you get married often appear even before the wedding. Buddies of the groom start joking about not going together to the singles' bars anymore. Friends of the bride let it be known that they're bored when the conversation turns to wedding plans and china patterns. The bride and groom find themselves fighting about whose friends they see more frequently. And the couple begins sharing their thoughts and feelings more with each other than with the friends in whom they formerly confided.

Many of the wedding and prewedding rituals ingeniously try to ease the passage from one phase of friendship to another. The traditional bridal shower and bachelor party help impress upon friends the reality of the impending marriage and offers them the opportunity to become involved in the event and demonstrate their good wishes and, perhaps, ambivalent feelings. The bride and groom express to best friends their desire to remain close in the years to come by asking them to participate in the wedding as bridesmaids and ushers.

Despite these symbolic customs, there is a tremendous amount of hurt that can result from the transformations that friendships undergo around the time of marriage. Single friends may especially feel excluded from the lives of the newlywed, and brides and grooms may feel deserted by old friends.

A 29-year-old female editor wrote:

> During my engagement many of my oldest friends seemed to desert me. It might have been envy or a sense that I was busy planning the wedding. I tried to downplay the event so that my friends without boyfriends wouldn't feel bad—but it put a damper on my excitement.

Another woman, who married at age 31, discovered that two of her female friends with whom she had spent lots of time

as a single in New York stopped calling her as soon as she
became engaged.

> They made it clear to me that they didn't like my choice
> of husband. They don't think he is exciting or suc-
> cessful enough for me. It really hurt me and still hurts
> me. They never gave him a chance. I don't think they
> could accept me in another role than the one they had
> been used to.

After years of joking about who will be the first to marry,
it frequently isn't a laughing matter when one is the first to
"go." A 27-year-old teacher writes:

> My relationships with my friends have remained good
> *except* with my childhood best friend who's not married.
> All the changes we promised would never happen to
> our friendship when we got married did anyway. That
> hurts because, though we're on good terms, the old
> closeness seems strained.

It's not uncommon for one person's good fortune to evoke
anxiety and anger in another person. The resentment of friends
about your new marriage may, nevertheless, come as a surprise
and cause you to seek refuge and protection in your relationship
with your spouse. In fact, envy or hostility demonstrated to you
by friends may lead you and your mate to band together in a
way that fortifies your couple relationship.[6]

Of course, if you're like many newlyweds, you may find
that you feel less of a need for friends now that your companionship needs are met by your spouse. Cathy, 30, married just
seven months, says:

> I hardly see my friends. My husband is my best friend.
> We are completely enmeshed. I'm not that interested
> in getting involved with other groups of people. I'm
> becoming more reclusive. It's pretty surprising. It's a
> lot different from the way I used to be. I used to run
> around to parties like a chicken without a head.

Many people expressed to us that, once married, they began to feel distanced from their single friends, with whom they
now had less in common. One 31-year-old newly married woman
wrote:

Most of my friends are still single. I enjoy hearing their stories but sometimes lose patience with them. They seem to call at times when my husband and I wish to spend quiet moments together, and when they call with their problems, it's very difficult to rush them off the phone. Even though I don't see my married friends too often—trying to plan around four people's schedules is difficult—when I talk with them, they and I understand each other's problems much better than I and my single friends do.

Even those who want to get together with friends discover that finding the time to do so is difficult. One recently remarried man wrote us: "My wife and I came to marriage with a lot of friends, and we're finding it tough to socialize with a double volume."

And one woman comments:

It's been difficult to maintain close friendships. My focus has shifted. In the list of priorities my friends are an unfortunate third, with my primary concerns being spending time with my husband and family.

As newlyweds become closer, they often find themselves sharing less with their friends, either because they have a decreased need to confide in someone other than their mate or because they consider it a betrayal of their spouse. One 31-year-old husband told us:

I used to tell my friends a lot more. Now I would feel like I'm involving them in a very personal time in my life. Unless it was really, really important, I wouldn't tell them about my quirks about my marriage. There's been this team spirit about getting married. I would feel disloyal talking about our marriage to others.

REASSESSING RELATIONSHIPS WITH SINGLE FRIENDS

While all of the reactions we've described are quite normal, they can culminate in what is essentially a turning point in a friendship—the friendship can either survive the change or not. From the viewpoint of the newlywed who feels themself drifting away from a single friend or is bitter about how a single friend has reacted to their marriage, there is usually a reevaluation of the former friendship.

That turning point came for Cecilia Clark, 26, when, married almost a year, she threw a dinner party in honor of one of her single friends. For months she had been feeling neglectful of her single friends. It seemed like she never had time for them anymore, and when she did speak with them, they didn't have as much in common. She decided to use her friend's birthday as an opportunity to get back in touch with them. She invited five female friends to the surprise dinner party, all of whom had known each other since high school. She purposely chose a night when her husband Max would be working late because she suspected that some of her friends didn't feel that comfortable with him.

From the moment her guests walked into her apartment, Cecilia felt strange about the evening. Cecilia had planned a simple dinner of eggplant parmagiana and spaghetti. But just the fact that she had put the dinner together and had set up a pretty table with place settings prompted "oohs" and "aahs" from her friends, who claimed that they never cooked and didn't know how. To Cecilia it seemed as though her friends were regarding her, a "married lady," as a member of a different species.

The clincher for the night, however, was the conversation. Sometime between the main course and dessert one of her friends announced that two of their high school acquaintances were marrying each other. The table started buzzing as each friend offered her own interpretation of the news. "Oh, she must have really wanted to get married—he's not her type at all! She wouldn't even speak to him in high school." "That's really sad—she must have been desperate." "I could never settle like that."

Cecilia stayed mum as she listened to one friend after another lambast their absent peer for compromising herself in marriage. The cynicism, the anger, the hostility that emanated from her friends shocked Cecilia. "They couldn't even for one minute imagine that perhaps Susan loves Stan," she complained to her husband later that evening. "Their attitude is that someone who marries is resigning themselves to second best."

As she sat listening to her friends ventilate their malicious, accusatory thoughts about their former schoolmates, Cecilia realized that a tremendous gap had formed between her and her old chums. While they seemed determined to put down marriage, Cecilia was devoting herself to building her marriage. As she watched her friends talk—ironically they were seated beneath an enlarged wedding portrait of her and her husband—she realized for the first time since she was married that she needn't feel guilty about growing apart from her single friends, for they were partially responsible for the distancing. She realized that they had as much trouble integrating her, as a married woman, into their minds as she had difficulty integrating them into her life.

Before she had married, Cecilia and her friends identified *with* each other, but now they were projecting their own insecurities *upon* each other. Being in Cecilia's presence seemed to trigger her friends to defend their single status. Perhaps her marriage stirred disappointment in them about where they want to be in their personal lives. And the cynicism that they expressed about their former schoolmates' marriage struck a sensitive chord in Cecilia, who took those comments personally— perhaps because she herself feels vulnerable, having recently given up her freedom as a single woman to enter marriage.

It was on the evening of her dinner party, Cecilia says, that she came to terms with the realization that, at least for the present time, she and her friends were traveling separate paths.

If you sense a gap between you and your single friends, the keys to surviving such a rocky period are:

1. Realize that there is an ebb and flow to all friendships. After all, as individuals grow and develop they sometimes take similar, sometimes different roads. When one friend is single and another is married, it's important for each to appreciate each other's position and concerns—and to accept the evolving changes in their relationship. Explain to your single friends that though you may not be quite as available for them as you were before you married, you still care for them deeply. To show your continued interest in them, you might set aside specific times to see or speak to them.

Now that you're married, you may even have an added appreciation for your single friends. A 25-year-old female bookkeeper told us:

> My girlfriends are a very important support system for
> me. My husband is wonderful, but he'll never be as
> attentive as my girlfriends. They remember the names
> of people I work with—he doesn't. They probe me
> with questions—he is only starting to now. At the be-
> ginning, when we first got married, I felt pressed that
> I couldn't see my friends on weekends. My husband
> doesn't like doing things without me. But now he doesn't
> get offended if I go off with them every once in a
> while. I know that if I'm not there, he won't do much.
> But I think it's good to have some independence from
> each other.

2. *Talk with your single friends about how it feels to be in
different life stages.* Acknowledging that you are in different
phases may alleviate some of the tension that arises if feelings
of envy or resentment or exclusion exist. Don't be embarrassed
by the feelings your getting married has stirred up. They're
probably all quite normal. Being able to accept your separate
situations will enable your friendship to continue to enrich your
lives.

GETTING ALONG WITH EACH
OTHER'S FRIENDS

One of the hardest issues for couples to grapple with is one
spouse's dislike of the other's friends. Nobody likes to be told
with whom they should or should not socialize. After all, friends
are by definition people with whom we choose to be. There can
be nothing more threatening to your sense of independence
than to be asked to give up attachments you cherish.

Husbands or wives offer all sorts of reasons why they don't
like their spouse's friends. A 21-year-old wife complained in
our survey that her husband's friends are a negative influence
on him. "His night out with the boys means gambling with
money that he should really spend on our home. I always wait
up for him, worrying the whole time how much he lost," she
wrote. One husband lamented to us that his wife's friends are
heavily into drugs and that whenever she gets together with

them, she also takes drugs. He wants her to cut off all contact with her girlfriends.

Conflicts over friends may unconsciously be triggered by differences between you and your spouse that you would prefer to ignore. For instance, rather than face that her husband is inept at handling money, the wife above may find it easier to accuse her husband's friends for poorly influencing him. Or if you find something in your spouse's past distasteful—for instance, if he or she came from a lower-class background—you may attack your mate's friends because they bring to mind an unpleasant issue. If you're more educated than your mate, any crude or vulgar remarks by your spouse's friends may remind you that you're from a more cultured home. Whatever the reason may be, if you feel uncomfortable with your mate's friends, the question of whether you as a couple are poorly matched is likely to gnaw at you.

Rona and Evan Silver, a couple with a 15-year age difference between them, found that their dislike of each other's friends was at first very threatening to their marriage. Evan, a 48-year-old businessman who had been married previously, regarded Rona's friends, all in their early 30s and artists, as immature, liberal, leftover hippies. He told us:

> When I met her, she was hanging out with people from a group house at the beach. I worried that if these people's values appealed to Rona that something was wrong—maybe we weren't meant to be together. I felt she was nondiscriminating about friends.

Rona, in the meantime, complained that she resented the didactic tone that Evan took with her friends as he tried to convince them of his conservative Republican philosophy.

> When I have my friends over for dinner he tends to stand on the soapbox. He's a very effective, forceful debater, and it makes me feel like he's taking over my friendships. I'd like my friends to like him. It would be nice to have their approval of the man I married.

You and your mate may find that you like each other's friends, but not their spouses. One groom bemoaned that his wife and his best friend's wife don't hit it off, which prevents them from getting together as a foursome.

If you and your spouse do not get along with each other's friends:

1. Exercise tolerance. Rather than creating a tug of war in which you or your spouse feels pulled between loyalty to your friends and each other, discuss what your friends mean in your lives and try to keep an open mind. Think about why it is that your friends and your mate, or you and your spouse's friends, don't get along:

- Is it a matter of just being different types of people?
- Is it a result of wanting to exert control over each other's choice of friends?
- Is it because there is something else you're really angry about?

2. Consider that it may not be realistic, or even necessary, for you both to like each other's friends. There may be no reason for you all to go out together. Why not get together with friends alone sometimes, without dragging a begrudging mate along? Being able to accept that you each are separate people with separate tastes and separate interests is a major step in loving and appreciating each other for who you are.

3. Don't be overdependent on your friends' (or anyone else's) opinions of your spouse. It's important to strive to make your marriage as free from group pressure as possible. What your friends or relatives or work colleagues think of your spouse really doesn't matter. It's what you want in your spouse that is important. Don't listen to friends who try to berate your mate.

4. Do not give up friends just because your mate doesn't like them. It's true that you may see certain friends differently after marrying and want to let some friendships lapse. But those decisions should be based *only* on your own feelings. Many of the longtime married people we interviewed regretted that in their newlywed year they gave up friends of which their spouse did not approve. One woman, now divorced, wrote to us: "My husband disapproved of most of my friends—he said they were very boring and I gradually stopped seeing them. Looking back, I should not have given in so much to his demands."

Each of you is an adult and entitled to your own opinions, and that includes your taste in friends.

FEELING COMPETITIVE WITH
YOUR SPOUSE'S FRIENDS

Closely linked with not liking the friends of one's spouse is feeling jealous of them, a common phenomenon. After all, your spouse's friends are a reminder of the life your mate led prior to marriage. Those friends are rivals for your mate's free time. Those friends share things in common with your spouse—private jokes, childhood or college memories—which may leave you feeling excluded. Those friends might bring out a side of your spouse's personality which makes you uncomfortable or threatened. One husband who is normally quite serious with his wife notes that his best friend sends him into peals of laughter.

Whenever I'm on the phone with Len, my wife starts pushing me to get off the phone. It's ridiculous—I'm rolling on the floor with laughter and she thinks of some nonsensical reason for me to get off. I think she gets upset because I don't find her particularly funny. But a male friendship is different from a husband–wife relationship.

A 21-year-old woman told us she was so enraged by her husband's hanging out with his buddies all weekend that she is planning to see a marital therapist.

It seems like the second we got married my husband began to take me for granted. He seems to have this incredible sense of security now and thinks he can just go off with his friends when he wants. If I ask him not to go, he complains that I'm on the "rag." He always drinks with his friends and he can't handle liquor. He tells me I should "lighten up."

The husband of this woman is probably "hanging out" with his buddies because he feels threatened about being married. He is probably very scared of losing his independence, and so he is overcompensating by spending as much time as he can with the "guys." With time, as he grows more accustomed to being married, he may feel less of a need to turn to his male friends. But, until then, his wife will probably be extremely resentful and jealous. And in a "catch-22," the more she articulates her resentment at her husband's socializing with his buddies, the more he will feel the need to spend time with them.

In some cases, jealousy over one's spouse's friends is more a result of psychological repercussions from childhood experiences than one's actual marital situation.

Jeffrey Kramer is a second-year medical student just married to Tanya, an occupational therapist. Whenever Jeffrey has free time at night and wants to go out with his male friends, Tanya gets furious. From his standpoint, he feels hemmed in by his demanding medical school program, and Tanya's possessiveness makes him feel restricted at home. From Tanya's perspective, she feels neglected and second-rate. As each talk about their feelings, it becomes clear that they are repeating childhood patterns. Jeffrey's mother was a nurturing woman but, Jeffrey says, very demanding and irrational. His view of Tanya is much the same. Tanya's parents, on the other hand, had separated when she was a child, and so whenever she feels Jeffrey is drawing away from her, it terrifies her that she will lose him—just the way she felt she lost her parents when they divorced.

If you resent the amount of time your spouse spends with friends:

1. Determine whether or not your feelings stem from a deep, emotional neediness by weighing your feelings against the actual situation. Do this by placing a check next to all of the following statements which are true in your marriage:

☐ Your spouse spends *all* of his or her free time with friends.

☐ Your spouse always excludes you when he or she is with friends.

☐ You rarely have time to be with your spouse without his or her friends also being included.

If you checked off *any* of the above statements, then your situation may merit the concern you feel. If you did *not* check off any of the above—in other words, if you *do* have time alone with your mate, if your spouse *does* invite you along to be with his or her friends—your resentment may indicate a neediness and desire on your part for a childlike, dependent marital relationship. If you feel incomplete inside yourself, insecure, or afraid of abandonment, you may tend to look for constant proof of your partner's love. You'll seek safety and protection in a symbiotic bond with your spouse and guard your relationship tenaciously from any possible intruders. Eventually, such a fear of letting anyone else in can be harmful.

2. Share your feelings with your spouse. Let him or her know if you feel their friendships are impinging on your marriage. Once you've talked things out, your mate may decide to reschedule the times he or she gets together with friends, or realize your hurt at not being included in their socializing, or be able to reassure you that you come first.

3. Look at the benefits of your spouse's friendships. Although this may be difficult to see in the early stages of marriage when togetherness is of prime concern, there *are* definite advantages to having a mate who has other people to turn to for advice, companionship, entertainment. And keep in mind that your spouse's ability to care about friends reflects well on your mate's character and capability for commitment. Also, the enjoyment that your spouse derives from friends is a potential source of enrichment in your marriage. The more you bring to your relationship, the more interesting and fulfilling it will be.

4. Recognize that with time your spouse may look to friends less as he or she feels more comfortable being married. If you feel that your mate is being immature by continuing to maintain very close and frequent contact with old friends, try to appreciate how vulnerable your spouse may feel about "merging" in marriage, and respect the function that these friendships are playing. Be patient and try not to be too demanding. Once your spouse feels reassured that he or she does *not have to* give up their friends just because he or she is married, there will probably be less compulsion to be with those friends all the time.

FRIENDS OF THE OPPOSITE SEX

To many newlyweds the most threatening of their spouse's friendships are those which they maintain with members of the opposite sex. While rationally you may know that your partner's friendship is platonic, emotionally you may not truly accept that any male–female relationship is nonsexual. You can't help it, but you're jealous.

Relating to people of the opposite sex may also feel uncomfortable, especially if you're accustomed to being flirtatious, seductive, sexual. One woman told us that she had never realized that she acted coy and coquettish with men, but now that she is married she realizes she's used to being a flirt. While she no longer wants to behave that way, she admits that she misses the flattery and attention she used to get from men.

With time, friendships with those of the opposite sex usually become less tense and threatening. One man, married just a year, said:

> I used to resent Jan's friendships with guys. I was especially jealous of the guys she lived with before she met me. Recently she cleaned out her old photo albums and threw out some of the pictures of her with those guys. But I didn't say anything about it. I realized that those people were an important part of her past and anyone worth loving has a past. I suppose the fact that she still keeps in touch with them shows that the relationships she had were solid, important ones to her. It's her ability to care so deeply that makes me love her.

When conflicts arise regarding friendships with members of the opposite sex, you have several options:

1. Include your mate when you socialize with a friend of the opposite sex—so that he or she feels included and thereby less threatened. If your friend is someone you work with, you might invite your spouse to join you for lunch to get to know your friend. Or invite the friend home for dinner. If you're the one feeling jealous, ask that you be included when your mate socializes with friends of the opposite sex.

2. Keep your friendships separate from your marriage. Your spouse may not mind you having friends of the opposite sex, as long as you don't talk about them all the time and bring them into your relationship. You might want to get together with friends of the opposite sex during lunch hours—or at other times that don't infringe on your marriage.

3. You can end the friendship. One 24-year-old man, married two years, told us:

> After I got married I wanted to keep in touch with an old girlfriend of mine from college. My wife was very upset about my having had a relationship with that girl, since it took place while I was dating my wife. One night, several months after our wedding, while my wife was out I began writing my old girlfriend a friendly letter. My wife came home just as I was finishing it. I quickly flung it into the desk drawer but she immediately picked up on who I was writing to and I could see the hurt cross her face. I realized right then that it wasn't worth causing my wife such pain to keep in touch with an old girlfriend. I care about her, but she's in my past.

4. Talk about the reasons for jealousy. There may be specific things that one of you is doing which are making the other jealous. Maybe it has to do with gift giving, phone calls, paying too many compliments to a friend of the opposite sex. Consider whether your heterosexual friendships are provoking your spouse in some way, the impact of which you are denying. Are you (or is your mate) really expressing hostility in the tendency to openly socialize or flirt with those of the opposite sex? Explore your motivations and tell each other how your friendships might be different and less threatening. If you realize that your jealousy is not well founded but results from childhood fears of being left, explain to your spouse your feelings. Try to empathize with each other's situation.

DEVELOPING MUTUAL FRIENDS

At some point in marriage a couple will usually find themselves socializing more with other couples than with single friends. Part of it may be convenience—going out in a foursome may be more comfortable than having a third hanging on. But this change also seems to reflect a transformation in the way newlyweds look at themselves. As a couple grows closer and begins to view themselves more as a unit, they look toward others who are in the same position and share common concerns. And being with others who are married, our survey illustrated, is reinforcing:

- 28 percent of newlyweds noted that their relationships with married friends improved since their wedding.
- Only 4 percent noted that their relationships with married friends had worsened.

Researchers[7] have pointed out that while individual friendships have a separating influence on a couple, couple relationships have a joining effect and, in fact, are an almost obligatory aspect of being married. One man who recently got divorced after three years of marriage told us that he and his wife had never shared *any* of the same friends. He now views their lack of mutual friends as an indication that they had never seen themselves as a couple. "My wife didn't have any friends who are married. She said she never could relate to couples."

Some newlyweds complain of finding it difficult to find couples they both enjoy. "The two of us tend to overanalyze people after we leave them," said one husband who wished he and his wife had more couple friends. "We get hypercritical, which I don't think is good." This gossiping about friends, which is so common among spouses, may actually serve an important marital function, according to one theorist,[8] by helping a couple project the hostility that exists between them outside the marriage.

Being with other couples often has the effect of generating comparisons—how does *our* marriage match up against *theirs*. One woman, who confided to us that she is beset with doubts about her marriage, told us:

When we go out with another couple, I'll see them looking at each other lovingly, or sharing private jokes, or hugging each other, and I want to have that same experience with my husband. I become dissatisfied, envious, critical. It's a horrible feeling.

Another female newlywed related the following incident:

This weekend we went out to dinner with a couple. I was looking at them as I do a lot of couples now. They're on the same wavelength. The looks they were giving

each other showed their love for each other. Maybe
I'm too impressed by what people say and how they
act to each other. But being with other couples brings
out all of my insecurity about our marriage.

Yet another woman noted that when they socialize with
other couples, she and her husband often end up arguing in
front of them. For reasons they don't quite understand, tensions
and gripes that they leave alone in private seem to become
aroused in the company of others. It is, in fact, not uncommon
for couples who are unable to contain their aggression within
their relationship to use social situations as a way to ventilate
and display some of their rage.[9] You may find that you tend to
argue in front of certain friends. These couples may unconsciously stir up conflict between you and your spouse—as a way
of assuring themselves about their own marriage—because of
the aggression they see demonstrated in yours.

If you have problems meeting, developing, or keeping mutual friends:

**1. Examine whether these troubles relating to friends are
caused by, or are indicative of, other difficulties in your marriage.**
For instance, are your social problems related to:

- a lack of shared interests between you and your spouse
- making too little effort to set aside leisure time
- a lack of self-confidence as individuals and as a couple
- anger at each other that leads to a desire to humiliate
  each other in public
- doubts about your marital partner that make you jealous
  of other seemingly happy spouses

**2. Remember, what works for one couple will not necessarily
work for you.** One of the major tasks in marriage is to recognize
that your marriage is your own—for you and your spouse
to create to suit your needs. Your marriage couldn't—and
shouldn't—be like anyone else's. And just because a couple
seems to be blissfully happy—that doesn't mean they don't have
their share of problems. Every couple experiences ups and downs.
It's impossible to tell from socializing with another couple what
is going on behind closed doors. In other words, all comparisons
with other couples are futile and inaccurate. Rather than finding fault with your marriage for not being like someone else's,
try to make yours the best it can be.

TO CONFIDE—OR NOT
CONFIDE—IN FRIENDS?

Sure you may joke to your friends about how your spouse is messy, can't cook, snores in his or her sleep, and is too attached to their family. But it's less likely that you feel as comfortable unburdening yourself to your friends about your deeper marital doubts, disappointments, and anxieties. As one husband told us:

> I'm embarrassed to tell my friends when things aren't going well at home, I guess because I feel a little bit like a failure—like I shouldn't be having the trouble with my wife that I am. But also, I'm afraid that if I share my doubts about my wife with my friends, it will color their view of her. I don't want them holding things against my wife long after we've worked through some of our problems.

How much you should or should not tell your friends regarding your deepest feelings about your marriage is a very individual decision. There are benefits to expressing some of one's anxieties about marriage to a friend. It's only once friends understand what you are experiencing that they can offer support, advice, and possibly confide that they too have experienced the same thing in their own marriage. And there is certainly nothing to be ashamed about in admitting to a friend that you are experiencing marital difficulties. Chances are your friend has gone through some rough periods in their own relationships too.

People have different needs regarding how much to tell others about what is going on in their life.

If you are considering confiding in a friend about your marital feelings and situation:

1. Ask yourself the following questions:
- Is my friend trustworthy?
- Can my friend keep a secret?
- Has my friend been sympathetic in the past to my concerns, or is he or she the type to say things like "I told you so!"

2. Consider your spouse's feelings before you confide in friends.
How upset will your mate be to know that you're planning to
talk about an explosive argument you recently had? Is it appropriate to talk with friends regarding this matter or should
you seek professional help?

There are pros and cons to sharing your marital concerns
with friends and only you can decide whether such confidences
are appropriate.

WORKSHOP: PLANNING
SOCIAL SCHEDULES

Each individual has different attitudes regarding how often
to see friends and how much closeness is desirable. If you and
your spouse are both social butterflies or homebodies, then you
are probably in general agreement about how often to socialize.
Or if one of you is a "sit at home" type, but perfectly happy to
let your mate draw you out of your shell by planning your social
life, then your opposite styles may suit you.

But more often than not, figuring out which friends to see
when takes a bit of juggling before you settle down to a social
schedule that suits you both. If you and your spouse are having
difficulty planning your social life, we suggest trying the following, very specific exercise. Undoubtedly, with time you won't
need to be so regimented about dividing your time amongst
the different people in your lives. But by putting down in black
and white exactly when you'd like to see which friends, you
quickly establish your individual visions for how you'd like friends
to fit into your lives.

Sit down with your spouse and on a pad of paper list:
- which friends you each would like to see individually
  next month
- which friends you'd like to socialize with together next
  month
- how many weekend days and nights you'd like to spend
  with each other, just the two of you, next month
- any occasions for which you have to get together with
  family members next month

Then take out a calendar, flip to next month, and pencil
in tentative dates based on your list—dates to have alone with

each other, with relatives, with individual friends, and mutual friends. Try to compromise on plans over which you disagree. For instance, if you think your spouse socializes too frequently alone with their friends, you might arrange that those get-togethers only take place weeknights, leaving weekends for each other. Perhaps you might plan to do one weekend "his" way (quiet dinners alone with a few friends) and one weekend "her" way (partying with lots of friends at clubs). If you can't think of any friends you'd both like to socialize with together, discuss things you might do to increase your opportunity of meeting other couples—whether it's joining a church or synagogue, becoming members of a book club, joining a bowling league, or enrolling together in a dance or cooking course.

PART 5

REFLECTIONS

*"Oh how we danced on the night
we were wed. . . ."*

Anniversary Waltz

TROUBLE IN PARADISE

Coping with Serious Marital Doubts and Problems

As you approach your first anniversary you may be disappointed because marriage is not as you thought it would be. Small problems that you had assumed would disappear may have grown; doubts about your mate and marriage may have lingered.

Throughout this book we've tried to demonstrate that experiencing marital problems is normal, even among newlyweds who feel, overall, very pleased about their marriages. In our survey of newlyweds, most of whom described themselves as feeling happy about their marriages:[1]

- 51 percent reported having at least occasional doubts that their marriage would last.
- 49 percent reported having significant marital problems.
- 41 percent reported finding marriage harder than they expected.[2]
- 18 percent reported that marriage has been either a pretty difficult or very difficult adjustment for them.[3]

Throughout this book we've explained why the transition into marriage may be rife with conflict and how couples may successfully cope with these challenges to strengthen and solidify their marriage.

Yet, there are some marriages that don't work out, almost right from the start. Statistics show[4] that the first five years of marriage are the highest risk period for divorce. More people get divorced within this initial stage than during any other time span in marriage. And so if you find yourself feeling overwhelmed by marital problems, personal anxieties, or doubts, you shouldn't hesitate to seek professional help. Consulting with a therapist does *not* mark you as weak, sick, or a failure. In fact, making the effort to improve your marriage is the *healthiest* step you can take.

How can you tell if your problems are more serious than the norm? How can you know when you need the help of an expert?

CHECKUP: DO YOU NEED PROFESSIONAL HELP?

The following is a list of symptoms of marital difficulties which indicate that professional help is called for. Place a check next to all of the symptoms which apply to you:

- ☐ feeling overwhelmed by marital problems you can't seem to solve yourselves
- ☐ feeling so angry or irritated at your spouse that you can't recall why you married in the first place
- ☐ experiencing recurring sexual difficulties
- ☐ feeling consumed by external stress—a job loss, a death in the family, an unexpected pregnancy, or other life crisis
- ☐ experiencing *constant* sexual fantasies about partners other than your spouse
- ☐ a total intolerance of the differences that exist between you and your spouse
- ☐ a persistent desire to end your marriage
- ☐ feeling or becoming violent toward yourself or your mate

The following is a list of symptoms of psychopathology that may or may not be due to marital problems but which certainly would contribute to marital difficulties. These symptoms indicate the need for a consultation with a psychiatrist, who can conduct both medical and psychological evaluations.

- ☐ feeling deeply depressed, with or without suicidal thoughts
- ☐ abusing drugs or alcohol
- ☐ experiencing sharp mood swings
- ☐ experiencing dramatic changes in appetite, sleep patterns, or weight
- ☐ experiencing severe panic or fear

☐ experiencing vague physical ailments, such as
    chronic headaches, backaches, or stomach pain
☐ experiencing hallucinations or hearing voices

As you can see, the above lists includes both physical and
emotional indicators for counseling. Before you consult a therapist, any physical symptom should be diagnosed by a psychiatrist or by a family physician.

SEEKING PROFESSIONAL
HELP

If you're feeling hopeless about your marriage, you may
be wondering what benefits a therapist can offer. A qualified
expert can help you:

*   identify underlying problems in your marriage (exam-
    ple: Is your sexual difficulty stemming from a physical
    problem or from an emotional one—perhaps a fear of
    intimacy?)
*   gain a more objective perspective in which to evaluate
    your problems
*   understand how you are at least partially responsible for
    your marital problems
*   find alternatives to approaching and handling problems

What a competent therapist will usually *not* do is tell you
who is "right" and "wrong" in your marriage, nor will a counselor be able to change your spouse into the person you'd like
him or her to be.

To find a qualified therapist, ask your physician or a member of your clergy for a recommendation. If there is a major
medical center in your area with a psychiatric department, the
head of the psychiatric staff can probably make a referral once
you've explained your needs and interest. Social service and
community organizations are also likely to be of help. Organizations of professional therapists—such as the American Psychiatric Association and the American Association for Marriage
and Family Therapy—can also refer you to someone in your
area. You might contact their national offices in Washington,
D.C., or check if these organizations have a local branch in your
area.

What kind of therapist you see should depend upon your

needs. If your problem has a physiological basis (for instance, if you suffer from depression or panic disorder), then you should see a psychiatrist, since he or she has been medically trained and can prescribe medication. But whether you see a psychiatrist, psychologist, social worker, or pastoral counselor, you should make sure to inquire about their training *and* certification. Also ask about their psychological orientation. There are several approaches to treating marital problems, depending on the orientation of the specialist:

A *psychodynamic* therapist examines the way conflicting desires, unconscious feelings, conscience, and reality lead to a sense of anxiety, depression, helplessness, and despair. Childhood roots may be explored to understand and change debilitating and emotionally harmful patterns of behavior. Feelings and reactions that emerge in the "here and now" of therapy may be used to add vivid dimension to understanding one's conflict and to help find solutions.

A *behavioral* therapist looks at the behaviors that are contributing to marital problems and focuses on replacing destructive patterns with positive, reinforcing behaviors. The emphasis is on changing behavior patterns rather than on understanding them.

A *systems, or family,* therapist views the entire family as a unit, with each member influencing the other.[5] If in-laws are a problem, a systems therapist might involve those relatives in therapy, with the goal of altering family patterns.

An *experiential* therapist concentrates on how spouses experience each other. A couple might be asked to role-play each other's part in order to better understand the emotions they evoke in each other.

Many professionals—including sex therapists—integrate various approaches in therapy. A sex therapist might encourage a couple to explore their childhood fears and guilt about sex, in addition to prescribing for them specific sexual behaviors and techniques to practice in the privacy of their home.

A good therapist will be able to evaluate what kind and what length of treatment is appropriate after a consultation has been completed. A few sessions may be sufficient for a couple experiencing a particular crisis. Prolonged treatment may be advised for someone seeking an in-depth understanding of the nature of their problems.

Whether you see a therapist alone or with your spouse depends on what you both want. If you're both eager to be in therapy together, you should look for a therapist to counsel you jointly. If one of you has no interest in going to a therapist, then the other can be seen alone in treatment. Some therapists see spouses both individually and together. Others strongly insist that a husband and wife should be seen by different therapists. Again, these are all questions to take up during an initial consultation. If, for some reason, you are not satisfied with the competency or comfortable with the technique of the first therapist you see, then pursue a second consultation with a different therapist to compare approaches.

Be aware that entering therapy may be painful. In the close relationship between patient and therapist, you may find yourself acknowledging and examining patterns in your life that you've long ignored or denied. But know that, ultimately, there is an even greater risk in not looking at those issues which are harming your marriage.

THOSE WHO DON'T MAKE IT
THROUGH THE FIRST YEAR

In our interviews, we met with several people whose marriages ended early on—either in their first year of marriage or shortly after. The stories of these couples are quite diverse. Some of them are more common—due to family pressures or interference. Others are more dramatic and unusual. We relate them not to demonstrate any "lessons" about what to do or what not to do, but rather to show some of the many ways and reasons why marriages may quickly sour.

Amy Minetti's story was probably the most stereotypical. Now a 30-year-old newspaper editor, Amy had gotten married when she was 19 and had sought an annulment within nine months of her wedding. Her explanation for their marital failure: she and her husband were too young when they married.

Amy met Ralph, whom she was to marry, when she was 17 and he was 18. They were both walking on the boardwalk in Coney Island, Brooklyn, with some friends. Ralph was Amy's first serious, long-term boyfriend. After a year of dating, getting married seemed the logical thing to do, she says. Amy's parents didn't approve of Ralph—they thought he was wild, brash, and irresponsible. But the more they disapproved, the more Amy wanted to stay with Ralph. "Getting married was my way of getting out of my parents' house. Also, there was an unspoken competition between me and some friends and cousins about who'd marry first," she recalls.

Amy's parents planned a big, traditional Italian wedding. Three weeks before her wedding Amy considered backing out after a huge fight with Ralph, but the bridesmaids already had their gowns, the down payment had been put on the hall. Amy said she couldn't deal with the humiliation of calling the wedding off.

Amy recalled that she and Ralph had their first marital squabble in a heart-shaped bathtub in a honeymoon Poconos resort.

> I realized right away that I had done a stupid thing. My husband was just a boy. I was brighter and couldn't always talk to him. He was intimidated. We'd both get very frustrated. Before marriage, we hung out with a crowd. In our apartment alone together, it didn't seem like there was much to talk about. One month after marriage he was fired from his job of fixing photocopying machines because he wouldn't cut his hair for his job. When our wedding money ran out so did our marriage.

While Amy told us she has never regretted ending her marriage, she also described how difficult it was for her to go back to her parents' house, abide by a curfew, and enter the dating scene.

> My self-confidence was very low after we had our marriage annulled. All my college friends felt young and carefree, and I felt unattractive and was very introverted. I went through a period of frigidity. It took me a long time to start feeling good about myself and to be able to date. But I realize now that you have to have self-esteem before becoming part of a couple.

While the desire to escape her parents helped catapult Amy into marriage, it was the wish to remain closely involved with his family that contributed to the breakup of Stewart Eisenman's marriage. Even five years later, Stewart, now 35, has difficulty finding fault with his wife, Gloria, from whom he sought a divorce after six months of marriage.

> Gloria was a great wife. She was always in an up mood when I came home from work. She loved to be physical. She was affectionate and loving. I'm sure she was shocked when I announced I wanted a divorce.

Part of the problem, according to Stewart, is that he didn't know Gloria very well when he married her. He proposed to her a month after they met. "I felt some pressure," he told us, "because when I met her, Gloria was dating someone who was eager to marry her." Of the love he felt in that initial stage, he said, "I haven't experienced that feeling of love before or after."

Stewart's parents made it clear from the beginning that they didn't like Gloria or her family. During Stewart and Gloria's four-month engagement, conflict arose between Stewart's parents and his future in-laws over who would pay what for the wedding. Stewart, an only son who runs a clothing business with his mother and father, began to sense that by marrying, he would be breaking up the cozy family unit he was used to. Yet, he told us, it was only several years after his divorce that he began to acknowledge how influenced he was by his parents' disapproval of his wife.

At the time, Stewart blamed his in-laws for a lot of his and Gloria's domestic problems. "They were very much in the picture and always butting into our business." Stewart was also rather taken aback by how much he and Gloria were fighting, something he hadn't witnessed in his own parents' marriage and with which he was intensely uncomfortable. "I don't like arguing. Gloria was very inflexible. I couldn't deal with that."

While Stewart may have unconsciously sought a wife who was strong enough to help him break away from his family, the pull between his feelings of loyalty toward his parents and his new wife became too frightening and uncomfortable to tolerate. Doubts that began during his engagement became accentuated as soon as he married.

Stewart said he felt badly about the blow he dealt to Gloria's ego. "I know she was very hurt," he commented. His parents, he recalled, were very supportive when he told them he was getting divorced. When we spoke with him, Stewart still seemed to be struggling with why he ran into marriage and why he panicked and ran out.

It was the desire to fulfill her parents' wishes that led Colleen Lee, a Chinese-American computer consultant, to marry at age 42. Colleen's husband, 50-year-old Paul Ling, is a Chinese engineer who is just the type of man Colleen's parents wanted her to wed. But when we met with Colleen, just six months after her wedding, it was already clear she was having a rough adjustment. "The longer you've lived alone the harder it is to adjust to having a mate. I feel kind of restricted, like in having to get back home after work," she told us.

One of the most blatant signs of Colleen's anxiety about her marriage was that within minutes of meeting us, she started talking about her previous 19-year relationship with a Jewish man. Asked why she hadn't married her Jewish boyfriend, she said that she had come to the conclusion that she wanted to marry somebody with the same cultural background as herself. Her boyfriend's Jewish family, she said, had never been accepting of her and she had never even told her old-world, elderly Chinese parents about her Jewish boyfriend.

Despite their shared Oriental heritage, Colleen noted to us that she and her husband are very different.

> He's Catholic and I'm Protestant. He's traditionally role-minded, and I believe in equality. He's very meticulous about every dime, and I believe in spending money and that it's important to enjoy life.

The differences did not end there. Paul had a vasectomy years ago; Colleen said she wants children. They talked about adopting a child, but, she told us, "for him it's not as crucial an issue as for me." Colleen also informed us that Paul suffers from premature ejaculation and sometimes has difficulty getting an erection.

> When I met Paul, I wasn't attracted to him physically. I didn't think of him as a sexual partner until later on. He has a lot of sexual problems and sexual guilt. My one condition before marrying him was that he'd continue seeing a therapist.

As Colleen walked us to the elevator at the end of our interview, she informed us that she was herself considering entering psychotherapy.

By our second interview with Colleen, two months later, she had separated from her husband. Her voice and face seemed pained as she tried to explain the rapid deterioration of her marriage.

> We went to see a marital therapist and we did not even agree upon the problems. Paul's concept was that our only problem was sex. He said he was going to have an operation so that he could function sexually. I didn't want him to do it—I felt it was treating the symptom, not the problem.

Colleen's view of their problems included: Paul's not having close friends, his preference for staying at home and watching TV rather than going to cultural events, his owing money to creditors, and his being secretive about where he spent his money.

> Before we married, he verbally agreed to certain financial arrangements, household responsibilities, and lifestyle arrangements. After we got married, he said he did that just because he didn't want to lose me. I felt suffocated in the relationship. Paul used to call me six, seven times a day, just to say, "How are you?" At the beginning it was sweet. But after a while it becomes unhealthy. I saw it as insecurity and mistrust.

In her stream of complaints Colleen seemed, like many newlyweds, to be confused by all the emotional turmoil she had experienced in her short-lived marriage. She knew she was unhappy, but she wasn't quite sure what was the major problem.

Months later, Colleen acknowledged to us that she had *not wanted* to stay married to Paul. Looking back, she told us that Paul was the kind of person she had felt she was *supposed* to marry. After all, that is what her traditional Chinese parents expected. And although Colleen was 42 years old, she had never truly broken away from her parents. She had never told them about her 19-year relationship with her Jewish boyfriend. In retrospect, Colleen said she realized that she was drawn to Paul out of sympathy and obligation.

> I was raised in a family where the motto is "Be good to others." Paul had a difficult life, and I wanted to rescue him by making him happy. But at some point I had to realize that *I* am very important. I had to stop thinking about what other people will think.

Several months after separating from Paul, Colleen described herself to us as feeling "liberated." It was as if by doing what her parents wanted her to do—getting married—and then rejecting the marriage, she was asserting her adulthood to her parents. She informed us that she had recently met a man in whom she was interested. "I told my parents, 'Look, this is someone I've met and I like. But I don't want to have pressure about marrying him.' " For the first time, as a divorced woman, Colleen was facing her parents as an adult.

Of course, just by the fact that Colleen had stayed in a 19-year relationship with someone who for her was "nonmarriage-able" (because he is Jewish and she is Chinese) indicates that Colleen had fears of marriage, commitment, and intimacy. Colleen's marriage demonstrated her ambivalence about wanting to be dependent and independent. As someone who manages other people at work, she tends to be a person in control. Yet, while she chose to marry a man who had few other people in his life so that he would depend totally upon her, she found that pressure unbearable. Some wives might love it if their husbands called them six or seven times a day; Colleen found such calls "unhealthy" and threatening. Despite her desire to be independent, marriage made Colleen realize that she also wants to be taken care of by a man—physically, financially, emotionally. Before marriage her massive denial of her need for anybody else was evidenced in her choosing a husband who could not sexually satisfy her. It was only after the failure of her marriage that Colleen was able to admit that her sexual and emotionally needy self is important.

The impact of family upon choice of mate was mentioned to us by yet another person who ended their marriage early on.

Brett Samuels, a tall, dark, 36-year-old social worker, called Dory for a blind date shortly after his dad had given him her phone number. Bret's dad and Dory's dad had been friends in high school. Although Dory's dad had recently died, Brett's father had become friendly with her mother. Both parents had recently discovered that both of their children were living near each other in Los Angeles.

After four months of dating, Brett and Dory became engaged. Brett said:

> It was magic. After spending my whole life being so ambivalent, I couldn't believe I felt such love for her.

So we rushed right into it. Figuring we didn't know each other that well, we planned an eight-month engagement.

Looking back after his nine-month marriage ended, Brett acknowledged that there were problems during their engagement but they swept them under the rug.

Her mother thought my two-bedroom apartment was a dump, but Dory had an objection to every other apartment that we looked at. She hated every neighborhood and became very complaining and very angry. She really regressed. I don't think she really wanted to get married. We ended up moving into her studio.

You see, my father is very, very wealthy. He offered to buy us a house, but I didn't want him to pay for our house. I'd take some help from him but I want to make it on my own. Dory and her mother took that to mean that I wouldn't take *any* money from my father. They couldn't understand or accept my values.

While Dory and Brett's honeymoon and first two months of marriage were pleasant enough, by the third month Dory became withdrawn, angry, and depressed, according to Brett. "Dory came home from work, turned on the TV in our studio apartment, and would watch all night." Brett, who despises watching TV, asked that some nights they just talk rather than watch television. She refused to compromise.

At first, said Brett, he couldn't admit that things were going so bad, so quickly.

I tried to be patient. I thought: Dory's only 28, be patient. But I realized that we have different values. At one point, I suggested that I might change jobs, which would bring in less money but give me more time at home if we were to have a child. But Dory wouldn't hear of it. She only wanted me to make money. She didn't care or understand about my doing what I like. I felt like she didn't love me. She didn't know who I was or what I value. She didn't act like a wife at all —she wouldn't talk to me. Unconsciously I think she wanted to force me to leave, because she didn't feel strong enough to leave herself.

Brett said that at first he blamed himself for the failure of his marriage, but he felt that he'd been very patient with her, and had she shown any desire to work out their problems, he would have stayed. "The last straw was that she refused to see a marriage therapist or seek any help," he commented.

In analyzing why he fell in love with Dory, Brett said that part of his attraction to her was related to the fact that his father had introduced them. *"It was a way of getting close to my father. We haven't shared very much. Dory is the only thing he ever gave to me besides money."*

Brett also hypothesized that by marrying him, Dory tried to regain her father, who had died shortly before she met Brett—and who'd been an old friend of Brett's father.

I think part of why she became depressed when we got married was that she was mourning over the loss of her father. She wanted a daddy. She wanted someone to take care of her. She was acting like a little girl rather than a married woman.

Like most people who are dissatisfied with their marriages, Brett focused on his spouse's problems—he talked to us about his wife's immature, regressive behavior and her lack of desire to stay married. What he didn't say—but what his comments suggested—is that his passivity, or rather his resistance to asserting and insisting that some of his own needs get met, may have also contributed to the failure of his marriage.

Looking back, everyone we spoke with who got divorced said there had been danger signs before they got married, but they ignored them. While in some cases the denial was of problems in a couple's interpersonal relationship, in other instances, as in the following two stories, the denial was of aspects of a spouse's psychological pathology.

Thirty-two-year-old Beatrice Powers admitted to us that when she got married four years before, she refused to read the signals that her husband was sending her.

Before we got married, Will told me a story of his once not having had any money in Florida and stealing things.

I remember filing that story away. He told me he was a thief, but I didn't want to believe it, so I didn't.

Despite living with Will for two years before marriage, Beatrice said she didn't recognize Will's chronic lying, stealing, forging of her checks, and drug-taking until she married him.

Tall, pencil-thin, with a no-nonsense style, Beatrice recalled:

I was more responsible than Will was and I didn't like that. But when I met Will, I was kind of amorphous and unopinionated. I thought to myself, "No one will ever love me like Will does." I had doubts about marrying Will but I didn't listen to them. Before our wedding, I had escape nightmares. I had a dream of a rabbit running along the fence, something running after it, and I couldn't get away. I lost 10 pounds and wasn't sleeping well. But I'm the middle of five kids— all overachievers. I always wanted recognition. I would be the first to get married in my family—that was a coup. I knew I was nervous but I couldn't separate what I was feeling from normal prewedding jitters.

Beatrice and Will went to see a premarital therapist, but as she put it:

I was hoping the therapist would be a mind reader. I didn't express my doubts. I was looking for someone to save me. Nobody picked up what I was trying to say by osmosis. I felt like I had given my word to marry Will and I should do it.

The day before their wedding, Will went to buy a gift for his best man.

We had agreed that he would spend $50. When the bill came in a month later, I saw he had spent $160. I told him in no uncertain terms that this was not a great thing to do. The whole thing of me being responsible got set in cement two seconds after we got married. I always paid all the bills. His big line was, "I'm not sure how much I can give you this week." We had conversations about this all the time. I said, "I don't get it.

You earn twice as much as I do. Where is it going?
Why are we not acting like we're married?"

Soon after their wedding Will stopped having sex with
Beatrice.

It wasn't that I wasn't interested. He just wasn't there,
like he wasn't there in every other area of the relationship. He didn't come home for dinner, never called
to say he'd be late. The low point came when I asked
him to give my diamond ring to his mother to put in
her safe deposit box. A month later I found this pawn-
shop ticket for a diamond ring. I confronted him. He
said, "Well, I needed the money." I freaked out. I don't
know from pawnshops. Being married to him was like
a descent into hell. I knew the money had to be going
somewhere—gambling, drugs, other women.

When Beatrice found a hypodermic needle and bottle cap
in her sofa, Will told her they must have been left by his brother,
who was enrolled in a methadone program.

The reason we didn't get a divorce for a while is that
I kept asking myself, "How much can I put up with?
Maybe things will change."

But when she discovered a canceled check of hers that Will had
forged, it was the final straw.

It suddenly dawned on me that Will left all this for me
to find—the pawn ticket, the hypodermic needle and
bottle cap, the canceled check. I realized that it would
never change. All my efforts to make this marriage
work were a complete waste.

Up until the time I decided to divorce, I was dependent
on what other people would say. I was scared of my
parents telling me, "What, you failed!" Before I got a
divorce, I had to be willing to risk other people not
approving of me.

The aftermath of Beatrice's experience, she said, is that

I'm a hundred years older than I was five years ago.
I was living in a cloudbank and I crashed down to

earth five minutes after I got married. I lost my illusions. I'm very big on reality now. I look at everything more analytically. Now I don't care what anyone else thinks about what I do for the rest of my life. My advice to someone about to get married? Try to seriously imagine living with this person for the next fifty years. Can you imagine being happy with this person—warts and all? Nothing will change magically. Things you don't like now, you'll hate later. If somebody tells you they used to drink, think about what they're telling you.

There was less cynicism, but as much determinism expressed by Lili Kartel, a 38-year-old divorced woman. When Lili, a Texan, and Tab, a New Englander, met several years ago and fell in love, they decided to get married so they could be together. Right before meeting Tab, Lili had discovered she was a diabetic, and his acceptance of the diabetes was very important to her. "I'm sure I felt less marriageable because of it," she explained in her Southern drawl. Nevertheless, Lili had not wanted to get married right away. She suggested that she move up to Massachusetts and they just live together. But "Tab wouldn't hear of it," she recalled.

He said he had just been through that with another woman and that it hadn't worked out. In my head I felt like we didn't know each other long enough when we became engaged—about 14 weeks. But in my heart it felt good. Everybody said, "Go ahead. He's so wonderful. You're so good together." I should have listened to my insecurity. But I agreed to get married.

Before they became engaged, Lili had visited Tab and met his roommate, a gay male psychiatrist.

Tab's explanation was very rational. They had lived across the hall from each other in an apartment house and discovered that they both wanted to live in a bigger place. That turned out not to be the truth. I sort of sensed it when I was there, but I ignored it. Tab's housemate looked at me very peculiarly when Tab told him we were engaged. That made me uneasy. The funny thing is I would always confront Tab. Tab said he always thought his housemate wanted a relationship with him and might be jealous. I later found out that Tab's former girlfriend left him when she found out that Tab and his housemate were having a homosexual relationship.

Lili and Tab had a passionate relationship in their five months before marriage. But on their wedding night it was different.

He just didn't seem to enjoy sex. He acted like it was something he wanted to get over with. I thought it was the strain of the wedding. We had basic intercourse the first two days of our honeymoon—that was it for the rest of the two-week trip. I tried to initiate sex, but Tab didn't respond. He had completely changed. Once we came back from our honeymoon, Tab would come home from work, go into our room, pull down the shades, and sleep. We had sex maybe ten times when we were married. The relationship became very strained. I began to feel like a monster. The sick thing was if there were people around, he'd be very physically affectionate and teasing. And after they'd leave, he'd stop. He'd put on a big show in front of his family that we were going to bed with each other—it was horrible.

While Tab refused to acknowledge that there was any problem, Lili sought guidance from a therapist. Eventually Tab agreed to go along with Lili to a sex therapist, and after a few sessions he told her he was ready to have intercourse.

It was very angry, very aggressive—there was no kissing, no loving. I just cried afterward. It wasn't that I just wanted sex. That was a symptom of everything that was missing from our relationship.

While at first Lili said she couldn't bear the responsibility of ending the marriage herself, after the last episode she decided she had no other choice. At no point did her husband admit to her that he was gay.

He traveled a lot for business, and I don't know what he did on trips. I do know of an interlude he had in our hometown. We visited friends, one of whom is gay. Our host said he had to go to the local hardware store. Tab said, "Goodness me, I have to get something too." When I finally asked Tab's gay former roommate about Tab's sexuality, he said, "That's just the problem. Tab doesn't know himself."

Looking back, Lili said she has not one doubt that getting a divorce was the right step for her to take. As much as she wanted her marriage to succeed, she realized it was impossible for that to happen without her husband sharing that desire. And as he withdrew from her physically and emotionally, "I began to disassociate my affection for him," she says.

We interviewed others whose marriages ended early on, and in each instance, the difficulties that caused the dissolution were unique. While having trouble does not forecast doom for a relationship, we did observe that the marriages that ended in divorce were characterized by one or more of the following underlying problems:

1. Poor individuation of one or both spouses from their family of origin. (This is evidenced in the marriages of Amy Minetti, whose marriage was a rebellious act against her parents; Stewart Eisenman, who felt anguished by shifting his allegiance from his parents to his wife; and Colleen Lee, who married to fulfill her parent's dream.)

2. Problems with aggression, anger, and assertiveness. (This is demonstrated in Brett Samuel's unwillingness to express certain needs and expectations and to insist that they be met, as well as in Stewart Eisenman's discomfort with arguing with his wife. The problem of controlling aggression was also evidenced among some other couples we interviewed whose marriages ended as a result of domestic violence.)

3. Denial of hidden psychopathology. (In our sample, this was seen in the marriage of Will and Beatrice Powers, both of whom resisted facing up to Will's drug abuse and lying, as well as Lili and Tab Kartel's denial of his unresolved bisexual tendencies.)

HOW TO DECIDE
WHEN TO GET OUT

Marriages that are short and sour do not fade easily into one's past. No matter how little time a marriage lasts, it leaves its imprint on the people involved. Those we spoke with whose marriages ended early on said the experience had been harrowing. The pain, anguish, regret, and embarrassment had left their scars.[6] The failure of one's marriage shakes one's confidence in one's ability to judge people. As Colleen Lee put it, "How can I manage other people at work and tell them what to do if I make such a mess out of my own life?"

But there are situations in which marriages just aren't right—when no matter how much time or effort you give them, they fail. There are circumstances when two people would be better off out of the marriage than in it.

How can you assess if your marital problems constitute a real malignancy or can be resolved through your own efforts or with the help of therapy?

The truth is that almost any problem can be dealt with without walking out on the marriage. One person might accept the fact that their mate is gay, while another refuses to stay in a marriage with someone who is homosexual. One person might stay in a marriage with an alcoholic, drug-abusing, or mentally ill spouse, while another finds such a situation intolerable. One person might stay in a miserable marriage because they are too afraid to leave it, while another has sufficient strength to risk ending it even though the alternative is unknown. One individual might try to involve their spouse in the new directions in which he or she is growing, while another decides that they have outgrown their mate, period. To a large degree the extent of a problem is based on one's view of it. *Only you can decide how much is too much. Only you can decide when to walk out.*

As we've discussed throughout this book, marriage is a major personal transformation, and when a couple experiences a tumultuous newlywed year, it behooves them to look at and understand these changes. Yet, while we think it's important for couples to give their marriage a chance and foolish not to give themselves time to make adjustments, we also think it is worthwhile to reflect on the indications of when it is time to get out of a marriage.

Dr. Leonard Diamond, a New York psychoanalyst, believes that divorce is probably indicated if a couple's marriage is characterized by the following three factors:[7]

1. No shared common goals. If you do not share a similar vision of how you want to live your life together, you may be unsuited to spend your life together. If you don't share any of the same hopes and aspirations—whether they involve raising children, pursuing careers, dedicating yourselves to causes, or living hedonistically—if you don't hold any of the same values or share any mutual purpose in life, then your marriage will probably not provide the day-to-day mutual involvements that are sustaining, reinforcing, and rewarding.

2. No like or love for each other. If you don't enjoy being together, if you feel many more negative feelings toward each other and few or no positive feelings, if your spouse isn't someone you would befriend if you weren't married to them—then at some point you may find it intolerable to stay in your marriage.

3. Not caring about one's spouse as much as oneself. If you don't feel invested in your mate's health, welfare, and happiness to the same degree that you care about your own, or at least to a substantial degree, then your marriage may be at risk. In a marriage where there is care and concern, one person empathizes with the other.

You're likely to experience all of the above feelings at some time or other. It is almost inevitable that at times you'll hate your mate or feel distant or be less concerned with their preoccupations than usual. It is only if your marriage is *always* characterized by one or more of the above three qualities, that you may be better off out of marriage than in it. But even if that is the case—don't make any impulsive decisions to get out of your marriage. It is better to give your marital relationship a little time than to end it quickly and later have regrets. And before making any final decisions, you may benefit from consulting a therapist to determine if and how you might save your marriage.

Because of the many feelings that getting married can stir up—about yourself, your family, and your mate—more often than not it can be difficult to tell early on whether your marriage will be able to withstand many of the difficulties you initially face. As George Bernard Shaw's character wisely advises in his play *You Never Can Tell*:[8]

> Cheer up, sir, cheer up: every man is frightened of marriage when it comes to the point; but it often turns out very comfortable, very enjoyable and happy indeed, sir—from time to time. I never was master in my own house, sir: my wife was like your young lady: she was of a commanding and masterful disposition, which my son has inherited. But if I had my life to live twice over, I'd do it again, I'd do it again, I assure you. You never can tell, sir: you never can tell.

THE FIRST ANNIVERSARY
Taking Stock

No matter how you choose to celebrate the occasion, your first anniversary marks a milestone in your relationship. While your wedding signifies the beginning of your marriage, your first anniversary connotes the start of your "settling in" phase. One year later the excitement of the wedding has subsided, the towels and flatware patterns have been selected, the thank-you notes have been sent.

If you've survived the turbulent ups and downs inherent in adjusting to marriage, you probably feel a tremendous sense of accomplishment and relief. If you're doubtful about the future of your marriage and confused about how the joy of your wedding day has deteriorated so badly, you are probably questioning just where your relationship has gone wrong, who is to blame, and what might be done. Either way, your first anniversary is likely to evoke a rich array of feelings and reactions. It will stimulate you to reflect on your marriage—where you have been and where you are going.

"WE'VE COME A LONG WAY"

In chapter 1 we discussed the different reactions that people have when they first get married. Among them, we described the "Disappointed Dreamers," who are dismayed when they discover that marriage isn't all "roses," and the "Ho-Hum Honeymooners," who assume a blasé attitude about marriage, assured that just signing a paper won't do anything to change their relationship or their lives.

We found it interesting that by their first anniversary many husbands and wives whom we interviewed had changed their attitude about marriage. Given the time, people are often willing to give up some of the fantasies with which they entered marriage. They realize that marriage does not magically solve

every problem, and that to make a success of marriage they
need to find ways to make it work. There is a growing recognition that one must see one's spouse as a separate individual
who needs to be accepted and appreciated for who he or she
is, and not expect that spouse to fulfill all of one's own expectations about who and how he or she should be. In fact, most
of the men and women who described their marriages in positive terms at the time of their first anniversary were, or had
grown to become, "Realistic Romantics." There was a more
knowing, open-eyed quality to their attitudes about their marriages. Life together was not always rosy, but it felt more sat-
isfyingly *real* than before. Even those who had denied that
marriage would change anything, admitted that marriage *had*
changed something. Married life, they said, was closer, deeper,
more connected.

Barbara Dobbs, whom we introduced in chapter 3, perfectly personified that change in attitude. After six months of
marriage, she had informed us that she was considering seeking
an annulment because of differences between her husband and
herself, but at her first anniversary Barbara described herself
as quite contented in her marriage. She told us:

> The second half of the first year is so much better. I'm
> not sure why. Part of it has to do with a business man-
> agement class I'm taking in which my professor spoke
> about taking responsibility for relationships. That idea
> really influenced me. It seems like my husband and I
> are communicating better. We're not fighting as much.
> I'm more relaxed and accepting of him. You know, I
> never expected a man to be so fussy about decorating,
> but Ned is. It's been a true compromise. I've tried to
> stop nagging him so much. Also, I don't think I notice
> annoying things about Ned as much as I did. When I
> changed careers recently, I realized how giving and
> supporting Ned is. He has done things like iron my
> blouses when I'm too tired after work. I mean that's
> *so* nice. I feel much closer to him now, like I know him
> a lot better.

After pausing for a moment, Barbara continued:

> Looking back, I realize that I thought I knew Ned
> before I married him, but I was missing a big piece of

the pie. We hadn't lived together, and dating is so artificial. You just don't know anyone until you live with them. In the last year we've really grown and developed together. I feel like I've got a nice buddy. We've still got a ways to go in working out some problems, but I think we'll both work at it. If we have anything going for us it's that we're both pretty much givers.

Even those who lived with their mates before marrying, acknowledged that one year after the wedding things were somewhat different. One man, who lived with his wife 10 years before marrying her, said:

I used to get angry with her and not verbalize it and think about leaving. Since I'm married, I don't really think of leaving. Now if I'm angry, I tell her, but we tend to settle things much faster than we used to. We don't want to be angry with each other. Years ago when we'd have fights, they'd linger. There's more of a family kind of feeling between us. We have more invested in each other's happiness.

By their first anniversary most couples have a perspective on their marriages. They know what their strong points are, what their weak spots are, what helps them get along better, and what triggers arguments. One 34-year-old husband noted that he and his wife seemed to have more control of their anger than they did in the early months of marriage. "If we sense that we're fighting for no good reason, we'll say, 'This is ridiculous, let's stop.' "

A remarried newlywed seemed almost tired as she reflected on how much had been accomplished during her newlywed year:

This year wasn't an easy carefree time. We tried to figure out how our kids from our previous marriages fit into our lives, we tried to work out finances, we tried to arrange on a daily basis what we're going to do and whom we're going to see, and we tried to plan for the future. It's been a lot of work, but there's been a real deepening of love between my husband and myself. Before marriage I was always analyzing the content of

Harold's conversation. I used to examine how he looked, talked, handled his relationship with his children. Now we know each other better. I care more for him. I have an investment in his well-being. I don't test him as much. We're functioning as a couple rather than two separate people. There's less defensiveness, less need to prove yourself and question the behavior of the other person. We're compromising more.

"ME" BECOMES "WE"

Much of the sense of accomplishment that people described to us as they approached their first anniversary centered on the strengthening of their image as a couple. Over the course of the year spouses develop a conception of themselves as a married couple—they think and talk a lot about who they are and are not, what they like and don't like, where they're similar and where they're different.[1] Much of the conflict they experience is often due to the different ways in which they see themselves as a married couple.

For many people, as they approach their first anniversary, there is not only a greater confidence in themselves as a unit, but also as individuals. In fact, in our survey:

- 47 percent of newlyweds noted that their feelings of self-confidence had increased since being married.

The excitement of having blossomed, of having become more aware of one's own strengths and capabilities, was articulated by many people in interviews. As one 30-year-old husband, married just a year, put it:

I feel changed over the last year. I feel much more secure in myself and more at ease with other people. I feel more lovable. There are qualities that seem to have blossomed in me. There's a kind of synergy between my wife and myself. There's a real comfortable feeling for me in being with her that was unanticipated to some degree. Before marrying, I thought marriage was a limited thing. Now I see it as opening up options. There's a sense of sharing, not only ideas and feelings—but also there are so many more varied people in our lives that we've each brought to our marriage. I feel more confident in our relationship, and also socially.

Roy Schafer, an eminent psychoanalyst,[2] has pointed out that in examining one's life, one may trace numerous possible narrative themes. Or to put it simply, there are various ways of acting, and of viewing one's life. A rich life, he says, entails a constant elaboration of different ways of thinking of oneself.

In marriage there is a wonderful potential for developing your vision of yourself. When marrying, you start a new life, at least symbolically. You become engaged with someone in a partnership within which you can work to change old patterns and cultivate new qualities.

A 26-year-old woman, whose childhood had been an unhappy one, said to us:

> Marriage has been a very positive thing for me. Before, I had doubts about myself—would I be too needy, want too much. I'm more aware of my own needs now. I realize that how I am as a person has a great deal to do with our marriage as a unit. I realize that if I don't take care of my own needs, my husband can't do it for me. I no longer run out of the room when we have an argument and I'm less anxious about having to be the perfect person. I still think there are parts of me that my husband doesn't know—the level of my pensiveness or depressiveness. But he's a very upbeat person, which helps me. Instead of looking at things in a maudlin way I feel now that I have a choice.

As you feel closer to your spouse, you may find that your image of yourself within the couple replaces the image of yourself within your family of origin, making it easier for you to break free from old-patterned ways of seeing yourself.

One husband acknowledged that within the security of marriage he felt more comfortable facing qualities in himself that he had previously denied or ignored.

> I've learned more about myself this year than any other year of my life. Before I got married I don't think I realized how selfish I could be. But slowly I feel myself becoming less selfish. There are all these little changes that have happened. I find that as we become closer,

I want to be the best husband I can be. My wife has surprised me with her strength, and caring, and understanding. I want to reciprocate.

You know, it's incredible how close you can feel to someone. After a while, you start to become conscious of the way a person smells and you like it. Even at night when my wife's sleeping she smells good. I'm feeling safer and safer with her. She draws out of me emotional things that I would have been ashamed of before. Sometimes marriage is so much better than I thought it would be. There's this incredible feeling of closeness—of excluding everyone else. We're more of a team. It's us against any problems we have. Before we married I didn't feel I could talk with my wife so much about what bothered me. Now I confide in her more and vice versa.

ANNIVERSARY
CELEBRATIONS

Not everyone makes a big deal of their first anniversary—some people are by nature more eager than others to celebrate and ritualize occasions. One couple we interviewed, determined not to make a fuss, had dinner at home and watched a football game on television. At the other end of the spectrum, one of our interviewee couples traveled to Europe to mark the event. A sentimental variation was planned by a husband and wife who lingered over a home-cooked dinner and champagne, while dressed in their wedding clothes and recalling everything they could from their wedding day one year before.

No matter what they ended up planning, we found it interesting that the people we spoke with spent quite a bit of time and thought in arranging how to celebrate their anniversary. Couples seem to regard their observance of their anniversary as a statement of how they relate to each other and to others. For instance, many of "our" couples deliberated about whether or not to include their families in their celebrations. One husband, who felt that his family was intrusive and overinvolved in his marriage, specifically made plans to go away with his wife for their anniversary weekend in order to make a statement to his parents that he and his wife were a separate unit. And a

40-year-old woman, trying to balance the needs of her husband with those of her daughters from a previous marriage, arranged to enjoy an anniversary dinner with her husband but planned a Sunday brunch in which they could all partake.

Often one spouse is more interested than the other in gift-giving and anniversary celebrations. When that's the case, it seems to work out best if the spouse who is eager to celebrate the occasion makes that fact known as clearly as possible. Being explicit about how you want to commemorate the event and making plans for carrying out those wishes leaves as little chance for disappointment as possible. Peggy Williams, a 26-year-old magazine writer who married her high school sweetheart, told us:

> Our anniversary really felt like a big thing to me. It was such a relief. The first year seemed like a major hurdle to get over. My husband doesn't really like to make events over things, but surprisingly he went along with me. We planned a special dinner at our weekend house.

Peggy obviously got her message across to her husband that she wanted their anniversary to be special, because his gift to her was especially sentimental. She told us:

> For our anniversary he bought me this beautiful desk set made of Florentine paper. He remembered that when we were in Florence for our honeymoon I bought it as a gift for others. I was surprised that he remembered a detail like that from a year ago. And I didn't even know that he knew the first anniversary is the paper anniversary. When he gave it to me he said he wanted me to know that he was proud of me being a writer. That's what touched me the most.

Such occasions as anniversaries are signposts of time passing. They send thoughts flashing back and forth between the past and the present and the future. Setting aside a day to celebrate your joining in marriage provides you with a special opportunity to evaluate your life together and express your appreciation for each other.

But how you spend your first anniversary really makes no difference—as long as it meets the needs and expectations of the two of you. One husband we know—a diehard baseball fan—spent his anniversary week in a Florida baseball camp batting at home plate with Mickey Mantle and other former New York Yankees. Playing professional baseball had been a lifelong dream for this New York husband, and when he heard about the special week-long program, he was itching to enroll. His wife good-naturedly went along with the idea, and flew down to Florida for their anniversary weekend. She took pictures of him and "The Mick" together and waved a big banner rooting for her husband in the week's final game. While a baseball theme wasn't basically her idea of a romantic anniversary, she agreed to her husband's wishes because she knew that for him playing with the Yankees would be a fantasy come true.

Their baseball anniversary affirmed for the couple their ability each to accept and appreciate the other, and help each other fulfill dreams and goals. For the wife it was an opportunity to watch her husband experience a major thrill of his life; and for the husband it evoked tremendous gratitude and love that he had found a woman who cared enough to want to make him happy.

WORKSHOP: ON PLANNING YOUR FIRST ANNIVERSARY

1. Consider the meaning your anniversary has for you. Even if you're not the sentimental type, it can be helpful to use this milestone as an opportunity to evaluate your feelings about your marriage. Ask yourself:

- What kind of feelings are being evoked in me by our anniversary?
- How have my feelings about my spouse and myself changed since I married?
- How has being married compared with the way I expected it to be?

If your feelings are very positive ones, your answers to those questions will probably make you feel very lucky and, perhaps, eager to celebrate your anniversary in a way that demonstrates your loving feelings to your spouse. If your feelings about the past year are less cheerful, you might focus on how you'd like things to be different—and think of your anniversary as the start of turning a new leaf.

2. Discuss anniversary plans with your mate, and together come up with at least three different possibilities for celebrations. There are all kinds of ways you might commemorate this occasion. Discuss the alternatives to make sure that you both express your wishes and expectations. Talk about whether you want to include any friends or relatives in your anniversary celebration. One couple we know decided to celebrate their anniversary on three separate occasions. They spent their anniversary night at home, eating by candlelight and poring over their wedding album. The following night was spent celebrating with relatives. And later in the week they invited friends over for an anniversary cake.

You may also want to be clear ahead of time regarding the extent of gift-giving you have in mind, so that one of you isn't disappointed if he or she receives no present, or so that there is not a tremendous discrepancy in the lavishness of gifts.

3. Remember that your first anniversary sets a precedent for future anniversaries. If you commemorate it in a big way, the occasion is likely always to be marked in your marriage as an important one. If you shrug it off as no big deal, then your mate will probably assume that in later years too, you don't care whether or not you receive gifts or go out to celebrate the occasion.

4. Try to be understanding if your mate doesn't value your anniversary in the same way you do. Don't be insulted if your spouse isn't as enthusiastic about anniversary partying as you. Ultimately, how your spouse feels and acts day-to-day is more important.

MEMORIES

Looking Back on the First Year of Marriage

Until now we've focused mostly on how people feel in their first year of marriage. But when conducting our research we were also interested in finding out how men and women *look back* on their newlywed year. Do they think their first year was indicative of what came later in their marriage? Was the first year the hardest, as everyone claims it is supposed to be? Given the benefit of hindsight, what do people wish they had done differently early on in their marriages? And how did people who were married ten, twenty, thirty, and forty years ago differ in their newlywed experience from people who are marrying today?

Memory, of course, is selective. But, with that in mind, we wanted to find out what stands out most in people's memories despite the passage of time. And the fact is, most people do seem to remember quite a bit from their honeymoon days. During our interviews we were struck by how emotionally connected men and women obviously felt in looking back on their newlywed year. Even if the details weren't vivid, the feelings associated with them were.

We present the recollections of veteran newlyweds so that you will gain a larger context within which to view your own newlywed experience—and a sense of the significance it may have for you in years to come.

THE WAY WE WERE:
THOUGHTS FROM VETERAN
NEWLYWEDS

There were 75 people in our "looking back" sample—42 of whom answered a special questionnaire and 33 others whom we spoke with in person or by telephone. These men and women either responded to notices about our study (which were published in newspapers and magazines or posted in clergy news-letters) or heard about our research by word of mouth. Among our sample there were three people who were widowed, 15 who were divorced, and five who were remarried. The longest-married respondent was an 80-year-old woman married almost 60 years; the one married the shortest period of time was a man wed just three years prior to our survey.

Our actual "looking back" questionnaire was much longer than the sampling we present here, and the responses we got in return are many more numerous. We selected the present responses because we found them to be among the most representative of the survey, and have ordered them chronologically by wedding date. That date appears after each respondent's statement. Persons married several times were placed according to the date of their first wedding. Unless otherwise indicated, respondents were still married when surveyed.

Was your first year of marriage indicative of what followed in your marriage?

• Yes and no. Our first year of marriage was horrendous and now I can say that our marriage is quite happy. But from the beginning I never questioned that we would stay together and was determined to work things out. That determination to work at it was there from the start and has been indicative of our attitude throughout our marriage. (male married in 1950)

• Yes. We both used sex as a weapon. We repressed anger—we were both withholding of sex towards each other. Also my husband held the purse strings. I wasn't strong enough to fight this. I needed to be a good girl—good girls don't need things and spend money. This continued when we had children. I didn't work. If you don't work and earn money, you have less rights and say-so—was my thinking. Also, when we got married we were torn between our loyalty to each other and our loyalty to our families. We are still pulled by our families. We continue to behave and do things for them—just like "good kids." (female married in 1952)

• Yes. We established some guidelines, i.e. that we were now a family and would make our own decisions. We had a big argument when we were newlyweds and I will never forget that my husband said, "You have to understand where I'm coming from." He then told me that once when he rinsed out a glass because he wanted some milk, his grandfather said to him, "What are you doing? There are women here to do that—*you* don't!" My husband and I had a big argument over this as I was working full-time also. We've had ongoing exchanges about this throughout our marriage. (female married in 1962)

• Yes. But we've tried to change my outlook on sex— which when we got married I thought was something you did, but didn't enjoy. Sex can be fun, enjoyable and exciting, but sometimes the old feelings come back that it's not something to enjoy. (female married in 1967)

• Yes. We established trust for each other and our future together. Freedom and respect for each other's interests. (male married in 1971)

• Yes. Nothing was shared, from the time we got married—not money, not feelings, not responsibility. (female married in 1974, later divorced)

• No. Things got very bad after five years. (male married in 1974, later divorced)

• No. In our second year we had a child and our relationship changed dramatically, as did our lifestyle. While we thought we were prepared for parenthood, we were not prepared for all the accompanying adjustments. It did set patterns however regarding money—my husband was considered financial head of household with me accountable to him for expenditures—which became a problem when I stopped earning to stay at home and raise a family. (female married in 1978)

• Yes. I believe it did set patterns but now we've accepted them more, i.e. who does the bills and who does certain chores, etc. We do share most of the chores, family commitments, decisions regarding money, etc. Sex is somewhat improved but still could be better. (male married in 1980)

• Yes. It was hard to treat my wife's child like my own and it still is. (male married in 1980)

To sum up: There was almost overwhelming agreement among the people we heard from that the first year of marriage had set patterns for what followed. However, quite a few noted that having children had disrupted the status quo previously established, shifted responsibilities, and brought new issues to the fore. Also, in some cases, problems from the first year were later resolved, patterns became more acceptable to spouses, disagreements became less intense. In other cases, mild problems later became exacerbated.

Looking back over your marriage, would you say the first year was the hardest? Why or why not?

• No. Our lives were structured by my being in the army, the demands of wartime, and my being in dental school. We were young and malleable and hopeful. (male married in 1943)

• Yes. We were both too attached to our families—couldn't separate from them and needed to please them. (female married in 1952)

• Yes. We were not comfortable with one another. (female married in 1957)

• In my second marriage the first year was definitely the hardest because of concern over children—his and mine. (female remarried in 1957)

• No. When children became teenagers, marriage got harder. (male married in 1961)

• No—the easiest. We shared the same hopes, interests, and dreams. We had a good double income. We had lots of time and no stresses. Children make it harder. The most important change is the wife is often too tired or distracted for lovemaking. (female married in 1965)

• No. In my first marriage, despite adjustments, it was one of the best years. It changed after the birth of our daughter. Looking back, I think my husband resented having another person I had to pay attention to. For my current second marriage, the first year was the hardest. The first three months were especially difficult because suddenly five teenagers were staying with us and we moved into a new house. I had only one daughter and suddenly was dealing with all kinds of teenage crises. (female married in 1965, divorced, remarried in 1980)

• Yes. We had to adjust to each other, to marriage and, because we moved, to big city living and a different lifestyle. (male married in 1967)

• No. For years it was difficult—not just the first year. Now it's calming down. After eighteen years marriage is great! (female married in 1967)

• No. In both instances, the romantic glow was still there and troubles were not that severe or persistent. (female married in 1967, divorced, remarried in 1978)

• Yes. I think the first year is the hardest because it's filled with all the negatives. You suddenly face the hardest realization which is that they're not going to change. (male married in 1972)

• Yes. It was hard mostly because I was sorting out who I was. (He always knew his own needs, expectations, etc. better.) (female married in 1973)

• No. It's nice to spend your life with someone you care about and who cares about you—with very little responsibility to anyone else. You can pick up and go and spend time together or alone, depending on your wishes. Children make life harder. Also, my husband was more anxious to make me happy that first year. (female married in 1974)

• No. We lived together for two years before we got married and every weekend I took out my suitcase and threatened I was going to leave. So our first year of marriage was a holiday by comparison. We had gone through all the terrible ups and downs when we were living together. (female married in 1977)

• Absolutely not—it was relatively carefree. The simplicity of the first year was heavenly. My wife and I worked, went out often to dinner and shows. I had expected greater difficulty in resolving roles and responsibilities. I experienced less constraints and restrictions than I had observed in others. When kids came, everything changed. Having that first year to look back on is helpful when things get rough. (male married in 1978)

• No. In years three and four we ran into real problems. I had begun therapy in my second year of marriage and was growing by leaps and bounds. I began learning how to meet my own needs more (i.e. spending time with friends, going back to school, etc.) and my husband perceived this as my not "being there" to take care of him. We hit a crisis in our fifth year of marriage with long periods of not talking to each other. We are not fighters and withdraw from each other. The first year was easier in some ways in that there was little overt conflict. (female married in 1978, later divorced)

• Our first year has, so far, been our hardest. In some ways it was wonderful. My husband's previous wife had died—and when we lived together we had gone through all the grief. When we got married we started to look forward instead of back. But it was also a very rough time. There were lots of arguments. I had never cared that much before to argue. We had quarrels about how his kids treated me, how his mother treated him, . . . I felt that maybe I had bitten off more than I could chew. Fighting was initiated by me. I was working out my frustration and anger. Also, I was testing him to see whose side he was on—mine or his kids'—and to see if he'd stick by me. It's gotten a lot calmer. (female married in 1980)

• Not in our case. There were adjustments in terms of living together but as the years go by major decisions have to be made, i.e. investing, money, children, job changes and advancement. In our case the second was the most difficult year due to unforeseen circumstances relating to many of the above subjects. (male married in 1980)

• Our first year *everything* was torment. Now we never fight. I can't believe how it's changed and I have no idea why. (female married in 1983, currently pregnant with twins)

To sum up: Few people feel neutral about their newlywed year. They view it either as the hardest year of their marriage or the easiest—and there seem to be equal numbers in both camps. In general, those who later became divorced felt that their first year of marriage was not the hardest. It seems that for those who later broke up, problems were glossed over at the beginning. Turmoil did not really strike until later. Those who felt relatively satisfied with the current state of their marriage seemed to be the ones who hammered away at their problems and faced emotional upheaval early on. Marriage became easier once they'd developed a pattern of dealing with prevailing demands. Also, for some people, the adjustments of the newlywed year became muted, or seemed relatively mild, after they'd begun to experience such challenges as raising children, facing severe financial crises, suffering illnesses, and other life stresses.

Looking back, what would you have done differently in your first year of marriage? Explain.

• Grown up! (female married in 1944)

• I would have moved far enough away from both sets of our parents. (female married in 1952)

• I got pregnant three months after our wedding. I was very naive—I didn't think it would happen so quickly. I would have waited at least one year before getting pregnant. I would spend more time with my husband and enjoy getting to know each other, without having the responsibility of a family. After many years, my husband used to say that he does not remember me not being pregnant and we missed time to get to know each other without the responsibility of children. I have four children. The first three are twenty-one months apart, then we waited for five years and I had my last baby. (female married in 1955, now widowed)

• Lived in our own apartment—we lived with my parents. (male married in 1957)

• Made my husband share more responsibilities, clean, shop, learn to budget and pay bills. (female married in 1961)

• I would have insisted that we discuss differences. Not be intimidated by his yelling and short temper. (female married in 1965, later divorced)

• I would have really tried to work harder on my ideas and feelings about sex. We talked about everything else, but never really brought that topic up. Nice girls did not talk about sex. Also, only later did I realize that I did not have to do things the way my mother did—like me being the one to take care of the home. I should have realized earlier that I could be my own person in the marriage. (female married in 1967)

• I would have communicated better and have made my demands better known. I would not have given in to so many of his demands, would have been more loving and understanding and compassionate, since he did not know if he liked being married. I would have been more of an individual. (female married in 1967, later divorced)

• I would have had us both seek therapy. (female married in 1969)

• Saved more money, invested in real estate—planned for the future. (male married in 1974)

• I would not have been so trusting. (female married in 1974, later divorced)

• I would have learned how to *argue* instead of just withdrawing. I would also have tried to live more like a couple. We each kept our own checking account, individual friends, etc. We had few joint goals or projects. (male married in 1978)

• Not worry about money so much. Trust my husband more. I think I put too much pressure on him to succeed. Give him more support rather than question him all the time. (female married in 1980)

To sum up: Our survey supported the notion that there are as many regrets about the first year of marriage as there are people who have been married. Almost all our respondents found something they wished they'd done at least a little differently. If there was any one common denominator, it was the wish to have been more active as an individual in asserting needs and goals in marriage, and so to have assumed more responsibility for the success of the relationship (even if that meant delegating responsibility to one's mate).

If you've been divorced or separated, were there signs in your newlywed year that your marriage would not work out?

• Yes. I had a better salary than my husband. I was better educated and desired to further it. He was not as motivated. I generally am calm and rational. He was quick tempered, often was insulting when angry. (female married in 1965)

• Yes. He did not know if he wanted to stay married. We went to a marriage counselor who worsened the situation. When I described the things I did not like about him she said, "I don't see how you can stay married to him." (female married in 1967)

• Yes. He stayed out late at night almost every night. I was very frustrated. When we eventually broke up, he said he didn't love me anymore. Also, he is a latent homosexual. (female married in 1970)

• Yes. We had completely different value systems and different emotional rhythms. (male married in 1975)

• Yes, definitely. He was depressed very often and was very moody and unwilling to resolve an issue peacefully. He showed great agitation over trivial issues and needed to dominate. He was very rigid and authoritative, had little compassion and much rage and hostility toward people. He put me down unmercifully and unnecessarily, was obsessive with cleaning. He distanced himself from me, which caused me to feel he does not love me, or is not capable of loving. His destructive criticism, which I did not deserve, was fierce. I tried to get him to go for marital counseling but the first time the counselor tried to tell him something about himself, he walked out. (female married in 1979)

To sum up: Yes. According to everyone we contacted who split up from their mate at some point after marrying, signs of trouble appeared on the horizon at the start of marriage—but, in retrospect, many realized they denied or ignored their marital problems until it was too late.

What stands out most vividly about your first year of marriage? What types of problems did you have?

• I tried to get rid of little mannerisms that bothered my husband—like my whistling during bridge. Also the noise of chewing celery or biting an apple was most annoying to him. I think he had very acute hearing. Also, I remember trying to adjust to my mother-in-law and my husband's older brother, since we lived in their home though in a separate second floor apartment sharing a bath. (female married in 1926)

• My mother-in-law was a source of irritation. During the first year, being young and well mannered, I took all her nonsense gracefully. Later on I became more determined to express my feelings. (female married in 1943)

• Adjusting to each other's children—each of us was widowed. (male married in 1957)

• We were novices about sex. (female married in 1957)

• In each marriage power struggles were evident as I struggled to maintain my individuality while at the same time I wanted my husband to be the stronger one. In my first marriage (at age twenty-two) I married too early, did not have sexual experience, did not live with anyone, was not prepared for life on my own. I often think back to my first marriage and wonder if my marital problems are any different now, or if I had remained married to number one how it could have worked out. (female married in 1961, divorced, remarried in 1978)

• There were some adjustments because I was rather "Victorian" in sex, but my husband wasn't. Eventually things changed, adjusted. My husband was understanding and patient. (female married in 1962)

• I think one of the biggest assets to my marriage was that we were away from family for the first two years of my marriage and established a lot of our own guidelines without the influence of relatives. (female married in 1962)

• We had no problems—seems unbelievable, but true. In the first year I think we were both "giving one hundred percent." (female married in 1965)

• In both cases I thought more critically of my spouses as I became aware of idiosyncrasies that were annoying. In my current marriage our sex life diminished in the first year from what it was beforehand. (female married in 1967, divorced, remarried in 1978)

• We both read the book *Open Marriage*. In one part of the book it mentioned that when the husband wanted time for himself, he'd put on a red cap. For months after that, whenever my husband wanted to establish that he wanted time separate from me he'd give me a signal. I came from a real Jewish home where everyone was on top of everyone else. In my husband's home privacy was the name of the game. Also, he had ten years as a bachelor before marrying me. I was twenty-one when we got married and I needed a constant someone around. (female married in 1968)

• The first year I was really sure there was not going to be a marriage, because there was no way I could live with his mother. To me, during the first year, it seemed like there was no light at the end of the tunnel. I thought, We're never going to get through this, I'm never going to survive this. I'd say if I hadn't gone into therapy, this marriage would never have worked. I worked like hell on this marriage. To this day, I'll sometimes say to my husband, "I don't know why I'm involved with you. You're the most ridiculous human being I've ever met." And he says, "I feel exactly the same way about you." But our marriage works. This is a solid marriage because it's based on reality. We know each other's faults and we just work on it. But the first year was miserable . . . miserable. (female married in 1973)

• Our biggest problem was dealing with each other's expectations based on things that our families expected. (male married in 1974)

• We talked a lot during our first year of marriage. There was always time to "talk it out." (male married in 1975)

• The moment we got married, I felt like I had to watch over my husband—this motherly instinct came over me. (female married in 1976)

• My wife had her girlfriends over to the house too much. She talked to them on the phone too much. Not enough privacy. (male married in 1979)

• Sex decreased. (male married in 1979)

• I initially felt somewhat trapped by marriage. I had a brief affair six months after marriage which made me realize the beauty and quality of my wife. I felt much more at ease about marriage after that. (male married in 1979)

• The immediate assumption of responsibility. (male married in 1980)

To sum up: It was in these responses that the greatest generational differences were evidenced. Those who married before the 1960s often commented about being ignorant about sex and being unfamiliar and uncomfortable with their mate during their newlywed year. Those who married after the "sexual revolution" commented about their sex life diminishing after marriage and noted more subtle changes in their already familiar relationship with their spouse.

During your first year of marriage, did you feel you could talk freely to your spouse, family, and friends about what you were feeling regarding your marriage?

• I did not talk with others—besides my spouse—about our marriage. I felt it would have been disloyal and if I did say anything, I only had good things to say. (female married in 1946)

• Only to my spouse. We felt any problems we had were our own. (male married in 1957)

• NO! My parents only wanted to hear how wonderful everything was. My husband could/would not argue or fight and would discount any complaints I had; my friends, well I guess I had a hard time letting friends see the real situation. I tended to paint a pretty picture. (female married in 1960)

• I could speak to only one friend. (female married in 1960)

• No. I wanted everything to be ideal. (female married in 1965)

• I did not know enough to articulate. I thought this is just what one goes through. (male married in 1966)

• I talked to one friend. My mother thinks that marriage is the answer to everything and didn't want to hear that anything was wrong. (female married in 1978, later separated)

• Sometimes talking about sensitive areas with my spouse did not occur as I did not want to hurt her feelings. (male married in 1980)

• I spoke with my wife. We are each other's best friend. I only spoke very superficially to friends and family and never to work colleagues. (male married in 1983)

To sum up: Most newlyweds don't feel very free to talk openly with many people about their marital problems. This attitude seems to have been especially true for newlyweds of previous generations, many of whom felt it would be a tremendous disloyalty to "hang out their dirty laundry." Newlyweds who married more recently seem to regard their mates as their good if not best friends and are more open to sharing their emotions with each other.

PHILOSOPHICAL THOUGHTS
FROM ONETIME NEWLYWEDS

At the end of our survey we asked respondents if there was anything they would like to add. The following are just a few of the many comments our newlywed veterans offered. We chose to present these voices because we find the attitudes they convey healthy and inspiring. We'd like to close this chapter with these reflections because they show that it is possible to be at once "realistic" about marriage and happy in it.

• The happiness of our marriage has resulted partly from the fact that we thoroughly agree on the "work" part—how to spend money, how to bring up children, growing vegetables organically, eating healthy foods. We miss out a little on the "play" part. I look at news, business news, serious drama and ballet on TV. He enjoys "Murder She Wrote" and football. I majored in English and psychology, he in chemistry. He reads technical journals, I read novels. He enjoys driving "to get there," I enjoy the scenery and rambling in new inviting roads. But I'm not the world's best housekeeper and he couldn't care less. He eats with relish whatever I put before him. Our four children and nineteen grandchildren adore him and so do I. Each year we get together at the shore for a week. There were thirty-one of us last July. Our children and grandchildren are our greatest joy. There are three Phi Beta Kappas and seven merit scholars so far—more to come! What greater happiness could anyone have? (female married in 1926)

• I think that the three most important factors in a successful marriage are trust, respect, and friendship. Marriage is a funny thing. Some days can be so fantastic. Then other days you think maybe it's not so great. There are many ups and downs in a marriage. I think you have to be mature enough to deal with successfully maintaining an important relationship and after investing so much in each other—weigh the pros and cons. I have questions sometimes whether I'm in the right place, but after much reflection I always come up to—I am. (male married in 1980)

• You mellow with age. Certain things become less important to you. You get to know each other better. You learn how to work around each other and with each other. Now I don't yell to get my way. If it's so important to him . . . then let him have his way. (female married in 1967)

• What I can't get over is that what my idea of love was when I first got married is so different from what my idea of love is now. What is love? Love is putting the bowl that I hate and he loves in the middle of the dining room table. Love is taking a day off from work because he asked me to go with him someplace and it's important to him. This is what it's all about—the constant small compromises. The big things you work out right away. It's these little things—like accepting that he never picks up his goddamn socks. That to me is love. (female married in 1973)

A PARTING WORD

We hope that the first year of your marriage will prove to be just the beginning—the first leg of a long journey together with your spouse. Whatever the future holds for you, you can be certain there will be surprises in store. Life is never static. As you experience job promotions and losses, move from one neighborhood to another, raise children, care for aging parents, and live in a constantly changing society, you are bound to experience many marital triumphs and crises, successes and failures. Over the years your outlook and attitude about yourselves, each other, and marriage will fluctuate.

Should you and your mate find that consulting this book has helped ease your transition to marriage, you probably will also find that you feel better equipped to cope with future turning points and vicissitudes in your relationship. Once you are able to taste the elixir of joy and fulfillment and discovery that can be distilled from meeting life's challenges together, you will, we hope, feel stronger, more united in your identity as a couple, and more confident in your ability as partners to handle any difficult times that may lie ahead.

We've focused on the problems newlyweds face—problems that come up again and again, in couples of all profiles and backgrounds. But as we interviewed each person, we kept asking ourselves: What makes the difference in how *this* person is adjusting to marriage? Interviewees often asked us one or another of the same two questions: "Why am I having such a difficult time being married?" or "Why isn't being married as hard as everyone said it would be?"

While conflict is normal in marriage, and especially so in the early stages, when there is so much interpersonal as well as internal negotiation regarding your own needs and expectations and those of your spouse, we concluded from our research that several factors influence how someone adjusts to marriage. As we see it, people who adjust the most successfully to marriage have the following five qualities:

1. An ability to acknowledge and handle aggression in all of its manifestations—whether of anger, competitiveness, self-assertion or envy. Having disagreements or differences need not mean major problems; the inability to communicate and try to work out these differences is what forebodes danger. Like any close relationship, marriage entails a wealth of complex emotions—love, hate, anger, disappointment, frustration, and ambivalence. In the healthiest marriages, spouses recognize their feelings and needs, and are able to overcome the kinds of inhibitions that prevent emotional and sexual intimacy. They are not fearful of expressing (even insistently) what their needs are and how they would like to have them met, nor do they run away, withdraw, or lash back at the first signs of their mate's aggression. They are able to appreciate that both they and their mate are individuals who deserve to have their reasonable needs articulated and fulfilled.

2. An ability to tolerate imperfections and differences that exist between spouses. Part of being able to love maturely is accepting the flaws and foibles as well as the strengths of your mate. No matter how you may work at them, some problems in your relationship may never go away. Only people who recognize that marriage isn't going to work magic on their lives— that it isn't going to solve all of their problems—are sufficiently free to enjoy the rewards that marriage does reap. Such people are secure enough in their own identity that they need not be constantly critical of their spouses.

3. A willingness to differentiate from family of origin. In the strongest marriages, spouses place each other as their highest priority—along with any children they might have. As close and loving as they may feel to their parents, siblings, or friends, their focus is on each other, on creating new life patterns together.

4. A desire and commitment to remain married. Maturity, even love, isn't enough to keep two people together. You need to *want* to stay married in order to withstand all of the challenges with which you will be faced.

5. A recognition that there will be ups and downs in marriage.
Acknowledging that getting married involves making a major
life change—a change bound to evoke some emotional turmoil—is enormously helpful in enabling couples to accept and
cope with the conflicts that arise in the first year of marriage.
Understanding that the first year of marriage *is* just that—your
first annual milestone, with many more to be attained—is crucial, because during a lifetime a couple is bound to go through
many life stages. In marriage it's important not only to take
advantage of the opportunities, but also to be able to withstand
the obstacles. You need to have a perspective—to recognize
that it is both the good times and the bad times that, shared
between you, contribute to your sense of selves as a couple and
offer potential for continuing enrichment and growth.

The adjustment to marriage that we speak about is not the
romantic fantasy seen in advertisements aimed at honeymooners. We're not convinced that such an idyllic, blissful accom-
modation to marriage is attainable ever, by anyone. Adjusting
to marriage does not mean becoming the picture-perfect couple
posed on the beach against the sunset. It doesn't mean having
the same kind of marriage that your parents have, or that your
friends have, or that others think you should have. More than
ever before, you have the opportunity to create the type of
marriage that you want. The definition of marriage has eased
enough so that your marriage can be as traditional or untra-
ditional as you like. The first year of marriage is the time to
become aware of and communicate about your and your spouse's
marital needs and desires. By clarifying your vision of marriage
early on, you can begin to realize your dreams.

ABOUT OUR RESEARCH

Initially we sent out a short-essay style questionnaire to newly-weds who responded to notices we placed in *Bride's* magazine, *Monthly Detroit* magazine, the *New York Daily News*, church newsletters, and college and neighborhood newspapers in the New York metropolitan area. Clergy were helpful in providing us with lists of brides and grooms whom they married, and acquaintances offered the names and addresses of newlyweds they knew personally. The 56 newlyweds who responded to this original questionnaire set the stage by sharing with us their thoughts, fears, problems, and impressions regarding their adjustment to marriage.

A second survey (Appendix B), from which we yielded statistical results, was sent to two thousand newlyweds from all fifty states. These names were procured from a mailing list broker. We received 353 responses. Seven were disqualified for various reasons, so our findings are based on 346 responses. Of the two thousand questionnaires we sent out, 156 were returned to us by the post office because the addressees had moved and left no forwarding address. Our 19 percent response rate is based therefore on a mailing of 1,844 questionnaires. The response compares very favorably with other questionnaire distributions of this kind. For instance, Shere Hite, who conducted a study on female sexuality for her book, *The Hite Report* (Macmillan, 1976), distributed one hundred thousand questionnaires and received a little more than three thousand in return—a 3 percent response rate.

As we found in a telephone follow-up to people who did not respond to our survey, 11 of the 15 couples we called had not received our questionnaire. Those people had moved since their wedding—either from their parents' or their own home and our survey had not been forwarded to them. Of the other nonrespondents, three said they had filled out the questionnaires, but then either lost them or were waiting until their mates filled them out, which never happened. ("He's terrible at things like that—he won't even write a letter," commented one wife.) One woman said she received the questionnaire, but having been married for three years, she realized she did not qualify to have counted in our survey.

Of the 346 respondents upon whom our findings are based, 41 percent were male, 59 percent were female (all percentages rounded to the nearest whole percent). The age range of our respondents was from 17 to 64. Fifty-four percent of our respondents lived with their mate before marriage, 23 percent were previously married, and 14 percent had children from a previous marriage. Most spouses knew each other between two and four years before marrying. At the time they filled out our survey, the respondents had been married from one month to 18 months, with the average time being six months. Only 1 percent of those we surveyed were separated or divorced since their wedding.

Geographic breakdown of our respondents was as follows:*

New England	5%
Middle Atlantic states	27%
North Central states	24%
South Atlantic states	5%
South Central states	14%
Mountain states	8%
Pacific states	6%
Hawaii and California	10%
outside U.S.	2%

Regarding the type of community in which they live, the breakdown was:

rural	9%
suburban	29%
small city	27%
big city	36%

The average combined family income of the newlyweds we surveyed was between thirty thousand and fifty thousand dol-

---

*Total of percentages in this and other tables may equal 101% due to rounding out of percentages to the nearest whole percent.

lars. Ninety-six percent of the respondents grew up in the United States and 94 percent of them were white, 3 percent Hispanic, 2 percent black, 1 percent Oriental, and 1 percent members of other racial groups. As for religion, 31 percent were Protestant, 23 percent were Catholic, 21 percent were Jewish, 13 percent were of other religions, and 12 percent specified no affiliation. The average education level for our respondents is completion of the second year of college. Regarding occupation, the break-down is as follows:

full-time homemaker	6%
student	13%
labor, services	12%
arts	3%
clerical	12%
sales	8%
managerial	7%
professional/technical	33%
other	7%

How representative is our sample of newlyweds? Ours is not a random sample, and so, technically speaking, our conclusions apply only to our sample of newlyweds. To compare the answers of our respondents with those of the people who did not return our survey, we telephoned and reached some non-respondents (many of whom it turned out had never received our questionnaire). We asked them the same questions as were on our form. In general, we found the two groups comparable—in terms of both demographics (age, type of community they live in, etc.) and experience in marriage (they rated themselves as happy, for the most part, and in general noted the same problems).

But in any survey of this kind, those who respond are a select group. And in the case of our subject matter, we think that those who had grave doubts about their marriages were probably less likely to return our questionnaire. Among the 15 nonrespondents that we talked with, two women told us they had separated from their husbands for several nights since their wedding because of disagreements. One woman whom we spoke with, who had filled out the questionnaire but never sent it in, admitted, "When I filled it out I was not very truthful. I didn't want to look at anything being wrong." This woman, 21 years old, added that she'd found marriage to be a lot more demanding emotionally than she had expected, and that she was unhappy in her marriage.

Just as we assume that those dissatisfied with their marriages were less likely to answer or submit their questionnaires, so too do we find it probable that some people who did respond painted a rosier picture of their marriage than strict truthfulness would reflect, out of a desire to deny their marital difficulties. With these qualifications in mind, we feel our statistical findings offer a valuable portrait of the contemporary newlywed experience.

QUESTIONNAIRE FOR NEWLYWEDS

The following questionnaire is one that we distributed to newly-weds in our study (although with minor changes in punctuation and grammar here). You may want to answer the questionnaires for yourself and ask your spouse to do the same. Use the questions to clarify your own thoughts and to serve as a springboard for discussion.

1. Are you (1) male ____ or 2) female ____? (Check one.)
2. What is your age? ____
3. What is your spouse's age? ____
4. How many months have you been married? _____
5. In what state do you live? _____

For questions 6–13: Please *circle the number* beside the *one* choice which best answers the question for you.

6. What kind of community do you live in?
    1. rural
    2. suburban
    3. small city
    4. big city
7. How long did you and your spouse know each other before marrying?
    1. less than six months
    2. six months–less than one year
    3. one year–less than two years
    4. two years–less than four years
    5. four years or more
8. How long did you and your spouse live together before marrying?
    1. does not apply
    2. less than one year

3. one year–less than two years
4. two years–less than four years
5. four years or more

9. How many times have *you* been married before?
  1. never   2. once
  3. twice   4. more than two times

10. How many times has *your spouse* been married before?
  1. never   2. once
  3. twice   4. more than two times

11. Do *you* have children from a previous marriage?
  1. yes   2. no

12. Does *your spouse* have children from a previous marriage?
  1. yes   2. no

Please answer all of the following questions in regard to your current marriage.

13. In the weeks before your wedding, do you recall questioning whether or not you were marrying the right person? (Circle *one* choice.)
  1. Yes, I had very strong doubts.
  2. Yes, I had mild doubts.
  3. No, I had no doubts at all.

14. Why did you decide to marry when you did? (Circle the numbers beside *all* those that apply.)
  1. The time was right. I wanted to be married.
  2. Family pressure.
  3. My mate convinced me to marry.
  4. I was in love.
  5. Other.

15. Before marrying, did you two (circle the numbers beside *all* those that apply):
  1. share household expenses
  2. vacation together
  3. make love together
  4. discuss having children
  5. buy a house or car together
  6. have children together

16. How did you feel during your honeymoon (or first two weeks of marriage if you didn't go on a honeymoon)? (Circle the numbers beside *all* those that apply.)
  1. I had a great time.

2. I felt anxious because I realized I didn't know my spouse as well as I had thought.
3. I felt pressured to live up to the traditional image of the romantic honeymoon couple.
4. I felt disappointed about sex.
5. I felt no different with my spouse than before.

Use the following scale to answer questions 17–20. For each question *circle* the number in parentheses that refers to the *one* response most appropriate for you.

(1)	(2)	(3)	(4)	(5)
greatly	somewhat	not	somewhat	greatly
improved	improved	changed	worsened	worsened

17. Since I married, my relationship with my family has: (circle *one* choice)

| (1) | (2) | (3) | (4) | (5) |

18. Since I married, my relationship with my spouse's family has: (circle *one* choice)

| (1) | (2) | (3) | (4) | (5) |

19. Since I married, my relationships with my single friends have: (circle *one* choice)

| (1) | (2) | (3) | (4) | (5) |

20. Since I married, my relationships with my married friends have: (circle *one* choice)

| (1) | (2) | (3) | (4) | (5) |

Use the following scale to answer questions 21–26. For each question *circle* the number in parentheses that refers to the *one* response most appropriate for you.

(1)	(2)	(3)	(4)	(5)
greatly	somewhat	not	somewhat	greatly
increased	increased	changed	decreased	decreased

21. Since I married, my ambitions about my work have: (circle *one* choice)

| (1) | (2) | (3) | (4) | (5) |

22. Since we married, the number of arguments between my spouse and me has: (circle *one* choice)

| (1) | (2) | (3) | (4) | (5) |

23. Since I married, my feelings of self-confidence have: (circle *one* choice)

    (1)   (2)   (3)   (4)   (5)

24. Since I married, my tendency to be critical of my spouse has: (circle *one* choice)

    (1)   (2)   (3)   (4)   (5)

25. Since we married, my spouse's tendency to be critical of me has: (circle *one* choice)

    (1)   (2)   (3)   (4)   (5)

26. Since I married, my desire to have a clean, attractive home has: (circle *one* choice)

    (1)   (2)   (3)   (4)   (5)

27. *Using the numbers in the following scale,* please indicate how problematic the following issues are in your marriage.

(1)	(2)	(3)	(4)	(5)
significant problems that threaten our marriage	significant problems, but we're working on them	some problems	very few problems	no problems at all

___	1.	money	___	2.	decision making
___	3.	dealing with family	___	4.	household tasks
___	5.	friendships	___	6.	job obligations
___	7.	differences in values	___	8.	religion
___	9.	sexual activities	___	10.	marital goals
___	11.	communication styles	___	12.	shared interests
___	13.	personal tastes and habits	___	14.	finding time for each other

28. Which *one* of the above issues listed in question 27 do you argue about *most* with your spouse? ___

Except where otherwise indicated, for all of the following questions please *circle* the number beside the *one* choice that *best* answers the question for you.

29. Regarding the most serious problems you mentioned in question 27, which *one* statement below best describes how you feel?

    1.   I feel confident we can work out *all* our problems.

2.   I feel confident we can work out *most* of our problems.
3.   I feel confident we can work out *some* of our problems.
4.   I doubt we'll work out a lot of our problems.
5.   I doubt we'll work out *any* of our problems.

30.   How often do you two have fights?
1.   every day
2.   two to three times a week
3.   once a week
4.   once or twice a month
5.   once every several months
6.   once a year
7.   never

31.   On average, how long do your fights last?
1. minutes   2. hours   3. days   4. weeks

32.   How do you two handle your big conflicts? (Circle the numbers beside *all* those that apply.)
1.   We discuss things calmly.
2.   We suffer silently, bottling up our feelings.
3.   One or both of us usually start screaming.
4.   One of us storms out of the house.
5.   One or both of us throw things.
6.   One or both of us pound walls.
7.   One or both of us hit the other.

33.   Please read the following four choices:
a.   This has *not* occurred in our first year of marriage.
b.   This has occurred. It has *strengthened* our marriage.
c.   This has occurred. It has *weakened* our marriage.
d.   This has occurred. It *has not affected* our marriage significantly.

Now, next to each item in the list below, please insert the letter *a, b, c,* or *d* for whichever choice above is most appropriate.

  ____ 1.   a wanted pregnancy
  ____ 2.   an unexpected pregnancy
  ____ 3.   a miscarriage
  ____ 4.   an abortion
  ____ 5.   the birth of a baby
  ____ 6.   a serious illness
  ____ 7.   the loss of a job
  ____ 8.   the death of a close relative
  ____ 9.   a relative becoming seriously ill

34.   Were you a virgin when you got married?
    1.   yes   2.   no

35.   How often do you recall having sexual intercourse with your mate before you got married?
    1.   four times a week or more
    2.   between two and four times a week
    3.   once a week
    4.   twice a month
    5.   once a month
    6.   less than once a month
    7.   never

36.   Did you have sexual intercourse with your spouse on your wedding night?
    1.   yes   2.   no

37.   How did you feel about your sexual/intimate experience on your wedding night? (circle *all* that apply.)
    1.   very satisfied   2.   satisfied
    3.   unsatisfied   4.   disappointed

38.   How anxious about having sex were you on your wedding night?
    1.   very   2.   somewhat   3.   not at all

39.   Since you married, how often do you and your spouse have sex on the average?
    1.   four times a week or more
    2.   between two and four times a week
    3.   once a week
    4.   twice a month
    5.   once a month
    6.   less than once a month
    7.   never

40.   Are you satisfied with your sex life since being married? (Circle *one* choice.)
    1.   very   2.   somewhat
    3.   I have mixed feelings.   4.   not at all

41.   I'd like to have sexual intercourse:
    1.   much more frequently
    2.   somewhat more frequently
    3.   somewhat less frequently
    4.   much less frequently
    5.   the same amount as we do now

42.   Regarding sexual activity:
    1.   I wish we were more open and adventurous.
    2.   It's just right.
    3.   I wish we were less open and adventurous.

43.   Regarding sexual activity:
    1.   I wish we were more intimate and tender (hugging, cuddling, etc.).
    2.   It's just right.
    3.   I wish we were less intimate and tender.

44.   Since I'm married my feelings of sexual attraction toward my spouse have:
    1.   greatly increased
    2.   somewhat increased
    3.   not changed
    4.   somewhat decreased
    5.   greatly decreased

45.   I have fantasies about sex with my spouse:
    1.   frequently   2.   sometimes   3.   never

46.   I have fantasies about sex involving people other than my spouse:
    1.   frequently   2.   sometimes   3.   never

47.   My sexual fantasies involving my spouse (circle *all* that apply):
    1.   excite me
    2.   bother me a little
    3.   bother me a lot
    4.   does not apply

48.   My sexual fantasies involving people other than my spouse (circle *all* that apply):
    1.   excite me
    2.   bother me a little
    3.   bother me a lot
    4.   does not apply

49.   Circle the numbers beside *all* factors below that *you* have difficulty with in your marriage. Also, circle the numbers beside all that apply to·*your spouse.*

husband	*wife*
1. lack of sexual desire	1. lack of sexual desire
2. getting erection	2. having an orgasm
3. having an orgasm	3. painful intercourse
4. premature ejaculation	

50. Have you had any extramarital affairs?
    1. yes   2. no

51. If you answered yes to question 50, how many extramarital partners have you had? _____

52. If you answered yes to question 50, were your affairs motivated by (circle *all* that apply):
    1. a desire to have more or better sex
    2. a desire to have more intimacy and tenderness
    3. anger at your spouse
    4. other

53. How important do you consider sex to be in your marriage? (Circle *one* number.)
    1. very   2. somewhat   3. not at all

54. Please *circle* the *number* above the *one* choice below that best describes how you feel about your marriage.

(1)	(2)	(3)	(4)	(5)	(6)	(7)
couldn't be more *un*happy	very *un*happy	pretty *un*happy	fair	pretty happy	very happy	couldn't be happier

55. How does being married compare with what you recall you expected it to be like? (Circle *one* choice.)
    1. It's been much harder than I expected.
    2. It's been a little harder than I expected.
    3. It's been a little easier than I expected.
    4. It's been much easier than I expected.
    5. I don't remember what I expected.

56. So far, which of the following best describes your feelings about adjusting to marriage? (Circle *one* choice.)
    1. It's been a very difficult adjustment for me.
    2. It's been a pretty difficult adjustment for me.
    3. It's been a pretty easy adjustment for me.
    4. It's been a very easy adjustment for me.

57. Do you have doubts that your marriage will last?
    1. frequently   2. sometimes   3. rarely   4. never

58. Besides your spouse, with whom do you talk about your marital doubts or arguments? (Circle numbers beside *all* that apply.)
    1. friend(s)
    2. relative(s)
    3. work colleague(s)

    4.   professional marriage counselor(s)
    5.   clergy
    6.   psychotherapist
    7.   no one

59.   Which *one* best describes your parents' marriage? They:
    1.   were very happy   2.   had a number of problems
    3.   had serious problems 4.   were divorced

60.   Which *one* best describes your relationship with your mother?
    1.   excellent   2.   good, but there are/were problems.
    3.   We have many problems, but we communicate.
    4.   awful

61.   Which *one* best describes your relationship with your father?
    1.   excellent   2.   good, but there are/were problems.
    3.   We have many problems, but we communicate.
    4.   awful

62.   Which *one* best describes how you felt growing up?
    1.   I felt loved and secure.
    2.   I had some problems feeling loved and secure.
    3.   I felt very unloved and insecure.

63a.   Have you ever been in any kind of psychotherapy?
    1.   yes   2. no

If you answered yes, please answer questions 63*b* and 63*c*. If you answered no, please go on to question 64.

63b.   What kind of therapy were/are you in?
    1.   individual   2. couple   3. family   4. group

63c.   How has your experience in therapy affected your ability to cope with married life?
    1.   It's been very helpful.
    2.   It's been a little helpful.
    3.   It's neither been helpful nor unhelpful.
    4.   It's been a little harmful.
    5.   It's been very harmful.

Now, we'd like to know a little more about your and your spouse's background.

64a.   Which of the occupations listed below best describes your occupation? (Please insert the appropriate number.) _____

1.   homemaker (full-time)
2.   student
3.   farm worker
4.   laborer, services
5.   arts and related
6.   clerical and related
7.   sales
8.   manager, administrator
9.   professional, technical
10.   other

64b. Which of the occupations listed above in 64a best describes your *spouse's* occupation? (Please insert the appropriate number.) ____

65. Which of these best describes *your* and *your spouse's* individual salaries?

your salary	spouse's salary		
( )	( )	1.	less than $4,999
( )	( )	2.	$5,000–$9,999
( )	( )	3.	$10,000–$14,999
( )	( )	4.	$15,000–$24,999
( )	( )	5.	$25,000–$49,999
( )	( )	6.	$50,000–$100,000
( )	( )	7.	$100,000+

66a. Did you grow up in the United States?
1.   yes   2.   no

66b. If not, in what country did you live until age 18? _____

_____

67a. Did your spouse grow up in the United States?
1.   yes   2.   no

67b. If not, in what country did your spouse live until age 18?

_____

68. What is *your* and *your spouse's* race?

your race	spouse's race		
( )	( )	1.	White
( )	( )	2.	Black
( )	( )	3.	Oriental
( )	( )	4.	Hispanic
( )	( )	5.	other

69. To what religion do *you* and *your spouse* belong?

your religion   *spouse's religion*

your religion	spouse's religion		
( )	( )	1.	Protestant
( )	( )	2.	Catholic
( )	( )	3.	Jewish
( )	( )	4.	Islamic
( )	( )	5.	no preference
( )	( )	6.	other

70. To what ethnic group do *you* and *your spouse* belong?

your ethnicity   *spouse's ethnicity*

your ethnicity	spouse's ethnicity		
( )	( )	1.	Anglo-Saxon
( )	( )	2.	Irish
( )	( )	3.	Italian
( )	( )	4.	Latin American
( )	( )	5.	Middle Eastern
( )	( )	6.	Eastern European
( )	( )	7.	other

71. What is the highest grade *you* and *your spouse* have completed in school? (Please circle.)

you: 1 2 3 4 5 6 7 8 / 9 10 11 12 / 13 14 15 16 / 17+

spouse: 1 2 3 4 5 6 7 8 / 9 10 11 12 / 13 14 15 16 / 17+

        (elementary)   (high school)   (college)   (graduate)

72. As for your present state of affairs, are you:

1. still married and living with your spouse
2. separated from your spouse
3. divorced
4. widowed

73. Have you and your spouse separated for more than one night since your wedding because of incompatibility?

    1. yes   2. no

74. In regard to your future, which best applies?

1. I am seriously considering separating from or divorcing my spouse.
2. I think my spouse and I will be together for the foreseeable future.
3. I'm sure my spouse and I will be together forever.

NOTES

Readers interested in the statistical correlations that led to our conclusions will find them, by chapter, in the notes below. In general: In a positive correlation, one variable increases or decreases in accordance with another variable—for instance, height and weight are usually positively correlated. In a negative correlation, one variable increases relative to a decrease in another variable—for instance, the *more* problems there are in a marriage, the *less* happy people feel in their marriage. In the notes that follow, the value of r represents the relationship between two variables. The following guide shows how we expressed the correlations we assessed. (The formulas are a commonly used interpretative standard.)

$r = 0-.15$ essentially no correlation
$r = .16-.25$ weak correlation
$r = .26-.40$ moderate correlation
$r = .41-.60$ strong correlation
$r = .61-1$ very strong correlation

In our text preceding these notes, all percentages have been rounded out to the nearest whole percent.

CHAPTER 1

1. According to the "Marital Status and Living Arrangements" report published by the U.S. Census Bureau, in March 1985 the average age of a woman at the time of her first marriage hit a record high of 23.3 years. In the same year, the average age of a man at the time of his first marriage was 25.5, a record high since 1910.

2. Data suggests that couples today are more familiar with each other when they marry than were people who married in past decades. According to a March 1984 study of "Marital Status and Living Arrangements" published by the U.S. Census Bureau, the number of unmarried couples living together totaled nearly two million, more than triple the number of people living together in 1970.

3. The correlation, r, between vacationing together before marriage and adjustment to marriage is a weak .1717.

4. The correlation, r, between buying a house or car together before marriage and adjustment to marriage is an insubstantial .0602.

5. The correlation, r, between length of time spouses know each other before marriage and adjustment to marriage is an insubstantial .0722.

6. The correlation, r, between living together before marriage and adjustment to marriage is a weak .1673.

7. The correlation, r, between living together before marriage and marital happiness is an insubstantial .0465.

8. The correlation, r, between living together before marriage and satisfaction about marital sex life is an insubstantial .0840.

9. Alfred DeMaris and Gerald R. Leslie, "Cohabitation with the Future Spouse: Its Influence Upon Marital Satisfaction and Communication," *Journal of Marriage and the Family*, February 1984, pp. 77–84.

10. The correlation, r, between living together before marriage and having doubts about one's marital choice before wedding is an insubstantial .0847.

11. The correlation, r, between length of time spouses know each other before marriage and having doubts about one's marital choice before wedding is an insubstantial .1202.

12. There is also essentially no correlation between having doubts about one's marital choice just before the wedding and a person's age (.0204) or being male or female (.1073).

13. The correlation, r, between having doubts about one's marital choice before the wedding and deciding to marry because "I was in love" is a weak .1662.

14. William Stephens, *The Family in Cross-Cultural Perspective*, (Lanham, Maryland: University Press of America, 1982).

15. Mary D. Ainsworth, Ph.D., "Attachments Across the Life Span," presented as the Thomas William Salmon Lecture for the Salmon Committee on Psychiatry and Mental Hygiene at the New York Academy of Medicine, New York, on December 6, 1984.

16. For further interesting reading on the recent evolution of the adult marital bond, see Lawrence Stone's monumental study

Family, Sex and Marriage: England 1500–1800 (New York: Harper Torchbooks, 1979), which traces the addition of the affection bond between spouses to the otherwise political, social, and economic features of the marriage union.

17. Rubin Blanck and Gertrude Blanck, *Marriage and Personal Development* (New York: Columbia University Press, 1968).

18. Personal communication.

19. Philosopher Martin Buber wrote: "The inmost growth of the self is not accomplished, as people like to suppose today, in man's relation to himself, but in the relation between the one and the other. . . . It is from one man to another that the heavenly bread of self-being is passed." Martin Buber, "Distance and Relation," The William Alanson White Memorial Lectures, Fourth Series, *Psychiatry,* 1957, vol. 20, p. 104.

20. Psychoanalyst Hans Loewald reinforces the point that life periods of chaos and crisis—that can occur in intense interpersonal relationships—can be vital opportunities for personality growth. He states: "We know from analytic as well as from life experience that new spurts of self development may be intimately connected with such 'regressive' rediscoveries of oneself as may occur through the establishment of new object relationships." Furthermore, he notes, "These later consolidations (of personality)—and this is important—follow periods of relative ego-disorganization and reorganization. . . ." See Hans Loewald, "The Therapeutic Action of Psychoanalysis," *International Journal of Psychoanalysis,* 1960, vol. 41, pp. 17–18. This is also the thrust of Erik Erikson's seminal work, "Growth and Crises of the Healthy Personality," *Identity and the Life Cycle: Psychological Issues,* Monograph I. (New York: International Universities Press, 1959) pp. 50–100.

21. We placed notices in *Bride's* magazine, *Monthly Detroit* magazine, the *New York Daily News,* and church newsletters and neighborhood newspapers in the New York metropolitan area. Clergy from across the country were helpful in providing us with lists of brides and grooms they had married, and friends offered the names and addresses of newlyweds they knew personally.

22. A full explanation of how we conducted our survey is offered in Appendix A.

23. Psychoanalyst Heinz Hartmann coined the term "social

compliance" to describe the way in which social/cultural institutions function in unison with intrapsychic phenomena. This theory is modeled after Freud's idea of "somatic compliance," which refers to the notion that certain body organs serve as a focus for psychic conflict—for example the bowels (constipation), lungs (asthma), neuromuscular system (conversion paralysis). Similarly, Hartmann felt that social institutions and psychic needs converge in ways that support both. Marriage, it seems to us, can be thought of as serving social as well as intrapsychic needs—which can explain the tenacity of marriage as an institution. Special problem areas within marriage may represent a point of confrontation for individual or group intrapsychic conflict. See Heinz Hartmann, "Psychoanalysis and Sociology," *Essays on Ego Psychology* (New York: International Universities Press, 1964).

CHAPTER 2

1. The family life cycle is discussed by Ira D. Glick, M.D., and David R. Kessler, M.D., in *Marital and Family Therapy* (New York: Grune & Stratton, 1974).

2. Elizabeth Carter and Monica McGoldrich, *The Family Life Cycle: A Framework for Family Therapy* (New York: Gardner Press, 1980).

3. Martin S. Bergmann, "On the Intrapsychic Function of Falling in Love," *Psychoanalytic Quarterly,* XLIX, 1980, pp. 56–77.

4. Among newlyweds surveyed, 23.2% argue most about money; 13.5% argue most about issues relating to family.

5. The correlation, *r,* between respondent's marital happiness and their having children from a previous marriage is an insubstantial .0701. The correlation, *r,* between respondent's marital happiness and their spouse's having children from a previous marriage is an insubstantial .0273. These correlations are potentially affected by the fact that the distribution of responses is quite limited. The restricted range of responses may result in lowering the correlation.

6. Although the following differences are small, and therefore not statistically significant, we found it interesting that there is a consistent tendency for people with children to state that they have problems related to value differences, religion, and job obligations.

Marital problems relating to:	Respondents with children from a previous marriage	Respondents without children
value differences	8.5%	2.4%
religion	5.1%	1.2%
job obligations	8.5%	1.6%

7. Otto F. Kernberg, M.D., "Mature Love: Prerequisites and Characteristics," *Journal of the American Psychoanalytic Association,* 1974, vol. 22, no. 4; and William W. Meissner, S.J., M.D., "The Conceptualization of Marriage and Family Dynamics from a Psychoanalytic Perspective," *Marriage and Marital Therapy: Psychoanalytic, Behavior and Systems Theory Perspectives,* ed. by T. S. Paolino and B. S. McCrady (New York: Brunner, Mazel, 1978).

8. Murray Bowen, *Family Therapy and Clinical Practice* (New York/ London: Jason Aronson Inc., 1978).

9. In his monumental study of primitive marriage and kinship patterns, Claude Levi-Strauss, anthropological researcher and theorist, asserts that marriage in primitive societies was based primarily on the need for alliances. Only half jokingly, he says that marriages were less about a man's taking a wife than about his taking a brother-in-law who would function as an ally. We've come a long way since the times of our early ancestors, yet some people confided to us during interviews that in making a marital choice they did take into account the family into which they were marrying. See Claude Levi-Strauss, *The Elementary Structure of Kinship* (Boston: Beacon Press, 1969). For a concise summary of Levi-Strauss's position, see his chapter on marriage in *The View From Afar* (New York: Basic Books, 1985).

10. Emily B. Visher presented her paper "The Role Played by the Remarried Parent in the Stepfamily System" at the Seventh Annual Meeting of the American Family Therapy Associaton in San Diego, CA, in June 1985.

CHAPTER 3

1. Sigmund Freud, "On Narcissism" (1914), vol. 14, p. 94f, and "Group Psychology and the Analysis of the Ego" (1921), vol. 18, p. 112f, in the *Standard Edition of the Complete Psychological Works of Sigmund Freud,* ed. James Strachey (London: Hogarth Press, 1981). See also, Karen Horney, "The Problem of the

Monogamous Ideal," *International Journal of Psychoanalysis*, 1928, vol. 9, pp. 318–331.

2. Melanie Klein, *Envy and Gratitude and Other Works 1946–1963* (London: Hogarth Press, 1984).

3. For further discussion of the process of idealization from a variety of psychoanalytic perspectives, see Martin S. Bergmann, "On the Intrapsychic Function of Falling in Love," *Psychoanalytic Quarterly*, 1980, XLIX, pp. 56–77; Carol C. Nadelson, Derek C. Polonsky, and Mary Alice Matthews, "Marriage as a Developmental Process," *Marriage and Divorce: A Contemporary Perspective*, edited by Carol C. Nadelson and Derek C. Polonsky, (New York: Guilford Press, 1984), pp. 127–141; and Otto F. Kernberg, "Mature Love: Prerequisites and Characteristics," *Journal of the American Psychoanalytic Association*, 1974, vol. 22, pp. 743–768.

Also see Ludwig Jekels and Edmund Bergler, "Transference and Love," *Psychoanalytic Quarterly*, 1949, vol. 18, pp. 325–350; Janine Chasseguet-Smirgel, "The Ego Ideal: Being-in-Love and Genitality" (New York: W. W. Norton, 1985); and David S. Werman and Theodore J. Jacobs, "Thomas Hardy's 'The Well-Beloved' and the Nature of Infatuation," *International Review of Psycho-Analysis*, 1983, vol. 10, pp. 447–457.

4. Bergmann, op cit.

5. Samuel Rogers, *Recollections of the Table-Talk of Samuel Rogers* (New York: D. Appleton and Co., 1856).

6. Murstein, an important theorist on marital choice, has described the following three-step process. His theory, called stimulus-value-role, is based on an exchange theory—namely that each person has something to "offer" as a marital choice and will seek to maximize what they can "get." Stage one is *stimulus:* I'm attracted to you for (any number of) variables (usually superficial) I know about you—looks, position, prestige, for example. Stage two is called *value.* In it, potential spouses begin to become acquainted with each other's ideals and values. In stage three, *role,* during an ongoing series of social encounters (dates), potential mates learn the actual roles that each plays, is willing to play, and expects the other in turn to play. Murstein feels that at the end of this process a couple has come to know increasingly more about each other realistically. We agree, but nevertheless find that a number of things change

after marriage that may cast prior evaluations into doubt and review. Bernard I. Murstein, "Marital Choice," *Handbook of Developmental Psychology*, ed. by Benjamin B. Wolman (Englewood, NJ: Prentice-Hall, 1982), pp. 652–666.

7. Albert Scheflan, "Regressive One to One Relationships," *Psychoanalytic Quarterly*, 1960, vol. 34, pp. 692–708. Also, for Ernst Kris's notion of regression in the service of the ego, see "On Preconscious Mental Processes," *Psychoanalytic Explorations in Art* (New York: International Universities Press, 1952), pp. 303–318.

8. Clifford J. Sager, M.D., *Marriage Contracts and Couples Therapy* (New York: Brunner/Mazel, 1986).

9. Horney, op. cit.

10. Eight percent of newlywed respondents reported that their feelings of self-confidence had decreased since their wedding.

11. Bateson's original, brilliant description of schizmogenesis, based on work with natives of New Guinea, can be found in *Naven* (Stanford, CA: Stanford University Press, 1958) (originally published in 1936).

12. The original description of *projective* identification can be found in the work of Melanie Klein, op. cit. For a summary of Klein's works, see Hanna Segal, *Introduction to the Work of Melanie Klein* (New York: Basic Books, 1974).

Some modern applications of this concept to marriage can be found in John Zinner, "The Implications of Projective Identification for Marital Interaction," *Contemporary Marriage: Structure, Dynamics, and Therapy* (Boston: Little, Brown, 1976); T. F. Main, "Mutual Projection in a Marriage," *Comprehensive Psychiatry*, October 1966, vol. 7, no. 5, pp. 432–449; and Stanley J. Greenspan and Fontine V. M. Annino, "A Model of Brief Intervention with Couples Based on Projective Identification," *American Journal of Psychiatry*, Oct. 1974, 131: 10, pp. 1103–1106.

13. Eric Berne, *Games People Play* (New York: Ballantine, 1978) and *Transactional Analysis Bulletin: Selected Articles from Volumes 1–9* (San Francisco, CA: Transactional Analysis Press, 1976).

14. William W. Meissner, "The Conceptualization of Marriage and Family Dynamics," *Marriage and Marital Therapy: Psychoanalytic, Behavior and Systems Theory Perspectives*, ed. by T. S. Paolino and B. S. McCrady (New York: Brunner/Mazel, 1978), pp. 25–83.

15. Joseph Sandler, "Countertransference and Role Responsiveness," *International Review of Psychoanalysis,* 1976, vol. 3, pp. 43–47.

16. Klein, op. cit.

17. Klein, op. cit.

18. Jacob A. Arlow, a prominent contemporary psychoanalyst, writes that splitting can occur in people operating at otherwise higher degrees of functioning and personality development when they experience enough stress. "The splitting of the representation of a person does not necessarily occur only in cases of severe personality regression. . . . When there is a painful interaction between two people, one can observe in the dreams and fantasies of the patient how the qualities of good and bad may become sharply disassociated in the mental representations of the object. The individual, in turn, may respond to the other person as if that person were the repetition of the earlier mental representation of the bad object. At the same time such an individual may be functioning at an advanced level of mental development" (pp. 118–119). From Jacob A. Arlow, "Object Concept and Object Choice," *Psychoanalytic Quarterly,* 1980, XLIX, pp. 109–133.

19. Meissner, op. cit.

20. Erich Fromm, *The Art of Loving* (New York: Harper & Row, 1956), p. 9.

21. On the desire to transform the love object, also see Freud, "A Special Type of Choice of Object Made by Men" ("Contributions to the Psychology of Love I") (1910), vol. XI *Standard Edition,* op. cit., pp. 163–176.

22. Thirty percent of our survey respondents are intermarried by religion.

23. Sager, op. cit.

24. J. F. Cuber and P. B. Haroff, "The More Total View: Relationships Among Men and Women in the Upper Middle Class," *Marriage and Family Living,* 1963, vol. 25, pp. 140–145.

25. Freud, "On Narcissism," op. cit. Freud notes that the first two love objects of one's life are *oneself* and one's mother. Consequently he feels that subsequent love choices are based on a mix of narcissistic and dependency needs. *Narcissistic* needs are related to qualities of the other that boost one's own self-esteem.

Dependency needs are ways of being or feeling cared for. Satisfying both of these needs vitally adds to our feeling loved and lovable. Freud's famous quote from this paper is:

A person may love:

   1) according to the narcissistic type:
      a) what he himself is
      b) what he himself was
      c) what he himself would like to be
      d) someone who was also part of himself
   2) according to the anaclitic (attachment) type:
      a) the woman who feeds him
      b) the man who protects him. . . . (p. 90)

For elaboration on some of these themes, see Annie Reich, "Narcissistic Object Choice in Women," *Journal of the American Psychoanalytic Association: Volume 1* (New York: International University Press, 1953), pp. 22–24, and Martin H. Stein, "The Marriage Bond," *Psychoanalytic Quarterly,* 1956, vol. 25, pp. 238–259.

26. Peter L. Giovacchini, M.D., "Characterological Aspects of Marital Interaction," *The Psychoanalytic Forum,* Spring 1967, vol. 2, no. 1, pp. 7–30, and "Symbiosis and Intimacy," *International Journal of Psychoanalytic Psychotherapy,* 1976, vol. 5, pp. 413–436. Also, Henry V. Dicks, *Marital Tensions: Clinical Studies Towards a Psychological Theory of Interaction* (New York: Basic Books, 1967), and Cuber, op. cit.

27. Dicks, op. cit. Dicks has a most interesting model, to our minds, of how and when couple differences become significant regarding breakup and when they remain tolerated. He describes three intrapsychic systems. The first consists of the social values and norms one inherits from one's parents. The second represents the extent to which one is trying to break from one's parents and establish an independent identity. One more or less adheres to or rebels from parental values and norms. The last represents the deepest "imago" of the desired parental love object along with the distortions that protect one from fears of incest. Dicks feels—and documents with his extensive clinical experience—that couples who mesh on two or more of the above systems generally "make it," while those who differ on two or more don't have enough in common to sustain their relationship.

28. Erik Erikson, "Growth and Crises of the Healthy Personality," *Identity and the Life Cycle: Psychological Issues, Monograph I* (New York: International Universities Press, 1959), pp. 50–100.

CHAPTER 4

1. Robert G. Ryder, Ph.D., D. Wells Goodrich, M.D., "Married Couples' Responses to Disagreement," *Family Process*, vol. 5, 1966, pp. 30–41.

2. The correlation, *r*, between fighting infrequently and happiness in marriage is a moderate .3282.

3. Although 50 percent of our respondents noted that they have significant problems in their marriage, we also found that the more confident newlyweds are about working out their marital problems, the happier they feel about their marriage. The correlation, *r*, between confidence in resolving marital problems and marital happiness is a robust .4181.

4. Hermann von Keyserling, ed. *The Book of Marriage* (New York: Harcourt, Brace & Company, 1927).

5. Martin Goldberg, "The Dynamics of Marital Interaction and Marital Conflict," *Psychiatric Clinics of North America* 5:3, December 1982, pp. 449–467.

6. Ibid.

7. Talcott Parsons and Robert F. Bales present their classic study on the division of marital roles along the axis of men taking on tasks that involve negotiations outside of the home, between the family and the world (instrumental roles), and women assuming roles related to the homeostasis of the family's emotional life (emotional roles) in *Family: Socialization and Interaction Process* (Glencoe, IL: Free Press, 1955). Philip Blumstein, Ph.D., and Pepper Schwartz, Ph.D., offer a historical perspective on male–female roles in "The American Couple in Perspective," *American Couples* (New York, Pocket Books, 1985).

8. Harold L. Rausch, Wells Goodrich, and John D. Campbell, "Adaptation to the First Years of Marriage," *Psychiatry*, 1963, vol. 26, pp. 368–380.

9. The importance of the husband's meeting his own and his wife's expectations of the male role—both strongly based on their father's role model—is discussed persuasively by Roland G. Thorp in his extensive literature review, "Psychological Pat-

terning in Marriage," *Psychological Bulletin,* March 1963, vol. 60, no. 2, pp. 97–117.

10. Constantina Safilios-Rothschild, "The Dimensions of Power Distribution in the Family," *Contemporary Marriage: Structure, Dynamics and Therapy,* ed. by Henry Grunebaum, M.D., and Jacob Christ, M.D. (Boston: Little, Brown, 1976).

11. Annie Reich speaks about women who enter ambivalently tinged love relationships in the submissive role. Overvaluing the husband's power is seen alongside masochistic submissiveness, with resulting anger and aggression when this expectation is frustrated. In the case described in our chapter, the "submissive" defense works less thoroughly, and Nancy periodically expresses her anger at her husband's controlling style. See Annie Reich, "A Contribution to the Psychoanalysis of Extreme Submissiveness in Women," *Psychoanalytic Quarterly,* 1940, vol. IX, pp. 470–480.

12. Martin Stein discusses the ambivalence and problems involved for men whose wives represent "phallic" or powerful additions to themselves. Adoration of this power alternates with resentment and attempts to punish or subdue one's wife, leading to sadomasochistic interactions. He writes: "The manipulation of the penis is transferred directly to treatment of the wife in a masturbatory fashion. 'Self-defense' becomes, as it were, 'wife abuse.' Thus it is a vehicle for true sadistic expression, whether by teasing or by some form of violence, having as its arm, the production of an orgastic equivalent in the wife—tears, a temper tantrum, or some other manifestation of loss of control. . . . The husband feels he cannot do without his wife, but he is hardly ready to dignify her by admitting that she has any more than material or even mechanical importance. Her presence as an object for reassurance, manipulation and exhibition are obvious; but she is not appreciated as a companion or helpmeet" (p. 252).

While Stein feels that *all* men seek, to some degree, a "phallus" in the women they court and marry, the intensity and pathogenic intrusiveness of this fantasy will vary markedly depending on one's early life determinants. See Martin Stein, "The Marriage Bond," *Psychoanalytic Quarterly,* 1956, vol. 25, pp. 238–259.

The issue of woman as phallus is further discussed in Martin Grotjahn's "About the Symbolization of Alice's Adventures in Wonderland," *American Image IV,* 1947, pp. 32–41; Bertram D. Lewin's "The Body as Phallus," *Psychoanalytic Quarterly,* 1933, vol. 2, pp. 24–47; and Otto Fenichel's "The Symbolic Equation: Girl = Phallus," originally published in Germany in 1936 and translated in English in the *Psychoanalytic Quarterly,* 1949, vol. 18, pp. 303–324.

13. There is an extensive psychiatric literature focusing on the systems aspects of family relationships. For a recent review written for professional audiences, see Peter Steinglass, M.D., "The Conceptualization of Marriage from a Systems Theory Perspective," *Marriage and Marital Therapy: Psychoanalytic, Behavioral and Systems Theory Perspectives,* edited by T. S. Paolino and B. S. McCrady (New York: Brunner/Mazel, 1978).

CHAPTER 5

1. Leslie Navran, Ph.D., "Communication and Adjustment in Marriage," *Family Process,* 1976, pp. 173–184; and Harold L. Rausch, Wells Goodrich, and John D. Campbell, "Adaptation to the First Years of Marriage," *Human Adaptation: Coping with Life Crises,* ed. by Rudolph Moos (Lexington, MA: D. C. Heath & Co., 1976).

2. Twenty-three percent of newlywed respondents reported arguing most about money; 14 percent about family issues; 12 percent about communication styles; another 12 percent about household tasks.

3. According to our newlywed respondents:
- 12 percent argue most about communication styles, while only:
- 11 percent argue most about personal tastes
- 5 percent argue most about decision making
- 5 percent argue most about sex
- 5 percent argue most about finding time for each other
- 4 percent argue most about value differences
- 3 percent argue most about job obligations
- 2 percent argue most about religion
- 2 percent argue most about friendships
- 1 percent argue most about shared interests
- less than 1 percent argue most about marital goals

That's not to say that those issues aren't important in marriage, but they just don't surface as the most common cause of arguing.

4. Israel W. Charny, Ph.D., "Marital Love and Hate," *Family Process*, March 1969, vol. 8, no. 1, p. 2.

5. It's been noted for some time by social scientists (Robert Winch) and psychoanalysts (Peter Giovacchini) that people with opposite but complementary qualities often form extremely enduring bonds. These complementary matches allow and often facilitate the mutual processes of projection and introjection, which in higher-functioning personalities can lead to a sense of joint understanding, fulfillment, harmony. However, people with poorly functioning personalities can each "project" that the other is "bad" and lock a couple into an enduring blame/attack (sadomasochistic) struggle. See Robert F. Winch, "Complementary Needs and Related Notions About Voluntary Mate Selection," *Selected Studies in Marriage and the Family*, ed. by Robert F. Winch and Graham Spanier (New York: Holt, Rinehart, & Winston, 1974) and Peter L. Giovacchini, M.D., "Characterological Aspects of Marital Interaction," *The Psychoanalytic Forum*, Spring 1967, vol. 2, no. 1, pp. 7–30.

6. Joseph Barnett, M.D., "Narcissism and Dependency in the Obsessional-Hysteric Marriage," *Family Process*, 1971, vol. 10, no. 1, pp. 75–83.

7. The subject of vicious cycles in marriage was discussed by Oliver Bjornstein in his lecture "Interactional Concepts of Marital Treatment Planning," given at the 1985 American Psychiatric Association meeting in Dallas, TX. An abstract of this presentation is in the Continuing Medical Education Syllabus and Proceedings Summary of the 138th Annual Meeting of the American Psychiatric Association, Dallas, TX 1985 (p. 103), which was published by the American Psychiatric Association in Washington, D.C. 1985. A classic, more general theoretical paper about negative feedback loops in human relations can be found in Paul H. Wender, "Vicious and Virtuous Cycles: The Role of Deviation Amplifying Feedback; The Origins and Perpetuation of Behavior" in *Brief Therapies*, ed. by Harvey H. Barton (New York: Behavioral Publication, 1971). A couple's mutual attempt at domination, locking them into a system of mutual attack, is described by Bela Mittelman in "Complemen-

tary Neurotic Reactions in Intimate Relationships," *Psychoanalytic Quarterly,* 1944, vol. 13.

8. The power of failures of empathy to unleash rage has been convincingly explicated by Heinz Kohut, "Thoughts on Narcissism and Narcissistic Rage," *The Psychoanalytic Study of the Child,* 1972, vol. 27, pp. 377–400. The ways in which this problem is played out in marriage are well described by Larry B. Feldman, "Dysfunctional Marital Conflict: An Integrative Interpersonal-Intrapsychic Model," *Journal of Marital and Family Therapy,* October 1982, pp. 417–428.

9. John P. Spiegel, "The Resolution of Role Conflict Within the Family," *Psychiatry,* vxx, 1957, pp. 1–16.

10. Melvin R. Lansky, M.D., offers a very comprehensive exploration of blaming transactions in his article "On Blame," published in the *International Journal of Psychoanalytic Psychotherapy,* 1980, vol. 8, pp. 429–460.

11. Feldman, op. cit.

12. Navran, op. cit.

13. In a study exploring communication among 24 married couples, clinical psychologists Gary R. Birchler, Robert L. Weiss, and John P. Vincent discovered that couples tend to display more nonfacilitative behaviors with their own partners than with strangers. This study is referred to in "Improving Communication in Marriage," by Herbert Yahraes, in Science Monography 1, *Families Today,* vol. 1, National Institute of Mental Health.

14. David H. Knox, Jr., Ph.D., discussed this technique in the course "Behavioral Marriage and Family Therapy," given at the 1986 American Psychiatric Association in Washington, D.C. See David Knox, "Behavior Contracts in Marriage Counseling," *Journal of Family Counseling,* 1973, vol. 1, pp. 22–28.

15. Domeena C. Renshaw, M.D., "Communication in Marriage," *Medical Aspects of Human Sexuality,* vol. 17, no. 6, 1983, pp. 31–46; also Malcolm Kahn, Ph.D., "Non–Verbal Communication and Marital Satisfaction," *Family Process,* 1970, vol. 9, pp. 449–456.

16. Richard Rabkin, M.D., "Uncoordinated Communication Between Marriage Partners," *Family Process,* 1967, vol. 6, no. 1, pp. 10–15.

17. Spiegel, op. cit., and R. William Betcher, "Intimate Play

and Marital Adaptation," *Psychiatry*, vol. 44, February 1981.

18. The importance of viewing one's self and one's spouse as team members was demonstrated in a finding that harmonious married couples use the word "we" more than "I." See Harold Rausch, Ph.D., Karol A. Marshall, M.A.; and Jo-Anna M. Featherman, B.A., "Relations at Three Early Stages of Marriage as Reflected by the Use of Personal Pronouns," *Family Process*, 1970, vol. 9, no. 1, pp. 69–82.

19. Spiegel, op. cit.

20. Child psychoanalyst David Winnicott offers a fascinating discussion of the development in childhood of the *need* and capacity both to communicate and *not to communicate,* at least about deeply personal issues. The latter is a way of protecting one's "core" sense of self. See David Winnicott, "Communicating and Not Communicating Leading to a Study of Certain Opposites," *The Maturational Processes and the Facilitating Environment* (New York: International Universities Press, 1965), pp. 179–192.

CHAPTER 6

1. Betty Friedan, *The Feminine Mystique* (New York: Dell, 1964).

2. Pepper Schwartz, Ph.D., and Philip Blumstein, Ph.D., *American Couples* (New York: Pocket Books, 1985).

3. Of our newlywed respondents, 11.9 percent said they argue most about household tasks. The same percentage of respondents said they argue most about communication styles.

4. Murray A. Straus, Richard J. Gelles, and Suzanne K. Steinmetz, *Behind Closed Doors: Violence in the American Family* (New York: Doubleday/Anchor Press, 1980).

5. Source: a 1982–1983 study of 239 families by Sara Yogev, Ph.D., and Jeanne Brett, Ph.D., of Northwestern University in Evanston, IL.

6. Jessie Bernard, *The Future of Marriage,* Rev. ed. (New Haven and London: Yale University Press, 1982) and J. Giele, "Changing Sex Roles and the Future of Marriage," *Contemporary Marriage: Structure, Dynamics and Theory,* ed. by H. Grunebaum and J. Christ (Boston: Little, Brown & Co., 1976).

7. Carol C. Nadelson, M.D., and Malkah T. Notman, M.D., "To Marry or Not to Marry," *The Woman Patient: Concepts of Femininity and the Life Cycle,* vol. 2, ed. by Carol C. Nadelson, M.D., and Malkah T. Notman, M.D. (New York and London:

Plenum Press, 1978). Also, William A. Barry in "Marriage Research and Conflict: An Integrative Review," *Psychological Bulletin*, 1970, vol. 73, no. 1, pp. 41–54, suggests that marriage constitutes a more difficult *transition* for women than for men. While marriage may be a "wrinkle" in a man's day-to-day lifestyle, work and business continue for him more or less as usual. The role of wife, however, with its added household responsibilities and anticipation of childbearing and child rearing, has a major impact on the life of a woman who chooses that track. Barry postulates, therefore, and his research bears out, that when husbands are secure in their own identities and thus capable of emotional and practical support of their wives the amount of conflict experienced in the young marriage will be diminished. Conversely, husbands who are coercive and punitive will elicit defensive reactions in their already stressed wives, increase the level of interpersonal conflict, and exacerbate the couple's sense of desperate plight.

8. Catherine White Berheide, "Women's Work in the Home: Seems Like Old Times," *Marriage and Family Review*, vol. 7 (New York: The Haworth Press, 1984).

9. Sigmund Freud, "Three Essays on the Theory of Sexuality" (1905), vol. VII, *Standard Edition of the Complete Psychological Works of Sigmund Freud,* ed. James Strachey (London: Hogarth Press, 1981).

10. Roland G. Thorpe, "Psychological Patterning in Marriage," *Psychological Bulletin,* March 1963, vol. 60, no. 2, pp. 97–117.

11. Roy Schafer, "Men Who Struggle Against Sentimentality," *The Psychology of Men,* ed. by Gerald Fagel, Frederick Lane, and Robert Liebert (New York: Basic Books, 1986).

CHAPTER 7

1. George Bernard Shaw, preface to *Major Barbara* (1907), *Collected Plays with Their Prefaces* (New York: Dodd, Mead & Co., 1971).

2. Of our survey respondents, 23.2 percent said that they argue more often about money than about any other issue in their marriage.

3. Of our survey respondents, 29.3 percent said they had significant problems in their marriage relating to money. Of those people, 1.4 percent said that money problems threatened their

marriage and 27.8 percent said they were working on their problems.

4. In their 1970s survey of 3,999 men and women from across the United States, Anthony Pietropinto, M.D., and Jacqueline Simenauer, authors of *Husbands and Wives: A Nationwide Survey of Marriage* (New York: Times Books, 1979), found that people who earn under ten thousand dollars a year stated that matters of finance were the main cause of arguments over 50 percent more often than those making more than that amount.

5. Judson T. Landis, "Length of Time Required to Achieve Adjustment in Marriage," *American Sociological Review,* 1946, vol. 11, pp. 666–677.

6. *The New York Times* editorial page, January 2, 1986.

7. Psychoanalytically, the fear of depletion relates not only to feeling loved and nurtured, but also—for men especially, although not exclusively—to primitive childhood castration fears. See Freud, "The Taboo of Virginity" ("Contributions to the Psychology of Love III") (1918), vol. XI, *Standard Edition of the Complete Psychological Works of Sigmund Freud,* ed. James Strachey (London: Hogarth Press, 1981). Although it's beyond the scope of this book, for his fascinating discussion equating, at deep, unconscious levels, money, phallus, feces, gifts, and baby, see Freud, "On Transformations of Instinct as Exemplified in Anal Eroticism" (1917), vol. XVII, *Standard Edition,* op. cit.

8. Philip Blumstein, Ph.D., and Pepper Schwartz, Ph.D., *American Couples* (New York: Pocket Books, 1985).

9. William M. Meissner explores spouses' capacity for closeness and distance in marriage in his paper, "The Conceptualization of Marriage and Family Dynamics from a Psychoanalytic Perspective," *Marriage and Marital Therapy: Psychoanalytic, Behavior and Systems Theory Perspectives,* ed. by T. S. Paolino and B. S. McCrady (New York: Brunner/Mazel, 1978).

CHAPTER 8

1. The correlation, *r,* between work ambitions increasing or decreasing after marriage and being male or female is a weak .2101.

2. According to one recent study, Americans are working longer hours and spending less time at leisure due to economic pressures. The national survey, conducted by Louis Harris and As-

sociates, Inc., showed that the median work week increased from 43.1 hours in 1975 to 47.3 hours in 1984, while the median time for leisure decreased from 24.3 hours in 1975 to 18.1 hours in 1984.

3. Philip Blumstein, Ph.D., and Pepper Schwartz, Ph.D., *American Couples* (New York: Pocket Books, 1985).

4. Jay B. Rohrlich, M.D., *Work and Love: The Crucial Balance* (New York: Summit Books, 1980).

5. Lord Thomas Robert Dewar, *Epigram.*

6. Based on data from a 1977 national employment survey of 1,515 American workers, psychologists Graham Staines, Ph.D., Kathleen Pottick, Ph.D., and Deborah Fudge, M.S., of Rutgers University analyzed two groups: 208 husbands whose wives work for pay, and 408 husbands whose wives do not work for pay and are described by their husbands as housewives. The researchers concluded that a husband's perception of his adequacy as breadwinner in the family is a central component of his mental health. The authors published their research findings in the article, "Wives' Employment and Husbands' Attitude Toward Work and Life," *Journal of Applied Psychology*, February 1986.

7. A thorough overview of studies relating to commuter marriages is provided in "Commuter Marriages: A Review" by Naomi Gerstel, Ph.D., and Harriet Engel Gross, Ph.D., *Marriage and Family Review*, vol. 5, no. 2, 1981.

CHAPTER 9

1. George Bernard Shaw, "Maxims for Revolutionists," *Collected Plays with Their Prefaces*, vol. II (New York: Dodd, Mead & Co., 1971).

2. This report by the National Center for Health Statistics is based on statistics collected in the 1982 National Survey of Family Growth.

3. The correlation, r, between frequency of sex before marriage (with marital partner) and frequency of sex in marriage is an insubstantial .1071.

4. The correlation, r, between having sex problems in marriage and living together before marriage is an insubstantial .0120.

5. Cathy Stein Greenblat, "The Salience of Sexuality in the Early Years of Marriage," *Journal of Marriage and the Family*, May 1983, pp. 289–299.

6. Arnold Van Gennep, *The Rites of Passage* (Chicago: University of Chicago Press, 1960).

7. Sigmund Freud, "The Taboo of Virginity" ("Contributions to the Psychology of Love III") (1918), vol. XI, *Standard Edition of the Complete Psychological Works of Sigmund Freud*, ed. James Strachey (London: Hogarth Press, 1981).

8. The correlation, *r*, between having a great time on the honeymoon and feeling happy about one's marriage is a moderate .2896.

9. William H. James, "The Honeymoon Effect on Marital Coitus," *The Journal of Sex Research*, May 1981, vol. 17, no. 2, pp. 114–123.

10. Philip Blumstein, Ph.D., and Pepper Schwartz, Ph.D., *American Couples* (New York: Pocket Books, 1985).

11. Ibid.

12. Denis de Rougemont, *Love in the Western World* (New York: Anchor, 1957).

13. Ibid., p. 52.

14. Sigmund Freud, "On the Universal Tendency to Debasement in the Sphere of Love" ("Contributions to the Psychology of Love II") (1912), vol. XI, "Three Essays on the Theory of Sexuality" (1905), vol. VII, and "Group Psychology and the Analysis of the Ego" (1921), vol. XVIII, *Standard ꞏ ꞏdition*, op. cit.; and Karen Horney, "The Problem of the Monogamous Ideal," *International Journal of Psychoanalysis*, 1928, vol. 9, pp. 318–331.

15. Sandor Ferenczi, "Psycho-analysis of Sexual Habits," *Further Contributions to the Theory and Technique of Psychoanalysis* (London: Hogarth Press, 1926), pp. 372–404.

16. Freud wrote, "Anyone who is to be really free and happy in love must have surmounted his respect for women and have come to terms with the idea of incest with his mother or sister." See Sigmund Freud, "On the Universal Tendency to Debasement in the Sphere of Love," op. cit., p. 186.

Jacob A. Arlow, an important contemporary psychoanalyst, notes a variation on this theme. Early childhood fantasies, he notes, play a prominent role in guiding and directing the activities of adult life. Psychoanalysts note that the child exposed to his parents having sex ("primal scenes") perceives this event as violent. The mother is seen as debased and rejecting of the jealous child. The pursuit, and perhaps rescue, of the debased love object represents the pursuit of this debased, lost parental figure. He notes that any individual will have their own special drama, based on childhood experiences, which they relive in love. See Jacob A. Arlow, "Object Concept and Object Choice," *Psychoanalytic Quarterly*, 1980, XLIX, pp. 109–133.

17. Peter L. Giovacchini, M.D., "Characterological Aspects of Marital Interaction," *The Psychoanalytic Forum*, Spring 1967, vol. 2, no. 1, pp. 7–30, and "Symbiosis and Intimacy," *International Journal of Psychoanalytic Psychotherapy*, 1976, vol. 5, pp. 413–436.

18. Otto Kernberg, M.D., "Mature Love: Prerequisites and Characteristics," *Journal of the American Psychoanalytic Association*, 1974, vol. 2, pp. 743–768.

19. We found almost no difference between males and females in their desire for more frequent sex in their marriages. The correlation, r, between gender and wanting more frequent marital sex is an insubstantial .1397.

20. The correlation, r, between having sex infrequently and feeling unhappy about one's marriage is a robust .4324.

21. Sidney Levin, M.D., "Further Comments on a Common Type of Marital Incompatibility," *Journal of the American Psychoanalytic Association*, vol. 17, pp. 1097–1113.

22. John N. Edwards, Ph.D., and Alan Booth, Ph.D., "The Cessation of Marital Intercourse," *American Journal of Psychiatry*, November 1976, vol. 133, no. 11, pp. 1333–1336. An interesting historical study of how the tapering or termination of a couple's sexual activity together leads to, at times, productive diversion of "sexual energy" can be found in a paper by Alan C. Elms, "Freud, Irma, Martha: Sex and Marriage in the 'Dream of Irma's Injection,' " *Psychoanalytic Review*, 1980, vol. 67, pp. 63–109. In it, Elms discusses how the drop-off in Freud's sex life due to his wife's sixth pregnancy may have found expression and sublimation in his clinical interests and theories, which were "coincidentally" all about competitive childhood sexual fantasies.

23. E. Frank, C. Anderson, and D. Kupfer, "Frequency of Sex-

ual Dysfunction in 'Normal' Couples," *New England Journal of Medicine,* 1978, vol. 299, pp. 111–115.

24. Helen Singer Kaplan, M.D., Ph.D., *The Illustrated Manual of Sex Therapy* (New York: Quadrangle-New York Times Book Co., 1985).

25. Harold I. Lief, M.D., and Ellen M. Berman, M.D., "Sexual Interviewing of the Individual Patient Through the Life Cycle," *Sex and the Life Cycle,* edited by Wilbur W. Oaks, M.D., and Gerald A. Melchiode, M.D., and Ilda Ficher, M.D. (New York: Grune & Stratton Inc., 1976).

26. Jane E. Brody, "Personal Health" column, *The New York Times,* October 31, 1984.

27. Douglas K. Snyder, Ph.D., and Phyllis Berg, Ph.D., "Determinants of Sexual Dissatisfaction in Sexually Distressed Couples," *Archives of Sexual Behavior,* 1983, vol. 12, no. 3, pp. 237–246.

28. Aaron Paley, M.D., "Adapting to a Spouse's Idiosyncrasy," *Medical Aspects of Human Sexuality,* April 1984, vol. 18, no. 4.

29. Sherryl Connelly, "Fantasy Lives," *New York Daily News,* May 1, 1984, YOU section, p. 29.

30. About the same percentage of newlywed men and women reported having fantasies about their spouse. The correlation, r, between gender and having fantasies about one's spouse is an insubstantial .1195. Gender also seems to have little influence on whether or not people have sex fantasies about partners other than their mates. . . . The correlation, r, between being male or female and having fantasies about someone other than one's spouse is a weak .2240.

31. Mark F. Schwartz, Sc.D., and William H. Masters, M.D., "The Masters and Johnson Treatment Program for Dissatisfied Homosexual Men," *The American Journal of Psychiatry,* February 1984, vol. 141, no. 2, pp. 173–181.

32. Otto F. Kernberg, "Boundaries and Structure in Love Relations," *Journal of the American Psychoanalytic Association,* 1977, vol. XXV, pp. 81–114.

33. John P. Docherty, M.D., and Jean Ellis, R.N., "A New Concept and Finding in Morbid Jealousy," *American Journal of Psychiatry,* June 1976, vol. 133, no. 6, pp. 679–683.

34. Sigmund Freud, "Some Neurotic Mechanisms in Jealousy,

Paranoia and Homosexuality" (1922), vol. XIII, *Standard Edition*, op. cit., pp. 223–234.

35. Ibid, pp. 224–256.

36. A. C. Kinsey, W. B. Pomeroy, and C. E. Martin, *Sexual Behavior in the Human Male* (Philadelphia: Saunders, 1948) and *Sexual Behavior in the Human Female* (Philadelphia: Saunders, 1953).

37. Linda Wolfe, *The Cosmo Report* (New York: Arbor House, 1981).

38. Otto F. Kernberg, M.D., "Love, the Couple, and the Group: A Psychoanalytic Frame," *Psychoanalytic Quarterly* XLIX, 1980, pp. 78–108.

39. Herbert S. Strean presents four reasons for marital infidelity, based on psychoanalytic clinical work:

1. running away from Oedipal incest fears
2. seeking someone who has not become the recipient of "superego" projections. ("He/she is always criticizing/nagging me.")
3. fears of bisexuality. In the "Don Juan syndrome," a male has frequent affairs as an assertion of his "macho" (or male) character to bolster a weak masculine identity, or to allay (usually unconscious) homosexual fears.
4. running from fears of symbiotic merging with a mother figure

Strean notes that these four motivators often blend together in the adulterous personality. He presents his theory in "The Extramarital Affair: A Psychoanalytic View," *Psychoanalytic Review*, 1976, vol. 63, pp. 101–113.

40. Harvey S. Waxman and Jancis V. F. Long, "Adultery and Marriage: Three Psychological Perspectives," *Marriage and Divorce: A Contemporary Perspective* (New York: Guilford Press, 1984), pp. 142–156.

41. Freud, "On the Universal Tendency to Debasement in the Sphere of Love," op. cit., p. 185.

42. Annie Reich, "Narcissistic Object Choice in Women," *Journal of the American Psychoanalytic Association: Volume 1* (New York: International University Press, 1953), pp. 22–24.

43. O. Fenichel, *The Psychoanalytic Theory of Neurosis* (New York: W. W. Norton, 1945).

CHAPTER 10

1. From *Letters of Rainer Maria Rilke 1892–1910* (New York: Norton, 1969).

2. A fundamental psychoanalytic precept, based upon findings about adults in psychoanalysis as well as upon developmental observations of children, is that childhood trauma will affect an adult's ability to relate to and to love others. The nature of the trauma and its effect, however, are hotly debated. The following are only a few of the important references for a wide spectrum of psychoanalytic viewpoints.

One major text about child development, which spells out the stages of a child's coming to be a separate human being capable of independent love attachments, is Margaret S. Mahler, Fred Pine, Anni Bergman, *Psychological Birth of the Human Infant: Symbiosis and Individuation* (New York: Basic Books, 1975).

Daniel Stern offers another developmental view of the unfolding relationship between mother and infant in *The Interpersonal World of the Infant* (New York: Basic Books, 1985). He writes: "To engage in sustained romantic love requires that the individual be given the opportunity through many life experiences to develop the ability to be imbued with the presence of an absent person, an almost constantly evoked companion" (p. 244).

In her paper, "Our Adult World and Its Roots in Intimacy," from *Envy and Gratitude and Other Works 1946–1963* (London: Hogarth Press, 1984), noted child observer and psychoanalyst Melanie Klein notes, "A strong identification with a good mother makes it easier for the child to identify also with a good father and later on with other friendly figures. As a result, his inner world comes to contain predominantly good objects (persons) and feelings and these good objects are felt to respond to the infant's love. All this contributes to a stable personality and *makes it possible to extend sympathy and friendly feelings to other people*. It is clear that a good relation of the parents to each other and to the child and a happy home atmosphere plays a vital role in the success of this process" (pp. 251–252).

Another important writer on how childhood hurts can later life relationships is Heinz Kohut. His classic text, based on adult psychoanalysis of the seriously narcissistic personality, is *The Analysis of the Self* (New York: International Universities Press, 1977).

3. Charlotte Kahn, "Proverbs of Love and Marriage: A Psychological Perspective," *Psychoanalytic Review,* Fall 1983, vol. 70, no. 3, pp. 359–371.

4. Martin S. Bergmann, "Psychoanalytic Observations on the Capacity to Love," *Separation Individuation Essays in Honor of Margaret S. Mahler,* ed. by John B. McDavitt and Calvin Settlage (New York: International Universities Press, 1971), pp. 15–40.

5. William A. Binstock, M.D., "On the Two Forms of Intimacy," *Journal of the American Psychoanalytic Association,* 1973, vol. 21, no. 1, pp. 93–107; and R. C. Bak, "Being in Love and Object Loss," *International Journal of Psychoanalysis,* 1973, vol. 54, pp. 1–8.

6. Carol Gilligan, *In a Different Voice: Psychological Theory and Women's Development* (Cambridge, MA: Harvard University Press, 1982).

7. Ibid.

8. Daniel Goleman, "Two Views of Marriage Explored: His and Hers," *The New York Times,* April 1, 1986, p. C1.

9. Ibid.

10. Kathleen M. White, Joseph C. Steisman, Doris Jackson, Scott Eartis, Daryl Costos, "Intimacy Maturity and Its Correlates in Young Married Couples," *The Journal of Personality and Social Psychology,* January 1986.

11. Joseph Barnett, M.D., "Narcissism and Dependency in the Obsessional-Hysteric Marriage," *Family Process,* 1971, vol. 10, no. 1, pp. 75–83.

12. E. M. Waring, M.D., Mary Pat Tillman, M.S.W., L. Frelick, M.D., Lila Russell, M.S.W., and G. Weisz, Ph.D., "Concepts of Intimacy in the General Population," *The Journal of Nervous and Mental Disease,* 1980, vol. 168, no. 8, pp. 471–474.

13. See footnote 2.

14. Erik Erikson, "Growth and Crises of the Healthy Personality," *Identity and the Life Cycle: Psychological Issues, Monograph I* (New York: International Universities Press, 1959), pp. 50–100; Roger L. Gould, M.D., "The Phases of Adult Life: A Study in Developmental Psychology," *The American Journal of Psychiatry,* November 1972, vol. 129, no. 5; Daniel J. Levinson, et. al., *The Seasons of a Man's Life* (New York: Ballantine Books, 1978).

15. T. H. Christensen, "The Timing of First Pregnancy as a

Factor in Divorce: A Cross-Cultural Analysis," *Eugenics Quarterly*, 1963, vol. 10, pp. 119–130; and Lillian Breslow Rubin, *Worlds of Pain* (New York: Basic Books, 1976).

16. H. Waldo Bird, M.D., Anthony I. Schuham, Ph.D., Lois Benson, M.S.W., Leslie L. Gans, B.A., "Stressful Life Events and Marital Dysfunction," *Hospital and Community Psychiatry*, July 1981, vol. 32, no. 7, pp. 486–490.

17. Benjamin Wolman, ed., *International Encyclopedia of Psychiatry, Psychology, Psychoanalysis and Neurology*, vol. 6 (New York: Aesculepius Publishers for Van Nostrand Reinhold Co., 1977), pp. 444–446.

18. Robert J. Sternberg and Susan Grajeck, "The Nature of Love," *Journal of Personality and Social Psychology*, 1984, vol. 47, no. 2, pp. 312–329. In their article, Sternberg and Grajeck especially focus on an article by J. A. Lee, "A Typology of Styles of Loving," *Personality and Social Psychology Bulletin 3*, 1977, pp. 173–182.

19. Michael Balint, "On Genital Love," *Primary Love and Psychoanalytic Technique* (New York: Tavistock, 1948), pp. 109–120.

20. Rollo May, *Love and Will* (New York: W. W. Norton, 1969), p. 289.

21. George Eliot, *George Eliot Letters,* 9 vols. ed. by Gordon Haight (New Haven, Yale University Press, 1954–78). Quote from a letter by Eliot to Mrs. Burne Jones, dated May 11, 1875.

22. Otto F. Kernberg, M.D., "Boundaries and Structure in Love Relations," *Journal of the American Psychoanalytic Association*, 1977, vol. XXV, pp. 81–114.

23. Kahlil Gibran, *The Prophet* (New York: Knopf, 1923), p. 15.

CHAPTER 11

1. Robert G. Ryder, Ph.D., John S. Kafka, M.D., and David H. Olson, Ph.D., "Separating and Joining Influences in Courtship and Early Marriage," *American Journal of Orthopsychiatry,* April 1971, pp. 450–464.

2. Stuart Rosenthal, M.D., "The Need for Friendships in Marriage," *Medical Aspects of Human Sexuality,* vol. 18, no. 11, Nov. 1984.

3. Jeanette Lauer and Robert Lauer, "Marriages Made to Last," *Psychology Today,* June 1985, pp. 22–26.

4. Psychoanalyst Otto Kernberg makes the point that "a couple that, for various realistic or neurotic reasons, isolates itself excessively from the surrounding social group is subject to danger from the internal effects of mutual aggression." Otto F. Kernberg, M.D., "Love, the Couple, and the Group: A Psychoanalytic Frame," *Psychoanalytic Quarterly*, 1980, XLIX, p. 98.

5. George E. Vaillant, *Adaptation to Life* (Boston: Little, Brown & Co., 1977).

6. Kernberg describes how a couple may become a strong target for oedipal idealization, anxiety, and envy from a group to which they belong and how the "couple's relationship (with each other) offers a liberation from the loss of identity and primitive aggression that is inherent in the large group." Kernberg, op. cit., p. 99.

7. Ryder, et al., op. cit.

8. Kernberg, op. cit.

9. Kernberg, op. cit.

CHAPTER 12

1. In our newlywed survey:
   - 35 percent said they "could not be happier" about their marriages
   - 45 percent said they feel "very happy" about their marriages
   - 11 percent said they feel "pretty happy" about their marriages
   - 5 percent said they feel "fair" about their marriages
   - 3 percent said they feel "very unhappy" about their marriages

2. Of our newlywed respondents, 9.1 percent stated that marriage was *much* harder than they had expected it to be, 32.4 percent reported that marriage was a little harder than they had expected it to be.

3. Of our newlywed respondents, 4.3 percent reported that marriage was a very difficult adjustment for them, 13.9 percent reported that marriage is a pretty difficult adjustment for them.

4. Source: June 1980 Marital History Survey, conducted by the U.S. Census Bureau. Another recent study demonstrating the frequency of divorce in the early stage of marriage was conducted by psychologist David H. Olson, who compared the ex-

pectations of each spouse three to four months before marriage and the state of a couple's marriage two to three years later. In his follow-up of the 164 engaged couples whom he had surveyed, Dr. Olson found that 52 couples had delayed or canceled their wedding plans, and of those who married, 31 couples had either divorced or separated. Twenty-two couples said they were dissatisfied with their marriages. David H. Olson and Blaine J. Fowers, "Predicting Marital Success: A Predictive Validity Study," *Journal of Marriage and Family Therapy*, October 1986, vol. 12, No. 4, pp. 403–413.

5. Nathan Ackerman, one of the pioneers and major theorists of family therapy, wrote: "The stability of the family and that of its members hinges on a delicate pattern of emotional balance and interchange. The behavior of each member is affected by every other. . . . A crisis in the life of the family may exert pervasive and far-reaching effects on the mental health of the family and its individual members." See Nathan W. Ackerman, M.D., "The Psychodynamics of the Family," *The Psychodynamics of Family Life: Diagnosis and Treatment of Family Relationships* (New York: Basic Books, 1958). Also, a state-of-the-art description of the issues and process of family therapy can be found in Ira D. Glick, M.D., and David R. Kessler, M.D., in *Marital and Family Therapy* (New York: Grune & Stratton, 1974).

6. A study conducted by Dr. Judith Wallerstein, executive director of the Center for the Family in Transition, in Corte Madera, California, has shown that 40 percent of women and 30 percent of men reported having intensely angry feelings about their failed marriages *ten* years after they had been divorced.

7. Personal communication.

8. George Bernard Shaw, *You Never Can Tell, Plays: Pleasant and Unpleasant*, vol. 2 (Chicago & N.Y.: Herdut S. Stake & Co., 1898), p. 122.

CHAPTER 13

1. Dorothy Witacker spoke about the "metaphor," or myth, that evolves for a group about itself. Her work was with groups in group therapy, but her concept seems relevant to the married couple's gradual development of an image of themselves. That

image serves many purposes, not least of which resides in its being a valued possession that spouses "carry around." Eventually this image becomes concretized, a permanent, internal possession of the mind, from which important, sustaining feelings can be drawn. This idea comes from Witacker's Grand Rounds presentation, entitled "On the Use of Metaphor in Psychotherapeutic Groups," February 22, 1985, at the Department of Psychiatry, Cornell University Medical College, New York Hospital-Westchester Division.

This idea seems to relate to David W. Winnicott's notion that young children develop "transitional objects"—teddy bears or dolls, for example. The object is not the love-object mother, nor an internalized mental representation of her, but something in between—an external object, but one about which rich, internal feelings are attached and aroused. The evolving image of the marriage—represented in some of the trinkets, gifts, and photos we carry with us—may serve as an adult manifestation of this "transitional object" phenomenon. See David W. Winnicott, "Transitional Objects and Transitional Phenomena," *The International Journal of Psycho-Analysis,* 1953, vol. XXXIV, pp. 89–96.

2. Schafer focuses on four narrative themes: the comic, the romantic, the tragic, the ironic. The *comic* is marked by a buoyant enthusiasm and unbounded optimism. The *romantic* is marked by a sense of quest, sometimes with danger. It lends purpose, meaning, and challenge to our lives. The *tragic* is characterized by a sense of one's limitations. It can include sad resignation, but also can be ennobling, as in trying against great odds to pursue a course one believes in. The *ironic* is typified in one's ability to stand outside oneself, and look back with an observing eye.

Schafer points out that there are many more narrative themes that could be developed. He notes that many of us limit our visions of ourselves, and therefore limit the potential richness with which we experience our lives. A depressed person, for instance, may be overimbued with the tragic vision to the exclusion of the lighter comic or romantic visions. Naive optimists, on the other hand, may be overromantic, and fail to adequately appreciate life's more difficult aspects, or the enriching qualities of the tragic and ironic perspectives.

Though Schafer's work refers to the intrapsychic experience one has in one's own life, his concept seems useful in thinking about the breadth or lack of breadth in how individual spouses think of their marriage as well as the range of myths, tales, stories, folklore, lies, beliefs, and mirages the couple evolve *together* as part of their shared possession in marriage. See Roy Schafer, "The Psychoanalytic Vision of Reality," *International Journal of Psycho-Analysis,* 1970, vol. 51, pp. 179–297.

BIBLIOGRAPHY

Ackerman, Nathan W. "The Psychodynamics of the Family." *The Psychodynamics of Family Life: Diagnosis and Treatment of Family Relationships.* New York: Basic Books, 1958.

Ainsworth, Mary D. "Attachments Across the Life Span." Presented as the Thomas William Salmon Lecture for the Salmon Committee on Psychiatry and Mental Hygiene at the New York Academy of Medicine, New York, on December 6, 1984.

Arlow, Jacob A. "Object Concept and Object Choice." *Psychoanalysis Quarterly,* 1980, XLIX, pp. 109–133.

Baks, R.C. "Being in Love and Object Loss." *International Journal of Psychoanalysis,* 1973, vol. 54, pp. 1–8.

Balint, Michael. "On Genital Love." *Primary Love and Psychoanalytic Technique.* New York: Tavistock, 1948, pp. 109–120.

Barnett, Joseph. "Narcissism and Dependency in the Obsessional–Hysteric Marriage." *Family Process,* 1971, vol. 10, no. 1, pp. 75–83.

Barry, William A. "Marriage Research and Conflicts: An Integrative Review." *Psychological Bulletin,* 1970, vol. 73, no. 1, pp. 41–54.

Bateson, Gregory. *Naven.* Stanford, CA: Stanford University Press, 1958 (originally published in 1936).

Bergmann, Martin S. "On the Intrapsychic Function of Falling in Love." *Psychoanalytic Quarterly,* 1980, XLIX, pp. 56–77.

Bergmann, Martin S. "Psychoanalytic Observations on the Capacity to Love." *Separation Individuations Essay in Honor of Margaret S. Mahler,* McDavitt, John B. and Settlage, Calvin, eds. New York: International Universities Press, 1971, pp. 15–40.

Berheide, Catherine White. "Women's Work in the Home: Seems Like Old Times." *Marriage and Family Review.* New York: The Haworth Press, 1984.

Bernard, Jessie. *The Future of Marriage.* Rev. ed. New Haven & London: Yale University Press, 1982.

Berne, Eric. *Transactional Analysis Bulletin: Selected Articles From Volumes 1–9*. San Francisco, CA: Transactional Analysis Press, 1976.

Berne, Eric. *Games People Play*. New York: Ballantine, 1978.

Betcher, William. "Intimate Play and Marital Adaptation." *Psychiatry*, vol. 44, February 1981.

Binstock, William A. "On the Two Forms of Intimacy." *Journal of the American Psychoanalytic Association*, 1973, vol. 21, no. 1, pp. 93–107.

Bird, H. Waldo; Schuham, Anthony I.; Benson, Lois; and Gans, Leslie L. "Stressful Life Events and Marital Dysfunction." *Hospital and Community Psychiatry*, July 1981, vol. 32, no. 7, pp. 487–490.

Blanck, Rubin and Blanck, Gertrude. *Marriage and Personal Development*. New York: Columbia University Press, 1968.

Bowen, Murray. *Family Therapy and Clinical Practice*. New York/London: Jason Aronson, Inc. 1978.

Brody, Jane E. "Personal Health" Column. *The New York Times*, October 31, 1984.

Buber, Martin. *"Distance and Relation."* The William Aronson White Memorial Lectures, Fourth Series. *Psychiatry*, 1957, vol. 20, p. 104.

Carter, Elizabeth and McGoldrich, Monica. *The Family Life Cycle: A Framework for Family Therapy*. New York: Gardner Press, 1980.

Charny, Israel W. "Marital Love and Hate." *Family Process*, March, 1969, vol. 8, no. 1, p. 2.

Chasseguet-Smirgel, Janine. "The Ego Ideal: Being-in-Love and Genitality." New York: W. W. Norton, 1985.

Christensen, T. H. "The Timing of Pregnancy as a Factor in Divorce: A Cross-Cultural Analysis." *Eugenics Quarterly*, 1963, vol. 10, pp. 119–130.

Connelly, Sherryl. "Fantasy Lives." *New York Daily News*, May, 1984, YOU Section, p. 29.

Cuber, J. F. and Harloff, P. B. "The More Total View: Relationships Among Men and Women in the Upper Middle Class." *Marriage and Family Living*, 1963, vol. 25, pp. 140–145.

DeMaris, Alfred and Leslie, Gerald R. "Cohabitation with the Future Spouse: Its Influence Upon Marital Satisfaction and Communication." *Journal of Marriage and the Family*, February, 1984, pp. 77–84.

de Rougemont, Denis. *Love in the Western World*. New York: Anchor Press, 1957.

Dicks, Henry V. *Marital Tensions: Clinical Studies Towards a Psychological Theory of Interaction*. New York: Basic Books, 1967.

Docherty, John P. and Ellis, Jean. "A New Concept and Finding in Morbid Jealousy." *American Journal of Psychiatry*, June, 1976, vol. 133, no. 6, pp. 679–683.

Edwards, John N. and Booth, Alan. "The Cessation of Marital Intercourse." *American Journal of Psychiatry*, November, 1976, vol. 133, no. 11, pp. 1333–1336.

Eliot, George. *George Eliot Letters*, 9 vols., Haight, Gordon, ed. New Haven: Yale University Press, 1954–78.

Elms, Alan C. "Freud, Irma, Martha: Sex and Marriage in the 'Dream of Irma's Injection.'" *Psychoanalytic Review*, 1980, vol. 67, pp. 63–109.

Erikson, Erik. "Growth Crises of the Healthy Personality: Identity and the Life Cycles. *Psychological Issues*, Monograph I. New York: International Universities Press, 1959, pp. 50–100.

Feldman, Larry B. "Dysfunctional Marital Conflict: An Integrative Interpersonal–Intrapsychic Model." *Journal of Marital and Family Therapy*, October, 1982, pp. 417–428.

Fenichel, O. *The Psychoanalytic Theory of Neurosis*. New York: W. W. Norton, 1945.

Fenichel, Otto. "The Symbolic Equation: Girl = Phallus," originally published in Germany in 1936 and translated in English in the *Psychoanalytic Quarterly*, 1949, vol. 18, pp. 303–324.

Ferenczi, Sandor. "Psycho-Analysis of Sexual Habits." *Further Contributions to the Theory and Technique of Psychoanalysis*. London: Hogarth Press, 1926, pp. 372–404.

Frank, E.; Anderson, C.; and Kupfer, D. "Frequency of Sexual Dysfunction in 'Normal Couples'." *New Journal of Medicine*, 1978, vol. 299, pp. 111–115.

Freud, Sigmund. "Three Essays on the Theory of Sexuality" vol. VIII. (1905), *Standard Edition of the Complete Psychological Works of Sigmund Freud*, Strachey, James, ed. London: Hogarth Press, 1981.

———. "A Special Type of Choice of Object Made by Men." ("Contributions to the Psychology of Love I") (1910), *Standard*

Edition, vol. XI. Strachey, James, ed. London: Hogarth Press, 1981.

————. "On the Universal Tendency to Debasement in the Sphere of Love." ("Contributions to the Psychology of Love II") (1912), *Standard Edition,* vol. XI. Strachey, James, ed. London: Hogarth Press, 1981.

————. "The Taboo of Virginity." ("Contributions to the Psychology of Love III") (1918), *Standard Edition,* vol. XI. Strachey, James, ed. London: Hogarth Press, 1981.

————. "Group Psychology and the Analysis of the Ego." (1912), *Standard Edition,* vol. XVIII. Strachey, James, ed. London: Hogarth Press, 1981.

————. "Some Neurotic Mechanisms in Jealousy, Paranoia and Homosexuality." (1922), *Standard Edition,* vol. XIII, pp. 223–234.

Friedan, Betty. *The Feminine Mystique.* New York: Dell, 1964.

Fromm, Erich. *The Art of Loving.* New York: Harper & Row, 1956.

Gerstel, Naomi and Gross, Harriety Engel. "Commuter Marriages: A Review." *Marriage and Family Review,* vol. 5, no. 2, 1981.

Gibran, Kaheil. *The Prophet.* New York: Knopf, 1923, p. 15.

Gilligan, Carol. *In A Different Voice: Psychological Theory and Women's Development.* Cambridge, MA: Harvard University Press, 1982.

Giovacchini, Peter L. "Characterological Aspects of Marital Interaction." *The Psychoanalytic Forum,* Spring, 1967, vol. 2, no. 1, pp. 7–30.

Giovacchini, Peter. "Symbiosis and Intimacy." *International Journal of Psychoanalytic Psychotherapy,* 1976, vol. 5, pp. 413–436.

Glick, Ira D. and Kessler, David R. *Marital and Family Therapy.* New York: Grune & Stratton, 1974.

Goldberg, Martin. "The Dynamics of Marital Interaction and Marital Interaction and Marital Conflict." *Psychiatric Clinics of North America* 5:3, December, 1982, pp. 449–467.

Goleman, Daniel. "Two Views of Marriage Explored: His and Hers." *The New York Times,* April 1, 1986, p. C1.

Gould, Roger. "The Phases of Adult Life: A Study in Developmental Psychology." *The American Journal of Psychiatry,* November, 1972, vol. 129, no. 5.

Greenblatt, Cathy Stein. "The Salience of Sexuality in the Early Years of Marriage." *Journal of Marriage and the Family,* May 1983, pp. 289–292.

Greenspan, Stanley J. and Annino, Fontire, V.M. "A Model of Brief Intervention with Couples Based on Projective Identification." *American Journal of Psychiatry,* Oct., 1974, 131:10, pp. 1103–1106.

Grotjahn, Martin. "About the Symbolization of Alice's Adventures in Wonderland." *American Image* IV, 1974, pp. 32–41.

Grunebaum, Henry and Christ, Jacob, eds. *Contemporary Marriage: Structure, Dynamics, Therapy.* Boston: Little, Brown, 1976.

Hartmann, Heinz. "Psychoanalysis and Sociology." *Essays on Ego Psychology.* New York: International Universities Press, 1964.

Horney, Karen. "The Problem of the Monogamous Ideal." *International Journal of Psychoanalysis,* 1928, vol. 9, pp. 318–331.

James, William H. "The Honeymoon Effect on Marital Coitus." *The Journal of Sex Research,* May, 1981, vol. 17, no. 2, pp. 114–123.

Jakels, Ludwig and Bengler, Edmund. "Transference and Love." *Psychoanalytic Quarterly,* 1949, vol. 18, pp. 325–350.

Kahn, Charlotte. "Proverbs of Love and Marriage: A Psychological Perspective." *Psychoanalytic Review,* Fall, 1983, vol. 70, no. 3, pp. 359–371.

Kahn, Malcolm. "Non-Verbal Communication and Marital Satisfaction." *Family Process,* 1970, vol. 9, pp. 449–456.

Kaplan, Helen Singer. *The Illustrated Manual of Sex Therapy.* New York: Quadrangle/New York Times Book Company, 1985.

Kernberg, Otto F. "Boundaries and Structure in Love Relations." *Journal of the American Psychoanalytic Association,* 1977, vol. XXV, pp. 81–114.

Kernberg, Otto F. "Love, the Couple, and the Group: A Psychoanalytic Frame." *Psychoanalytic Quarterly* XLIX, 1980, pp. 78–108.

Kernberg, Otto F. "Mature Love: Prerequisites and Characteristics." *Journal of the American Psychoanalytic Association,* 1974, vol. 22, no. 4, pp. 743–768.

Kinsey, A. C.; Pomeroy, W. B.; and Martin, C. E. *Sexual Behavior in the Human Male.* Philadelphia: Saunders, 1948.

Kinsey, A. C.; Pomeroy, W. B.; and Martin, C. E. *Sexual Behavior in the Human Female*. Philadelphia: Saunders, 1953.

Klein, Melanie. *Envy and Gratitude and Other Works 1946–1963*. London: Hogarth Press, 1984.

Knox, David Jr. "Behavior Contracts in Marriage Counseling." *Journal of Family Counseling*, 1973, vol. 1, pp. 22–28.

Kohut, Heinz. *The Analysis of the Self*. New York: International Universities Press, 1977.

Kohut, Heinz. "Thoughts on Narcissism and Narcissistic Rage." *The Psychoanalytic Study of the Child*, 1972, vol. 27, pp. 377–400.

Kris, Ernst. "On Preconscious Mental Process." *Psychoanalytic Exploration in Art*. New York: International Universities Press, 1952, pp. 303–318.

Landis, Judson T. "Length of Time Required to Achieve Adjustment in Marriage." *American Sociological Review*, 1946, vol. II, pp. 666–667.

Lansky, Melvin. "On Blame." *International Journal of Psychoanalytic Psychotherapy*, 1980, vol. 8, pp. 429–460.

Lauer, Jeanette and Lauer, Robert. "Marriages Made to Last." *Psychology Today*, June, 1985, pp. 22–26.

Lee, J. A. "A Typology of Styles of Loving." *Personality and Social Psychology Bulletin 3*, 1977, pp. 173–182.

Levi-Strauss, Claude. *The View From Afar*. New York: Basic Books, 1985.

Levi-Strauss, Claude. *The Elementary Structure of Kinship*. Boston: Beacon Press, 1969.

Levin, Sidney. "Further Comments on a Common Type of Marital Incompatability." *Journal of the American Psychoanalytic Association*, vol. 17, pp. 1097–1113.

Levinson, Daniel. *The Seasons of a Man's Life*. New York: Ballantine Books, 1978.

Lief, Harold I. and Berman, Ellen. "Sexual Interviewing of the Individual Patient Through the Life Cycle." *Sex and the Life Cycle*, Oaks, Wilbur W.; Melchiode, Gerald A.; and Ficher, Ilda, eds. New York: Grune & Stratton, Inc., 1976.

Lewin, Bertram D. "The Body as Phallus." *Psychoanalytic Quarterly*, 1933, vol. 2, pp. 24–47.

Loewwald, Hans. "The Therapeutic Action of Psychoanalysis." *International Journal of Psychoanalysis*, 1960, vol. 41, pp. 17–18.

Mahler, Margaret S.; Pine, Fred; and Bergman, Anni. *Psycho-*

logical Birth of the Human Infant: Symbiosis and Individuation. New York: Basic Books, 1975.

Main, T. F. "Mutual Projection in a Marriage." *Comprehensive Psychiatry,* October, 1976, vol. 7, no. 5, pp. 432–449.

May, Rollo. *Love and Will.* New York: W. W. Norton, 1969, p. 289.

Mittelman, Bella. "Complementary Neurotic Reactions in Intimate Relationships." *Psychoanalytic Quarterly,* 1944, vol. 13.

Murstein, Bernard I. "Marital Choice." *Handbook of Developmental Psychology,* Wolman, Benjamin B., ed. Englewood, N.J.: Prentice-Hall, 1982, pp. 652–666.

Nadelson, Carol C. and Notman, Malkah T. "To Marry or Not to Marry." *The Woman Patient: Concepts of Femininity and the Life Cycle,* vol. 2, Nadelson, Carol C. and Notman, Malkah T., eds. New York & London: Plenum Press, 1978.

Nadelson, Carol C.; Polansky, Derek C.; and Matthews, Mary Alice. "Marriage as a Developmental Process." *Marriage and Divorce: A Contemporary Perspective,* Nadelson, Carol C. and Polansky, Derek C., eds. New York: Guilford Press, 1984, pp. 127–141.

Navran, Leslie. "Communication and Adjustment in Marriage." *Family Process,* 1976, pp. 173–184.

Olson, David H. and Fowers, Blaine J. "Predicting Marital Success: A Predictive Validity Study." *Journal of Marriage and Family Therapy,* October, 1986, vol. 12, no. 4, pp. 403–413.

Paley, Aaron. "Adapting to a Spouse's Idiosyncrasy." *Medical Aspects of Human Sexuality,* April, 1984, vol. 18, no. 4.

Paolino, T. S. and McCrady, B. S. *Marriage and Marital Therapy: Psychoanalytic, Behavior and Systems Theory.* New York: Brunner, Mazel, 1978.

Parsons, Talcott and Bales, Robert F. *Family: Socialization and Interaction Process.* Glencoe, Il: Free Press, 1955.

Pietropinto, Anthony and Simenauer, Jacqueline. *Husbands and Wives: A Nationwide Survey of Marriage.* New York: Times Books, 1979.

Rabkin, Richard. "Uncoordinated Communication Between Marriage Partners." *Family Process,* 1967, vol. 6, pp. 10–15.

Rausch, Harold; Marshall, Karol A.; and Featherman, Jo-Anna M. "Relations at Three Early Stages of Marriage as

Reflected by the Use of Personal Pronouns." *Family Process*, 1970, vol. 9, no. 1, pp. 69–82.

Rausch, Harold; Goodrich, Wells; and Campbell, John D. "Adaptation to the First Years of Marriage." *Psychiatry*, 1963, vol. 26, pp. 368–380.

Reich, Annie. "A Contribution to the Psychoanalysis of Extreme Submissiveness in Women." *Psychoanalytic Quarterly*, 1940, vol. IX, pp. 470–480.

Reich, Annie. "Narcissistic Object Choice in Women." *Journal of the American Psychoanalytic Association: Volume I*. New York International Universities Press, 1953, pp. 22–24.

Renshaw, Domeena. "Communication in Marriage." *Medical Aspects of Human Sexuality*, vol. 17, no. 6, 1983, pp. 31–46.

Rilke, Rainer Maria *Letters of Rainer Maria Rilke 1892–1910*. New York: Norton, 1969.

Rohrlich, Jay B. *Work and Love: The Crucial Balance*. New York: Summit Books, 1980.

Rosenthal, Stuart. "The Need for Friendship in Marriage." *Medical Aspects of Human Sexuality*, vol. 18, no. 11, November, 1984.

Rubin, Lillian Breslow. *Worlds of Pain*. New York: Basic books, 1976.

Ryder, Robert G.; Kafka, John S.; and Olson, David H. "Separating and Joining Influences in Courtship and Early Marriage." *American Journal of Orthopsychiatry*, April, 1971, pp. 450–464.

Ryder, Robert and Goodrich, Wells. "Married Couples' Responses to Disagreement." *Family Process*, vol. 5, 1966, pp. 30–41.

Sager, Clifford J. *Marriage Contracts and Couples Therapy*. New York: Brunner/Mazel, 1986.

Sandler, Joseph. "Countertransference and Role Responsiveness." *International Review of Psychoanalysis*, 1976, vol. 3, pp. 43–47.

Schafer, Roy. "The Psychoanalytic Vision of Reality." *International Journal of Psycho-Analysis*, 1970, vol. 51, pp. 179–297.

Schafer, Roy. "Men Who Struggle Against Sentimentality." *The Psychology of Men*, Fagel, Gerald; Lane, Frederick; and Liebert, Robert, eds. New York: Basic Books, 1986.

Scheflan, Albert. "Regressive One to One Relationships." *Psychoanalytic Quarterly*, 1960, vol. 34, pp. 692–708.

Schwartz, Mark E. and Masters, William H. "The Masters and Johnson Treatment Program for Dissatisfied Homosexual Men." *The American Journal of Psychiatry*, February, 1984, vol. 141, no. 2, pp. 173–181.

Schwartz, Pepper and Blumstein, Philip. *American Couples*. New York: Pocket Books, 1985.

Segal, Hanna. *Introduction to the Work of Melanie Klein*. New York: Basic Books, 1974.

Shaw, George Bernard. "You Never Can Tell," *Plays: Pleasant and Unpleasant*, vol. 2. Chicago and New York: Herdut S. Stake and Company, 1898, p. 122.

Shaw, George Bernard. "Maxims for Revolutionists." *Collected Plays With Their Prefaces*, vol. II. New York: Dodd, Mead & Co., 1971.

Shaw, George Bernard. "Major Barbara." *Collected Plays and Their Prefaces*. New York: Dodd, Mead & Co., 1971.

Snyder, Douglas K. and Berg, Phyllis. "Determinants of Sexual Dissatisfaction in Sexually Distressed Couples." *Archives of Sexual Behavior*, 1983, vol. 12, no. 3, pp. 237–246.

Spiegel, John P. "The Resolution of Role Conflict Within the Family," *Psychiatry*, VXX, 1957, pp. 1–16.

Staines, Graham; Pottick, Kathleen; and Fudge, Deborah. "Wives' Employment Husbands' Attitude Toward Work and Life." *Journal of Applied Psychology*, February, 1986.

Stein, Martin H. "The Marriage Bond." *Psychoanalytic Quarterly*, 1956, vol. 25, pp. 238–259.

Stern, Daniel. *The Interpersonal World of the Infant*. New York: Basic Books, 1985.

Sternberg, Robert J. and Grajeck, Susan. "The Nature of Love." *Journal of Personality and Social Psychology*, 1984, vol. 47, no. 2, pp. 312–329.

Stone, Lawrence. *Family Sex and Marriage: England 1500–1800*. New York: Harper Torchbooks, 1979.

Straus, Murray A.; Gelles, Richard J.; and Steinmetz, Suzanne K. *Behind Closed Doors: Violence in the American Family*. New York: Doubleday/Anchor Press, 1980.

Strean, Herbert S. "The Extramarital Affair: A Psychoanalytic View." *Psychoanalytic Review*, 1976, vol. 63, pp. 101–113.

Thorp, Roland G. "Psychological Patterning in Marriage." *Psychological Bulletin*. March, 1963, vol. 60, no. 2, pp. 97–117.

Van Gennep, Arnold. *The Rites of Passage*. Chicago: University of Chicago Press, 1960.

Visher, Emily B. "The Role Played by the Remarried Parent in the Stepfamily System." Presented at the Seventh Annual Meeting of the American Family Therapy Association, San Diego, CA, in June, 1985.

Von Keyserling, Hermann, ed. *The Book of Marriage*. New York: Harcourt, Brace & Company, 1927.

Waring, E. M.; Tillman, Mary Pat; Frelick, L.; Russell, Lila; and Weisz, G. "Concepts of Intimacy in the General Population." *The Journal of Nervous and Mental Disease*, 1980, vol. 168, no. 8, pp. 471–474.

Wender, Paul H. "Vicious and Virtuous Cycles: The Roles of Deviation Amplifying Feedback; The Origins and Perpetuation of Behavior." *Brief Therapies*, Barton, Harvey H., ed. New York: Behavioral Publication, 1971.

Werman, David S. and Jacobs, Theodore J. "Thomas Hardy's 'The Well-Beloved' and the Nature of Infatuation." *International Review of Psycho-Analysis*, 1983, vol. 10, pp. 447–457.

White, Kathleen; Steisman, Joseph C.; Jackson, Doris; Eartis, Scott; and Costos, Daryl. "Intimacy, Maturity and Its Correlates in Young Married Couples." *The Journal of Personality and Social Psychology*, January, 1986.

Winch, Robert F. "Complementary Needs and Related Notions about Voluntary Mate Selection." *Selected Studies in Marriage and Family*, Winch, Robert F. and Spanier, Graham, eds. New York: Holt, Rinehart & Winston, 1974.

Wolman, Benjamin, ed. *International Encyclopedia of Psychiatry, Psychology, Psychoanalysis and Neurology*, vol. 6. New York: Aesculepius Publishers of Van Nostrand Reinhold Co., 1977, pp. 444–446.

Wolfe, Linda. *The Cosmo Report*. New York: Arbor House, 1981.

Yahraes, Herbert. "Improving Communication in Marriage." *Science Monography 1, Families Today*, vol. 1, National Institute of Health.

Waxman, Harvey S. and Long, Janis, V.F. "Adultery and Marriage: Three Psychological Perspectives." *Marriage and Divorce: A Contemporary Perspective*. New York: Guilford Press, 1984, pp. 142–156.

Winnicott, David W. "Transitional Objects and Transitional

Phenomena." *The International Journal of Psycho-Analysis,* 1953, vol. XXXIV, pp. 89–96.

Winnicott, David. "Communicating and Not Communicating Leading to a Study of Certain Opposites." *The Maturational Process and the Facilitating Environment.* New York: International Universities Press, 1965, pp. 179–192.

INDEX